THE STORY OF FLORENCE

BY

EDMUND G. GARDNER

Copyright © 2013 Read Books Ltd.
This book is copyright and may not be
reproduced or copied in any way without
the express permission of the publisher in writing

British Library Cataloguing-in-Publication Data
A catalogue record for this book is available from the
British Library

Contents

PREFACE. 5

CHAPTER I. The People and Commune of Florence. 9

CHAPTER II. The Times of Dante and Boccaccio 46

CHAPTER III. The Medici and the Quattrocento 90

CHAPTER IV. From Fra Girolamo to Duke Cosimo 139

CHAPTER V. The Palazzo Vecchio–The Piazza della Signoria–The Uffizi 183

    The Uffizi. 199

    Ritratti dei Pittori–Primo Corridore. 201

    Tribuna. 203

    Scuola Toscana. 207

    Sala di maestri diversi Italiani. 218

    Scuola Veneta. 219

    Sala di Lorenzo Monaco. 222

CHAPTER VI. Or San Michele and the Sesto di San Piero . 229

CHAPTER VII. From the Bargello past Santa Croce. 262

CHAPTER VIII. The Baptistery, the Campanile, and the Duomo 299

CHAPTER IX. The Palazzo Riccardi–San Lorenzo San Marco. 344

CHAPTER X. The Accademia delle Belle Arti–
The Santissima Annunziata–And other Buildings.......... 381

CHAPTER XI. The Bridges–The Quarter of Santa Maria
Novella 410

CHAPTER XII. Across the Arno 449

CHAPTER XIII. Conclusion 491

CHRONOLOGICAL INDEX OF
ARCHITECTSSCULPTORS & PAINTERS 510

Pallas taming a Centaur,
by Botticelli.
(THE TRIUMPH OF LORENZO.)

The Story of Florence
by Edmund G. Gardner
Illustrated by Nelly Erichsen

To
MY SISTER
MONICA MARY GARDNER

PREFACE

THE present volume is intended to supply a popular history of the Florentine Republic, in such a form that it can also be used as a guide-book. It has been my endeavour, while keeping within the necessary limits of this series of *Mediæval Towns*, to point out briefly the most salient features in the story of Florence, to tell again the tale of those of her streets and buildings, and indicate those of her artistic treasures, which are either most intimately connected with that story or most beautiful in themselves. Those who know best what an intensely fascinating and many-sided history that of Florence has been, who have studied most closely the work and characters of those strange and wonderful personalities who have lived within (and, in the case of the greatest, died without) her walls, will best appreciate my difficulty in compressing even a portion of all this wealth and profusion into the narrow bounds enjoined by the aim and scope of this book. Much has necessarily been curtailed over which it would have been tempting to linger, much inevitably omitted which the historian could not have passed over, nor the compiler of a guide-book failed to mention. In what I have selected for treatment and what omitted, I have usually let myself be guided by the remembrance of my own needs when I first commenced to visit Florence and to study her arts and history.

It is needless to say that the number of books, old and new, is very considerable indeed, to which anyone venturing in these days to write yet another book on Florence must have had recourse, and to whose authors he is bound to be indebted–from the earliest Florentine chroniclers down to the most recent biographers of Lorenzo the Magnificent, of Savonarola, of Michelangelo–from Vasari down to our modern scientific art critics–from Richa and Moreni down to the Misses Horner. My obligations can hardly be acknowledged here in detail; but, to mention a few modern works alone, I am most largely indebted to Capponi's *Storia della Repubblica di Firenze*, to various writings of Professor Pasquale Villari, and to Mr Armstrong's *Lorenzo de' Medici*; to the works of Ruskin and J. A. Symonds, of M. Reymond and Mr Berenson; and, in the domains of topography, to Baedeker's *Hand Book*. In judging of the merits and the authorship of individual pictures and statues, I have usually given more weight to the results of modern criticism than to the pleasantness of old tradition.

Carlyle's translation of the *Inferno* and Mr Wicksteed's of the *Paradiso* are usually quoted.

If this little book should be found helpful in initiating the English-speaking visitor to the City of Flowers into more of the historical atmosphere of Florence and her monuments than guide-books and catalogues can supply, it will amply have fulfilled its object.

E. G. G.

Roehampton, *May* 1900.

CHAPTER I.

THE PEOPLE AND COMMUNE OF FLORENCE

"La bellissima e famosissima figlia di Roma, Fiorenza."
–*Dante.*

BEFORE the imagination of a thirteenth century poet, one of the sweetest singers of the *dolce stil novo*, there rose a phantasy of a transfigured city, transformed into a capital of Fairyland, with his lady and himself as fairy queen and king:

"Amor, eo chero mea donna in domino,
l'Arno balsamo fino,
le mura di Fiorenza inargentate,
le rughe di cristallo lastricate,
fortezze alte e merlate,
mio fedel fosse ciaschedun Latino."[2]

But is not the reality even more beautiful than the dreamland Florence of Lapo Gianni's fancy? We stand on the heights of San Miniato, either in front of the Basilica itself or lower down in the Piazzale Michelangelo. Below us, on either bank of the silvery Arno, lies outstretched Dante's "most famous and most beauteous daughter of Rome," once the Queen of Etruria and centre of the most wonderful culture that the world has known since Athens, later the first capital of United Italy, and still, though shorn of much of her former splendour and beauty, one of the loveliest cities of Christendom. Opposite to us, to the north, rises the hill upon which stands Etruscan Fiesole, from which the people of Florence originally came: "that ungrateful and malignant people," Dante once called them, "who of old came down from Fiesole." Behind us stand the fortifications which mark the death of the Republic, thrown up or at least strengthened by Michelangelo in the city's last agony, when she barred her gates and defied the united power of Pope and Emperor to take the State that had once chosen Christ for her king.

"O foster-nurse of man's abandoned glory
Since Athens, its great mother, sunk in splendour;
Thou shadowest forth that mighty shape in story,
As ocean its wrecked fanes, severe yet tender:
The light-invested angel Poesy
Was drawn from the dim world to welcome thee.

"And thou in painting didst transcribe all taught
By loftiest meditations; marble knew
The sculptor's fearless soul—and as he wrought,
The grace of his own power and freedom grew."

The Story of Florence

Between Fiesole and San Miniato, then, the story of the Florentine Republic may be said to be written.

The beginnings of Florence are lost in cloudy legend, and her early chroniclers on the slenderest foundations have reared for her an unsubstantial, if imposing, fabric of fables— the tales which the women of old Florence, in the *Paradiso*, told to their house-holds—

"dei Troiani, di Fiesole, e di Roma."

FLORENCE FROM THE BOBOLI GARDENS

Setting aside the Trojans ("Priam" was mediæval for "Adam," as a modern novelist has remarked), there is no doubt that both Etruscan Fiesole and Imperial Rome united to found the "great city on the banks of the Arno." Fiesole or Faesulae upon its hill was an important Etruscan city, and a place of consequence in the days of the Roman Republic; fallen though it now is, traces of its old greatness remain. Behind the Romanesque cathedral are considerable remains of Etruscan walls and of a Roman theatre. Opposite it to the west we may ascend to enjoy the glorious view from the Convent of the Franciscans, where once the old citadel of Faesulae stood. Faesulae was ever the centre of Italian and democratic discontent against Rome and her Senate (*sempre ribelli di Roma*, says Villani of its inhabitants); and it was here, in October b.c. 62, that Caius Manlius planted the Eagle of revolt–an eagle which Marius had borne in the war against the Cimbri–and thus commenced the Catilinarian war, which resulted in the annihilation of Catiline's army near Pistoia.

This, according to Villani, was the origin of Florence. According to him, Fiesole, after enduring the stupendous siege, was forced to surrender to the Romans under Julius Cæsar, and utterly razed to the ground. In the second sphere of Paradise, Justinian reminds Dante of how the Roman Eagle "seemed bitter to that hill beneath which thou wast born." Then, in order that Fiesole might never raise its head again, the Senate ordained that the greatest lords of Rome, who had been at the siege, should join with Cæsar in building a new city on the banks of the Arno. Florence, thus founded by Cæsar, was populated by the noblest citizens of Rome, who received into their number those of the inhabitants of fallen Fiesole who wished to live there. "Note then," says the old chronicler, "that it is not wonderful that the Florentines are always at war and in dissensions among themselves, being drawn and born from two peoples, so contrary and hostile and diverse in habits, as were the noble and virtuous Romans, and the savage and contentious folk of Fiesole." Dante similarly, in Canto XV. of the *Inferno*, ascribes the injustice of the Florentines towards himself to this mingling of the people of Fiesole with the true Roman nobility (with special reference, however, to the union of Florence with conquered Fiesole in the twelfth century):–

"che tra li lazzi sorbi
si disconvien fruttare al dolce fico."[3]

And Brunetto Latini bids him keep himself free from their pollution:–

"Faccian le bestie Fiesolane strame
di lor medesme, e non tocchin la pianta,
s'alcuna surge ancor nel lor letame,
in cui riviva la semente santa
di quei Roman che vi rimaser quando
fu fatto il nido di malizia tanta."[4]

The truth appears to be that Florence was originally founded by Etruscans from Fiesole, who came down from their mountain to the plain by the Arno for commercial purposes. This Etruscan colony was probably destroyed during the wars between Marius and Sulla, and a Roman military colony established here–probably in the time of Sulla, and augmented later by Cæsar and by Augustus. It has, indeed, been urged of late that the old Florentine story has some truth in it, and that Cæsar, not only in legend but in fact, may be regarded as the true first founder of Florence. Thus the Roman colony of Florentia gradually grew into a little city–*come una altra piccola Roma*, declares her patriotic chronicler. It had its capitol and its forum in the centre of the city, where the Mercato Vecchio once stood; it had an amphitheatre outside the walls, somewhere near where the Borgo dei Greci and the Piazza Peruzzi are to-day. It had baths and temples, though doubtless on a small scale. It had the shape and form of a Roman camp, which (together with the Roman walls in which it was inclosed) it may be said to have retained down to the middle of the twelfth century, in spite of legendary demolitions by Attila and Totila, and equally legendary reconstructions by Charlemagne. Above all, it had a grand temple to Mars, which almost certainly occupied the site of the present Baptistery, if not actually identical with it. Giovanni Villani tells us–and we shall have to return to his statement–that the wonderful octagonal building, now known as the Baptistery or the Church of St John, was consecrated as a temple by the Romans in honour of Mars, for their victory over the Fiesolans, and that Mars was the patron of the Florentines as long as paganism lasted. Round the equestrian statue that was supposed to have once stood in the midst of this temple, numberless legends have gathered. Dante refers to it again and again. In Santa Maria Novella you shall see how a great painter of the early Renaissance, Filippino Lippi, conceived of his city's first patron. When Florence changed him for the Baptist, and the people of Mars became the sheepfold of St John, this statue was removed from the temple and set upon a tower by the side of the Arno:–

"The Florentines took up their idol which they called the God Mars, and set him upon a high tower near the river Arno; and they would not break or shatter it, seeing that in their ancient records they found that the said idol of Mars had been consecrated under the ascendency of such a planet, that if it should be broken or put in a dishonourable place, the city would suffer danger and damage and great mutation. And although the Florentines had newly become Christians, they still retained many customs of paganism, and retained them for a long time; and they greatly feared their ancient idol of Mars; so little perfect were they as yet in the Holy Faith."

This tower is said to have been destroyed like the rest of Florence by the Goths, the statue falling into the Arno, where it lurked in hiding all the time that the city lay in ruins. On the legendary rebuilding of Florence by Charlemagne, the statue, too–or rather the mutilated fragment that remained–was restored to light and honour. Thus Villani:–

"It is said that the ancients held the opinion that there was no power to rebuild the city, if that marble image, consecrated by necromancy to Mars by the first Pagan builders, was not first found again and drawn out of the Arno, in which it had been from the destruction of Florence down to that time. And, when found, they set it upon a pillar on the bank of the said river, where is now the head of the Ponte Vecchio. This we neither affirm nor believe, inasmuch as it appeareth to us to be the opinion of augurers and pagans, and not reasonable, but great folly, to hold that a statue so made could work thus; but commonly it was said by the ancients that, if it were changed, our city would needs suffer great mutation."

Thus it became *quella pietra scema che guarda il ponte*, in Dantesque phrase; and we shall see what terrible sacrifice its clients unconsciously paid to it. Here it remained, much honoured by the Florentines; street boys were solemnly warned of the fearful judgments that fell on all who dared to throw mud or stones at it; until at last, in 1333, a great flood carried away bridge and statue alike, and it was seen no more. It has recently been suggested that the statue was, in reality, an equestrian monument in honour of some barbaric king, belonging to the fifth or sixth century.

Florence, however, seems to have been—in spite of Villani's describing it as the Chamber of the Empire and the like—a place of very slight importance under the Empire. Tacitus mentions that a deputation was sent from Florentia to Tiberius to prevent the Chiana being turned into the Arno. Christianity is said to have been first introduced in the days of Nero; the Decian persecution raged here as elsewhere, and the soil was hallowed with the blood of the martyr, Miniatus. Christian worship is said to have been first offered up on the hill where a stately eleventh century Basilica now bears his name. When the greater peace of the Church was established under Constantine, a church dedicated to the Baptist on the site of the Martian temple and a basilica outside the walls, where now stands San Lorenzo, were among the earliest churches in Tuscany.

In the year 405, the Goth leader Rhadagaisus, *omnium antiquorum praesentiumque hostium longe immanissimus*, as Orosius calls him, suddenly inundated Italy with more than 200,000 Goths, vowing to sacrifice all the blood of the Romans to his gods. In their terror the Romans seemed about to return to their old paganism, since Christ had failed to protect them. *Fervent tota urbe blasphemiae*, writes Orosius. They advanced towards Rome through the Tuscan

Apennines, and are said to have besieged Florence, though there is no hint of this in Orosius. On the approach of Stilicho, at the head of thirty legions with a large force of barbarian auxiliaries, Rhadagaisus and his hordes—miraculously struck helpless with terror, as Orosius implies—let themselves be hemmed in in the mountains behind Fiesole, and all perished, by famine and exhaustion rather than by the sword. Villani ascribes the salvation of Florence to the prayers of its bishop, Zenobius, and adds that as this victory of "the Romans and Florentines" took place on the feast of the virgin martyr Reparata, her name was given to the church afterwards to become the Cathedral of Florence.

Zenobius, now a somewhat misty figure, is the first great Florentine of history, and an impressive personage in Florentine art. We dimly discern in him an ideal bishop and father of his people; a man of great austerity and boundless charity, almost an earlier Antoninus. Perhaps the fact that some of the intervening Florentine bishops were anything but edifying, has made these two—almost at the beginning and end of the Middle Ages—stand forth in a somewhat ideal light. He appears to have lived a monastic life outside the walls in a small church on the site of the present San Lorenzo, with two young ecclesiastics, trained by him and St Ambrose, Eugenius and Crescentius. They died before him and are commonly united with him by the painters. Here he was frequently visited by St Ambrose—here he dispensed his charities and worked his miracles (according to the legend, he had a special gift of raising children to life)–here at length he died in the odour of sanctity, a.d. 424. The beautiful legend of his translation should be familiar to every student of Italian painting. I give it in the words of a monkish writer of the fourteenth century:–

"About five years after he had been buried, there was made bishop one named Andrew, and this holy bishop summoned a great chapter of bishops and clerics, and said in the chapter that it was meet to bear the body of St Zenobius to the Cathedral Church of San Salvatore; and so it was ordained. Wherefore, on the 26th of January, he caused him to be unburied and borne to the Church of San Salvatore by four bishops; and these bishops bearing the body of St Zenobius were so pressed upon by the people that they fell near an elm, the which was close unto the Church of St John the Baptist; and when they fell, the case where the body of St Zenobius lay was broken, so that the body touched the elm, and gradually, as the elm was touched, it brought forth flowers and leaves, and lasted all that year with the flowers and leaves. The people, seeing the miracle, broke up all the elm, and with devotion carried the branches away. And the Florentines, beholding what was done, made a column of marble with a cross where the elm had been, so that the miracle should ever be remembered by the people."

Like the statue of Mars, this column was destroyed by the flood of 1333, and the one now standing to the north of the Baptistery was set up after that year. It was at one time the custom for the clergy on the feast of the translation to go in procession and fasten a green bough to this column. Zenobius now stands with St Reparata on the cathedral façade. Domenico Ghirlandaio painted him, together with his pupils Eugenius and Crescentius, in the Sala dei Gigli of the Palazzo della Signoria; an unknown follower of Orcagna had painted a similar picture for a pillar in the Duomo. Ghiberti cast his miracles in bronze for the shrine in the Chapel of the Sacrament; Verrocchio and Lorenzo di Credi at Pistoia placed him and the Baptist on either side of Madonna's throne. In a picture by some other follower of Verrocchio's in the Uffizi he is seen offering up a model of his city to the Blessed Virgin. Two of the most famous of his miracles, the raising of a child to life and the flowering of the elm tree at his translation, are superbly rendered in two pictures by Ridolfo Ghirlandaio. On May 25th the people still throng the Duomo with bunches of roses and other flowers, which they press to the reliquary which contains his head, and so obtain the "benedizione di San Zenobio." Thus does his memory live fresh and green among the people to whom he so faithfully ministered.

Another barbarian king, the last Gothic hero Totila, advancing upon Rome in 542, took the same shorter but more difficult route across the Apennines. According to the legend, he utterly destroyed all Florence, with the exception of the Church of San Giovanni, and rebuilt Fiesole to oppose Rome and prevent Florence from being restored. The truth appears to be that he did not personally attack Florence, but sent a portion of his troops under his lieutenants. They were successfully resisted by Justin, who commanded the imperial garrison, and, on the advance of reinforcements from Ravenna, they drew off into the valley of the Mugello, where they turned upon the pursuing "Romans" (whose army consisted of worse barbarians than Goths) and completely routed them. Fiesole, which had apparently recovered from its old destruction, was probably too difficult to be assailed; but it appears to have been gradually growing at the expense of Florence–the citizens of the latter emigrating to it for greater safety. This was especially the case during the Lombard invasion, when the fortunes of Florence were at their lowest, and, indeed, in the second half of the eighth century, Florence almost sank to being a suburb of Fiesole.

With the advent of Charlemagne and the restoration of the Empire, brighter days commenced for Florence,–so much so that the story ran that he had renewed the work of Julius Caesar and founded the city again. In 786 he wintered here with his court on his third visit to Rome; and, according to legend, he was here again in great wealth and pomp in 805, and founded the Church of Santissimi Apostoli–the oldest existing Florentine building after the Baptistery. Upon its façade you may still read a pompous inscription concerning the Emperor's reception in Florence, and how the Church was consecrated by Archbishop Turpin in the presence of Oliver and Roland, the Paladins! Florence was becoming a power in Tuscany, or at least beginning to see more of Popes and Emperors. The Ottos stayed within her walls on their way to be crowned at Rome; Popes, flying from their rebellious subjects, found shelter here. In 1055 Victor II. held a council in Florence. Beautiful Romanesque churches began to rise–notably the SS. Apostoli and San Miniato, both probably dating from the eleventh century. Great churchmen appeared among her sons, as San Giovanni Gualberto–the "merciful knight" of Burne-Jones' unforgettable picture–the reformer of the Benedictines and the founder of Vallombrosa. The early reformers, while Hildebrand was still "Archdeacon of the Roman Church," were specially active in Florence; and one of them, known as Peter Igneus, in 1068 endured the ordeal of fire and is said to have passed unhurt through the flames, to convict the Bishop of Florence of simony. This, with other matters relating to the times of Giovanni Gualberto and the struggles of the reformers of the clergy, you may see in the Bargello in a series of noteworthy marble bas-reliefs (terribly damaged, it is true), from the hand of Benedetto da Rovezzano.

Although we already begin to hear of the "Florentine people" and the "Florentine citizens," Florence was at this time subject to the Margraves of Tuscany. One of them, Hugh the Great, who is said to have acted as vicar of the Emperor Otto III., and who died at the beginning of the eleventh century, lies buried in the Badia which had been founded by his mother, the Countess Willa, in 978. His tomb, one of the most noteworthy monuments of the fifteenth century, by Mino da Fiesole, may still be seen, near Filippino Lippi's Vision of St Bernard.

It was while Florence was nominally under the sway of Hugo's most famous successor, the Countess Matilda of Tuscany, that Dante's ancestor Cacciaguida was born; and, in the fifteenth and sixteenth cantos of the *Paradiso*, he draws an ideal picture of that austere old Florence, *dentro dalla cerchia antica*, still within her Roman walls. We can still partly trace and partly conjecture the position of these walls. The city stood a little way back from the river, and had four master gates; the Porta San Piero on the east, the Porta del Duomo on the north, the Porta San Pancrazio on the west, the Porta Santa Maria on the south (towards the Ponte Vecchio). The heart of the city, the Forum or, as it came to be called, the Mercato Vecchio, has indeed been destroyed of late years to make way for the cold and altogether hideous Piazza Vittorio Emanuele; but we can still perceive that at its south-east corner the two main streets of this old

Florentia quadrata intersected,–Calimara, running from the Porta Santa Maria to the Porta del Duomo, south to north, and the Corso, running east to west from the Porta San Piero to the Porta San Pancrazio, along the lines of the present Corso, Via degli Speziali, and Via degli Strozzi. The Porta San Piero probably stood about where the Via del Corso joins the Via del Proconsolo, and there was a suburb reaching out to the Church of San Piero Maggiore. Then the walls ran along the lines of the present Via del Proconsolo and Via dei Balestrieri, inclosing Santa Reparata and the Baptistery, to the Duomo Gate beyond the Bishop's palace–probably somewhere near the opening of the modern Borgo San Lorenzo. Then along the Via Cerretani, Piazza Antinori, Via Tornabuoni, to the Gate of San Pancrazio, which was somewhere near the present Palazzo Strozzi; and so on to where the Church of Santa Trinità now stands, near which there was a postern gate called the Porta Rossa. Then they turned east along the present Via delle Terme to the Porta Santa Maria, which was somewhere near the end of the Mercato Nuovo, after which their course back to the Porta San Piero is more uncertain. Outside the walls were churches and ever-increasing suburbs, and Florence was already becoming an important commercial centre. Matilda's beneficent sway left it in practical independence to work out its own destinies; she protected it from imperial aggressions, and curbed the nobles of the contrada, who were of Teutonic descent and who, from their feudal castles round, looked with hostility upon the rich burgher city of pure Latin blood that was gradually reducing their power and territorial sway. At intervals the great Countess entered Florence, and either in person or by her deputies and judges (members of the chief Florentine families) administered justice in the Forum. Indeed she played the part of Dante's ideal Emperor in the *De Monarchia*; made Roman law obeyed through her dominions; established peace and curbed disorder; and therefore, in spite of her support of papal claims for political empire, when the *Divina Commedia* came to be written, Dante placed her as guardian of the Earthly Paradise to which the Emperor should guide man, and made her the type of the glorified active life. Her praises, *la lauda di Matelda*, were long sung in the Florentine churches, as may be gathered from a passage in Boccaccio.

It is from the death of Matilda in 1115 that the history of the Commune dates. During her lifetime she seems to have gradually, especially while engaged in her conflicts with the Emperor Henry, delegated her powers to the chief Florentine citizens themselves; and in her name they made war upon the aggressive nobility in the country round, in the interests of their commerce. For Dante the first half of this twelfth century represents the golden age in which his ancestor lived, when the great citizen nobles—Bellincion Berti, Ubertino Donati, and the heads of the Nerli and Vecchietti and the rest–lived simple and patriotic lives, filled the offices of state and led the troops against the foes of the Commune. In a grand burst of triumph that old Florentine crusader, Cacciaguida, closes the sixteenth canto of the *Paradiso*:

"Con queste genti, e con altre con esse,
vid'io Fiorenza in sì fatto riposo,
che non avea cagion onde piangesse;
con queste genti vid'io glorioso,
e giusto il popol suo tanto, che'l giglio
non era ad asta mai posto a ritroso,
nè per division fatto vermiglio."[5]

When Matilda died, and the Popes and Emperors prepared to struggle for her legacy (which thus initiated the strifes of Guelfs and Ghibellines), the Florentine Republic asserted its independence: the citizen nobles who had been her delegates and judges now became the Consuls of the Commune and the leaders of the republican forces in war. In 1119 the Florentines assailed the castle of Monte Cascioli, and killed the imperial vicar who defended it; in 1125 they took and destroyed Fiesole, which had always been a refuge for robber nobles and all who hated the Republic. But already signs of division were seen in the city itself, though it was a century before it came to a head; and the great family of the Uberti–who, like the nobles of the contrada, were of Teutonic descent—were prominently to the front, but soon to be *disfatti per la lor superbia*. Scarcely was Matilda dead than they appear to have attempted to seize on the supreme power, and to have only been defeated with much bloodshed and burning of houses. Still the Republic pursued its victorious course through the twelfth century—putting down the feudal barons, forcing them to enter the city and join the Commune, and extending their commerce and influence as well as their territory on all sides. And already these nobles within and without the city were beginning to build their lofty towers, and to associate themselves into Societies of the Towers; while the people were grouped into associations which afterwards became the Greater and Lesser Arts or Guilds. Villani sees the origin of future contests in the mingling of races, Roman and Fiesolan; modern writers find it in the distinction, mentioned already, between the nobles, of partly Teutonic origin and imperial sympathies, and the burghers, who were the true Italians, the descendants of those over whom successive tides of barbarian conquest had swept, and to whom the ascendency of the nobles would mean an alien yoke. This struggle between a landed military and feudal nobility, waning in power and authority, and a commercial democracy of more purely Latin descent, ever increasing in wealth and importance, is what lies at the bottom of the contest between Florentine Guelfs and

Ghibellines; and the rival claims of Pope and Emperor are of secondary importance, as far as Tuscany is concerned.

In 1173 (as the most recent historian of Florence has shown, and not in the eleventh century as formerly supposed), the second circle of walls was built, and included a much larger tract of city, though many of the churches which we have been wont to consider the most essential things in Florence stand outside them. A new Porta San Piero, just beyond the present façade of the ruined church of San Piero Maggiore, enclosed the Borgo di San Piero; thence the walls passed round to the Porta di Borgo San Lorenzo, just to the north of the present Piazza, and swept round, with two gates of minor importance, past the chief western Porta San Pancrazio or Porta San Paolo, beyond which the present Piazza di Santa Maria Novella stands, down to the Arno where there was a Porta alla Carraia, at the point where the bridge was built later. Hence a lower wall ran along the Arno, taking in the parts excluded from the older circuit down to the Ponte Vecchio. About half-way between this and the Ponte Rubaconte, the walls turned up from the Arno, with several small gates, until they reached the place where the present Piazza di Santa Croce lies—which was outside. Here, just beyond the old site of the Amphitheatre, there was a gate, after which they ran straight without gate or postern to San Piero, where they had commenced.

Instead of the old Quarters, named from the gates, the city was now divided into six corresponding Sesti or sextaries; the Sesto di Porta San Piero, the Sesto still called from the old Porta del Duomo, the Sesto di Porta Pancrazio, the Sesto di San Piero Scheraggio (a church near the Palazzo Vecchio, but now totally destroyed), and the Sesto di Borgo Santissimi Apostoli–these two replacing the old Quarter of Porta Santa Maria. Across the river lay the Sesto d'Oltrarno–then for the most part unfortified. At that time the inhabitants of Oltrarno were mostly the poor and the lower classes, but not a few noble families settled there later on. The Consuls, the supreme officers of the state, were elected annually, two for each sesto, usually nobles of popular tendencies; there was a council of a hundred, elected every year, its members being mainly chosen from the Guilds as the Consuls from the Towers; and a Parliament of the people could be summoned in the Piazza. Thus the popular government was constituted.

Hardly had the new walls risen when the Uberti in 1177 attempted to overthrow the Consuls and seize the government of the city; they were partially successful, in that they managed to make the administration more aristocratic, after a prolonged civil struggle of two years' duration. In 1185 Frederick Barbarossa took away the privileges of the Republic and deprived it of its contrada; but his son, Henry VI., apparently gave it back. With the beginning of the thirteenth century we find the Consuls replaced by a Podestà, a foreign noble elected by the citizens themselves; and the Florentines, not content with having back their contrada, beginning to make wars of conquest upon their neighbours, especially the Sienese, from whom they exacted a cession of territory in 1208.

THE BUONDELMONTE TOWER

In 1215 there was enacted a deed in which poets and chroniclers have seen a turning point in the history of Florence. Buondelmonte dei Buondelmonti, "a right winsome and comely knight," as Villani calls him, had pledged himself for political reasons to marry a maiden of the Amidei family–the kinsmen of the proud Uberti and Fifanti. But, at the instigation of Gualdrada Donati, he deserted his betrothed and married Gualdrada's own daughter, a girl of great beauty. Upon this the nobles of the kindred of the deserted girl held a council together to decide what vengeance to take, in which "Mosca dei Lamberti spoke the evil word: *Cosa fatta, capo ha*; to wit, that he should be slain; and so it was done." On Easter Sunday the Amidei and their associates assembled, after hearing mass in San Stefano, in a palace of the Amidei, which was on the Lungarno at the opening of the present Via Por Santa Maria; and they watched young Buondelmonte coming from Oltrarno, riding over the Ponte Vecchio "dressed nobly in a new robe all white and on a white palfrey," crowned with a garland, making his way towards the palaces of his kindred in Borgo Santissimi Apostoli. As soon as he had reached this side, at the foot of the pillar on which stood the statue of Mars, they rushed out upon him. Schiatta degli Uberti struck him from his horse with a mace, and Mosca dei Lamberti, Lambertuccio degli Amidei, Oderigo Fifanti, and one of the Gangalandi, stabbed him to death with their daggers at the foot of the statue. "Verily is it shown," writes Villani, "that the enemy of human nature by reason of the sins of the Florentines had power in this idol of Mars, which the pagan Florentines adored of old; for at the foot of his figure was this murder committed, whence such great evil followed to the city of Florence." The body was placed upon a bier, and, with the young bride supporting the dead head of her bridegroom, carried through the streets to urge the people to vengeance. Headed by the Uberti, the older and more aristocratic families took up the cause of the Amidei; the burghers and the democratically inclined nobles supported the Buondelmonti, and from this the chronicler dates the beginning of the Guelfs and Ghibellines in Florence.

But it was only the names that were then introduced, to intensify a struggle which had in reality commenced a century before this, in 1115, on the death of Matilda. As far as Guelf and Ghibelline meant a struggle of the commune of burghers and traders with a military aristocracy of Teutonic descent and feudal imperial tendencies, the thing is already clearly defined in the old contest between the Uberti and the Consuls. This, however, precipitated matters, and initiated fifty years of perpetual conflict. Dante, through Cacciaguida, touches upon the tragedy in his great way in *Paradiso* XVI., where he calls it the ruin of old Florence.

"La casa di che nacque il vostro fleto,
per lo giusto disdegno che v'ha morti
e posto fine al vostro viver lieto,
era onorata ed essa e suoi consorti.
O Buondelmonte, quanto mal fuggisti
le nozze sue per gli altrui conforti!
Molti sarebbon lieti, che son tristi,
se Dio t'avesse conceduto ad Ema
la prima volta che a città venisti.
Ma conveniasi a quella pietra scema
che guarda il ponte, che Fiorenza fesse
vittima nella sua pace postrema."[6]

And again, in the Hell of the sowers of discord, where they are horribly mutilated by the devil's sword, he meets the miserable Mosca.

"Ed un, ch'avea l'una e l'altra man mozza,
levando i moncherin per l'aura fosca,
sì che il sangue facea la faccia sozza,
gridò: Ricorderaiti anche del Mosca,
che dissi, lasso! 'Capo ha cosa fatta,'
che fu il mal seme per la gente tosca."[7]

For a time the Commune remained Guelf and powerful, in spite of dissensions; it adhered to the Pope against

Frederick II., and waged successful wars with its Ghibelline rivals, Pisa and Siena. Of the other Tuscan cities Lucca was Guelf, Pistoia Ghibelline. A religious feud mingled with the political dissensions; heretics, the Paterini, Epicureans and other sects, were multiplying in Italy, favoured by Frederick II. and patronised by the Ghibellines. Fra Pietro of Verona, better known as St Peter Martyr, organised a crusade, and, with his white-robed captains of the Faith, hunted them in arms through the streets of Florence; at the Croce al Trebbio, near Santa Maria Novella, and in the Piazza di Santa Felicità over the Arno, columns still mark the place where he fell furiously upon them, *con l'uficio apostolico*. But in 1249, at the instigation of Frederick II., the Uberti and Ghibelline nobles rose in arms; and, after a desperate conflict with the Guelf magnates and the people, gained possession of the city, with the aid of the Emperor's German troops. And, on the night of February 2nd, the Guelf leaders with a great following of people armed and bearing torches buried Rustico Marignolli, who had fallen in defending the banner of the Lily, with military honours in San Lorenzo, and then sternly passed into exile. Their palaces and towers were destroyed, while the Uberti and their allies with the Emperor's German troops held the city. This lasted not two years. In 1250, on the death of Frederick II., the Republic threw off the yoke, and the first democratic constitution of Florence was established, the *Primo Popolo*, in which the People were for the first time regularly organised both for peace and for war under a new officer, the Captain of the People, whose appointment was intended to outweigh the Podestà, the head of the Commune and the leader of the nobles. The Captain was intrusted with the white and red Gonfalon of the People, and associated with the central government of the Ancients of the people, who to some extent corresponded to the Consuls of olden time.

This *Primo Popolo* ran a victorious course of ten years, years of internal prosperity and almost continuous external victory. It was under it that the banner of the Commune was changed from a white lily on a red field to a red lily on a white field–*per division fatto vermiglio*, as Dante puts it–after the Uberti and Lamberti with the turbulent Ghibellines had been expelled. Pisa was humbled; Pistoia and Volterra forced to submit. But it came to a terrible end, illuminated only by the heroism of one of its conquerors. A conspiracy on the part of the Uberti to take the government from the people and subject the city to the great Ghibelline prince, Manfredi, King of Apulia and Sicily, son of Frederick II., was discovered and severely punished. Headed by Farinata degli Uberti and aided by King Manfredi's German mercenaries, the exiles gathered at Siena, against which the Florentine Republic declared war. In 1260 the Florentine army approached Siena. A preliminary skirmish, in which a band of German horsemen was cut to pieces and the royal banner captured, only led a few months later to the disastrous defeat of Montaperti, *che fece l'Arbia colorata in rosso*; in which, after enormous slaughter and loss of the Carroccio, or battle car of the Republic, "the ancient people of Florence was broken and annihilated" on September 4th, 1260. Without waiting for the armies of the conqueror, the Guelf nobles with their families and many of the burghers fled the city, mainly to Lucca; and, on the 16th of September, the Germans under Count Giordano, Manfredi's vicar, with Farinata and the exiles, entered Florence as conquerors. All liberty was destroyed, the houses of Guelfs razed to the ground, the Count Guido Novello–the lord of Poppi and a ruthless Ghibelline–made Podestà. The Via Ghibellina is his record. It was finally proposed in a great Ghibelline council at Empoli to raze Florence to the ground; but the fiery eloquence of Farinata degli Uberti, who declared that, even if he stood alone, he would defend her sword in hand as long as life lasted, saved his city. Marked out with all his house for the relentless hate of the Florentine people, Dante has secured to him a lurid crown of glory even in Hell. Out of the burning tombs of the heretics he rises, *come avesse l'inferno in gran dispitto*, still the unvanquished hero who, when all consented to destroy Florence, "alone with open face defended her."

For nearly six years the life of the Florentine people was suspended, and lay crushed beneath an oppressive despotism of Ghibelline nobles and German soldiery under Guido Novello, the vicar of King Manfredi. Excluded from all political interests, the people imperceptibly organised their greater and lesser guilds, and waited the event. During this gloom Farinata degli Uberti died in 1264, and in the following year, 1265, Dante Alighieri was born. That same year, 1265, Charles of Anjou, the champion of the Church, invited by Clement IV. to take the crown of the kingdom of Naples and Sicily, entered Italy, and in February 1266 annihilated the army of Manfredi at the battle of Benevento. Foremost in the ranks of the crusaders–for as such the French were regarded–fought the Guelf exiles from Florence, under the Papal banner specially granted them by Pope Clement–a red eagle clutching a green dragon on a white field. This, with the addition of a red lily over the eagle's head, became the arms of the society known as the Parte Guelfa; you may see it on the Porta San Niccolò and in other parts of the city between the cross of the People and the red lily of the Commune. Many of the noble Florentines were knighted by the hand of King Charles before the battle, and did great deeds of valour upon the field. "These men cannot lose to-day," exclaimed Manfredi, as he watched their advance; and when the silver eagle of the house of Suabia fell from Manfredi's helmet and he died in the melée crying *Hoc est signum Dei*, the triumph of the Guelfs was complete and German rule at an end in Italy. Of Manfredi's heroic death and the dishonour done by the Pope's legate to his body, Dante has sung in the *Purgatorio*.

When the news reached Florence, the Ghibellines trembled for their safety, and the people prepared to win back their own. An attempt at compromise was first made, under the auspices of Pope Clement. Two *Frati Gaudenti* or "Cavalieri di Maria," members of an order of warrior monks from Bologna, were made Podestàs, one a Guelf and one a Ghibelline, to come to terms with the burghers. You may still trace the place where the Bottega and court of the Calimala stood in Mercato Nuovo (the Calimala being the Guild of dressers of foreign cloth–panni franceschi, as Villani calls it), near where the Via Porta Rossa now enters the present Via Calzaioli. Here the new council of thirty-six of the best citizens, burghers and artizans, with a few trusted members of the nobility, met every day to settle the affairs of the State. Dante has branded these two warrior monks as hypocrites, but, as Capponi says, from this Bottega issued at once and almost spontaneously the Republic of Florence. Their great achievement was the thorough organisation of the seven greater Guilds, of which more presently, to each of which were given consuls and rectors, and a gonfalon or ensign of its own, around which its followers might assemble in arms in defence of People and Commune. To counteract this, Guido Novello brought in more troops from the Ghibelline cities of Tuscany, and increased the taxes to pay his Germans;

until he had fifteen hundred horsemen in the city under his command. With their aid the nobles, headed by the Lamberti, rushed to arms. The people rose *en masse* and, headed by a Ghibelline noble, Gianni dei Soldanieri, who apparently had deserted his party in order to get control of the State (and who is placed by Dante in the Hell of traitors), raised barricades in the Piazza di Santa Trinità and in the Borgo SS. Apostoli, at the foot of the Tower of the Girolami, which still stands. The Ghibellines and Germans gathered in the Piazza di San Giovanni, held all the north-east of the town, and swept down upon the people's barricades under a heavy fire of darts and stones from towers and windows. But the street fighting put the horsemen at a hopeless disadvantage, and, repulsed in the assault, the Count and his followers evacuated the town. This was on St Martin's day, November 11th, 1266. The next day a half-hearted attempt to re-enter the city at the gate near the Ponte alla Carraia was made, but easily driven off; and for two centuries and more no foreigner set foot as conqueror in Florence.

Not that Florence either obtained or desired absolute independence. The first step was to choose Charles of Anjou, the new King of Naples and Sicily, for their suzerain for ten years; but, cruel tyrant as he was elsewhere, he showed himself a true friend to the Florentines, and his suzerainty seldom weighed upon them oppressively. The Uberti and others were expelled, and some, who held out among the castles, were put to death at his orders. But the government became truly democratic. There was a central administration of twelve Ancients, elected annually, two for each sesto; with a council of one hundred "good men of the People, without whose deliberation no great thing or expense could be done"; and, nominally at least, a parliament. Next came the Captain of the People (usually an alien noble of democratic sympathies), with a special council or *credenza*, called the Council of the Captain and Capetudini (the Capetudini composed of the consuls of the Guilds), of 80 members; and a general council of 300 (including the 80), all *popolani* and Guelfs. Next came the Podestà, always an alien noble (appointed at first by King Charles), with the Council of the Podestà of 90 members, and the general Council of the Commune of 300–in both of which nobles could sit as well as popolani. Measures presented by the 12 to the 100 were then submitted successively to the two councils of the Captain, and then, on the next day, to the councils of the Podestà and the Commune. Occasionally measures were concerted between the magistrates and a specially summoned council of *richiesti*, without the formalities and delays of these various councils. Each of the seven greater Arts[8] was further organised with its own officers and councils and banners, like a miniature republic, and its consuls (forming the Capetudini) always sat in the Captain's council and usually in that of the Podestà likewise.

THE PALACE OF THE PARTE GUELFA

There was one dark spot. A new organisation was set on foot, under the auspices of Pope Clement and King Charles, known as the Parte Guelfa—another miniature republic within the republic—with six captains (three nobles and three popolani) and two councils, mainly to persecute the Ghibellines, to manage confiscated goods, and uphold Guelf principles in the State. In later days these Captains of the Guelf Party became exceedingly powerful and oppressive, and were the cause of much dissension. They met at first in the Church of S. Maria sopra la Porta (now the Church of S. Biagio), and later had a special palace of their own—which still stands, partly in the Via delle Terme, as you pass up it from the Via Por Santa Maria on the right, and partly in the Piazza di San Biagio. It is an imposing and somewhat threatening mass, partly of the fourteenth and partly of the early fifteenth century. The church, which retains in part its structure of the thirteenth century, had been a place of secret meeting for the Guelfs during Guido Novello's rule; it still stands, but converted into a barracks for the firemen of Florence.

Thus was the greatest and most triumphant Republic of the Middle Ages organised—the constitution under which the most glorious culture and art of the modern world was to flourish. The great Guilds were henceforth a power in the State, and the *Secondo Popolo* had arisen—the democracy that Dante and Boccaccio were to know.

ARMS OF PARTE GUELFA

CHAPTER II.

THE TIMES OF DANTE AND BOCCACCIO

"Godi, Fiorenza, poi che sei sì grande
che per mare e per terra batti l'ali,
e per l'inferno il tuo nome si spande."
–*Dante.*

THE century that passed from the birth of Dante in 1265 to the deaths of Petrarch and Boccaccio, in 1374 and 1375 respectively, may be styled the *Trecento*, although it includes the last quarter of the thirteenth century and excludes the closing years of the fourteenth. In general Italian history, it runs from the downfall of the German Imperial power at the battle of Benevento, in 1266, to the return of the Popes from Avignon in 1377. In art, it is the epoch of the completion of Italian Gothic in architecture, of the followers and successors of Niccolò and Giovanni Pisano in sculpture, of the school of Giotto in painting. In letters, it is the great period of pure Tuscan prose and verse. Dante and Giovanni Villani, Dino Compagni, Petrarch, Boccaccio and Sacchetti, paint the age for us in all its aspects; and a note of mysticism is heard at the close (though not from a Florentine) in the Epistles of St. Catherine of Siena, of whom a living Italian poet has written—*Nel Giardino del conoscimento di sè ella è come una rosa di fuoco*. But at the same time it is a century full of civil war and sanguinary factions, in which every Italian city was divided against itself; and nowhere were these divisions more notable or more bitterly fought out than in Florence. Yet, in spite of it all, the Republic proceeded majestically on its triumphant course. Machiavelli lays much stress upon this in the Proem to his *Istorie Fiorentine*. "In Florence," he says, "at first the nobles were divided against each other, then the people against the nobles, and lastly the people against the populace; and it ofttimes happened that when one of these parties got the upper hand, it split into two. And from these divisions there resulted so many deaths, so many banishments, so many destructions of families, as never befell in any other city of which we have record. Verily, in my opinion, nothing manifests more clearly the power of our city than the result of these divisions, which would have been able to destroy every great and most potent city. Nevertheless ours seemed thereby to grow ever greater; such was the virtue of those citizens, and the power of their genius and disposition to make themselves and their country great, that those who remained free from these evils could exalt her with their virtue more than the malignity of those accidents, which had diminished them, had been able to cast her down. And without doubt, if only Florence, after her liberation from the Empire, had had the felicity of adopting a form of government which would have kept her united, I know not what republic, whether modern or ancient, would have surpassed her—with such great virtue in war and in peace would she have been filled."

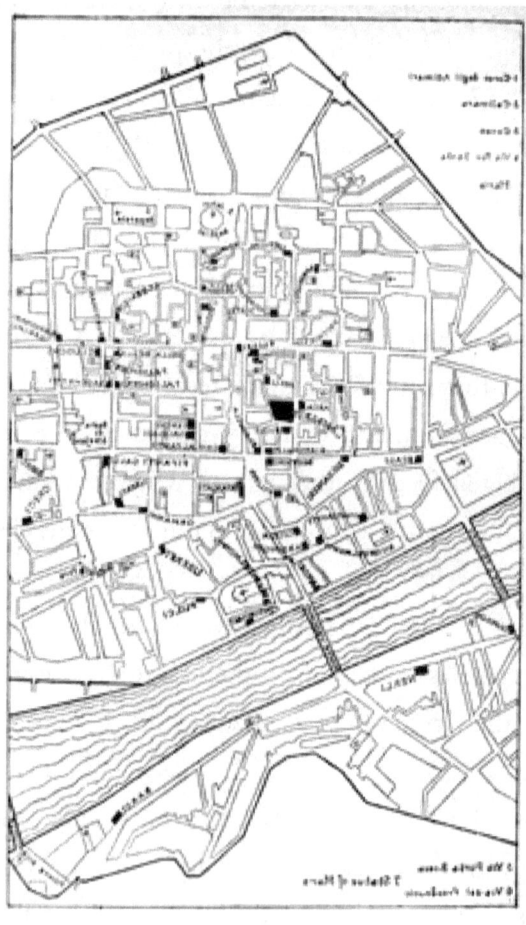

The Story of Florence

FLORENTINE FAMILIES,
EARLY THIRTEENTH CENTURY,
WITH A PORTION OF THE SECOND
WALLS INDICATED
(Temple Classics: Paradiso).
(The representation is approximate only: the Cerchi Palace near the Corso degli Adimari should be more to the right.)

The first thirty-four years of this epoch are among the brightest in Florentine history, the years that ran from the triumph of the Guelfs to the sequel to the Jubilee of 1300, from the establishment of the *Secondo Popolo* to its split into Neri and Bianchi, into Black Guelfs and White Guelfs. Externally Florence became the chief power of Tuscany, and all the neighbouring towns gradually, to a greater or less extent, acknowledged her sway; internally, in spite of growing friction between the burghers and the new Guelf nobility, between *popolani* and *grandi* or magnates, she was daily advancing in wealth and prosperity, in beauty and artistic power. The exquisite poetry of the *dolce stil novo* was heard. Guido Cavalcanti, a noble Guelf who had married the daughter of Farinata degli Uberti, and, later, the notary Lapo Gianni and Dante Alighieri, showed the Italians what true lyric song was; philosophers like Brunetto Latini served the state; modern history was born with Giovanni Villani. Great palaces were built for the officers of the Republic; vast

Gothic churches arose. Women of rare beauty, eternalised as Beatrice, Giovanna, Lagia and the like, passed through the streets and adorned the social gatherings in the open loggias of the palaces. Splendid pageants and processions hailed the Calends of May and the Nativity of the Baptist, and marked the civil and ecclesiastical festivities and state solemnities. The people advanced more and more in power and patriotism; while the magnates, in their towers and palace-fortresses, were partly forced to enter the life of the guilds, partly held aloof and plotted to recover their lost authority, but were always ready to officer the burgher forces in time of war, or to extend Florentine influence by serving as Podestàs and Captains in other Italian cities.

Dante was born in the Sesto di San Piero Maggiore in May 1265, some eighteen months before the liberation of the city. He lost his mother in his infancy, and his father while he was still a boy. This father appears to have been a notary, and came from a noble but decadent family, who were probably connected with the Elisei, an aristocratic house of supposed Roman descent, who had by this time almost entirely disappeared. The Alighieri, who were Guelfs, do not seem to have ranked officially as *grandi* or magnates; one of Dante's uncles had fought heroically at Montaperti. Almost all the families connected with the story of Dante's life had their houses in the Sesto di San Piero Maggiore, and their sites may in some instances still be traced. Here were the Cerchi, with whom he was to be politically associated in after years; the Donati, from whom sprung one of his dearest friends, Forese, with one of his deadliest foes, Messer Corso, and Dante's own wife, Gemma; and the Portinari, the house according to tradition of Beatrice, the "giver of blessing" of Dante's *Vita Nuova*, the mystical lady of the *Paradiso*. Guido Cavalcanti, the first and best of all his friends, lived a little apart from this Sesto di Scandali–as St Peter's section of the town came to be called–between the Mercato Nuovo and San Michele in Orto. Unlike the Alighieri, though not of such ancient birth as theirs, the Cavalcanti were exceedingly rich and powerful, and ranked officially among the *grandi*, the Guelf magnates. At this epoch, as Signor Carocci observes in his *Firenze scomparsa*, Florence must have presented the aspect of a vast forest of towers. These towers rose over the houses of powerful and wealthy families, to be used for offence or defence, when the faction fights raged, or to be dismantled and cut down when the people gained the upper hand. The best idea of such a mediæval city, on a smaller scale, can still be got at San Gemignano, "the fair town called of the Fair Towers," where dozens of these *torri* still stand; and also, though to a less extent, at Gubbio. A few have been preserved here in Florence, and there are a number of narrow streets, on both sides of the Arno, which still retain some of their mediæval characteristics. In the Borgo Santissimi Apostoli, for instance, and in the Via Lambertesca, there are several striking towers of this kind, with remnants of palaces of the *grandi*; and, on the other side of the river, especially in the Via dei Bardi and the Borgo San Jacopo. When one family, or several associated families, had palaces on either side of a narrow street defended by such towers, and could throw chains and barricades across at a moment's notice, it will readily be understood that in times of popular tumult Florence bristled with fortresses in every direction.

In 1282, the year before that in which Dante received the "most sweet salutation," *dolcissimo salutare*, of "the glorious lady of my mind who was called by many Beatrice, that knew not how she was called," and saw the vision of the Lord of terrible aspect in the mist of the colour of fire (the vision which inspired the first of his sonnets which has been preserved to us), the democratic government of the *Secondo Popolo* was confirmed by being placed entirely in the hands of the *Arti Maggiori* or Greater Guilds. The Signoria was henceforth to be composed of the Priors of the Arts, chosen from the chief members of the Greater Guilds, who now became the supreme magistrates of the State. They were, at this epoch of Florentine history, six in number, one to represent each Sesto, and held office for two months only; on leaving office, they joined with the Capetudini, and other citizens summoned for the purpose, to elect their successors. At a later period this was done, ostensibly at least, by lot instead of election. The glorious Palazzo Vecchio had not yet been built, and the Priors met at first in a house belonging to the monks of the Badia, defended by the Torre della Castagna; and afterwards in a palace belonging to the Cerchi (both tower and palace are still standing). Of the seven Greater Arts—the *Calimala*, the Money-changers, the Wool-merchants, the Silk-merchants, the Physicians and Apothecaries, the traders in furs and skins, the Judges and Notaries—the latter alone do not seem at first to have been represented in the Priorate; but to a certain extent they exercised control over all the Guilds, sat in all their tribunals, and had a Proconsul, who came next to the Signoria in all state processions, and had a certain jurisdiction over all the Arts. It was thus essentially a government of those who were actually engaged in industry and commerce. "Henceforth," writes Pasquale Villari, "the Republic is properly a republic of merchants, and only he who is ascribed to the Arts can govern it: every grade of nobility, ancient or new, is more a loss than a privilege." The double organisation of the People under the Captain with his two councils, and the Commune under the Podestà with his special council and the general council (in these two latter alone, it will be remembered, could nobles sit and vote) still remained; but the authority of the Podestà was naturally diminished.

CORSO DONATI'S TOWER

Florence was now the predominant power in central Italy; the cities of Tuscany looked to her as the head of the Guelfic League, although, says Dino Compagni, "they love her more in discord than in peace, and obey her more for fear than for love." A protracted war against Pisa and Arezzo, carried on from 1287 to 1292, drew even Dante from his poetry and his study; it is believed that he took part in the great battle of Campaldino in 1289, in which the last efforts of the old Tuscan Ghibellinism were shattered by the Florentines and their allies, fighting under the royal banner of the House of Anjou. Amerigo di Narbona, one of the captains of King Charles II. of Naples, was in command of the Guelfic forces. From many points of view, this is one of the more interesting battles of the Middle Ages. It is said to have been almost the last Italian battle in which the burgher forces, and not the mercenary soldiery of the Condottieri, carried the day. Corso Donati and Vieri dei Cerchi, soon to be in deadly feud in the political arena, were among the captains of the Florentine host; and Dante himself is said to have served in the front rank of the cavalry. In a fragment of a letter ascribed to him by one of his earlier biographers, Dante speaks of this battle of Campaldino; "wherein I had much dread, and at the end the greatest gladness, by reason of the varying chances of that battle." One of the Ghibelline leaders, Buonconte da Montefeltro, who was mortally wounded and died in the rout, meets the divine poet on the shores of the Mountain of Purgation, and, in lines of almost ineffable pathos, tells him the whole story of his last moments. Villani, ever mindful of Florence being the daughter of Rome, assures us that the news of the great victory was miraculously brought to the Priors in the Cerchi Palace, in much the same way as the tidings of Lake Regillus to the expectant Fathers at the gate of Rome. Several of the exiled Uberti had fallen in the ranks of the enemy, fighting against their own country. In the cloisters of the Annunziata you will find a contemporary monument of the battle, let into the west wall of the church near the ground; the marble figure of an armed knight on horseback, with the golden lilies of France over his surcoat, charging down upon the foe. It is the tomb of the French cavalier, Guglielmo Berardi, "balius" of Amerigo di Narbona, who fell upon the field.

The eleven years that follow Campaldino, culminating in the Jubilee of Pope Boniface VIII. and the opening of the fourteenth century, are the years of Dante's political life. They witnessed the great political reforms which confirmed the democratic character of the government, and the marvellous artistic embellishment of the city under Arnolfo di Cambio and his contemporaries. During these years the Palazzo Vecchio, the Duomo, and the grandest churches of Florence were founded; and the Third Walls, whose gates and some scanty remnants are with us to-day, were begun. Favoured by the Popes and the Angevin sovereigns of

Naples, now that the old Ghibelline nobility, save in a few valleys and mountain fortresses, was almost extinct, the new nobles, the *grandi* or Guelf magnates, proud of their exploits at Campaldino, and chafing against the burgher rule, began to adopt an overbearing line of conduct towards the people, and to be more factious than ever among themselves. Strong measures were adopted against them, such as the complete enfranchisement of the peasants of the contrada in 1289–measures which culminated in the famous Ordinances of Justice, passed in 1293, by which the magnates were completely excluded from the administration, severe laws made to restrain their rough usage of the people, and a special magistrate, the *Gonfaloniere* or "Standard-bearer of Justice," added to the Priors, to hold office like them for two months in rotation from each sesto of the city, and to rigidly enforce the laws against the magnates. This Gonfaloniere became practically the head of the Signoria, and was destined to become the supreme head of the State in the latter days of the Florentine Republic; to him was publicly assigned the great Gonfalon of the People, with its red cross on a white field; and he had a large force of armed popolani under his command to execute these ordinances, against which there was no appeal allowed.[9] These Ordinances also fixed the number of the Guilds at twenty-one–seven Arti Maggiori, mainly engaged in wholesale commerce, exportation and importation, fourteen Arti Minori, which carried on the retail traffic and internal trade of the city—and renewed their statutes.

The hero of this Magna Charta of Florence is a certain Giano della Bella, a noble who had fought at Campaldino and had now joined the people; a man of untractable temper, who knew not how to make concessions; somewhat anti-clerical and obnoxious to the Pope, but consumed by an intense and savage thirst for justice, upon which the craftier politicians of both sides played. "Let the State perish, rather than such things be tolerated," was his constant political formula: *Perisca innanzi la città, che tante opere rie si sostengano.* But the magnates, from whom he was endeavouring to snatch their last political refuge, the Parte Guelfa, muttered, "Let us smite the shepherd, and the sheep shall be scattered"; and at length, after an ineffectual conspiracy against his life, Giano was driven out of the city, on March 5th, 1295, by a temporary alliance of the burghers and magnates against him. The *popolo minuto* and artizans, upon whom he had mainly relied and whose interests he had sustained, deserted him; and the government remained henceforth in the hands of the wealthy burghers, the *popolo grosso*. Already a cleavage was becoming visible between these Arti Maggiori, who ruled the State, and the Arti Minori whose gains lay in local merchandise and traffic, partly dependent upon the magnates. And a butcher, nicknamed Pecora, or, as we may call him, Lambkin, appears prominently as a would-be politician; he cuts a quaintly fierce figure in Dino Compagni's chronicle. In this same year, 1295, Dante Alighieri entered public life, and, on July 6th, he spoke in the General Council of the Commune in support of certain modifications in the Ordinances of Justice, whereby nobles, by leaving their order and matriculating in one or other of the Arts, even without exercising it, could be free from their disabilities, and could share in the government of the State, and hold office in the Signoria. He himself, in this same year, matriculated in the Arte dei Medici e Speziali, the great guild which included the painters and the book-sellers.

The growing dissensions in the Guelf Republic came to a head in 1300, the famous year of jubilee in which the Pope was said to have declared that the Florentines were the "fifth element." The rival factions of Bianchi and Neri, White Guelfs and Black Guelfs, which were now to divide the whole city, arose partly from the deadly hostility of two families each with a large following, the Cerchi and the Donati, headed respectively by Vieri dei Cerchi and Corso Donati, the two heroes of Campaldino; partly from an analogous feud in Pistoia, which was governed from Florence; partly from the political discord between that party in the State that clung to the (modified) Ordinances of Justice and supported the Signoria, and another party that hated the Ordinances and loved the tyrannical Parte Guelfa. They were further complicated by the intrigues of the "black" magnates with Pope Boniface VIII., who apparently hoped by their means to repress the burgher government and unite the city in obedience to himself. With this end in view, he had been endeavouring to obtain from Albert of Austria the renunciation, in favour of the Holy See, of all rights claimed by the Emperors over Tuscany. Dante himself, Guido Cavalcanti, and most of the best men in Florence either directly adhered to, or at least favoured, the Cerchi and the Whites; the populace, on the other hand, was taken with the dash and display of the more aristocratic Blacks, and would gladly have seen Messer Corso–"il Barone," as they called him–lord of the city. Rioting, in which Guido Cavalcanti played a wild and fantastic part, was of daily occurrence, especially in the Sesto di San Piero. The adherents of the Signoria had their head-quarters in the Cerchi Palace, in the Via della Condotta; the Blacks found their legal fortress in that of the Captains of the Parte Guelfa in the Via delle Terme. At last, on May 1st, the two factions "came to blood" in the Piazza di Santa Trinità on the occasion of a dance of girls to usher in the May. On June 15th Dante was elected one of the six Priors, to hold office till August 15th, and he at once took a strong line in resisting all interference from Rome, and in maintaining order within the city. In consequence of an assault upon the officers of the Guilds on St. John's Eve, the Signoria, probably on Dante's initiative, put under bounds a certain number of factious magnates, chosen impartially from both parties, including Corso Donati and Guido Cavalcanti. From his place of banishment at Sarzana, Guido, sick to death, wrote the most pathetic of all his lyrics:–

> "Because I think not ever to return,
> Ballad, to Tuscany,–
> Go therefore thou for me
> Straight to my lady's face,
> Who, of her noble grace,
> Shall show thee courtesy.

> * * * * *

> "Surely thou knowest, Ballad, how that Death
> Assails me, till my life is almost sped:
> Thou knowest how my heart still travaileth
> Through the sore pangs which in my soul are bred:–
> My body being now so nearly dead,
> It cannot suffer more.
> Then, going, I implore
> That this my soul thou take
> (Nay, do so for my sake),
> When my heart sets it free."[10]

And at the end of August, when Dante had left office, Guido returned to Florence with the rest of the Bianchi, only to die. For more than a year the "white" burghers were supreme, not only in Florence, but throughout a greater part of Tuscany; and in the following May they procured the expulsion of the Blacks from Pistoia. But Corso Donati at Rome was biding his time; and, on November 1st, 1301, Charles of Valois, brother of King Philip of France, entered Florence with some 1200 horsemen, partly French and partly Italian,—ostensibly as papal peacemaker, but preparing to "joust with the lance of Judas." In Santa Maria Novella he solemnly swore, as the son of a king, to preserve the peace and well-being of the city; and at once armed his followers. Magnates and burghers alike, seeing themselves betrayed, began to barricade their houses and streets. On the same day (November 5th) Corso Donati, acting in unison with the French, appeared in the suburbs, entered the city by a postern gate in the second walls, near S. Piero Maggiore, and swept through the streets with an armed force, burst open the prisons, and drove the Priors out of their new Palace. For days the French and the Neri sacked the city and the contrada at their will, Charles being only intent upon securing a large share of the spoils for himself. But even he did not dare to alter the popular constitution, and was forced to content himself with substituting "black" for "white" burghers in the Signoria, and establishing a Podestà of his own following, Cante de' Gabbrielli of Gubbio, in the Palace of the Commune. An apparently genuine attempt on the part of the Pope, by a second "peacemaker," to undo the harm that his first had done, came to nothing; and the work of proscription commenced, under the direction of the new Podestà. Dante was one of the first victims. The two sentences against him (in each case with a few other names) are dated January 27th, 1302, and March 10th—and there were to be others later. It is the second decree that contains the famous clause, condemning him to be burned to death, if ever he fall into the power of the Commune. At the beginning of April all the leaders of the "white" faction, who had not already fled or turned "black," with their chief followers, magnates and burghers alike, were hounded into exile; and Charles left Florence to enter upon an almost equally shameful campaign in Sicily.

ACROSS THE PONTE VECCHIO

Dante is believed to have been absent from Florence on an embassy to the Pope when Charles of Valois came, and to have heard the news of his ruin at Siena as he hurried homewards–though both embassy and absence have been questioned by Dante scholars of repute. His ancestor, Cacciaguida, tells him in the *Paradiso*:–

> "Tu lascerai ogni cosa diletta
> più caramente, e questo è quello strale
> che l'arco dello esilio pria saetta.
> Tu proverai sì come sa di sale
> lo pane altrui, e com'è duro calle
> lo scendere e il salir per l'altrui scale."[11]

The rest of Dante's life was passed in exile, and only touches the story of Florence indirectly at certain points. "Since it was the pleasure of the citizens of the most beautiful and most famous daughter of Rome, Florence," he tells us in his *Convivio*, "to cast me forth from her most sweet bosom (in which I was born and nourished up to the summit of my life, and in which, with her good will, I desire with all my heart to rest my weary soul and end the time given me), I have gone through almost all the parts to which this language extends, a pilgrim, almost a beggar, showing against my will the wound of fortune, which is wont unjustly to be ofttimes reputed to the wounded."

Attempts of the exiles to win their return to Florence by force of arms, with aid from the Ubaldini and the Tuscan Ghibellines, were easily repressed. But the victorious Neri themselves now split into two factions; the one, headed by Corso Donati and composed mainly of magnates, had a kind of doubtful support in the favour of the populace; the other, led by Rosso della Tosa, inclined to the Signoria and the *popolo grosso*. It was something like the old contest between Messer Corso and Vieri dei Cerchi, but with more entirely selfish ends; and there was evidently going to be a hard tussle between Messer Corso and Messer Rosso for the possession of the State. Civil war was renewed in the city, and the confusion was heightened by the restoration of a certain number of Bianchi, who were reconciled to the Government. The new Pope, Benedict XI., was ardently striving to pacify Florence and all Italy; and his legate, the Cardinal Niccolò da Prato, took up the cause of the exiles. Pompous peace-meetings were held in the Piazza di Santa Maria Novella, for the friars of St Dominic–to which order the new Pope belonged–had the welfare of the city deeply at heart; and at one of these meetings the exiled lawyer, Ser Petracco dall'Ancisa (in a few days to be the father of Italy's second poet), acted as the representative of his party. Attempts were made to revive the May-day pageants of brighter days–but they only resulted in a horrible disaster on the Ponte alla Carraia, of which more presently. The fiends of faction broke loose again; and in order to annihilate the Cavalcanti, who were still rich and powerful round about the Mercato Nuovo, the leaders of the Neri deliberately burned a large portion of the city. On July 20th, 1304, an attempt by the now allied Bianchi and Ghibellines to surprise the city proved a disastrous failure; and, on that very day (Dante being now far away at Verona, forming a party by himself), Francesco di Petracco–who was to call himself Petrarca and is called by us Petrarch–was born in exile at Arezzo.

MERCATO NUOVO, THE FLOWER MARKET

This miserable chapter of Florentine history ended tragically in 1308, with the death of Corso Donati. In his old age he had married a daughter of Florence's deadliest foe, the great Ghibelline champion, Uguccione della Faggiuola; and, in secret understanding with Uguccione and the Cardinal Napoleone degli Orsini (Pope Clement V. had already transferred the papal chair to Avignon and commenced the Babylonian captivity), he was preparing to overthrow the Signoria, abolish the Ordinances, and make himself Lord of Florence. But the people anticipated him. On Sunday morning, October 16th, the Priors ordered their great bell to be sounded; Corso was accused, condemned as a traitor and rebel, and sentence pronounced in less than an hour; and with the great Gonfalon of the People displayed, the forces of the Commune, supported by the swordsmen of the Della Tosa and a band of Catalan mercenaries in the service of the King of Naples, marched upon the Piazza di San Piero Maggiore. Over the Corbizzi tower floated the banner of the Donati, but only a handful of men gathered round the fierce old noble who, himself unable by reason of his gout to bear arms, encouraged them by his fiery words to hold out to the last. But the soldiery of Uguccione never came, and not a single magnate in the city stirred to aid him. Corso, forced at last to abandon his position, broke through his enemies, and, hotly pursued, fled through the Porta alla Croce. He was overtaken, captured, and barbarously slain by the lances of the hireling soldiery, near the Badia di San Salvi, at the instigation, as it was whispered, of Rosso della Tosa and Pazzino dei Pazzi. The monks carried him, as he lay dying, into the Abbey, where they gave him humble sepulchre for fear of the people. With all his crimes, there was nothing small in anything that Messer Corso did; he was a great spirit, one who could have accomplished mighty things in other circumstances, but who could not breathe freely in the atmosphere of a mercantile republic. "His life was perilous," says Dino Compagni sententiously, "and his death was blame-worthy."

A brief but glorious chapter follows, though denounced in Dante's bitterest words. Hardly was Corso dead when, after their long silence, the imperial trumpets were again heard in the Garden of the Empire. Henry of Luxemburg, the last hero of the Middle Ages, elected Emperor as Henry VII., crossed the Alps in September 1310, resolved to heal the wounds of Italy, and to revive the fading mediæval dream of the Holy Roman Empire. In three wild and terrible letters, Dante announced to the princes and peoples of Italy the advent of this "peaceful king," this "new Moses"; threatened the Florentines with the vengeance of the Imperial Eagle; urged Cæsar on against the city–"the sick sheep that infecteth all the flock of the Lord with her contagion." But the Florentines rose to the occasion, and with the aid of their ally, the King of Naples, formed what was practically an Italian confederation to oppose the imperial invader. "It was at this moment," writes Professor Villari, "that the small merchant republic initiated a truly national policy, and became a great power in Italy." From the middle of September till the end of October, 1312, the imperial army lay round Florence. The Emperor, sick with fever, had his head-quarters in San Salvi. But he dared not venture upon an attack, although the fortifications were unfinished; and, in the following August, the Signoria of Florence could write exultantly to their allies, and announce "the blessed tidings" that "the most savage tyrant, Henry, late Count of Luxemburg, whom the rebellious persecutors of the Church, and treacherous foes of ourselves and you, called King of the Romans and Emperor of Germany," had died at Buonconvento.

But in the Empyrean Heaven of Heavens, in the mystical convent of white stoles, Beatrice shows Dante the throne of glory prepared for the soul of the noble-hearted Cæsar:–

> "In quel gran seggio, a che tu gli occhi tieni
> per la corona che già v'è su posta,
> prima che tu a queste nozze ceni,
> sederà l'alma, che fia giù agosta,
> dell'alto Enrico, ch'a drizzare Italia
> verrà in prima che ella sia disposta."[12]

After this, darker days fell upon Florence. Dante, with a renewed sentence of death upon his head, was finishing his *Divina Commedia* at Verona and Ravenna,– until, on September 14th, 1321, he passed away in the latter city, with the music of the pine-forest in his ears and the monuments of dead emperors before his dying eyes. Petrarch, after a childhood spent at Carpentras, was studying law at Montpellier and Bologna–until, on that famous April morning in Santa Chiara at Avignon, he saw the golden-haired girl who made him the greatest lyrist of the Middle Ages. It was in the year 1327 that Laura–if such was really her name–thus crossed his path. Boccaccio, born at Certaldo in 1313, the year of the Emperor Henry's death, was growing up in Florence, a sharp and precocious boy. But the city was in a woeful plight; harassed still by factious magnates and burghers, plundered by foreign adventurers, who pretended to serve her, heavily taxed by the Angevin sovereigns–the *Reali*–of Naples. Florence had taken first King Robert, and then his son, Charles of Calabria, as overlord, for defence against external foes (first Henry VII., then Uguccione della Faggiuola, and then Castruccio Interminelli); and the vicars of these Neapolitan princes replaced for a while the Podestàs; their marshals robbed and corrupted; their Catalan soldiers clamoured for pay. The wars with Uguccione and Castruccio were most disastrous to the Republic; and the fortunate coincidence of the deaths of Castruccio and Charles of

Calabria, in 1328, gave Florence back her liberty at the very moment when she no longer needed a defender. Although the Florentines professed to regard this suzerainty of the Reali di Napoli as an alliance rather than a subjection,– *compagnia e non servitù* as Machiavelli puts it–it was an undoubted relief when it ended. The State was reorganised, and a new constitution confirmed in a solemn Parliament held in the Piazza. Henceforth the nomination of the Priors and Gonfaloniere was effected by lot, and controlled by a complicated process of scrutiny; the old councils were all annulled; and in future there were to be only two chief councils–the Council of the People, composed of 300 *popolani*, presided over by the Captain, and the Council of the Commune, of 250, presided over by the Podestà, in which latter (as in former councils of the kind) both *popolani* and *grandi* could sit. Measures proposed by the Government were submitted first to the Council of the People, and then, if approved, to that of the Commune.

Within the next few years, in spite of famine, disease, and a terrible inundation of the Arno in 1333, the Republic largely extended its sway. Pistoia, Arezzo, and other places of less account owned its signory; but an attempt to get possession of Lucca–with the incongruous aid of the Germans–failed. After the flood, the work of restoration was first directed by Giotto; and to this epoch we owe the most beautiful building in Florence, the Campanile. The discontent, excited by the mismanagement of the war against Lucca, threw the Republic into the arms of a new and peculiarly atrocious tyrant, Walter de Brienne, Duke of Athens, a French soldier of fortune, connected by blood with the *Reali* of Naples. Elected first as war captain and chief justice, he acquired credit with the populace and the magnates by his executions of unpopular burghers; and finally, on September 8th, 1342, in the Piazza della Signoria, he was appointed Lord of Florence for life, amidst the acclamations of the lowest sections of the mob and the paid retainers of the treacherous nobles. The Priors were driven from their palace, the books of the Ordinances destroyed, and the Duke's banner erected upon the People's tower, while the church bells rang out the *Te Deum*. Arezzo, Pistoia, Colle di Val d'Elsa, San Gemignano, and Volterra acknowledged his rule; and with a curious mixture of hypocrisy, immorality, and revolting cruelty, he reigned as absolute lord until the following summer, backed by French and Burgundian soldiers who flocked to him from all quarters. By that time he had utterly disgusted all classes in the State, even the magnates by whose favour he had won his throne and the populace who had acclaimed him; and on the Feast of St. Anne, July 26th, 1343, there was a general rising. The instruments of his cruelty were literally torn to pieces by the people, and he was besieged in the Palazzo Vecchio, which he had transformed into a fortress, and at length capitulated on August 3rd. The Sienese and

Count Simone de' Conti Guidi, who had come to mediate, took him over the Ponte Rubaconte, through the Porta San Niccolò and thence into the Casentino, where they made him solemnly ratify his abdication.

"Note," says Giovanni Villani, who was present at most of these things and has given us a most vivid picture of them, "that even as the Duke with fraud and treason took away the liberty of the Republic of Florence on the day of Our Lady in September,[13] not regarding the reverence due to her, so, as it were in divine vengeance, God permitted that the free citizens with armed hand should win it back on the day of her mother, Madonna Santa Anna, on the 26th day of July 1343; and for this grace it was ordained by the Commune that the Feast of St. Anne should ever be kept like Easter in Florence, and that there should be celebrated a solemn office and great offerings by the Commune and all the Arts of Florence." St. Anne henceforth became the chief patroness and protectoress of the Republic, as Fra Bartolommeo painted her in his great unfinished picture in the Uffizi; and the solemn office and offerings were duly paid and celebrated in Or San Michele. One of Villani's minor grievances against the Duke is that he introduced frivolous French fashions of dress into the city, instead of the stately old Florentine costume, which the republicans considered to be the authentic garb of ancient Rome. That there was some ground for this complaint will readily be seen, by comparing the figure of a French cavalier in the Allegory of the Church in the Spanish Chapel at Santa Maria Novella (the figure formerly called Cimabue and now sometimes said to represent Walter de Brienne himself), with the simple grandeur and dignity of the dress worn by the burghers on their tombs in Santa Croce, or by Dante in the Duomo portrait.

Only two months after the expulsion of the Duke of Athens, the great quarrel between the magnates and the people was fought to a finish, in September 1343. On the northern side of the Arno, the magnates made head at the houses of the Adimari near San Giovanni, at the opening of the present Via Calzaioli, where one of their towers still stands, at the houses of the Pazzi and Donati in the Piazza di San Pier Maggiore, and round those of the Cavalcanti in Mercato Nuovo. The people under their great gonfalon and the standards of the companies, led by the Medici and Rondinelli, stormed one position after another, forcing the defenders to surrender. On the other side of the Arno, the magnates and their retainers held the bridges and the narrow streets beyond. The Porta San Giorgio was in their hands, and, through it, reinforcements were hurried up from the country. Repulsed at the Ponte Vecchio and the Ponte Rubaconte, the forces of the people with their victorious standards at last carried the Ponte alla Carraia, which was held by the Nerli; and next, joined by the populace of the Oltrarno, forced the Rossi and Frescobaldi to yield. The Bardi alone remained; and, in that narrow street which still bears their name, and on the Ponte Vecchio and the Ponte Rubaconte, they withstood single-handed the onslaught of the whole might of the people, until they were assailed in the rear from the direction of the Via Romana. The infuriated populace sacked their houses, destroyed and burned the greater part of their palaces and towers. The long struggle between *grandi* and *popolani* was thus ended at last. "This was the cause," says Machiavelli, "that Florence was stripped not only of all martial skill, but also of all generosity." The government was again reformed, and the minor arts admitted to a larger share; between the *popolo grosso* and them, between burghers and populace, lay the struggle now, which was to end in the Medicean rule.

But on all these perpetual changes in the form of the government of Florence the last word had, perhaps, been said in Dante's sarcastic outburst a quarter of a century before:–

"Atene e Lacedemone, che fenno
l'antiche leggi, e furon sì civili,
fecero al viver bene un picciol cenno
verso di te, che fai tanto sottili
provvedimenti, che a mezzo novembre
non giunge quel che tu d'ottobre fili.
Quante volte del tempo che rimembre,
legge, moneta, offizio, e costume

hai tu mutato, e rinnovato membre?
E se ben ti ricordi, e vedi lume,
vedrai te simigliante a quella inferma,
che non può trovar posa in su le piume,
ma con dar volta suo dolore scherma."[14]

The terrible pestilence, known as the Black Death, swept over Europe in 1348. During the five months in which it devastated Florence three-fifths of the population perished, all civic life was suspended, and the gayest and most beautiful of cities seemed for a while to be transformed into the dim valley of disease and sin that lies outstretched at the bottom of Dante's Malebolge. It has been described, in all its horrors, in one of the most famous passages of modern prose—that appalling introduction to Boccaccio's *Decameron*. From the city in her agony, Boccaccio's three noble youths and seven "honest ladies" fled to the villas of Settignano and Fiesole, where they strove to drown the horror of the time by their music and dancing, their feasting and too often sadly obscene stories. Giovanni Villani was among the victims in Florence, and Petrarch's Laura at Avignon. The first canto of Petrarch's *Triumph of Death* appears to be, in part, an allegorical representation—written many years later—of this fearful year.

During the third quarter of this fourteenth century—the years which still saw the Popes remaining in their Babylonian exile at Avignon–the Florentines gradually regained their lost supremacy over the cities of Tuscany: Colle di Val d'Elsa, San Gemignano, Prato, Pistoia, Volterra, San Miniato dei Tedeschi. They carried on a war with the formidable tyrant of Milan, the Archbishop Giovanni Visconti, whose growing power was a perpetual menace to the liberties of the Tuscan communes. They made good use of the descent of the feeble emperor, Charles IV., into Italy; waged a new war with their old rival, Pisa; and readily accommodated themselves to the baser conditions of warfare that prevailed, now that Italy was the prey of the companies of mercenaries, ready to be hired by whatever prince or republic could afford the largest pay, or to fall upon whatever city seemed most likely to yield the heaviest ransom. Within the State itself the *popolo minuto* and the Minor Guilds were advancing in power; Florence was now divided into four quarters (San Giovanni, Santa Maria Novella, Santa Croce, Santo Spirito), instead of the old Sesti; and the Signoria was now composed of the Gonfaloniere and *eight* Priors, two from each quarter (instead of the former six), of whom two belonged to the Minor Arts. These, of course, still held office for only two months. Next came the twelve Buonuomini, who were the counsellors of the Signoria, and held office for three months; and the sixteen Gonfaloniers of the city companies, four from each quarter, holding office for four months. And there were, as before, the two great Councils of the People and the Commune; and still the three great officers who carried out their decrees, the Podestà, the Captain, the Executor of Justice. The feuds of Ricci and Albizzi kept up the inevitable factions, much as the Buondelmonti and Uberti, Cerchi and Donati had done of old; and an iniquitous system of "admonishing" those who were suspected of Ghibelline descent (the *ammoniti* being excluded from office under heavy penalties) threw much power into the hands of the captains of the Parte Guelfa, whose oppressive conduct earned them deadly hatred. "To such arrogance," says Machiavelli, "did the captains of the Party mount, that they were feared more than the members of the Signoria, and less reverence was paid to the latter than to the former; the palace of the Party was more esteemed than that of the Signoria, so that no ambassador came to Florence without having commissions to the captains."

THE CAMPANILE

Pope Gregory XI preceded his return to Rome by an attempted reconquest of the States of the Church, by means of foreign legates and hireling soldiers, of whom the worst were Bretons and English; although St. Catherine of Siena implored him, in the name of Christ, to come with the Cross in hand, like a meek lamb, and not with armed bands. The horrible atrocities committed in Romagna by these mercenaries, especially at Faenza and Cesena, stained what might have been a noble pontificate. Against Pope Gregory and his legates, the Florentines carried on a long and disastrous war; round the Otto della Guerra, the eight magistrates to whom the management of the war was intrusted, rallied those who hated the Parte Guelfa. The return of Gregory to Rome in 1377 opens a new epoch in Italian history. Echoes of this unnatural struggle between Florence and the Pope reach us in the letters of St Catherine and the canzoni of Franco Sacchetti; in the latter is some faint sound of Dante's *saeva indignatio* against the unworthy pastors of the Church, but in the former we are lifted far above the miserable realities of a conflict carried on by political intrigue and foreign mercenaries, into the mystical realms of pure faith and divine charity.

In 1376, the Loggia dei Priori, now less pleasantly known as the Loggia dei Lanzi, was founded; and in 1378 the bulk of the Duomo was practically completed. This may be taken as the close of the first or "heroic" epoch of Florentine Art, which runs simultaneously with the great democratic period of Florentine history, represented in literature by Dante and Boccaccio. The Duomo, the Palace of the Podestà, the Palace of the Priors, Santa Maria Novella, Santa Croce, Or San Michele, the Loggia of the Bigallo, and the Third Walls of the City (of which, on the northern side of the Arno, the gates alone remain), are its supreme monuments in architecture. Its heroes of greatest name are Arnolfo di Cambio, Giotto di Bondone, Andrea Pisano, Andrea di Cione or Orcagna (the "Archangel"), and, lastly and but recently recognised, Francesco Talenti.

"No Italian architect," says Addington Symonds, "has enjoyed the proud privilege of stamping his own individuality more strongly on his native city than Arnolfo." At present, the walls of the city (or what remains of them)–*le mura di Fiorenza* which Lapo Gianni would fain see *inargentate*–and the bulk of the Palazzo Vecchio and Santa Croce, alone represent Arnolfo's work. But the Duomo (mainly, in its present form, due to Francesco Talenti) probably still retains in part his design; and the glorious Church of Or San Michele, of which the actual architect is not certainly known, stands on the site of his Loggia.

Giovanni Cimabue, the father of Florentine painting as Arnolfo of Florentine architecture, survives only as a name in Dante's immortal verse. Not a single authentic work remains from his hand in Florence. His supposed portrait in the cloisters of Santa Maria Novella is now held to be that of a French knight; the famous picture of the Madonna and Child with her angelic ministers, in the Rucellai Chapel, is shown to be the work of a Sienese master; and the other paintings once ascribed to him have absolutely no claims to bear his name. But the Borgo Allegro still bears its title from the rejoicings that hailed his masterpiece, and perhaps it is best that his achievement should thus live, only as a holy memory:–

> "Credette Cimabue nella pittura
> tener lo campo, ed ora ha Giotto il grido,
> sì che la fama di colui è oscura."[15]

Of Cimabue's great pupil, Dante's friend and contemporary, Giotto, we know and possess much more. Through him mediæval Italy first spoke out through painting, and with no uncertain sound. He was born some ten years later than Dante. Cimabue–or so the legend runs, which is told by Leonardo da Vinci amongst others–found him among the mountains, guarding his father's flocks and drawing upon the stones the movements of the goats committed to his care. He was a typical Florentine craftsman; favoured by popes, admitted to the familiarity of kings, he remained to the end the same unspoilt shepherd whom Cimabue had found. Many choice and piquant tales are told by the novelists about his ugly presence and rare personality, his perpetual good humour, his sharp and witty answers to king and rustic alike, his hatred of all pretentiousness, carried to such an extent that he conceived a rooted objection to hearing himself called *maestro*. Padua and Assisi possess some of his very best work; but Florence can still show much. Two chapels in Santa Croce are painted by his hand; of the smaller pictures ascribed to him in churches and galleries, there is one authentic–the Madonna in the Accademia; and, perhaps most beautiful of all, the Campanile which he designed and commenced still rises in the midst of the city. Giotto died in 1336; his work was carried on by Andrea Pisano and practically finished by Francesco Talenti.

Andrea di Ugolino Pisano (1270-1348), usually simply called Andrea Pisano, is similarly the father of Florentine sculpture. Vasari's curiously inaccurate account of him has somewhat blurred his real figure in the history of art. His great achievements are the casting of the first gate of the Baptistery in bronze, his work–apparently from Giotto's designs–in the lower series of marble reliefs round the Campanile, and his continuation of the Campanile itself after Giotto's death. He is said by Vasari to have built the Porta di San Frediano.

There is little individuality in the followers of Giotto, who carried on his tradition and worked in his manner. They are very much below their master, and are often surpassed by the contemporary painters of Siena, such as Simone Martini and Ambrogio Lorenzetti. Taddeo Gaddi and his son, Agnolo, Giovanni di Milano, Bernardo Daddi, are their leaders; the chief title to fame of the first-named being the renowned Ponte Vecchio. But their total achievement, in conjunction with the Sienese, was of heroic magnitude. They covered the walls of churches and chapels, especially those connected with the Franciscans and Dominicans, with the scenes of Scripture, with the lives of Madonna and her saints; they set forth in all its fullness the whole Gospel story, for those who could neither read nor write; they conceived vast allegories of human life and human destinies; they filled the palaces of the republics with painted parables of good government. "By the grace of God," says a statute of Sienese painters, "we are the men who make manifest to the ignorant and unlettered the miraculous things achieved by the power and virtue of the Faith." At Siena, at Pisa and at Assisi, are perhaps the greatest works of this school; but here, in Santa Croce and Santa Maria Novella, there is much, and of a very noble and characteristic kind. Spinello Aretino (1333-1410) may be regarded as the last of the Giotteschi; you may see his best series of frescoes in San Miniato, setting forth with much skill and power the life of the great Italian monk, whose face Dante so earnestly prayed to behold unveiled in Paradise.

This heroic age of sculpture and painting culminated in Andrea Orcagna (1308-1368), Andrea Pisano's great pupil. Painter and sculptor, architect and poet, Orcagna is at once the inheritor of Niccolò and Giovanni Pisano, and of Giotto. The famous frescoes in the Pisan Campo Santo are now known to be the work of some other hand; his paintings in Santa Croce, with their priceless portraits, have perished; and, although frequently consulted in the construction of the Duomo, it is tolerably certain that he was not the architect of any of the Florentine buildings once ascribed to him. The Strozzi chapel of St Thomas in Santa Maria Novella, the oratory of the Madonna in San Michele in Orto, contain all his extant works; and they are sufficient to prove him, next to Giotto, the greatest painter of his century, with a feeling for grace and beauty even above Giotto's, and only less excellent in marble. Several of his poems have been preserved, mostly of a slightly satirical character; one, a sonnet on the nature of love, *Molti volendo dir che fosse Amore*, has had the honour of being ascribed to Dante.

With the third quarter of the century, the first great epoch of Italian letters closes also. On the overthrow of the House of Suabia at Benevento, the centre of culture had shifted from Sicily to Tuscany, from Palermo to Florence. The prose and poetry of this epoch is almost entirely Tuscan, although the second of its greatest poets, Francesco Petrarca, comparatively seldom set foot within its boundaries. "My old nest is restored to me," he wrote to the Signoria, when they sent Boccaccio to invite his friend to return to Florence,

"I can fly back to it, and I can fold there my wandering wings." But, save for a few flying visits, Petrarch had little inclination to attach himself to one city, when he felt that all Italy was his country.

Dante had set forth all that was noblest in mediæval thought in imperishable form, supremely in his *Divina Commedia*, but appreciably and nobly in his various minor works as well, both verse and prose. Villani had started historical Italian prose on its triumphant course. Petrarch and Boccaccio, besides their great gifts to Italian literature, in the ethereal poetry of the one, painting every varying mood of the human soul, and the licentious prose of the other, hymning the triumph of the flesh, stand on the threshold of the Renaissance. Other names crowd in upon us at each stage of this epoch. Apart from his rare personality, Guido Cavalcanti's *ballate* are his chief title to poetic fame, but, even so, less than the monument of glory that Dante has reared to him in the *Vita Nuova*, in the *De Vulgari Eloquentia*, in the *Divina Commedia*. Dino Compagni, the chronicler of the Whites and Blacks, was only less admirable as a patriot than as a historian. Matteo Villani, the brother of Giovanni, and Matteo's son, Filippo, carried on the great chronicler's work. Fra Jacopo Passavanti, the Dominican prior of Santa Maria Novella, in the middle of the century, showed how the purest Florentine vernacular could be used for the purpose of simple religious edification. Franco Sacchetti, politician, novelist and poet, may be taken as the last Florentine writer of this period; he anticipates the popular lyrism of the Quattrocento, rather in the same way as a group of scholars who at the same time gathered round the Augustinian, Luigi Marsili, in his cell at Santo Spirito heralds the coming of the humanists. It fell to Franco Sacchetti to sing the dirge of this heroic period of art and letters, in his elegiac canzoni on the deaths of Petrarch and Boccaccio:–

> "Sonati sono i corni
> d'ogni parte a ricolta;
> la stagione è rivolta:
> se tornerà non so, ma credo tardi."

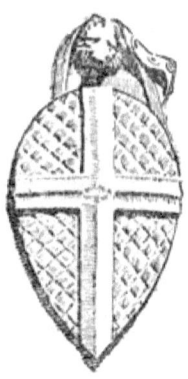

CROSS OF THE FLORENTINE PEOPLE
(FROM OLD HOUSE ON NORTH SIDE OF DUOMO)

CHAPTER III.

THE MEDICI AND THE QUATTROCENTO

"Tiranno è nome di uomo di mala vita, e pessimo fra tutti gli altri uomini, che per forza sopra tutti vuol regnare, massime quello che di cittadino è fatto tiranno."–*Savonarola.*

"The Renaissance of the fifteenth century was in many things great, rather by what it designed or aspired to do, than by what it actually achieved."–*Walter Pater.*

NON già Salvestro ma Salvator mundi, "thou that with noble wisdom hast saved thy country." Thus in a sonnet does Franco Sacchetti hail Salvestro dei Medici, the originator of the greatness of his house. In 1378, while the hatred between the Parte Guelfa and the adherents of the Otto della Guerra–the rivalry between the Palace of the Party and the Palace of the Signory–was at its height, the Captains of the Party conspired to seize upon the Palace of the Priors and take possession of the State. Their plans were frustrated by Salvestro dei Medici, a rich merchant and head of his ambitious and rising family, who was then Gonfaloniere of Justice. He proposed to restore the Ordinances against the magnates, and, when this petition was rejected by the Signoria and the Colleges,[16] he appealed to the Council of the People. The result was a riot, followed by a long series of tumults throughout the city; the *Arti Minori* came to the front in arms; and, finally, the bloody revolution known as the Tumult of the Ciompi burst over Florence. These Ciompi, the lowest class of artizans and all those who were not represented in the Arts, headed by those who were subject to the great Arte della Lana, had been much favoured by the Duke of Athens, and had been given consuls and a standard with an angel painted upon it. On the fall of the Duke, these Ciompi, or *popolo minuto*, had lost these privileges, and were probably much oppressed by the consuls of the Arte della Lana. Secretly instigated by Salvestro–who thus initiated the Medicean policy of undermining the Republic by means of the populace–they rose *en masse* on July 20th, captured the Palace of the Podestà, burnt the houses of their enemies and the Bottega of the Arte della Lana, seized the standard of the people, and, with it and the banners of the Guilds displayed, came into the Piazza to demand a share in the government. On July 22nd they burst into the Palace of the Priors, headed by a wool-comber, Michele di Lando, carrying in his hands the great Gonfalon; him they acclaimed Gonfaloniere and lord of the city.

This rough and half-naked wool-comber, whose mother made pots and pans and whose wife sold greens, is one of the heroes of Florentine history; and his noble simplicity throughout the whole affair is in striking contrast with the self-seeking and intrigues of the rich aristocratic merchants whose tool, to some extent, he appears to have been. The pious historian, Jacopo Nardi, likens him to the heroes of ancient Rome, Curius and Fabricius, and ranks him as a patriot and deliverer of the city, far above even Farinata degli Uberti. The next day the Parliament was duly summoned in the Piazza, Michele confirmed in his office, and a Balìa (or commission) given to him, together with the Eight and the Syndics of the Arts, to reform the State and elect the new Signoria—in which the newly constituted Guilds of the populace were to have a third with those of the greater and minor Arts. But, before Michele's term of office was over, the Ciompi were in arms again, fiercer than ever and with more outrageous demands, following the standards of the Angel and some of the minor Arts (who appear to have in part joined them). From Santa Maria Novella, their chosen head-quarters, on the last day of August they sent two representatives to overawe the Signoria. But Michele di Lando, answering their insolence with violence, rode through the city with the standard of Justice floating before him, while the great bell of the Priors' tower called the Guilds to arms; and by evening the populace had melted away, and the government of the people was re-established. The new Signoria was greeted in a canzone by Sacchetti, in which he declares that Prudence, Justice, Fortitude, and Temperance are once more reinstated in the city.

For the next few years the Minor Arts predominated in the government. Salvestro dei Medici kept in the background, but was presently banished. Michele di Lando seemed contented to have saved the State, and took little further share in the politics of the city. He appears later on to have been put under bounds at Chioggia; but to have returned to Florence before his death in 1401, when he was buried in Santa Croce. There were still tumults and conspiracies, resulting in frequent executions and banishments; while, without, inglorious wars were carried on by the companies of mercenary soldiers. This is the epoch in which the great English captain, Hawkwood, entered the service of the Florentine State. In 1382, after the execution of Giorgio Scali and the banishment of Tommaso Strozzi (noble burghers who headed the populace), the newly constituted Guilds were abolished, and the government returned to the greater Arts, who now held two-thirds of the offices–a proportion which was later increased to three-quarters.

The period which follows, from 1382 to 1434, sees the close of the democratic government of Florence. The Republic, nominally still ruled by the greater Guilds, is in reality sustained and swayed by the *nobili popolani* or *Ottimati*, members of wealthy families risen by riches or talent out of these greater Guilds into a new kind of burgher aristocracy. The struggle is now no longer between the Palace of the Signory and the Palace of the Party–for the days of the power of the Parte Guelfa are at an end—but between the Palace and the Piazza. The party of the Minor Arts and the Populace is repressed and ground down with war taxes; but behind them the Medici lurk and wait—first Vieri, then Giovanni di Averardo, then Cosimo di Giovanni—ever on the watch to put themselves at their head, and through them overturn the State. The party of the Ottimati is first led by Maso degli Albizzi, then by Niccolò da Uzzano, and lastly by Rinaldo degli Albizzi and his adherents—illustrious citizens not altogether unworthy of the great Republic that they swayed—the sort of dignified civic patricians whose figures, a little later, were to throng the frescoes of Masaccio and Ghirlandaio. But they were divided among themselves, persecuted their adversaries with proscription and banishment, thus making the exiles a perpetual source of danger to the State, and they were hated by the populace because of the war taxes. These wars were mainly carried on by mercenaries—who were now more usually Italians than foreigners—and, in spite of frequent defeats, generally ended well for Florence. Arezzo was purchased in 1384. A fierce struggle was carried on a few years later (1390-1402) with the "great serpent," Giovanni Galeazzo Visconti, who hoped to make himself King of Italy by violence as he had made himself Duke of Milan by treachery, and intended to be crowned in Florence. Pisa was finally and cruelly conquered in 1406; Cortona was obtained as the result of a prolonged war with King Ladislaus of Naples in 1414, in which the Republic had seemed once more in danger of falling into the hands of a foreign tyrant; and in 1421 Leghorn was sold to the Florentines by the Genoese, thus opening the sea to their merchandise.

The deaths of Giovanni Galeazzo and Ladislaus freed the city from her most formidable external foes; and for a while she became the seat of the Papacy, the centre of Christendom. In 1419, after the schism, Pope Martin V. took up his abode in Florence; the great condottiere, Braccio, came with his victorious troops to do him honour; and the deposed John XXIII. humbled himself before the new Pontiff, and was at last laid to rest among the shadows of the Baptistery. In his *Storia Florentina* Guicciardini declares that the government at this epoch was the wisest, the most glorious and the happiest that the city had ever had. It was the dawn of the Renaissance, and Florence was already full of artists and scholars, to whom these *nobili popolani* were as generous and as enlightened patrons as their successors, the Medici, were to be. Even Cosimo's fervent admirer, the librarian Vespasiano Bisticci, endorses Guicciardini's verdict: "In that time," he says, "from 1422 to 1433, the city of Florence was in a most blissful state, abounding with excellent men in every faculty, and it was full of admirable citizens."

Maso degli Albizzi died in 1417; and his successors in the oligarchy–the aged Niccolò da Uzzano, who stood throughout for moderation, and the fiery but less competent Rinaldo degli Albizzi–were no match for the rising and unscrupulous Medici. With the Albizzi was associated the noblest and most generous Florentine of the century, Palla Strozzi. The war with Filippo Visconti, resulting in the disastrous rout of Zagonara, and an unjust campaign against Lucca, in which horrible atrocities were committed by the Florentine commissioner, Astorre Gianni, shook their government. Giovanni dei Medici, the richest banker in Italy, was now the acknowledged head of the opposition; he had been Gonfaloniere in 1421, but would not put himself actively forward, although urged on by his sons, Cosimo and Lorenzo. He died in 1429; Niccolò da Uzzano followed him to the grave in 1432; and the final struggle between the fiercer spirits, Rinaldo and Cosimo, was at hand. "All these citizens," said Niccolò, shortly before his death, "some through ignorance, some through malice, are ready to sell this republic; and, thanks to their good fortune, they have found the purchaser."

Shortly before this date, Masaccio painted all the leading spirits of the time in a fresco in the cloisters of the Carmine. This has been destroyed, but you may see a fine contemporary portrait of Giovanni in the Uffizi. The much admired and famous coloured bust in the Bargello, called the portrait of Niccolò da Uzzano by Donatello, has probably nothing to do either with Niccolò or with Donatello. Giovanni has the air of a prosperous and unpretending Florentine tradesman, but with a certain obvious parade of his lack of pushfulness.

In 1433 the storm broke. A Signory hostile to Cosimo being elected, he was summoned to the Palace and imprisoned in an apartment high up in the Tower, a place known as the Alberghettino. Rinaldo degli Albizzi held the Piazza with his soldiery, and Cosimo heard the great bell ringing to call the people to Parliament, to grant a Balìa to reform the government and decide upon his fate. But he was too powerful at home and abroad; his popularity with those whom he had raised from low estate, and those whom he had relieved by his wealth, his influence with the foreign powers, such as Venice and Ferrara, were so great that his foes dared not take his life; and, indeed, they were hardly the men to have attempted such a crime. Banished to Padua (his brother Lorenzo and other members of his family being put under bounds at different cities), he was received everywhere, not as a fugitive, but as a prince; and the library of the Benedictines, built by Michelozzo at his expense, once bore witness to his stay in Venice. Hardly a year had passed when a new Signory was chosen, favourable to the Medici; Rinaldo degli Albizzi, after a vain show of resistance, laid down his arms on the intervention of Pope Eugenius, who was then at Santa Maria Novella, and was banished for ever from the city with his principal adherents. And finally, in a triumphant progress from Venice, "carried back to his country upon the shoulders of all Italy," as he said, Cosimo and his brother Lorenzo entered Florence on October 6th, 1434, rode past the deserted palaces of the Albizzi to the Palace of the Priors, and next day returned in triumph to their own house in the Via Larga.

The Republic had practically fallen; the head of the Medici was virtually prince of the city and of her fair dominion. But Florence was not Milan or Naples, and Cosimo's part as tyrant was a peculiar one. The forms of the government were, with modifications, preserved; but by means of a Balìa empowered to elect the chief magistrates for a period of five years, and then renewed every five years, he secured that the Signoria should always be in his hands, or in those of his adherents. The grand Palace of the Priors was still ostensibly the seat of government; but, in reality, the State was in the firm grasp of the thin, dark-faced merchant in the Palace in the Via Larga, which we now know as the Palazzo Riccardi. Although in the earlier part of his reign he was occasionally elected Gonfaloniere, he otherwise held no office ostensibly, and affected the republican manner of a mere wealthy citizen. His personality, combined with the widely ramifying banking relations of the Medici, gave him an almost European influence. His popularity among the mountaineers and in the country districts, from which armed soldiery were ever ready to pour down into the city in his defence, made him the fitting man for the ever increasing external sway of Florence. The forms of the Republic were preserved, but he consolidated his power by a general levelling and disintegration, by severing the nerves of the State and breaking the power of the Guilds. He had certain hard and cynical maxims for guidance: "Better a city ruined than a city lost," "States are not ruled by Pater-Nosters," "New and worthy citizens can be made by a few ells of crimson cloth." So he elevated to wealth and power men of low kind, devoted to and dependent on himself; crushed the families opposed to him, or citizens who seemed too powerful, by wholesale banishments, or by ruining them with fines and taxation, although there was comparatively little blood shed. He was utterly ruthless in all this, and many of the noblest Florentine citizens fell victims. One murder must be laid to his charge, and it is one of peculiar, for him, unusual atrocity. Baldaccio d'Anghiari, a young captain of infantry, who promised fair to take a high place among the condottieri of the day, was treacherously invited to speak with the Gonfaloniere in the Palace of the Priors, and there stabbed to death by hireling assassins from the hills, and his body flung ignominiously into the Piazza. Cosimo's motive is said to have been partly jealousy of a possible rival, Neri Capponi, who had won popularity by his conquest of the Casentino for Florence in 1440, and who was intimate with Baldaccio; and partly desire to gratify Francesco Sforza, whose treacherous designs upon Milan he was furthering by the gold wrung from his over-taxed Florentines, and to whose plans Baldaccio was prepared to offer an obstacle.

Florence was still for a time the seat of the Papacy. In January 1439, the Patriarch Joseph of Constantinople, and the Emperor of the East, John Paleologus, came to meet Pope Eugenius for the Council of Florence, which was intended to unite the Churches of Christendom. The Patriarch died here, and is buried in Santa Maria Novella. In the Riccardi Palace you may see him and the Emperor, forced, as it were, to take part in the triumph of the Medici in Benozzo Gozzoli's fresco–riding with them in the gorgeous train, that sets out ostensibly to seek the Babe of Bethlehem, and evidently has no intention of finding Him. Pope Eugenius returned to Rome in 1444; and in 1453 Mahomet II. stormed Constantinople, and Greek exiles thronged to Rome and Florence. In 1459, marvellous pageants greeted Pius II. in the city, on his way to stir up the Crusade that never went.

In his foreign policy Cosimo inaugurated a totally new departure for Florence; he commenced a line of action which was of the utmost importance in Italian politics, and which his son and grandson carried still further. The long wars with which the last of the Visconti, Filippo Maria, harassed Italy and pressed Florence hard (in the last of these Rinaldo degli Albizzi and the exiles approached near enough to catch a distant glimpse of the city from which they were relentlessly shut out), ended with his death in 1447. Cosimo dei Medici now allied himself with the great condottiere, Francesco Sforza, and aided him with money to make good his claims upon the Duchy of Milan. Henceforth this new alliance between Florence and Milan, between the Medici and the Sforza, although most odious in the eyes of the Florentine people, became one of the chief factors in the balance of power in Italy. Soon afterwards Alfonso, the Aragonese ruler of Naples, entered into this triple alliance; Venice and Rome to some extent being regarded as a double alliance to counterbalance this. To these foreign princes Cosimo was almost as much prince of Florence as they of their dominions; and by what was practically a *coup d'état* in 1459, Cosimo and his son Piero forcibly overthrew the last attempt of their opponents to get the Signoria out of their hands, and, by means of the creation of a new and permanent Council of a hundred of their chief adherents, more firmly than ever secured their hold upon the State.

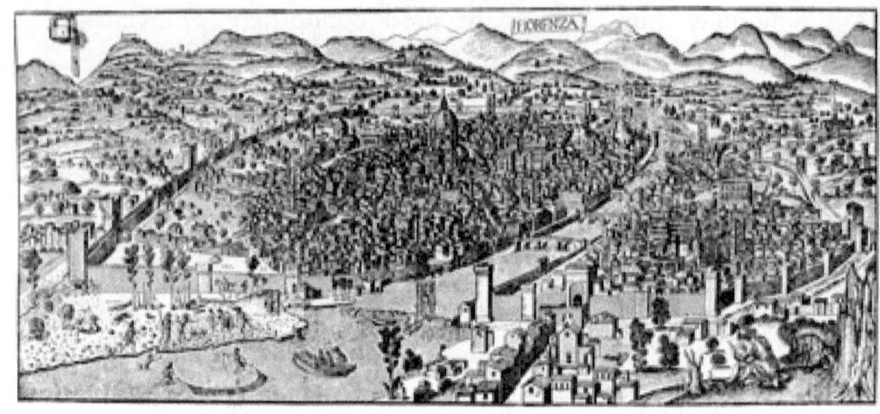

**FLORENCE IN THE DAYS OF LORENZO
THE MAGNIFICENT**
From an engraving, of about 1490, in the Berlin Museum

In his private life Cosimo was the simplest and most unpretentious of tyrants, and lived the life of a wealthy merchant-burgher of the day in its nobler aspects. He was an ideal father, a perfect man of business, an apparently kindly fellow-citizen to all. Above all things he loved the society of artists and men of letters; Brunelleschi and Michelozzo, Donatello and Fra Lippo Lippi–to name only a few more intimately connected with him–found in him the most generous and discerning of patrons; many of the noblest Early Renaissance churches and convents in Florence and its neighbourhood are due to his munificence–San Lorenzo and San Marco and the Badia of Fiesole are the most typical–and he even founded a hospital in Jerusalem. To a certain extent this was what we should now call "conscience money." His friend and biographer, Vespasiano Bisticci, writes: "He did these things because it appeared to him that he held money, not over well acquired; and he was wont to say that to God he had never given so much as to find Him on his books a debtor. And likewise he said: I know the humours of this city; fifty years will not pass before we are driven out; but the buildings will remain." The Greeks, who came to the Council of Florence or fled from the in-coming Turk, stimulated the study of their language and philosophy–though this had really commenced in the days of the Republic, before the deaths of Petrarch and Boccaccio–and found in Cosimo an ardent supporter. He founded great libraries in San Marco and in the Badia of Fiesole, the former with part of the codices collected by the scholar Niccolò Niccoli; although he had banished the old Palla Strozzi, the true renovator of the Florentine University, into hopeless exile. Into the Neo-Platonism of the Renaissance Cosimo threw himself heart and soul. "To Cosimo," writes Burckhardt, "belongs the special glory of recognising in the Platonic philosophy the fairest flower of the ancient world of thought, of inspiring his friends with the same belief, and thus of fostering within humanistic circles themselves another and a higher resuscitation of antiquity." In a youth of Figline, Marsilio Ficino, the son of a doctor, Cosimo found a future high priest of this new religion of love and beauty; and bidding him minister to the minds of men rather than to their bodies, brought him into his palace, and gave him a house in the city and a beautiful farm near Careggi. Thus was founded the famous Platonic Academy, the centre of the richest Italian thought of the century. As his end drew near, Cosimo turned to the consolations of religion, and would pass long hours in his chosen cell in San Marco, communing with the Dominican Archbishop, Antonino, and Fra Angelico, the painter of mediæval Paradise. And with these thoughts, mingled with the readings of Marsilio's growing translation of Plato, he passed away at his villa at Careggi in 1464, on the first of August. Shortly before his death he had lost his favourite son, Giovanni; and had been carried through his palace, in the Via Larga, sighing that it was now too large a house for so small a family. Entitled by public decree *Pater Patriae*, he was buried at his own request without any pompous funeral, beneath a simple marble in front of the high altar of San Lorenzo.

THE BADIA OF FIESOLE

Cosimo was succeeded, not without some opposition from rivals to the Medici within their own party, by his son Piero. Piero's health was in a shattered condition–il Gottoso, he was called–and for the most part he lived in retirement at Careggi, occasionally carried into Florence in his litter, leaving his brilliant young son Lorenzo to act as a more ornamental figure-head for the State. The personal appearance of Piero is very different to that of his father or son; in his portrait bust by Mino da Fiesole in the Bargello, and in the picture by Bronzino in the National Gallery, there is less craft and a certain air of frank and manly resolution. In his daring move in support of Galeazzo Maria Sforza, when, on the death of Francesco, it seemed for a moment that the Milanese dynasty was tottering, and his promptness in crushing the formidable conspiracy of the "mountain" against himself, Piero showed that sickness had not destroyed his faculty of energetic action at the critical moment. He completely followed out his father's policy, drawing still tighter the bonds which united Florence with Milan and Naples, lavishing money on the decoration of the city and the corruption of the people. The opposition was headed by Luca Pitti, Agnolo Acciaiuoli, Dietisalvi Neroni and others, who had been reckoned as Cosimo's friends, but who were now intriguing with Venice and Ferrara to overthrow his son. Hoping to eclipse the Medici in their own special field of artistic display and wholesale corruption, Luca Pitti commenced that enormous palace which still bears the name of his family, filled it with bravos and refugees, resorted to all means fair or foul to get money to build and corrupt. It seemed for a moment that the adherents of the Mountain (as the opponents of the Medici were called, from this highly situated Pitti Palace) and the adherents of the Plain (where the comparatively modest Medicean palace–now the Palazzo Riccardi–stood in the Via Larga) might renew the old factions of Blacks and Whites. But in the late summer of 1466 the party of the Mountain was finally crushed; they were punished with more mercy than the Medici generally showed, and Luca Pitti was practically pardoned and left to a dishonourable old age in the unfinished palace, which was in after years to become the residence of the successors of his foes. About the same time Filippo Strozzi and other exiles were allowed to return, and another great palace began to rear its walls in the Via Tornabuoni, in after years to be a centre of anti-Medicean intrigue.

The brilliancy and splendour of Lorenzo's youth–he who was hereafter to be known in history as the Magnificent–sheds a rich glow of colour round the closing months of Piero's pain-haunted life. Piero himself had been content with a Florentine wife, Lucrezia dei Tornabuoni, and he had married his daughters to Florentine citizens, Guglielmo Pazzi and Bernardo Rucellai; but Lorenzo must make a great foreign match, and was therefore given Clarice Orsini, the daughter of a great Roman noble. The splendid pageant in the Piazza Santa Croce, and the even more gorgeous marriage festivities in the palace in the Via Larga, were followed by a triumphal progress of the young bridegroom through Tuscany and the Riviera to Milan, to the court of that faithful ally of his house, but most abominable monster, Giovanni Maria Sforza. Piero died on December 3rd, 1469, and, like Cosimo, desired the simple burial which his sons piously gave him. His plain but beautiful monument designed by Verrocchio is in the older sacristy of San Lorenzo, where he lies with his brother Giovanni.

"The second day after his death," writes Lorenzo in his diary, "although I, Lorenzo, was very young, in fact only in my twenty-first year, the leading men of the city and of the ruling party came to our house to express their sorrow for our misfortune, and to persuade me to take upon myself the charge of the government of the city, as my grandfather and father had already done. This proposal being contrary to the instincts of my age, and entailing great labour and danger, I accepted against my will, and only for the sake of protecting my friends, and our own fortunes, for in Florence one can ill live in the possession of wealth without control of the government."[17]

These two youths, Lorenzo and Giuliano, were now, to all intents and purposes, lords and masters of Florence. Lorenzo was the ruling spirit; outwardly, in spite of his singularly harsh and unprepossessing appearance, devoted to the cult of love and beauty, delighting in sport and every kind of luxury, he was inwardly as hard and cruel as tempered steel, and firmly fixed from the outset upon developing the hardly defined prepotency of his house into a complete personal despotism. You may see him as a gallant boy in Benozzo Gozzoli's fresco in the palace of his father and grandfather, riding under a bay tree, and crowned with roses; and then, in early manhood, in Botticelli's famous Adoration of the Magi; and lastly, as a fully developed, omniscient and all-embracing tyrant, in that truly terrible picture by Vasari in the Uffizi, constructed out of contemporary materials–surely as eloquent a sermon against the iniquity of tyranny as the pages of Savonarola's *Reggimento di Firenze*. Giuliano was a kindlier and gentler soul, completely given up to pleasure and athletics; he lives for us still in many a picture from the hand of Sandro Botticelli, sometimes directly portrayed, as in the painting which Morelli bequeathed to Bergamo, more often idealised as Mars or as Hermes; his love for the fair Simonetta inspired Botticellian allegories and the most finished and courtly stanzas of Poliziano. The sons of both these brothers were destined to sit upon the throne of the Fisherman.

A long step in despotism was gained in 1488, when the two great Councils of the People and the Commune were deprived of all their functions, which were now invested in the thoroughly Medicean Council of the Hundred. The next year Lorenzo's friend and ally, Galeazzo Maria Sforza, with his Duchess and courtiers, came to Florence. They were sumptuously received in the Medicean palace. The licence and wantonness of these Milanese scandalised even the lax Florentines, and largely added to the growing corruption of the city. The accidental burning of Santo Spirito during the performance of a miracle play was regarded as a certain sign of divine wrath. During his stay in Florence the Duke, in contrast with whom the worst of the Medici seems almost a saint, sat to one of the Pollaiuoli for the portrait still seen in the Uffizi; by comparison with him even Lorenzo looks charming; at the back of the picture there is a figure of Charity–but the Duke has very appropriately driven it to the wall. Unpopular though this Medicean-Sforza alliance was in Florence, it was undoubtedly one of the safe-guards of the harmony which, superficially, still existed between the five great powers of Italy. When Galeazzo Maria met the fate he so richly deserved, and was stabbed to death in the Church of San Stefano at Milan on December 20th, 1476, Pope Sixtus gave solemn utterance to the general dismay: *Oggi è morta la pace d'Italia.*

But Sixtus and his nephews did not in their hearts desire peace in Italy, and were plotting against Lorenzo with the Pazzi, who, although united to the Medici by marriage, had secret and growing grievances against them. On the morning of Sunday April 26th, 1478, the conspirators set upon the two brothers at Mass in the Duomo; Giuliano perished beneath nineteen dagger-stabs; Lorenzo escaped with a slight wound in the neck. The Archbishop Salviati of Pisa in the meantime attempted to seize the Palace of the Priors, but was arrested by the Gonfaloniere, and promptly hung out of the window for his trouble. Jacopo Pazzi rode madly through the streets with an armed force, calling the people to arms, with the old shout of *Popolo e Libertà*, but was only answered by the ringing cries of *Palle, Palle*.[18] The vengeance taken by the people upon the conspirators was so prompt and terrible that Lorenzo had little left him to do (though that little he did to excess, punishing the innocent with the guilty); and the result of the plot simply was to leave him alone in the government, securely enthroned above the splash of blood. The Pope appears not to have been actually privy to the murder, but he promptly took up the cause of the murderers. It was followed by a general break-up of the Italian peace and a disastrous war, carried on mainly by mercenary soldiers, in which all the powers of Italy were more or less engaged; and Florence was terribly hard pressed by the allied forces of Naples and Rome. The plague broke out in the city; Lorenzo was practically deserted by his allies, and on the brink of financial ruin. Then was it that he did one of the most noteworthy, perhaps the noblest, of the actions of his life, and saved himself and the State by voluntarily going to Naples and putting himself in the power of King Ferrante, an infamous tyrant, who would readily have murdered his guest, if it had seemed to his advantage to do so. But, like all the Italians of the Renaissance, Ferrante was open to reason, and the eloquence of the Magnifico won him over to grant an honourable peace, with which Lorenzo returned to Florence in March 1480. "If Lorenzo was great when he left Florence," writes Machiavelli, "he returned much greater than ever; and he was received with such joy by the city as his great qualities and his fresh merits deserved, seeing that he had exposed his own life to restore peace to his country." Botticelli's noble allegory of the olive-decked Medicean Pallas, taming the Centaur of war and disorder, appears to have been painted in commemoration of this event. In the following August the Turks landed in Italy and stormed Otranto, and the need of union, in the face of "the common enemy Ottoman," reconciled the Pope to Florence, and secured for the time an uneasy peace among the powers of Italy.

Lorenzo's power in Florence and influence throughout Italy was now secure. By the institution in 1480 of a Council of Seventy, a permanent council to manage and control the election of the Signoria (with two special committees drawn from the Seventy every six months, the *Otto di pratica* for foreign affairs and the *Dodici Procuratori* for internal), the State was firmly established in his hands—the older councils still remaining, as was usual in every Florentine reformation of government. Ten years later, in 1490, this council showed signs of independence; and Lorenzo therefore reduced the authority of electing the Signoria to a small committee with a reforming Balìa of seventeen, of which he was one. Had he lived longer, he would undoubtedly have crowned his policy either by being made Gonfaloniere for life, or by obtaining some similar constitutional confirmation of his position as head of the State. Externally his influence was thrown into the scale for peace, and, on the death of Sixtus IV. in 1484, he established friendly relations and a family alliance with the new Pontiff, Innocent VIII. Sarzana with Pietrasanta were won back for Florence, and portions of the Sienese territory which had been lost during the war with Naples and the Church; a virtual protectorate was established over portions of Umbria and Romagna, where the daggers of assassins daily emptied the thrones of minor tyrants. Two attempts on his life failed. In the last years of his foreign policy and diplomacy he showed himself truly the magnificent. East and West united to do him honour; the Sultan of the Turks and the Soldan of Egypt sent ambassadors and presents; the rulers of France and Germany treated him as an equal. Soon the torrent of foreign invasion was to sweep over the Alps and inundate all the "Ausonian" land; Milan and Naples were ready to rend each other; Ludovico Sforza was plotting his own rise upon the ruin of Italy, and already intriguing with France; but, for the present, Lorenzo succeeded in maintaining the balance of power between the five great Italian states, which seemed as though they might present a united front for mutual defence against the coming of the barbarians.

Sarebbe impossibile avesse avuto un tiranno migliore e più piacevole, writes Guicciardini: "Florence could not have had a better or more delightful tyrant." The externals of life were splendid and gorgeous indeed in the city where Lorenzo ruled, but everything was in his hands and had virtually to proceed from him. His spies were everywhere; marriages might only be arranged and celebrated according to his good pleasure; the least sign of independence was promptly and severely repressed. By perpetual festivities and splendid shows, he strove to keep the minds of the citizens contented and occupied; tournaments, pageants, masques and triumphs filled the streets; and the strains of licentious songs, of which many were Lorenzo's own composition, helped to sap the morality of that people which Dante had once dreamed of as *sobria e pudica*. But around the Magnifico were grouped the greatest artists and scholars of the age, who found in him an enlightened Maecenas and most charming companion. *Amava maravigliosamente qualunque era in una arte eccellente*, writes Machiavelli of him; and that word—*maravigliosamente*—so entirely characteristic of Lorenzo and his ways, occurs again and again, repeated with studied persistence, in the chapter which closes Machiavelli's History. He was said to have sounded the depths of Platonic philosophy; he was a true poet, within certain limitations; few men have been more keenly alive to beauty in all its manifestations, physical and spiritual alike. Though profoundly immoral, *nelle cose veneree maravigliosamente involto*, he was a tolerable husband, and the fondest of fathers with his children, whom he adored. The delight of his closing days was the elevation of his favourite son, Giovanni, to the Cardinalate at the age of fourteen; it gave the Medici a voice in the Curia like the other princes of Europe, and pleased all Florence; but more than half Lorenzo's joy proceeded from paternal pride and love, and the letter of advice which he wrote for his son on the occasion shows both father and boy in a very amiable, even edifying light. And yet this same man had ruined the happiness of countless homes, and had even seized upon the doweries of Florentine maidens to fill his own coffers and pay his mercenaries.

But the *bel viver italiano* of the Quattrocento, with all its loveliness and all its immorality–more lovely and far less immoral in Florence than anywhere else–was drawing to an end. A new prophet had arisen, and, from the pulpits of San Marco and Santa Maria del Fiore, the stern Dominican, Fra Girolamo Savonarola, denounced the corruption of the day and announced that speedy judgment was at hand; the Church should be chastised, and that speedily, and renovation should follow. Prodigies were seen. The lions tore and rent each other in their cages; lightning struck the cupola of the Duomo on the side towards the Medicean palace; while in his villa at Careggi the Magnifico lay dying, watched over by his sister Bianca and the poet Poliziano. A visit from the young Pico della Mirandola cheered his last hours. He received the Last Sacraments, with every sign of contrition and humility. Then Savonarola came to his bedside. There are two accounts of what happened between these two terrible men, the corruptor of Florence and the prophet of renovation, and they are altogether inconsistent. The ultimate source of the one is apparently Savonarola's fellow-martyr, Fra Silvestro, an utterly untrustworthy witness; that of the other, Lorenzo's intimate, Poliziano. According to Savonarola's biographers and adherents, Lorenzo, overwhelmed with remorse and terror, had sent for the Frate to give him the absolution which his courtly confessor dared not refuse (*io non ho mai trovato uno che sia vero frate, se non lui*); and when the Dominican, seeming to soar above his natural height, bade him restore liberty to Florence, the Magnifico sullenly turned his back upon him and shortly afterwards died in despair.[19] According to Poliziano, an eyewitness and an absolutely whole-hearted adherent of the Medici, Fra Girolamo simply spoke a few words of priestly exhortation to the dying man; then, as he turned away, Lorenzo cried, "Your blessing, father, before you depart" (*Heus, benedictionem, Pater, priusquam a nobis proficisceris*) and the two together repeated word for word the Church's prayers for the departing; then Savonarola returned to his convent, and Lorenzo passed away in peace and consolation. Reverently and solemnly the body was brought from Careggi to Florence, rested for a while in San Marco, and was then buried, with all external simplicity, with his murdered brother in San Lorenzo. It was the beginning of April 1492, and the Magnifico was only in his forty-fourth year. The words of old Sixtus must have risen to the lips of many: *Oggi è morta la pace d'Italia.* "This man," said Ferrante of Naples, "lived long enough to make good his own title to immortality, but not long enough for Italy."

Lorenzo left three sons—Piero, who virtually succeeded him in the same rather undefined princedom; the young Cardinal Giovanni; and Giuliano. Their father was wont to call Piero the "mad," Giovanni the "wise," Giuliano the "good"; and to a certain extent their after-lives corresponded with his characterisation. There was also a boy Giulio, Lorenzo's nephew, an illegitimate child of Giuliano the elder by a girl of the lower class; him Lorenzo left to the charge of Cardinal Giovanni—the future Pope Clement to the future Pope Leo. Piero had none of his father's abilities, and was not the man to guide the ship of State through the storm that was rising; he was a wild licentious young fellow, devoted to sport and athletics, with a great shock of dark hair; he was practically the only handsome member of his family, as you may see in a peculiarly fascinating Botticellian portrait in the Uffizi, where he is holding a medallion of his great grandfather Cosimo, and gazing out of the picture with a rather pathetic expression, as if the Florentines who set a price upon his head had misunderstood him.

Piero's folly at once began to undo his father's work. A part of Lorenzo's policy had been to keep his family united, including those not belonging to the reigning branch. There were two young Medici then in the city, about Piero's own age; Lorenzo and Giovanni di Pier Francesco, the grandsons of Cosimo's brother Lorenzo (you may see Giovanni with his father in a picture by Filippino Lippi in the Uffizi). Lorenzo the Magnificent had made a point of keeping on good terms with them, for they were beloved of the people. Giovanni was destined, in a way, to play the part of Banquo to the Magnificent's Macbeth, had there been a Florentine prophet to tell him, "Thou shalt get kings though thou be none." But Piero disliked the two; at a dance he struck Giovanni, and then, when the brothers showed resentment, he arrested both and, not daring to take their lives, confined them to their villas. And these were times when a stronger head than Piero's might well have reeled. Italy's day had ended, and she was now to be the battle-ground for the gigantic forces of the monarchies of Europe. That same year in which Lorenzo died, Alexander VI. was elected to the Papacy he had so shamelessly bought. A mysterious terror fell upon the people; an agony of apprehension consumed their rulers throughout the length and breadth of the land. In 1494 the crash came. The old King Ferrante of Naples died, and his successor Alfonso prepared to meet the torrent of French arms which Ludovico Sforza, the usurping Duke of Milan, had invited into Italy.

In art and in letters, as well as in life and general conduct, this epoch of the Quattrocento is one of the most marvellous chapters in the history of human thought; the Renaissance as a wave broke over Italy, and from Italy surged on to the bounds of Europe. And of this "discovery by man of himself and of the world," Florence was the centre; in its hothouse of learning and culture the rarest personalities flourished, and its strangest and most brilliant flower, in whose hard brilliancy a suggestion of poison lurked, was Lorenzo the Magnificent himself.

In both art and letters, the Renaissance had fully commenced before the accession of the Medici to power. Ghiberti's first bronze gates of the Baptistery and Masaccio's frescoes in the Carmine were executed under the regime of the *nobili popolani*, the Albizzi and their allies. Many of the men whom the Medici swept relentlessly from their path were in the fore-front of the movement, such as the noble and generous Palla Strozzi, one of the reformers of the Florentine Studio, who brought the Greek, Emanuel Chrysolaras, at the close of the fourteenth century, to make Florence the centre of Italian Hellenism. Palla lavished his wealth in the hunting of codices, and at last, when banished on Cosimo's return, died in harness at Padua at the venerable age of ninety-two. His house had always been full of learned men, and his reform of the university had brought throngs of students to Florence. Put under bounds for ten years at Padua, he lived the life of an ancient philosopher and of exemplary Christian virtue. Persecuted at the end of every ten years with a new sentence, the last—of ten more years—when he was eighty-two; robbed by death of his wife and sons; he bore all with the utmost patience and fortitude, until, in Vespasiano's words, "arrived at the age of ninety-two years, in perfect health of body and of mind, he gave up his soul to his Redeemer like a most faithful and good Christian."

In 1401, the first year of the fifteenth century, the competition was announced for the second gates of the Baptistery, which marks the beginning of Renaissance sculpture; and the same year witnessed the birth of Masaccio, who, in the words of Leonardo da Vinci, "showed with his perfect work how those painters who follow aught but Nature, the mistress of the masters, laboured in vain," Morelli calls this Quattrocento the epoch of "character";

"that is, the period when it was the principal aim of art to seize and represent the outward appearances of persons and things, determined by inward and moral conditions." The intimate connection of arts and crafts is characteristic of the Quattrocento, as also the mutual interaction of art with art. Sculpture was in advance of painting in the opening stage of the century, and, indeed, influenced it profoundly throughout; about the middle of the century they met, and ran henceforth hand in hand. Many of the painters and sculptors, as, notably, Ghiberti and Botticelli, had been apprentices in the workshops of the goldsmiths; nor would the greatest painters disdain to undertake the adornment of a *cassone*, or chest for wedding presents, nor the most illustrious sculptor decline a commission for the button of a prelate's cope or some mere trifle of household furniture. The medals in the National Museum and the metal work on the exterior of the Strozzi Palace are as typical of the art of Renaissance Florence as the grandest statues and most elaborate altar-pieces.

The Story of Florence

"IN THE SCULPTOR'S WORKSHOP"
By Nanni di Banco
(For the Guild of Masters in Stone and Timber)

With the work of the individual artists we shall become better acquainted in subsequent chapters. Here we can merely name their leaders. In architecture and sculpture respectively, Filippo Brunelleschi (1377-1446) and Donatello (1386-1466) are the ruling spirits of the age. Their mutual friendship and brotherly rivalry almost recall the loves of Dante and Cavalcanti in an earlier day. Although Lorenzo Ghiberti (1378-1455) justly won the competition for the second gates of the Baptistery, it is now thought that Filippo ran his successful rival much more closely than the critics of an earlier day supposed. Mr Perkins remarks that "indirectly Brunelleschi was the master of all the great painters and sculptors of his time, for he taught them how to apply science to art, and so far both Ghiberti and Donatello were his pupils, but the last was almost literally so, since the great architect was not only his friend, but also his counsellor and guide." Contemporaneous with these three *spiriti magni* in their earlier works, and even to some extent anticipating them, is Nanni di Banco (died in 1421), a most excellent master, both in large monumental statues and in bas-reliefs, whose works are to be seen and loved outside and inside the Duomo, and in the niches round San Michele in Orto. A pleasant friendship united him with Donatello, although to regard him as that supreme master's pupil and follower, as Vasari does, is an anachronism. To this same earlier portion of the Quattrocento belong Leo Battista Alberti (1405-1472), a rare genius, but a wandering stone who, as an architect, accomplished comparatively little; Michelozzo Michelozzi (1396-1472), who worked as a sculptor with Ghiberti and Donatello, but is best known as the favoured architect of the Medici, for whom he built the palace so often mentioned in these pages, and now known as the Palazzo Riccardi, and the convent of San Marco; and Luca della Robbia (1399-1482), that beloved master of marble music, whose enamelled terracotta Madonnas are a perpetual fund of the purest delight. To Michelozzo and Luca in collaboration we owe the bronze gates of the Duomo sacristy, a work only inferior to Ghiberti's "Gates of Paradise."

Slightly later come Donatello's great pupils, Desiderio da Settignano (1428-1464), Andrea Verrocchio (1435-1488), and Antonio Pollaiuolo (1429-1498). The two latter are almost equally famous as painters. Contemporaneous with them are Mino da Fiesole, Bernardo and Antonio Rossellino, Giuliano da San Gallo, Giuliano and Benedetto da Maiano, of whom the last-named was the first architect of the Strozzi Palace. The last great architect of the Quattrocento is Simone del Pollaiuolo, known as Cronaca (1457-1508); and its last great sculptor is Andrea della Robbia, Luca's nephew, who was born in 1435, and lived on until 1525. Andrea's best works—and they are very numerous indeed, in the same enamelled terra-cotta—hardly yield in charm and fascination to those of Luca himself; in some of them, devotional art seems to reach its last perfection in sculpture. Giovanni, Andrea's son, and others of the family carried on the tradition—with cruder colours and less delicate feeling.

Masaccio (1401-1428), one of "the inheritors of unfulfilled renown," is the first great painter of the Renaissance, and bears much the same relation to the fifteenth as Giotto to the fourteenth century. Vasari's statement that Masaccio's master, Masolino, was Ghiberti's assistant appears to be incorrect; but it illustrates the dependence of the painting of this epoch upon sculpture. Masaccio's frescoes in the Carmine, which became the school of all Italian painting, were entirely executed before the Medicean regime. The

Dominican, Fra Angelico da Fiesole (1387-1455), seems in his San Marco frescoes to bring the denizens of the Empyrean, of which the mediæval mystics dreamed, down to earth to dwell among the black and white robed children of St Dominic. The Carmelite, Fra Lippo Lippi (1406-1469), the favourite of Cosimo, inferior to the angelical painter in spiritual insight, had a keener eye for the beauty of the external world and a surer touch upon reality. His buoyant humour and excellent colouring make "the glad monk's gift" one of the most acceptable that the Quattrocento has to offer us. Andrea del Castagno (died in 1457) and Domenico Veneziano (died in 1461), together with Paolo Uccello (died in 1475), were all absorbed in scientific researches with an eye to the extension of the resources of their art; but the two former found time to paint a few masterpieces in their kind—especially a Cenacolo by Andrea in Santa Appollonia, which is the grandest representation of its sublime theme, until the time that Leonardo da Vinci painted on the walls of the Dominican convent at Milan. Problems of the anatomical construction of the human frame and the rendering of movement occupied Antonio Pollaiuolo (1429-1498) and Andrea Verrocchio (1435-1488); their work was taken up and completed a little later by two greater men, Luca Signorelli of Cortona and Leonardo da Vinci.

The Florentine painting of this epoch culminates in the work of two men–Sandro di Mariano Filipepi, better known as Sandro Botticelli (1447-1510), and Domenico Ghirlandaio (1449-1494). If the greatest pictures were painted poems, as some have held, then Sandro Botticelli's masterpieces would be among the greatest of all time. In his rendering of religious themes, in his intensely poetic and strangely wistful attitude towards the fair myths of antiquity, and in his Neo-Platonic mingling of the two, he is the most complete and typical exponent of the finest spirit of the Quattrocento, to which, in spite of the date of his death, his art entirely belongs. Domenico's function, on the other hand, is to translate the external pomp and circumstance of his times into the most uninspired of painted prose, but with enormous technical skill and with considerable power of portraiture; this he effected above all in his ostensibly religious frescoes in Santa Maria Novella and Santa Trinità. Elsewhere he shows a certain pathetic sympathy with humbler life, as in his Santa Fina frescoes at San Gemignano, and in the admirable Adoration of the Shepherds in the Accademia; but this is a less characteristic vein. Filippino Lippi (1457-1504), the son of the Carmelite and the pupil of Botticelli, has a certain wayward charm, especially in his earlier works, but as a rule falls much below his master. He may be regarded as the last direct inheritor of the traditions of Masaccio. Associated with these are two lesser men, who lived considerably beyond the limits of the fifteenth century, but whose artistic methods never went past it; Piero di Cosimo (1462-1521) and Lorenzo di Credi (1459-1537). The former (called after Cosimo Rosselli, his master) was one of the most piquant personalities in the art world of Florence, as all readers of *Romola* know. As a painter, he has been very much overestimated; at his best, he is a sort of Botticelli, with the Botticellian grace and the Botticellian poetry almost all left out. He was magnificent at designing pageants; and of one of his exploits in this kind, we shall hear more presently. Lorenzo di Credi, Verrocchio's favourite pupil, was later, like Botticelli and others, to fall under the spell of Fra Girolamo; his pictures breathe a true religious sentiment and are very carefully finished; but for the most part, though there are exceptions, they lack virility.

Before this epoch closed, the two greatest heroes of Florentine art had appeared upon the scenes, but their great work lay still in the future. Leonardo da Vinci (born in 1452) had learned to paint in the school of Verrocchio; but painting was to occupy but a small portion of his time and labour. His mind roamed freely over every field of human activity, and plunged deeply into every sphere of human thought; nor is he adequately represented even by the greatest of the pictures that he has left. There is nothing of him now in Florence, save a few drawings in the Uffizi and an unfinished picture of the Epiphany. Leonardo finished little, and, with that little, time and man have dealt hardly. Michelangelo Buonarroti was born in the Casentino in

1475, and nurtured among the stone quarries of Settignano. At the age of thirteen, his father apprenticed him to the Ghirlandaii, Domenico and his brother David; and, with his friend and fellow-student, Francesco Granacci, the boy began to frequent the gardens of the Medici, near San Marco, where in the midst of a rich collection of antiquities Donatello's pupil and successor, Bertoldo, directed a kind of Academy. Here Michelangelo attracted the attention of Lorenzo himself, by the head of an old satyr which he had hammered out of a piece of marble that fell to his hand; and the Magnifico took him into his household. This youthful period in the great master's career was occupied in drinking in culture from the Medicean circle, in studying the antique and, of the moderns, especially the works of Donatello and Masaccio. But, with the exception of a few early fragments from his hand, Michelangelo's work commenced with his first visit to Rome, in 1496, and belongs to the following epoch.

Turning from art to letters, the Quattrocento is an intermediate period between the mainly Tuscan literary movement of the fourteenth century and the general Italian literature of the sixteenth. The first part of this century is the time of the discovery of the old authors, of the copying of manuscripts (printing was not introduced into Florence until 1471), of the eager search for classical relics and antiquities, the comparative neglect of Italian when Latinity became the test of all. Florence was the centre of the Humanism of the Renaissance, the revival of Grecian culture, the blending of Christianity and Paganism, the aping of antiquity in theory and in practice. In the pages of Vespasiano we are given a series of lifelike portraits of the scholars of this epoch, who thronged to Florence, served the State as Secretary of the Republic or occupied chairs in her newly reorganised university, or basked in the sun of Strozzian or Medicean patronage. Niccolò Niccoli, who died in 1437, is one of the most typical of these scholars; an ardent collector of ancient manuscripts, his library, purchased after his death by Cosimo dei Medici, forms the nucleus of the Biblioteca Laurenziana. His house was adorned with all that was held most choice and precious; he always wore long sweeping red robes, and had his table covered with ancient vases and precious Greek cups and the like. In fact he played the ancient sage to such perfection that simply to watch him eat his dinner was a liberal education in itself! *A vederlo in tavola, così antico come era, era una gentilezza.*

Vespasiano tells a delightful yarn of how one fine day this Niccolò Niccoli, "who was another Socrates or another Cato for continence and virtue," was taking a constitutional round the Palazzo del Podestà, when he chanced to espy a youth of most comely aspect, one who was entirely devoted to worldly pleasures and delights, young Piero Pazzi. Calling him and learning his name, Niccolò proceeded to question him as to his profession. "Having a high old time," answered the ingenuous youth: *attendo a darmi buon tempo*. "Being thy father's son and so handsome," said the Sage severely, "it is a shame that thou dost not set thyself to learn the Latin language, which would be a great ornament to thee; and if thou dost not learn it, thou wilt be esteemed of no account; yea, when the flower of thy youth is past, thou shalt find thyself without any *virtù*." Messer Piero was converted on the spot; Niccolò straightway found him a master and provided him with books; and the pleasure-loving youth became a scholar and a patron of scholars. Vespasiano assures us that, if he had lived, *lo inconveniente che seguitò*–so he euphoniously terms the Pazzi conspiracy–would never have happened.

Leonardo Bruni is the nearest approach to a really great figure in the Florentine literary world of the first half of the century. His translations of Plato and Aristotle, especially the former, mark an epoch. His Latin history of Florence shows genuine critical insight; but he is, perhaps, best known at the present day by his little Life of Dante in Italian, a charming and valuable sketch, which has preserved for us some fragments of Dantesque letters and several bits of really precious information about the divine poet, which seem to be authentic and which we do not find elsewhere. Leonardo appears to have undertaken it as a kind of holiday task, for recreation after the work of composing his more ponderous history. As Secretary of the Republic he exercised considerable political influence; his fame was so great that people came to Florence only to look at him; on his death in 1444, he was solemnly crowned on the bier as poet laureate, and buried in Santa Croce with stately pomp and applauded funeral orations. Leonardo's successors, Carlo Marsuppini (like him, an Aretine by birth) and Poggio Bracciolini– the one noted for his frank paganism, the other for the foulness of his literary invective–are less attractive figures; though the latter was no less famous and influential in his day. Giannozzo Manetti, who pronounced Bruni's funeral oration, was noted for his eloquence and incorruptibility, and stands out prominently amidst the scholars and humanists by virtue of his nobleness of character; like that other hero of the new learning, Palla Strozzi, he was driven into exile and persecuted by the Mediceans.

Far more interesting are the men of light and learning who gathered round Lorenzo dei Medici in the latter half of the century. This is the epoch of the Platonic Academy, which Marsilio Ficino had founded under the auspices of Cosimo. The discussions held in the convent retreat among the forests of Camaldoli, the meetings in the Badia at the foot of Fiesole, the mystical banquets celebrated in Lorenzo's villa at Careggi in honour of the anniversary of Plato's birth and death, may have added little to the sum of man's philosophic thought; but the Neo-Platonic religion of love and beauty, which was there proclaimed to the modern world, has left eternal traces in the poetic literature both of Italy and of England. Spenser and Shelley might have sat with the nine guests, whose number honoured the nine Muses, at the famous Platonic banquet at Careggi, of which Marsilio Ficino himself has left us an account in his commentary on the *Symposium*. You may read a later Italian echo of it, when Marsilio Ficino had passed away and his academy was a thing of the past, in the impassioned and rapturous discourse on love and beauty poured forth by Pietro Bembo, at that wonderful daybreak which ends the discussions of Urbino's courtiers in Castiglione's treatise. In a creed that could find one formula to cover both the reception of the Stigmata by St Francis and the mystical flights of the Platonic Socrates and Plotinus; that could unite the Sibyls and Diotima with the Magdalene and the Virgin Martyrs; many a perplexed Italian of that epoch might find more than temporary rest for his soul.

Simultaneously with this new Platonic movement there came a great revival of Italian literature, alike in poetry and in prose; what Carducci calls *il rinascimento della vita italiana nella forma classica*. The earlier humanists had scorned, or at least neglected the language of Dante; and the circle that surrounded Lorenzo was undoubtedly instrumental in this Italian reaction. Cristoforo Landini, one of the principal members of the Platonic Academy, now wrote the first Renaissance commentary upon the *Divina Commedia*; Leo Battista Alberti, also a leader in these Platonic disputations, defended the dignity of the Italian language, as Dante himself had done in an earlier day. Lorenzo himself compiled the so-called *Raccolta Aragonese* of early Italian lyrics, and sent them to Frederick of Aragon, together with a letter full of enthusiasm for the Tuscan tongue, and with critical remarks on the individual poets of the thirteenth and fourteenth centuries. Upon the popular poetry of Tuscany Lorenzo himself, and his favourite Angelo Ambrogini of Montepulciano, better known as Poliziano, founded a new school of Italian song. Luigi Pulci, the gay scoffer and cynical sceptic, entertained the festive gatherings in the Medicean palace with his wild tales, and, in his *Morgante Maggiore*, was practically the first to work up the popular legends of Orlando and the Paladins into a noteworthy poem—a poem of which Savonarola and his followers were afterwards to burn every copy that fell into their hands.

Poliziano is at once the truest classical scholar, and, with the possible exception of Boiardo (who belongs to Ferrara, and does not come within the scope of the present volume), the greatest Italian poet of the fifteenth century. He is, indeed, the last and most perfect fruit of Florentine Humanism. His father, Benedetto Ambrogini, had been murdered in Montepulciano by the faction hostile to the Medici; and the boy Angelo, coming to Florence, and studying under Ficino and his colleagues, was received into Lorenzo's household as tutor to the younger Piero. His lectures at the Studio attracted students from all Europe, and his labours in the field of textual criticism won a fame that has lasted to the present day. In Italian he wrote the *Orfeo* in two days for performance at Mantua, when he was eighteen, a lyrical tragedy which stamps him as the father of Italian dramatic opera; the scene of the descent of Orpheus into Hades contains lyrical passages of great melodiousness. Shortly before the Pazzi conspiracy, he composed his famous *Stanze* in celebration of a tournament given by Giuliano dei Medici, and in honour of the *bella Simonetta*. There is absolutely no "fundamental brain work" about these exquisitely finished stanzas; but they are full of dainty mythological pictures quite in the Botticellian style, overladen, perhaps, with adulation of the reigning house and its *ben nato Lauro*. In his lyrics he gave artistic form to the *rispetti* and *strambotti* of the people, and wrote exceedingly musical *ballate*, or *canzoni a ballo*, which are the best of their kind in the whole range of Italian poetry. There is, however, little genuine passion in his love poems for his lady, Madonna Ippolita Leoncina of Prato; though in all that he wrote there is, as Villari puts it, "a fineness of taste that was almost Greek."

Lorenzo dei Medici stands second to his friend as a poet; but he is a good second. His early affection for the fair Lucrezia Donati, with its inevitable sonnets and a commentary somewhat in the manner of Dante's *Vita Nuova*, is more fanciful than earnest, although Poliziano assures us of

"La lunga fedeltà del franco Lauro."

But Lorenzo's intense love of external nature, his power of close observation and graphic description, are more clearly shown in such poems as the *Caccia col Falcone* and the *Ambra*, written among the woods and hills in the country round his new villa of Poggio a Caiano. Elsewhere he gives free scope to the animal side of his sensual nature, and in his famous *Canti carnascialeschi*, songs to be sung at carnival and in masquerades, he at times revelled in pruriency, less for its own sake than for the deliberate corruption of the Florentines. And, for a time, their music drowned the impassioned voice of Savonarola, whose stern cry of warning and exhortation to repentance had for the nonce passed unheeded.

There is extant a miracle play from Lorenzo's hand, the acts of the martyrs Giovanni and Paolo, who suffered in the days of the emperor Julian. Two sides of Lorenzo's nature are ever in conflict—the Lorenzo of the ballate and the carnival songs—the Lorenzo of the *laude* and spiritual poems, many of which have the unmistakable ring of sincerity. And, in the story of his last days and the summoning of Savonarola to his bed-side, the triumph of the man's spiritual side is seen at the end; he is, indeed, in the position of the dying Julian of his own play:—

"Fallace vita! O nostra vana cura!
Lo spirto è già fuor del mio petto spinto:
O Cristo Galileo, tu hai vinto."

Such was likewise the attitude of several members of the Medicean circle, when the crash came. Poliziano followed his friend and patron to the grave, in September 1494; his last hours received the consolations of religion from Savonarola's most devoted follower, Fra Domenico da Pescia (of whom more anon); after death, he was robed in the habit of St Dominic and buried in San Marco. Pico della Mirandola, too, had been present at the Magnifico's death-bed, though not there when the end actually came; he too, in 1494, received the Dominican habit in death, and was buried by Savonarola's friars in San Marco. Marsilio Ficino outlived his friends and denied Fra Girolamo; he died in 1499, and lies at rest in the Duomo.

Of all these Medicean Platonists, Pico della Mirandola is the most fascinating. A young Lombard noble of almost feminine beauty, full of the pride of having mastered all the knowledge of his day, he first came to Florence in 1480 or 1482, almost at the very moment in which Marsilio Ficino finished his translation of Plato. He became at once the chosen friend of all the choicest spirits of Lorenzo's circle. Not only classical learning, but the mysterious East and the sacred lore of the Jews had rendered up their treasures for his intellectual feast; his mysticism shot far beyond even Ficino; all knowledge and all religions were to him a revelation of the Deity. Not only to Lorenzo and his associates did young Pico seem a phœnix of earthly and celestial wisdom, *uomo quasi divino* as Machiavelli puts it; but even Savonarola in his *Triumphus Crucis*, written after Pico's death, declares that, by reason of his loftiness of intellect and the sublimity of his doctrine, he should be numbered amongst the miracles of God and Nature. Pico had been much beloved of many women, and not always a Platonic lover, but, towards the close of his short flower-like life, he burnt "fyve bokes that in his youthe of wanton versis of love with other lyke fantasies he had made," and all else seemed absorbed in the vision of love Divine. "The substance that I have left," he told his nephew, "I intend to give out to poor people, and, fencing myself with the crucifix, barefoot walking about the world, in every town and castle I purpose to preach of Christ." Savonarola, to whom he had confided all the secrets of his heart, was not the only martyr who revered the memory of the man whom Lorenzo the Magnificent had loved. Thomas More translated his life and letters, and reckoned him a saint. He would die at the time of the lilies, so a lady had told Pico; and he died indeed on the very day that the golden lilies on the royal standard of France were borne into Florence through the Porta San Frediano—consoled with wondrous visions of the Queen of Heaven, and speaking as though he beheld the heavens opened.

A month or two earlier, the pen had dropped from the hand of Matteo Maria Boiardo, as he watched the French army descending the Alps; and he brought his unfinished *Orlando Innamorato* to an abrupt close, too sick at heart to sing of the vain love of Fiordespina for Brandiamante:–

> "Mentre che io canto, o Dio Redentore,
> Vedo l'Italia tutta a fiamma e foco,
> Per questi Galli, che con gran valore
> Vengon, per disertar non so che loco."

"Whilst I sing, Oh my God, I see all Italy in flame and fire, through these Gauls, who with great valour come, to lay waste I know not what place." On this note of vague terror, in the onrush of the barbarian hosts, the Quattrocento closes.

ARMS OF THE PAZZI

CHAPTER IV.

FROM FRA GIROLAMO TO DUKE COSIMO

"Vedendo lo omnipotente Dio multiplicare li peccati della Italia, maxime nelli capi così ecclesiastici come seculari, non potendo più sostenere, determinò purgare la Chiesa sua per uno gran flagello. Et perchè come è scripto in Amos propheta, Non faciet Dominus Deus verbum nisi revelaverit secretum suum ad servos suos prophetas: volse per la salute delli suoi electi acciò che inanzi al flagello si preparassino ad sofferire, che nella Italia questo flagello fussi prenuntiato. Et essendo Firenze in mezzo la Italia come il core in mezzo il corpo, s'è dignato di eleggere questa città; nella quale siano tale cose prenuntiate: acciò che per lei si sparghino negli altri luoghi."–*Savonarola*.

GLADIUS Domini super terram cito et velociter, "the Sword of the Lord upon the earth soon and speedily." These words rang ever in the ears of the Dominican friar who was now to eclipse the Medicean rulers of Florence. Girolamo Savonarola, the grandson of a famous Paduan physician who had settled at the court of Ferrara, had entered the order of St Dominic at Bologna in 1474, moved by the great misery of the world and the wickedness of men, and in 1481 had been sent to the convent of San Marco at Florence. The corruption of the Church, the vicious lives of her chief pastors, the growing immorality of the people, the tyranny and oppression of their rulers, had entered into his very soul—had found utterance in allegorical poetry, in an ode *De Ruina Mundi*, written whilst still in the world, in another, *De Ruina Ecclesiae*, composed in the silence of his Bolognese cloister—that cloister which, in better days, had been hallowed by the presence of St Dominic and the Angelical Doctor, Thomas Aquinas. And he believed himself set by God as a watchman in the centre of Italy, to announce to the people and princes that the sword was to fall upon them: "If the sword come, and thou hast not announced it," said the spirit voice that spoke to him in the silence as the dæmon to Socrates, "and they perish unwarned, I will require their blood at thy hands and thou shalt bear the penalty."

But at first the Florentines would not hear him; the gay dancings and the wild carnival songs of their rulers drowned his voice; courtly preachers like the Augustinian of Santo Spirito, Fra Mariano da Gennazano, laid more flattering unction to their souls. Other cities were more ready; San Gemignano first heard the word of prophecy that was soon to resound beneath the dome of Santa Maria del Fiore, even as, some two hundred years before, she had listened to the speech of Dante Alighieri. At the beginning of 1490, the Friar returned to Florence and San Marco; and, on Sunday, August 1st, expounding the Apocalypse in the Church of San

Marco, he first set forth to the Florentines the three cardinal points of his doctrine; first, the Church was to be renovated; secondly, before this renovation, God would send a great scourge upon all Italy; thirdly, these things would come speedily. He preached the following Lent in the Duomo; and thenceforth his great work of reforming Florence, and announcing the impending judgments of God, went on its inspired way. "Go to Lorenzo dei Medici," he said to the five citizens who came to him, at the Magnifico's instigation, to urge him to let the future alone in his sermons, "and bid him do penance for his sins, for God intends to punish him and his"; and when elected Prior of San Marco in this same year, 1491, he would neither enter Lorenzo's palace to salute the patron of the convent, nor welcome him when he walked among the friars in the garden.

Fra Girolamo was preaching the Lent in San Lorenzo, when the Magnifico died; and, a few days later, he saw a wondrous vision, as he himself tells us in the *Compendium Revelationum*. "In 1492," he says, "while I was preaching the Lent in San Lorenzo at Florence, I saw, on the night of Good Friday, two crosses. First, a black cross in the midst of Rome, whereof the head touched the heaven and the arms stretched forth over all the earth; and above it were written these words, *Crux irae Dei*. After I had beheld it, suddenly I saw the sky grow dark, and clouds fly through the air; winds, flashes of lightning and thunderbolts drove across, hail, fire and swords rained down, and slew a vast multitude of folk, so that few remained on the earth. And after this, there came a sky right calm and bright, and I saw another cross, of the same greatness as the first but of gold, rise up over Jerusalem; the which was so resplendent that it illumined all the world, and filled it all with flowers and joy; and above it was written, *Crux misericordiae Dei*. And I saw all generations of men and women come from all parts of the world, to adore it and embrace it."

In the following August came the simoniacal election of Roderigo Borgia to the Papacy, as Alexander VI.; and in Advent another vision appeared to the prophet in his cell, which can only be told in Fra Girolamo's own words:–

"I saw then in the year 1492, the night before the last sermon which I gave that Advent in Santa Reparata, a hand in Heaven with a sword, upon the which was written: *The sword of the Lord upon the earth, soon and speedily*; and over the hand was written, *True and just are the judgments of the Lord*. And it seemed that the arm of that hand proceeded from three faces in one light, of which the first said: *The iniquity of my sanctuary crieth to me from the earth*. The second replied: *Therefore will I visit with a rod their iniquities, and with stripes their sins*. The third said: *My mercy will I not remove from it, nor will I harm it in my truth, and I will have mercy upon the poor and the needy*. In like manner the first answered: *My people have forgotten my commandments days without number*.

The second replied: *Therefore will I grind and break in pieces and will not have mercy.* The third said: *I will be mindful of those who walk in my precepts.* And straightway there came a great voice from all the three faces, over all the world, and it said: *Hearken, all ye dwellers on the earth; thus saith the Lord: I, the Lord, am speaking in my holy zeal. Behold, the days shall come and I will unsheath my sword upon you. Be ye converted therefore unto me, before my fury be accomplished; for when the destruction cometh, ye shall seek peace and there shall be none.* After these words it seemed to me that I saw the whole world, and that the Angels descended from Heaven to earth, arrayed in white, with a multitude of spotless stoles on their shoulders and red crosses in their hands; and they went through the world, offering to each man a white robe and a cross. Some men accepted them and robed themselves with them. Some would not accept them, although they did not impede the others who accepted them. Others would neither accept them nor permit that the others should accept them; and these were the tepid and the sapient of this world, who made mock of them and strove to persuade the contrary. After this, the hand turned the sword down towards the earth; and suddenly it seemed that all the air grew dark with clouds, and that it rained down swords and hail with great thunder and lightning and fire; and there came upon the earth pestilence and famine and great tribulation. And I saw the Angels go through the midst of the people, and give to those who had the white robe and the cross in their hands a clear wine to drink; and they drank and said: *How sweet in our mouths are thy words, O Lord.* And the dregs at the bottom of the chalice they gave to drink to the others, and they would not drink; and it seemed that these would fain have been converted to penitence and could not, and they said: *Wherefore dost thou forget us, Lord?* And they wished to lift up their eyes and look up to God, but they could not, so weighed down were they with tribulations; for they were as though drunk, and it seemed that their hearts had left their breasts, and they went seeking the lusts of this world and found them not. And they walked like senseless beings without heart. After this was done, I heard a very great voice from those three faces, which said: *Hear ye then the word of the Lord: for this have I waited for you, that I may have mercy upon you. Come ye therefore to me, for I am kind and merciful, extending mercy to all who call upon me. But if you will not, I will turn my eyes from you for ever.* And it turned then to the just, and said: *But rejoice, ye just, and exult, for when my short anger shall have passed, I will break the horns of sinners, and the horns of the just shall be exalted.* And suddenly everything disappeared, and it was said to me: *Son, if sinners had eyes, they would surely see how grievous and hard is this pestilence, and how sharp the sword.*"[20]

The French army, terrible beyond any that the Italians had seen, and rendered even more terrible by the universal dread that filled all men's minds at this moment, entered Italy. On September 9th, 1494, Charles VIII. arrived at Asti, where he was received by Ludovico and his court, while the Swiss sacked and massacred at Rapallo. Here was the new Cyrus whom Savonarola had foretold, the leader chosen by God to chastise Italy and reform the Church. While the vague terror throughout the land was at its height, Savonarola, on September 21st, ascended the pulpit of the Duomo, and poured forth so terrible a flood of words on the text *Ecce ego adducam aquas diluvii super terram*, that the densely packed audience were overwhelmed in agonised panic. The bloodless mercenary conflicts of a century had reduced Italy to helplessness; the Aragonese resistance collapsed, and, sacking and slaughtering as they came, the French marched unopposed through Lunigiana upon Tuscany. Piero dei Medici, who had favoured the Aragonese in a half-hearted way, went to meet the French King, surrendered Sarzana and Pietrasanta, the fortresses which his father had won back for Florence, promised to cede Pisa and Leghorn, and made an absolute submission. "Behold," cried Savonarola, a few days later, "the sword has descended, the scourge has fallen, the prophecies are being fulfilled; behold, it is the Lord who is leading on these armies." And he bade the citizens fast and pray throughout the city: it was for the sins of Italy and of Florence that these things had happened; for the corruption of the Church, this tempest had arisen.

It was the republican hero, Piero Capponi, who now gave utterance to the voice of the people. "Piero dei Medici," he said in the Council of the Seventy called by the Signoria on November 4th, "is no longer fit to rule the State: the Republic must provide for itself: the moment has come to shake off this baby government." They prepared for defence, but at the same time sent ambassadors to the "most Christian King," and amongst these ambassadors was Savonarola. In the meantime Piero dei Medici returned to Florence to find his government at an end; the Signoria refused him admittance into the palace; the people assailed him in the Piazza. He made a vain attempt to regain the State by arms, but the despairing shouts of *Palle, Palle,* which his adherents and mercenaries raised, were drowned in the cries of *Popolo e Libertà,* as the citizens, as in the old days of the Republic, heard the great bell of the Palace tolling and saw the burghers once more in arms. On the 9th of November Piero and Giuliano fled through the Porta di San Gallo; the Cardinal Giovanni, who had shown more courage and resource, soon followed, disguised as a friar. There was some pillage done, but little bloodshed. The same day Pisa received the French troops, and shook off the Florentine yoke—an example shortly followed by other Tuscan cities. Florence had regained her liberty, but lost her empire. But the King had listened to the words of Savonarola—words preserved to us by the Friar himself in his *Compendium Revelationum*—who had hailed him as the Minister of Christ, but warned him sternly and fearlessly that, if he abused his power over Florence, the strength which God had given him would be shattered.

On November 17th Charles, clad in black velvet with mantle of gold brocade and splendidly mounted, rode into Florence, as though into a conquered city, with lance levelled, through the Porta di San Frediano. With him was that priestly Mars, the terrible Cardinal della Rovere (afterwards Julius II.), now bent upon the deposition of Alexander VI. as a simoniacal usurper; and he was followed by all the gorgeous chivalry of France, with the fierce Swiss infantry, the light Gascon skirmishers, the gigantic Scottish bowmen–*uomini bestiali* as the Florentines called them–in all about 12,000 men. The procession swept through the gaily decked streets over the Ponte Vecchio, wound round the Piazza della Signoria, and then round the Duomo, amidst deafening cries of *Viva Francia* from the enthusiastic people. But when the King descended and entered the Cathedral, there was a sad disillusion–*parve al popolo un poco diminuta la fama*, as the good apothecary Luca Landucci tells us–for, when off his horse, he appeared a most insignificant little man, almost deformed, and with an idiotic expression of countenance, as his bust portrait in the Bargello still shows. This was not quite the sort of Cyrus that they had expected from Savonarola's discourses; but still, within and without Santa Maria del Fiore, the thunderous shouts of *Viva Francia* continued, until he was solemnly escorted to the Medicean palace which had been prepared for his reception.

That night, and each following night during the French occupation, Florence shone so with illuminations that it seemed mid-day; every day was full of feasting and pageantry; but French and Florentines alike were in arms. The royal "deliverer"–egged on by the ladies of Piero's family and especially by Alfonsina, his young wife–talked of restoring the Medici; the Swiss, rioting in the Borgo SS. Apostoli, were severely handled by the populace, in a way that showed the King that the Republic was not to be trifled with. On November 24th the treaty was signed in the Medicean (now the Riccardi) palace, after a scene never forgotten by the Florentines. Discontented with the amount of the indemnity, the King exclaimed in a threatening voice, "I will bid my trumpets sound" (*io farò dare nelle trombe*). Piero Capponi thereupon snatched the treaty from the royal secretary, tore it in half, and exclaiming, "And we will sound our bells" (*e noi faremo dare nelle campane*), turned with his colleagues to leave the room. Charles, who knew Capponi of old (he had been Florentine Ambassador in France), had the good sense to laugh it off, and the Republic was saved. There was to be an alliance between the Republic and the King, who was henceforth to be called "Restorer and Protector of the Liberty of Florence." He was to receive a substantial indemnity. Pisa and the fortresses were for the present to be retained, but ultimately restored; the decree against the Medici was to be revoked, but they were still banished from Tuscany. But the King would not go. The tension every day grew greater, until at last Savonarola sought the royal presence, solemnly warned him that God's anger would fall upon him if he lingered, and sent him on his way. On November 28th the French left Florence, everyone, from Charles himself downwards, shamelessly carrying off everything of value that they could lay hands on, including the greater part of the treasures and rarities that Cosimo and Lorenzo had collected.

It was now that all Florence turned to the voice that rang out from the Convent of San Marco and the pulpit of the Duomo; and Savonarola became, in some measure, the pilot of the State. Mainly through his influence, the government was remodelled somewhat on the basis of the Venetian constitution with modifications. The supreme authority was vested in the *Greater Council*, which created the magistrates and approved the laws; and it elected the *Council of Eighty*, with which the Signoria was bound to consult, which, together with the Signoria and the Colleges, made appointments and discussed matters which could not be debated in the Greater Council. A law was also passed, known as the "law of the six beans," which gave citizens the right of appeal from the decisions of the Signoria or the sentences of the *Otto di guardia e balìa* (who could condemn even to death by six votes or "beans")–not to a special council to be chosen from the Greater Council, as Savonarola wished, but to the Greater Council itself. There was further a general amnesty proclaimed (March 1495). Finally, since the time-honoured calling of parliaments had been a mere farce, an excuse for masking revolution under the pretence of legality, and was the only means left by which the Medici could constitutionally have overthrown the new regime, it was ordained (August) that no parliament should ever again be held under pain of death. "The only purpose of parliament," said Savonarola, "is to snatch the sovereign power from the hands of the people." So enthusiastic–to use no harsher term–did the Friar show himself, that he declared from the pulpit that, if ever the Signoria should sound the bell for a parliament, their houses should be sacked, and that they themselves might be hacked to pieces by the crowd without any sin being thereby incurred; and that the Consiglio Maggiore was the work of God and not of man, and that whoever should attempt to change this government should for ever be accursed of the Lord. It was now that the Sala del Maggior Consiglio was built by Cronaca in the Priors' Palace, to accommodate this new government of the people; and the Signoria set up in the middle of the court and at their gate the two bronze statues by Donatello, which they took from Piero's palace–the *David*, an emblem of the triumphant young republic that had overthrown the giant of tyranny, the *Judith* as a warning of the punishment that the State would inflict upon whoso should attempt its restoration; *exemplum salutis publicae cives posuere*, 1495, ran the new inscription put by these stern theocratic republicans upon its base.

But in the meantime Charles had pursued his triumphant march, had entered Rome, had conquered the kingdom of Naples almost without a blow. Then fortune turned against him; Ludovico Sforza with the Pope formed an Italian league, including Venice, with hope of Germany and Spain, to expel the French from Italy–a league in which all but Florence and Ferrara joined. Charles was now in full retreat to secure his return to France, and was said to be marching on Florence with Piero dei Medici in his company–no reformation of the Church accomplished, no restoration of Pisa to his ally. The Florentines flew to arms. But Savonarola imagined that he had had a special Vision of the Lilies vouchsafed to him by the Blessed Virgin, which pointed to an alliance with France and the reacquisition of Pisa.[21] He went forth to meet the King at Poggibonsi, June 1495, overawed the fickle monarch by his prophetic exhortation, and at least kept the French out of Florence. A month later, the battle of Fornovo secured Charles' retreat and occasioned (what was more important to posterity) Mantegna's Madonna of the Victory. And of the lost cities and fortresses, Leghorn alone was recovered.

But all that Savonarola had done, or was to do, in the political field was but the means to an end—the reformation and purification of Florence. It was to be a united and consecrated State, with Christ alone for King, adorned with all triumphs of Christian art and sacred poetry, a fire of spiritual felicity to Italy and all the earth. In Lent and Advent especially, his voice sounded from the pulpit, denouncing vice, showing the beauty of righteousness, the efficacy of the sacraments, and interpreting the Prophets, with special reference to the needs of his times. And for a while Florence seemed verily a new city. For the wild licence of the Carnival, for the Pagan pageantry that the Medicean princes had loved, for the sensual songs that had once floated up from every street of the City of Flowers—there were now bonfires of the vanities in the public squares; holocausts of immoral books, indecent pictures, all that ministered to luxury and wantonness (and much, too, that was very precious!); there were processions in honour of Christ and His Mother, there were new mystical lauds and hymns of divine love. A kind of spiritual inebriation took possession of the people and their rulers alike. Tonsured friars and grave citizens, with heads garlanded, mingled with the children and danced like David before the Ark, shouting, "*Viva Cristo e la Vergine Maria nostra regina.*" They had indeed, like the Apostle, become fools for Christ's sake. "It was a holy time," writes good Luca Landucci, "but it was short. The wicked have prevailed over the good. Praised be God that I saw that short holy time. Wherefore I pray God that He may give it back to us, that holy and pure living. It was indeed a blessed time." Above all, the children of Florence were the Friar's chosen emissaries and agents in the great work he had in hand; he organised them into bands, with standard-bearers and officers like the time-honoured city companies with their gonfaloniers, and sent them round the city to seize vanities, forcibly to stop gambling, to collect alms for the poor, and even to exercise a supervision over the ladies' dresses. *Ecco i fanciugli del Frate*, was an instant signal for gamblers to take to flight, and for the fair and frail ladies to be on their very best behaviour. They proceeded with olive branches, like the children of Jerusalem on the first Palm Sunday; they made the churches ring with their hymns to the Madonna, and even harangued the Signoria on the best method of reforming the morals of the citizens. "Out of the mouths of babes and sucklings Thou hast perfected praise," quotes Landucci: "I have written these things because they are true, and I have seen them and have felt their sweetness, and some of my own children were among these pure and blessed bands."[22]

But the holy time was short indeed. Factions were still only too much alive. The *Bigi* or *Palleschi* were secretly ready to welcome the Medici back; the *Arrabbiati*, the powerful section of the citizens who, to some extent, held the traditions of the so-called *Ottimati* or *nobili popolani*, whom the Medici had overthrown, were even more bitter in their hatred to the *Frateschi* or *Piagnoni*, as the adherents of the Friar were called, though prepared to make common cause with them on the least rumour of Piero dei Medici approaching the walls. The *Compagnacci*, or "bad companions," dissolute young men and evil livers, were banded together under Doffo Spini, and would gladly have taken the life of the man who had curtailed their opportunities for vice. And to these there were now added the open hostility of Pope Alexander VI., and the secret machinations of his worthy ally, the Duke of Milan. The Pope's hostility was at first mainly political; he had no objection whatever to Savonarola reforming faith and morals (so long as he did not ask Roderigo Borgia to reform himself), but could not abide the Friar declaring that he had a special mission from God and the Madonna to oppose the Italian league against France. At the same time the Pope would undoubtedly have been glad to see Piero dei Medici restored to power. But in the early part of 1496, it became a war to the death between these two–the Prophet of Righteousness and the Church's Caiaphas–a war which seemed at one moment about to convulse all Christendom, but which ended in the funeral pyre of the Piazza della Signoria.

On Ash Wednesday, February 17th, Fra Girolamo, amidst the vastest audience that had yet flocked to hear his words, ascended once more the pulpit of Santa Maria del Fiore. He commenced by a profession of most absolute submission to the Church of Rome. "I have ever believed, and do believe," he said, "all that is believed by the Holy Roman Church, and have ever submitted, and do submit, myself to her.... I rely only on Christ and on the decisions of the Church of Rome." But this was a prelude to the famous series of sermons on Amos and Zechariah which he preached throughout this Lent, and which was in effect a superb and inspired denunciation of the wickedness of Alexander and his Court, of the shameless corruption of the Papal Curia and the Church generally, which had made Rome, for a while, the sink of Christendom. Nearly two hundred years before, St Peter had said the same thing to Dante in the Heaven of the Fixed Stars:–

> "Quegli ch'usurpa in terra il loco mio,
> il loco mio, il loco mio, che vaca
> nella presenza del Figliuol di Dio,
> fatto ha del cimitero mio cloaca
> del sangue e della puzza, onde il perverso
> che cadde di quassù, laggiù si placa."[23]

These were, perhaps, the most terrible of all Savonarola's sermons and prophecies. Chastisement was to come upon Rome; she was to be girdled with steel, put to the sword, consumed with fire. Italy was to be ravaged with pestilence and famine; from all sides the barbarian hordes would sweep down upon her. Let them fly from this corrupted Rome, this new Babylon of confusion, and come to repentance. And for himself, he asked and hoped for nothing but the lot of the martyrs, when his work was done. These sermons echoed through all Europe; and when the Friar, after a temporary absence at Prato, returned to the pulpit in May with a new course of sermons on Ruth and Micah, he was no less daring; as loudly as ever he rebuked the hideous corruption of the times, the wickedness of the Roman Court, and announced the scourge that was at hand:–

"I announce to thee, Italy and Rome, that the Lord will come forth out of His place. He has awaited thee so long that He can wait no more. I tell thee that God will draw forth the sword from the sheath; He will send the foreign nations; He will come forth out of His clemency and His mercy; and such bloodshed shall there be, so many deaths, such cruelty, that thou shalt say: O Lord, Thou hast come forth out of Thy place. Yea, the Lord shall come; He will come down and tread upon the high places of the earth. I say to thee, Italy and Rome, that the Lord will tread upon thee. I have bidden thee do penance; thou art worse than ever. The feet of the Lord shall tread upon thee; His feet shall be the horses, the armies of the foreign nations that shall trample upon the great men of Italy; and soon shall priests, friars, bishops, cardinals and great masters be trampled down....

"Trust not, Rome, in saying: Here we have the relics, here we have St Peter and so many bodies of martyrs. God will not suffer such iniquities! I warn thee that their blood cries up to Christ to come and chastise thee."[24]

But, in the meanwhile, the state of Florence was dark and dismal in the extreme. Pestilence and famine ravaged her streets; the war against Pisa seemed more hopeless every day; Piero Capponi had fallen in the field in September; and the forces of the League threatened her with destruction, unless she deserted the French alliance. King Charles showed no disposition to return; the Emperor Maximilian, with the Venetian fleet, was blockading her sole remaining port of Leghorn. A gleam of light came in October, when, at the very moment that the miraculous Madonna of the Impruneta was being borne through the streets in procession by the Piagnoni, a messenger brought the news that reinforcements and provisions had reached Leghorn from Marseilles; and it was followed in November by the dispersion of the imperial fleet by a tempest. At the opening of 1497 a Signory devoted to Savonarola, and headed by Francesco Valori as Gonfaloniere, was elected; and the following carnival witnessed an even more emphatic burning of the vanities in the great Piazza, while the sweet voices of the "children of the Friar" seemed to rise louder and louder in intercession and in praise. Savonarola was at this time living more in seclusion, broken in health, and entirely engaged upon his great theological treatise, the *Triumphus Crucis*; but in Lent he resumed his pulpit crusade against the corruption of the Church, the scandalous lives of her chief pastors, in a series of sermons on Ezekiel; above all in one most tremendous discourse on the text: "And in all thy abominations and thy fornications thou hast not remembered the days of thy youth." In April, relying upon the election of a new Signoria favourable to the Mediceans (and headed by Bernardo del Nero as Gonfaloniere), Piero dei Medici—who had been leading a most degraded life in Rome, and committing every turpitude imaginable—made an attempt to surprise Florence, which merely resulted in a contemptible fiasco. This threw the government into the hands of the Arrabbiati, who hated Savonarola even more than the Palleschi did, and who were intriguing with the Pope and the Duke of Milan. On Ascension Day the Compagnacci raised a disgraceful riot in the Duomo, interrupted Savonarola's sermon, and even attempted to take his life. Then at last there came from Rome the long-expected bull of excommunication, commencing, "We have heard from many persons worthy of belief that a certain Fra Girolamo Savonarola, at this present said to be vicar of San Marco in Florence, hath disseminated pernicious doctrines to the scandal and great grief of simple souls." It was published on June 18th in the Badia, the Annunziata, Santa Croce, Santa Maria Novella, and Santo Spirito, with the usual solemn ceremonies of ringing bells and dashing out of the lights–in the last-named church, especially, the monks "did the cursing in the most orgulist wise that might be done," as the compiler of the *Morte Darthur* would put it.

The Arrabbiati and Compagnacci were exultant, but the Signoria that entered office in July seemed disposed to make Savonarola's cause their own. A fresh plot was discovered to betray Florence to Piero dei Medici, and five of the noblest citizens in the State–the aged Bernardo del Nero, who had merely known of the plot and not divulged it, but who had been privy to Piero's coming in April while Gonfaloniere, among them–were beheaded in the courtyard of the Bargello's palace, adjoining the Palazzo Vecchio. In this Savonarola took no share; he was absorbed in tending those who were dying on all sides from the plague and famine, and in making the final revision of his *Triumph of the Cross*, which was to show to the Pope and all the world how steadfastly he held to the faith of the Church of Rome.[25] The execution of these conspirators caused great indignation among many in the city. They had been refused the right of appeal to the Consiglio Maggiore, and it was held that Fra Girolamo might have saved them, had he so chosen, and that his ally, Francesco Valori, who had relentlessly hounded them to their deaths, had been actuated mainly by personal hatred of Bernardo del Nero.

But Savonarola could not long keep silence, and in the following February, 1498, on Septuagesima Sunday, he again ascended the pulpit of the Duomo. Many of his adherents, Landucci tells us, kept away for fear of the excommunication: "I was one of those who did not go there." Not faith, but charity it is that justifies and perfects man—such was the burden of the Friar's sermons now: if the Pope gives commands which are contrary to charity, he is no instrument of the Lord, but a broken tool. The excommunication is invalid, the Lord will work a miracle through His servant when His time comes, and his only prayer is that he may die in defence of the truth. On the last day of the Carnival, after communicating his friars and a vast throng of the laity, Savonarola addressed the people in the Piazza of San Marco, and, holding on high the Host, prayed that Christ would send fire from heaven upon him that should swallow him up into hell, if he were deceiving himself, and if his words were not from God. There was a more gorgeous burning of the Vanities than ever; but all during Lent the unequal conflict went on, and the Friar began to talk of a future Council. This was the last straw. An interdict would ruin the commerce of Florence; and on the 17th of March the Signoria bowed before the storm, and forbade Savonarola to preach again. On the following morning, the third Sunday in Lent, he delivered his last sermon:—

"If I am deceived, Christ, Thou hast deceived me, Thou. Holy Trinity, if I am deceived, Thou hast deceived me. Angels, if I am deceived, ye have deceived me. Saints of Paradise, if I am deceived, ye have deceived me. But all that God has said, or His angels or His saints have said, is most true, and it is impossible that they should lie; and, therefore, it is impossible that, when I repeat what they have told me, I should lie. O Rome, do all that thou wilt, for I assure thee of this, that the Lord is with me. O Rome, it is hard for thee to kick against the pricks. Thou shalt be purified yet.... Italy, Italy, the Lord is with me. Thou wilt not be able to do aught. Florence, Florence, that is, ye evil citizens of Florence, arm yourselves as ye will, ye shall be conquered this time, and ye shall not be able to kick against the pricks, for the Lord is with me, as a strong warrior." "Let us leave all to the Lord; He has been the Master of all the Prophets, and of all the holy men. He is the Master who wieldeth the hammer, and, when He hath used it for His purpose, putteth it not back into the chest, but casteth it aside. So did He unto Jeremiah, for when He had used him as much as He wished, He cast him aside and had him stoned. So will it be also with this hammer; when He shall have used it in His own way, He will cast it aside. Yea, we are content, let the Lord's will be done; and by the more suffering that shall be ours here below, so much the greater shall the crown be hereafter, there on high."

"We will do with our prayers what we had to do with our preaching. O Lord, I commend to Thee the good and the pure of heart; and I pray Thee, look not at the negligence of the good, because human frailty is great, yea, their frailty is great. Bless, Lord, the good and pure of heart. Lord, I pray Thee that Thou delay no longer in fulfilling Thy promises."

It was now, in the silence of his cell, that Savonarola prepared his last move. He would appeal to the princes of Christendom–the Emperor, Ferdinand and Isabella of Spain, Henry VII. of England, the King of Hungary, and above all, that "most Christian King" Charles VIII. of France–to summon a general council, depose the simoniacal usurper who was polluting the chair of Peter, and reform the Church. He was prepared to promise miracles from God to confirm his words. These letters were written, but never sent; a preliminary message was forwarded from trustworthy friends in Florence to influential persons in each court to prepare them for what was coming; and the despatch to the Florentine ambassador in France was intercepted by the agents of the Duke of Milan. It was at once placed in the hands of Cardinal Ascanio Sforza in Rome, and the end was now a matter of days. The Signoria was hostile, and the famous ordeal by fire lit the conflagration that freed the martyr and patriot. On Sunday, March 25th, the Franciscan Francesco da Puglia, preaching in Santa Croce and denouncing Savonarola, challenged him to prove his doctrines by a miracle, to pass unscathed through the fire. He was himself prepared to enter the flames with him, or at least said that he was. Against Savonarola's will his lieutenant, Fra Domenico, who had taken his place in the pulpit, drew up a series of conclusions (epitomising Savonarola's teaching and declaring the nullity of the excommunication), and declared himself ready to enter the fire to prove their truth.

Huge was the delight of the Compagnacci at the prospect of such sport, and the Signoria seized upon it as a chance of ending the matter once for all. Whether the Franciscans were sincere, or whether it was a mere plot to enable the Arrabbiati and Compagnacci to destroy Savonarola, is still a matter of dispute. The Piagnoni were confident in the coming triumph of their prophet; champions came forward from both sides, professedly eager to enter the flames–although it was muttered that the Compagnacci and their Doffo Spini had promised the Franciscans that no harm should befall them. Savonarola misliked it, but took every precaution that, if the ordeal really came off, there should be no possibility of fraud or evasion. Of the amazing scene in the Piazza on April 7th, I will speak in the following chapter; suffice it to say here that it ended in a complete fiasco, and that Savonarola and his friars would never have reached their convent alive, but for the protection of the armed soldiery of the Signoria. Hounded home under the showers of stones and filth from the infuriated crowd, whose howls of execration echoed through San Marco, Fra Girolamo had the *Te Deum* sung, but knew in his heart that all was lost. That very same day his Cyrus, the champion of his prophetic dreams, Charles VIII. of France, was struck down by an apoplectic stroke at Amboise; and, as though in judgment for his abandonment of what the prophet had told him was the work of the Lord, breathed his last in the utmost misery and ignominy.

The next morning, Palm Sunday, April 8th, Savonarola preached a very short sermon in the church of San Marco, in which he offered himself in sacrifice to God and was prepared to suffer death for his flock. *Tanto fu sempre questo uomo simile a sè stesso*, says Jacopo Nardi. Hell had broken loose by the evening, and the Arrabbiati and Compagnacci, stabbing and hewing as they came, surged round the church and convent. In spite of Savonarola and Fra Domenico, the friars had weapons and ammunition in their cells, and there was a small band of devout laymen with them, prepared to hold by the prophet to the end. From vespers till past midnight the attack and defence went on; in the Piazza, in the church, and through the cloisters raged the fight, while riot and murder wantoned through the streets of the city. Francesco Valori, who had escaped from the convent in the hope of bringing reinforcements, was brutally murdered before his own door. The great bell of the convent tolled and tolled, animating both besieged and besiegers to fresh efforts, but bringing no relief from without. Savonarola, who had been prevented from following the impulses of his heart and delivering himself up to the infernal crew that thirsted for his blood in the Piazza, at last gathered his friars round him before the Blessed Sacrament, in the great hall of the Greek library, solemnly confirmed his doctrine, exhorted them to embrace the Cross alone, and then, together with Fra Domenico, gave himself into the hands of the forces of the Signoria. The entire cloisters were already swarming with his exultant foes. "The work of the Lord shall go forward without cease," he said, as the mace-bearers bound him and Domenico, "my death will but hasten it on." Buffeted and insulted by the Compagnacci and the populace, amidst the deafening uproar, the two Dominicans were brought to the Palazzo Vecchio. It seemed to the excited imaginations of the Piagnoni that the scenes of the first Passiontide at Jerusalem were now being repeated in the streets of fifteenth century Florence.

The Signoria had no intention of handing over their captives to Rome, but appointed a commission of seventeen–including Doffo Spini and several of Savonarola's bitterest foes–to conduct the examination of the three friars. The third, Fra Silvestro, a weak and foolish visionary, had hid himself on the fatal night, but had been given up on the following day. Again and again were they most cruelly tortured–but in all essentials, though ever and anon they wrung some sort of agonised denial from his lips, Savonarola's testimony as to his divine mission was unshaken. Fra Domenico, the lion-hearted soul whom the children of Florence had loved, and to whom poets like Poliziano had turned on their death-beds, was as heroic on the rack or under the torment of the boot as he had been throughout his career. Out of Fra Silvestro the examiners could naturally extort almost anything they pleased. And a number of laymen and others, supposed to have been in their counsels, were similarly "examined," and their shrieks rang through the Bargello; but with little profit to the Friar's foes. So they falsified the confessions, and read the falsification aloud in the Sala del Maggior Consiglio, to the bewilderment of all Savonarola's quondam disciples who were there. "We had believed him to be a prophet," writes Landucci in his diary, "and he confessed that he was not a prophet, and that he had not received from God the things that he preached; and he confessed that many things in his sermons were the contrary to what he had given us to understand. And I was there when this process was read, whereat I was astounded, stupified, and amazed. Grief pierced my soul, when I saw so great an edifice fall to the ground, through being sadly based upon a single lie. I expected Florence to be a new Jerusalem, whence should proceed the laws and splendour and example of goodly living, and to see the renovation of the Church, the conversion of the infidels and the consolation of the good. And I heard the very contrary, and indeed took the medicine: *In voluntate tua, Domine, omnia sunt posita.*"

A packed election produced a new Signoria, crueller than the last. They still refused to send the friars to Rome, but invited the Pope's commissioners to Florence. These arrived on May 19th–the Dominican General, Torriani, a well-intentioned man, and the future Cardinal Romolino, a typical creature of the Borgias and a most infamous fellow. It was said that they meant to put Savonarola to death, even if he were a second St John the Baptist. The torture was renewed without result; the three friars were sentenced to be hanged and then burnt. Fra Domenico implored that he might be cast alive into the fire, in order that he might suffer more grievous torments for Christ, and desired only that the friars of Fiesole, of which convent he was prior, might bury him in some lowly spot, and be loyal to the teachings of Fra Girolamo. On the morning of May 23rd, Savonarola said his last Mass in the Chapel of the Priors, and communicated his companions. Then they were led out on to the Ringhiera overlooking the Piazza, from which a temporary *palchetto* ran out towards the centre of the square to serve as scaffold. Here, the evening before, the gallows had been erected, beam across beam; but a cry had arisen among the crowd, *They are going to crucify him.* So it had been hacked about, in order that it might not seem even remotely to resemble a cross.

But in spite of all their efforts, Jacopo Nardi tells us, that gallows still seemed to represent the figure of the Cross.

THE DEATH OF SAVONAROLA
(From an old, but quite contemporary, representation)

The guards of the Signoria kept back the crowds that pressed thicker and thicker round the scaffold, most of them bitterly hostile to the Friars and heaping every insult upon them. When Savonarola was stripped of the habit of Saint Dominic, he said, "Holy dress, how much did I long to wear thee; thou wast granted to me by the grace of God, and to this day I have kept thee spotless. I do not now leave thee, thou art taken from me." They were now degraded by the Bishop of Vasona, who had loved Fra Girolamo in better days; then in the same breath sentenced and absolved by Romolino, and finally condemned by the Eight—or the seven of them who were present—as representing the secular arm. The Bishop, in degrading Savonarola, stammered out: *Separo te ab Ecclesia militante atque triumphante*; to which the Friar calmly answered, in words which have become famous: *Militante, non triumphante; hoc enim tuum non est.* Silvestro suffered first, then Domenico. There was a pause before Savonarola followed; and in the sudden silence, as he looked his last upon the people, a voice cried: "Now, prophet, is the time for a miracle." And then another voice: "Now can I burn the man who would have burnt me"; and a ruffian, who had been waiting since dawn at the foot of the scaffold, fired the pile before the executioner could descend from his ladder. The bodies were burnt to ashes amidst the ferocious yells of the populace, and thrown into the Arno from the Ponte Vecchio. "Many fell from their faith," writes Landucci. A faithful few, including some noble Florentine ladies, gathered up relics, in spite of the crowd and the Signory, and collected what floated on the water. It was the vigil of Ascension Day.

Savonarola's martyrdom ends the story of mediæval Florence. The last man of the Middle Ages–born out of his due time–had perished. A portion of the prophecy was fulfilled at once. The people of Italy and their rulers alike were trampled into the dust beneath the feet of the foreigners–the Frenchmen, the Switzers, the Spaniards, the Germans. The new King of France, Louis XII., who claimed both the Duchy of Milan and the kingdom of the Two Sicilies, entered Milan in 1499; and, after a brief restoration, Ludovico Sforza expiated his treasons by being sold by the Swiss to a lingering life-in-death in a French dungeon. The Spaniards followed; and in 1501 the troops of Ferdinand the Catholic occupied Naples. Like the dragon and the lion in Leonardo's drawing, Spain and France now fell upon each other for the possession of the spoils of conquered Italy; the Emperor Maximilian and Pope Julius II. joined in the fray; fresh hordes of Swiss poured into Lombardy. The battle of Pavia in 1525 gave the final victory to Spain; and, in 1527, the judgment foretold by Savonarola fell upon Rome, when the Eternal City was devastated by the Spaniards and Germans, nominally the armies of the Emperor Charles V. The treaty of Câteau-Cambresis in 1559 finally forged the Austrian and Spanish fetters with which Italy was henceforth bound.

The death of Savonarola did not materially alter the affairs of the Republic. The Greater Council kept its hold upon the people and city, and in 1502 Piero di Tommaso Soderini was elected Gonfaloniere for life. The new head of the State was a sincere Republican and a genuine wholehearted patriot; a man of blameless life and noble character, but simple-minded almost to a fault, and of abilities hardly more than mediocre. Niccolò Machiavelli, who was born in 1469 and had entered political life in 1498, shortly after Savonarola's death, as Secretary to the Ten (the Dieci di Balìa), was much employed by the Gonfaloniere both in war and peace, especially on foreign legations; and, although he sneered at Soderini after his death for his simplicity, he co-operated faithfully and ably with him during his administration. It was under Soderini that Machiavelli organised the Florentine militia. Pisa was finally reconquered for Florence in 1509; and, although Machiavelli cruelly told the Pisan envoys that the Florentines required only their obedience, and cared nothing for their lives, their property, nor their honour, the conquerors showed unusual magnanimity and generosity in their triumph.

These last years of the Republic are very glorious in the history of Florentine art. In 1498, just before the French entered Milan, Leonardo da Vinci had finished his Last Supper for Ludovico Sforza; in the same year, Michelangelo commenced his Pietà in Rome which is now in St Peter's; in

1499, Baccio della Porta began a fresco of the Last Judgment in Santa Maria Nuova, a fresco which, when he entered the Dominican order at San Marco and became henceforth known as Fra Bartolommeo, was finished by his friend, Mariotto Albertinelli. These three works, though in very different degrees, represent the opening of the Cinquecento in painting and sculpture. While Soderini ruled, both Leonardo and Michelangelo were working in Florence, for the Sala del Maggior Consiglio, and Michelangelo's gigantic David—the Republic preparing to meet its foes—was finished in 1504. This was the epoch in which Leonardo was studying those strange women of the Renaissance, whose mysterious smiles and wonderful hair still live for us in his drawings; and it was now that he painted here in Florence his Monna Lisa, "the embodiment of the old fancy, the symbol of the modern idea." At the close of 1504 the young Raphael came to Florence (as Perugino had done before him), and his art henceforth shows how profoundly he felt the Florentine influence. We know how he sketched the newly finished David, studied Masaccio's frescoes, copied bits of Leonardo's cartoon, was impressed by Bartolommeo's Last Judgment. Although it was especially Leonardo that he took for a model, Raphael found his most congenial friend and adviser in the artist friar of San Marco; and there is a pleasant tradition that he was himself influential in persuading Fra Bartolommeo to resume the brush. Leonardo soon went off to serve King Francis I. in France; Pope Julius summoned both Michelangelo and Raphael to Rome. These men were the masters of the world in painting and sculpture, and cannot really be confined to one school. Purely Florentine painting in the Cinquecento now culminated in the work of Fra Bartolommeo (1475-1517) and Andrea del Sarto (1486-1531), who had both been the pupils of Piero di Cosimo, although they felt other and greater influences later. After Angelico, Fra Bartolommeo is the most purely religious of all the Florentine masters; and, with the solitary exception of Andrea del Sarto, he is their only really great colourist. Two pictures of his at Lucca—one in the Cathedral, the other now in the Palazzo Pubblico—are among the greatest works of the Renaissance. In the latter especially, "Our Lady of Mercy," he shows himself the heir in painting of the traditions of Savonarola. Many of Bartolommeo's altar-pieces have grown very black, and have lost much of their effect by being removed from the churches for which they were painted; but enough is left in Florence to show his greatness. With him was associated that gay Bohemian and wild liver, Mariotto Albertinelli (1474-1515), who deserted painting to become an innkeeper, and who frequently worked in partnership with the friar. Andrea del Sarto, the tailor's son who loved not wisely but too well, is the last of a noble line of heroic craftsmen. Although his work lacks all inspiration, he is one of the greatest of colourists. "Andrea del Sarto," writes Mr Berenson, "approached, perhaps, as closely to a Giorgione or a Titian as could a Florentine, ill at ease in the neighbourhood of Leonardo and Michelangelo." He entirely belongs to these closing days of the Republic; his earliest frescoes were painted during Soderini's gonfalonierate; his latest just before the great siege.

In the Carnival of 1511 a wonderfully grim pageant was shown to the Florentines, and it was ominous of coming events. It was known as the *Carro della Morte*, and had been designed with much secrecy by Piero di Cosimo. Drawn by buffaloes, a gigantic black chariot, all painted over with dead men's bones and white crosses, slowly passed through the streets. Upon the top of it, there stood a large figure of Death with a scythe in her hand; all round her, on the chariot, were closed coffins. When at intervals the Triumph paused, harsh and hoarse trumpet-blasts sounded; the coffins opened, and horrible figures, attired like skeletons, half issued forth. "We are dead," they sang, "as you see. So shall we see you dead. Once we were even as you are, soon shall you be as we." Before and after the chariot, rode a great band of what seemed to be mounted deaths, on the sorriest steeds that could be found. Each bore a great black banner with skull and cross-bones upon it, and each ghastly cavalier was attended by four skeletons with black torches. Ten black standards followed the Triumph; and, as it slowly moved on, the whole procession chanted the *Miserere*. Vasari tells us that this spectacle, which filled the city with terror and wonder, was supposed to signify the return of the Medici to Florence, which was to be "as it were, a resurrection from death to life."

And, sure enough, in the following year the Spaniards under Raimondo da Cardona fell upon Tuscany, and, after the horrible sack and massacre of Prato, reinstated the Cardinal Giovanni dei Medici and Giuliano in Florence–their elder brother, Piero, had been drowned in the Garigliano eight years before. Piero Soderini went into exile, the Greater Council was abolished, and, while the city was held by their foreign troops, the Medici renewed the old pretence of summoning a parliament to grant a balìa to reform the State. At the beginning of 1513 two young disciples of Savonarola, Pietro Paolo Boscoli and Agostino Capponi, resolved to imitate Brutus and Cassius, and to liberate Florence by the death of the Cardinal and his brother. Their plot was discovered, and they died on the scaffold. "Get this Brutus out of my head for me," said Boscoli to Luca della Robbia, kinsman of the great sculptor, "that I may meet my last end like a Christian"; and, to the Dominican friar who confessed him, he said, "Father, the philosophers have taught me how to bear death manfully; do you help me to bear it out of love for Christ." In this same year the Cardinal Giovanni was elected Pope, and entered upon his splendid and scandalous pontificate as

Leo X. "Let us enjoy the Papacy," was his maxim, "since God has given it to us."

Although Machiavelli was ready to serve the Medici, he had been deprived of his posts at the restoration, imprisoned and tortured on suspicion of being concerned in Boscoli's conspiracy, and now, released in the amnesty granted by the newly elected Pope, was living in poverty and enforced retirement at his villa near San Casciano. It was now that he wrote his great books, the *Principe* and the *Discorsi sopra la prima deca di Tito Livio*. Florence was ruled by the Pope's nephew, the younger Lorenzo, son of Piero by Alfonsina Orsini. The government was practically what it had been under the Magnificent, save that this new Lorenzo, who had married a French princess, discarded the republican appearances which his grandfather had maintained, and surrounded himself with courtiers and soldiers. For him and for Giuliano, the Pope cherished designs of carving out large princedoms in Italy; and Machiavelli, in dedicating his *Principe* first to Giuliano, who died in 1516, and then to Lorenzo, probably dreamed that some such prince as he described might drive out the foreigner and unify the nation. In his nobler moments Leo X., too, seems to have aspired to establish the independence of Italy. When Lorenzo died in 1519, leaving one daughter, who was afterwards to be the notorious Queen of France, there was no direct legitimate male descendant of Cosimo the elder left; and the Cardinal

Giulio, son of the elder Giuliano, governed Florence with considerable mildness, and even seemed disposed to favour a genuine republican government, until a plot against his life hardened his heart. It was to him that Machiavelli, who was now to some extent received back into favour, afterwards dedicated his *Istorie Fiorentine*. In 1523 the Cardinal Giulio, in spite of his illegitimate birth, became Pope Clement VII., that most hapless of Pontiffs, whose reign was so surpassingly disastrous to Italy. In Florence the Medici were now represented by two young bastards, Ippolito and Alessandro, the reputed children of the younger Giuliano and the younger Lorenzo respectively; while the Cardinal Passerini misruled the State in the name of the Pope. But more of the true Medicean spirit had passed into the person of a woman, Clarice, the daughter of Piero (and therefore the sister of the Duke Lorenzo), who was married to the younger Filippo Strozzi, and could ill bear to see her house end in these two base-born lads. And elsewhere in Italy Giovanni delle Bande Nere (as he was afterwards called, from the mourning of his soldiers for his death) was winning renown as a captain; he was the son of that Giovanni dei Medici with whom Piero had quarrelled, by Caterina Sforza, the Lady of Forlì, and had married Maria Salviati, a grand-daughter of Lorenzo the Magnificent. But the Pope would rather have lost Florence than that it should fall into the hands of the younger line.

But the Florentine Republic was to have a more glorious sunset. In 1527, while the imperial troops sacked Rome, the Florentines for the third time expelled the Medici and re-established the Republic, with first Niccolò Capponi and then Francesco Carducci as Gonfaloniere. In this sunset Machiavelli died; Andrea del Sarto painted the last great Florentine fresco; Michelangelo returned to serve the State in her hour of need. The voices of the Piagnoni were heard again from San Marco, and Niccolò Capponi in the Greater Council carried a resolution electing Jesus Christ king of Florence. But the plague fell upon the city; and her liberty was the price of the reconciliation of Pope and Emperor. From October 1529 until August 1530, their united forces—first under the Prince of Orange and then under Ferrante Gonzaga—beleaguered Florence. Francesco Ferrucci, the last hope of the Republic, was defeated and slain by the imperialists near San Marcello; and then, betrayed by her own infamous general Malatesta Baglioni, the city capitulated on the understanding that, although the form of the government was to be regulated and established by the Emperor, her liberty was preserved. The sun had indeed set of the most noble Republic in all history.

Alessandro dei Medici, the reputed son of Lorenzo by a mulatto woman, was now made hereditary ruler of Florence by the Emperor, whose illegitimate daughter he married, and by the Pope. For a time, the Duke behaved with some decency; but after the death of Clement in 1534, he showed himself in his true light as a most abominable tyrant, and would even have murdered Michelangelo, who had been working upon the tombs of Giuliano and Lorenzo. "It was certainly by God's aid," writes Condivi, "that he happened to be away from Florence when Clement died." Alessandro appears to have poisoned his kinsman, the Cardinal Ippolito, the other illegitimate remnant of the elder Medicean line, in whom he dreaded a possible rival. Associated with him in his worst excesses was a legitimate scion of the younger branch of the house, Lorenzino–the *Lorenzaccio* of Alfred de Musset's drama–who was the grandson of the Lorenzo di Pier Francesco mentioned in the previous chapter.[26] On January 5th, 1537, this young man–a reckless libertine, half scholar and half madman–stabbed the Duke Alessandro to death with the aid of a bravo, and fled, only to find a dishonourable grave some ten years later in Venice.

THE DAWN
By Michelangelo

Florence now fell into the hands of the ablest and most ruthless of all her rulers, Cosimo I. (the son of Giovanni delle Bande Nere), who united Medicean craft with the brutality of the Sforzas, conquered Siena, and became the first Grand Duke of Tuscany. At the opening of his reign the Florentine exiles, headed by the Strozzi and by Baccio Valori, attempted to recover the State, but were defeated by Cosimo's mercenaries. Their leaders were relentlessly put to death; and Filippo Strozzi, after prolonged torture, was either murdered in prison or committed suicide. A word will be said presently, in chapter ix., on Cosimo's descendants, the Medicean Grand Dukes who reigned in Tuscany for two hundred years.

The older generation of artists had passed away with the Republic. After the siege Michelangelo alone remained, compelled to labour upon the Medicean tombs in San Lorenzo, which have become a monument, less to the tyrants for whom he reared them, than to the *saeva indignatio* of the great master himself at the downfall of his country. A madrigal of his, written either in the days of Alessandro or at the beginning of Cosimo's reign, expresses what was in his heart. Symonds renders it:–

"Lady, for joy of lovers numberless
Thou wast created fair as angels are;
Sure God hath fallen asleep in heaven afar,
When one man calls the bliss of many his."

But the last days and last works of Michelangelo belong to the story of Rome rather than to that of Florence. Jacopo Carucci da Pontormo (1494-1557), who had been Andrea del Sarto's scholar, and whose earlier works had been painted before the downfall of the Republic, connects the earlier with the later Cinquecento; but of his work, as of that of his pupil Angelo Bronzino (1502-1572), the portraits alone have any significance for us now. Giorgio Vasari (1512-

1574), although painter and architect–the Uffizi and part of the Palazzo Vecchio are his work–is chiefly famous for his delightful series of biographies of the artists themselves. Benvenuto Cellini (1500-1571), that most piquant of personalities, and the Fleming Giambologna or Giovanni da Bologna (1524-1608), the master of the flying Mercury, are the last noteworthy sculptors of the Florentine school. When Michelangelo–*Michel, più che mortale, Angel divino*, as Ariosto calls him–passed away on February 18th, 1564, the Renaissance was over as far as Art was concerned. And not in Art only. The dome of St Peter's, that was slowly rising before Michelangelo's dying eyes, was a visible sign of the new spirit that was moving within the Church itself, the spirit that reformed the Church and purified the Papacy, and which brought about the renovation of which Savonarola had prophesied.

CHAPTER V.

THE PALAZZO VECCHIO–THE PIAZZA DELLA SIGNORIA–THE UFFIZI

"Ecco il Palagio de' Signori si bello
che chi cercasse tutto l'universo,
non credo ch'é trovasse par di quello."
–*Antonio Pucci.*

THE PALAZZO VECCHIO

The Story of Florence

AT the eastern corner of the Piazza della Signoria—that great square over which almost all the history of Florence may be said to have passed—rises the Palazzo Vecchio, with its great projecting parapets and its soaring tower: the old Palace of the Signoria, originally the Palace of the Priors, and therefore of the People. It is often stated that the square battlements of the Palace itself represent the Guelfs, while the forked battlements of the tower are in some mysterious way connected with the Ghibellines, who can hardly be said to have still existed as a real party in the city when they were built; there is, it appears, absolutely no historical foundation for this legend. The Palace was commenced by Arnolfo di Cambio in 1298, when, in consequence of the hostility between the magnates and the people, it was thought that the Priors were not sufficiently secure in the Palace of the Cerchi; and it may be taken to represent the whole course of Florentine history, from this government of the Secondo Popolo, through Savonarola's Republic and the Medicean despotism, down to the unification of Italy. Its design and essentials, however, are Arnolfo's and the people's, though many later architects, besides Vasari, have had their share in the completion of the present building. Arnolfo founded the great tower of the Priors upon an older tower of a family of magnates, the Foraboschi, and it was also known as the Torre della Vacca. When, in those fierce democratic days, its great bell rang to summon a Parliament in the Piazza, or to call the companies of the city to arms, it was popularly said that "the cow" was lowing. The upper part of the tower belongs to the fifteenth century. Stupendous though the Palazzo is, it would have been of vaster proportions but for the prohibition given to Arnolfo to raise the house of the Republic where the dwellings of the Uberti had once stood–*ribelli di Firenze e Ghibellini*. Not even the heroism of Farinata could make this stern people less "fierce against my kindred in all its laws," as that great Ghibelline puts it to Dante in the *Inferno*.

The present steps and platform in front of the Palace are only the remnants of the famous Ringhiera constructed here in the fourteenth century, and removed in 1812. On it the Signoria used to meet to address the crowd in the Piazza, or to enter upon their term of office. Here, at one time, the Gonfaloniere received the Standard of the People, and here, at a somewhat later date, the batons of command were given to the condottieri who led the mercenaries in the pay of the Republic. Here the famous meeting took place at which the Duke of Athens was acclaimed *Signore a vita* by the mob; and here, a few months later, his Burgundian followers thrust out the most unpopular of his agents to be torn to pieces by the besiegers. Here the Papal Commissioners and the Eight sat on the day of Savonarola's martyrdom, as told in the last chapter.

The inscription over the door, with the monogram of Christ, was placed here by the Gonfaloniere Niccolò Capponi in February 1528, in the last temporary restoration of the Republic; it originally announced that Jesus Christ had been chosen King of the Florentine People, but was modified by Cosimo I. The huge marble group of Hercules and Cacus on the right, by Baccio Bandinelli, is an atrocity; in Benvenuto Cellini's autobiography there is a rare story of how he and Baccio wrangled about it in the Duke's presence, on which occasion Bandinelli was stung into making a foul–but probably true–accusation against Cellini, which might have had serious consequences. The Marzocco on the left, the emblematical lion of Florence, is a copy from Donatello.

The court is the work of Michelozzo, commenced in 1434, on the return of the elder Cosimo from exile. The stucco ornamentations and grotesques were executed in 1565, on the occasion of the marriage of Francesco dei Medici, son of Cosimo I., with Giovanna of Austria; the faded frescoes are partly intended to symbolise the ducal exploits, partly views of Austrian cities in compliment to the bride. The bronze boy with a dolphin, on the fountain in the centre of the court, was made by Andrea Verrocchio for Lorenzo the Magnificent; it is an exquisite little work, full of life and motion–"the little boy who for ever half runs and half flits across the courtyard of the Palace, while the dolphin ceaselessly struggles in the arms, whose pressure sends the water spurting from the nostrils."[27]

On the first floor is the *Sala del Consiglio Grande,* frequently called the *Salone dei Cinquecento*. It was mainly constructed in 1495 by Simone del Pollaiuolo, called Cronaca from his capacity of telling endless stories about Fra Girolamo. Here the Greater Council met, which the Friar declared was the work of God and not of man. And here it was that, in a famous sermon preached before the Signoria and chief citizens on August 20th, 1496, he cried: "I want no hats, no mitres great or small; nought would I have save what Thou hast given to Thy saints—death; a red hat, a hat of blood—this do I desire." It was supposed that the Pope had offered to make him a cardinal. In this same hall on the evening of May 22nd, 1498, the evening before their death, Savonarola was allowed an hour's interview with his two companions; it was the first time that they had met since their arrest, and in the meanwhile Savonarola had been told that the others had recanted, and Domenico and Silvestro had been shown what purported to be their master's confession, seeming, in part at least, to abjure the cause for which Fra Domenico was yearning to shed his blood. A few years later, in 1503, the Gonfaloniere Piero Soderini intrusted the decoration of these walls to Leonardo da Vinci and Michelangelo; and it was then that this hall, so consecrated to liberty, became *la scuola del mondo*, the school of all the world in art; and Raphael himself was among the most ardent of its scholars. Leonardo drew his famous scene of the Battle of the Standard, and appears to have actually commenced painting on the wall. Michelangelo sketched the cartoon of a group of soldiers bathing in the Arno, suddenly surprised by the sound of the trumpet calling them to arms; but he did not proceed any further. These cartoons played the same part in the art of the Cinquecento as Masaccio's Carmine frescoes in that of the preceding century; it is the universal testimony of contemporaries that they were the supremely perfect works of the Renaissance. Vasari gives a full description of each—but no traces of the original works now remain. One episode from Leonardo's cartoon is preserved in an engraving by Edelinck after a copy, which is hardly likely to have been a faithful one, by Rubens; and there is an earlier engraving as well. A few figures are to be seen in a drawing at Venice, doubtfully ascribed to Raphael. Drawings and engravings of Michelangelo's soldiers have made a portion of his composition familiar—enough at least to make the world realise something of the extent of its loss.

On the restoration of the Medici in 1512, the hall was used as a barracks for their foreign soldiers; and Vasari accuses Baccio Bandinelli of having seized the opportunity to destroy Michelangelo's cartoon—which hardly seems probable. The frescoes which now cover the walls are by Vasari and his school, the statues of the Medici partly by Bandinelli, whilst that of Fra Girolamo is modern. It was in this hall that the first Parliament of United Italy met, during the short period when Florence was the capital. The adjoining rooms, called after various illustrious members of the Medicean family, are adorned with pompous uninspiring frescoes of their exploits by Vasari; in the Salotto di Papa Clemente there is a representation of the siege of Florence by the papal and imperial armies, which gives a fine idea of the magnitude of the third walls of the city, Arnolfo's walls, though even then the towers had been in part shortened.

On the second floor, the hall prettily known as the Sala dei Gigli contains some frescoes by Domenico Ghirlandaio, executed about 1482. They represent St Zenobius in his majesty, enthroned between Eugenius and Crescentius, with Roman heroes as it were in attendance upon this great patron of the Florentines. In a lunette, painted in imitation of bas-relief, there is a peculiarly beautiful Madonna and Child with Angels, also by Domenico Ghirlandaio. This room is sometimes called the Sala del Orologio, from a wonderful old clock that once stood here. The following room, into which a door with marble framework by Benedetto da Maiano leads, is the audience chamber of the Signoria; it was originally to have been decorated by Ghirlandaio, Botticelli, Perugino, and Filippino Lippi–but the present frescoes are by Salviati in the middle of the sixteenth century. Here, on the fateful day of the *Cimento* or Ordeal, the two Franciscans, Francesco da Puglia and Giuliano Rondinelli, consulted with the Priors and then passed into the Chapel to await the event. Beyond is the Priors' Chapel, dedicated to St Bernard and decorated with frescoes in imitation of mosaic by Ridolfo Ghirlandaio (Domenico's son). Here on the morning of his martyrdom Savonarola said Mass, and, before actually communicating, took the Host in his hands and uttered his famous prayer:—

"Lord, I know that Thou art that very God, the Creator of the world and of human nature. I know that Thou art that perfect, indivisible and inseparable Trinity, distinct in three Persons, Father, Son, and Holy Ghost. I know that Thou art that Eternal Word, who didst descend from Heaven to earth in the womb of the Virgin Mary. Thou didst ascend the wood of the Cross to shed Thy precious Blood for us, miserable sinners. I pray Thee, my Lord; I pray Thee, my Salvation; I pray Thee, my Consoler; that such precious Blood be not shed for me in vain, but may be for the remission of all my sins. For these I crave Thy pardon, from the day that I received the water of Holy Baptism even to this moment; and I confess to Thee, Lord, my guilt. And so I crave pardon of Thee for what offence I have done to this city and all this people, in things spiritual and temporal, as well as for all those things wherein of myself I am not conscious of having erred. And humbly do I crave pardon of all those persons who are here standing round. May they pray to God for me, and may He make me strong up to the last end, so that the enemy may have no power over me. Amen."

Beyond the Priors' chapel are the apartments of Duke Cosimo's Spanish wife, Eleonora of Toledo, with a little chapel decorated by Bronzino. It was in these rooms that the Duchess stormed at poor Benvenuto Cellini, when he passed through to speak with the Duke—as he tells us in his autobiography. Benvenuto had an awkward knack of suddenly appearing here whenever the Duke and Duchess were particularly busy; but their children were hugely delighted at seeing him, and little Don Garzia especially used to pull him by the cloak and "have the most pleasant sport with me that such a *bambino* could have."

A room in the tower, discovered in 1814, is supposed to be the Alberghettino, in which the elder Cosimo was imprisoned in 1433, and in which Savonarola passed his last days—save when he was brought down to the Bargello to be tortured. Here the Friar wrote his meditations upon the *In te, Domine, speravi* and the *Miserere*—meditations which became famous throughout Christendom. The prayer, quoted above, is usually printed as a pendant to the *Miserere*.

On the left of the palace, the great fountain with Neptune and his riotous gods and goddesses of the sea, by Bartolommeo Ammanati and his contemporaries, is a characteristic production of the later Cinquecento. No less characteristic, though in another way, is the equestrian statue in bronze of Cosimo I., as first Grand Duke of Tuscany, by Giovanni da Bologna; the tyrant sits on his steed, gloomily guarding the Palace and Piazza where he has finally extinguished the last sparks of republican liberty. It was finished in 1594, in the days of his son Ferdinand I., the third Grand Duke.

At the beginning of the Via Gondi, adjoining the custom-house and now incorporated in the Palazzo Vecchio, was the palace of the Captain, the residence of the Bargello and Executor of Justice. It was here that the Pazzi conspirators were hung out of the windows in 1478; here that Bernardo del Nero and his associates were beheaded in 1497; and here, in the following year, the examination of Savonarola and his adherents was carried on. Near here, too, stood in old times the Serraglio, or den of the lions, which was also incorporated by Vasari into the Palace; the Via del Leone, in which Vasari's rather fine rustica façade stands, is named from them still.

The Piazza saw the Pisan captives forced ignominiously to kiss the Marzocco in 1364, and to build the so-called Tetto dei Pisani, which formerly stood on the west, opposite the Palace. In this Piazza, too, the people assembled in parliament at the sounding of the great bell. In the fifteenth century, this simply meant that whatever party in the State desired to alter the government, in their own favour, occupied the openings of the Piazza with troops; and the noisy rabble that appeared on these occasions, to roar out their assent to whatever was proposed, had but little connection with the real People of Florence. Among the wildest scenes that this Piazza has witnessed were those during the rising of the Ciompi in 1378, when again and again the populace surged round the Palace with their banners and wild cries, until the terrified Signoria granted their demands. Here, too, took place Savonarola's famous burnings of the Vanities in Carnival time; large piles of these "lustful things" were surmounted by allegorical figures of King Carnival, or of Lucifer and the seven deadly sins, and then solemnly fired; while the people sang the *Te Deum*, the bells rang, and the trumpets and drums of the Signoria pealed out their loudest. But sport of less serious kind went on here too–tournaments and shows of wild beasts and the like–things that the Florentines dearly loved, and in which their rulers found it politic to fool them to the top of their bent. For instance, on June 25th, 1514, there was a *caccia* of a specially magnificent kind; a sort of glorified bull-fight, in which a fountain surrounded by green woods was constructed in the middle of the Piazza, and two lions, with bears and leopards, bulls, buffaloes, stags, horses, and the like were driven into the arena. Enormous prices were paid for seats; foreigners came from all countries, and four Roman cardinals were conspicuous, including Raphael's Bibbiena, disguised as Spanish gentlemen. Several people were killed by the beasts. It was always a sore point with the

Florentines that their lions were such unsatisfactory brutes and never distinguished themselves on these occasions; they were no match for your Spanish bull, at a time when, in politics, the bull's master had yoked all Italy to his triumphal car.

The *Loggia dei Priori*, now called the *Loggia dei Lanzi* after the German lancers of Duke Cosimo who were stationed here, was originally built for the Priors and other magistrates to exercise public functions, with all the display that mediæval republics knew so well how to use. It is a kind of great open vaulted hall; a throne for a popular government, as M. Reymond calls it. Although frequently known as the Loggia of Orcagna, it was commenced in 1376 by Benci di Cione and Simone Talenti, and is intermediate in style between Gothic and Renaissance (in contrast to the pure Gothic of the Bigallo). The sculptures above, frequently ascribed to Agnolo Gaddi and representing the Virtues, are now assigned to Giovanni d'Ambrogio and Jacopo di Piero, and were executed between 1380 and 1390. Among the numerous statues that now stand beneath its roof (and which include Giambologna's Rape of the Sabines) are two of the finest bronzes in Florence: Donatello's *Judith and Holofernes*, cast for Cosimo the elder, and originally in the Medicean Palace, but, on the expulsion of the younger Piero, set up on the Ringhiera with the threatening inscription: *exemplum Salutis Publicae*; and Benvenuto Cellini's *Perseus with the head of Medusa*, cast in 1553 for the Grand Duke Cosimo (then only Duke), and possibly intended as a kind of despotic counter-blast to the Judith. The pedestal (with the exception of the bas-relief in front, of which the original is in the Bargello) is also Cellini's. Cellini gives us a rare account of the exhibiting of this Perseus to the people, while the Duke himself lurked behind a window over the door of the palace to hear what was said. He assures us that the crowd gazed upon him—that is, the artist, not the statue—as something altogether miraculous for having accomplished such a work, and that two noblemen from Sicily accosted him as he walked in the Piazza, with such ceremony as would have been too much even towards the Pope. He took a holiday in honour of the event, sang psalms and hymns the whole way out of Florence, and was absolutely convinced that the *ne plus ultra* of art had been reached.

But it is of Savonarola, and not of Benvenuto Cellini, that the Loggia reminds us; for here was the scene of the *Cimento di Fuoco*, the ordeal of fire, on April 7th, 1498. An immense crowd of men filled the Piazza; women and children were excluded, but packed every inch of windows, roofs, balconies. The streets and entrances were strongly held by troops, while more were drawn up round the Palace under Giovacchino della Vecchia. The platform bearing the intended pyre—a most formidable death-trap, which was to be fired behind the champions as soon as they were well within it–ran out from the Ringhiera towards the centre of the Piazza. In spite of the strict proclamation to armed men not to enter, Doffo Spini appeared with three hundred Compagnacci, "all armed like Paladins," says Simone Filipepi,[28] "in favour of the friars of St Francis." They entered the Piazza with a tremendous uproar, and formed up under the Tetto dei Pisani, opposite the Palace. Simone says that there was a pre-arranged plot, in virtue of which they only waited for a sign from the Palace to cut the Dominicans and their adherents to pieces. The Loggia was divided into two parts, the half nearer the Palace assigned to the Franciscans, the other, in which a temporary altar had been erected, to the Dominicans. In front of the Loggia the sun flashed back from the armour of a picked band of soldiers, under Marcuccio Salviati, apparently intended as a counter demonstration to Doffo Spini and his young aristocrats. The Franciscans were first on the field, and quietly took their station. Their two champions entered the Palace, and were seen no more during the proceedings. Then with exultant strains of the *Exsurgat Deus*, the Dominicans slowly made their way down the Corso degli Adimari and through the Piazza in procession, two and two. Their fierce psalm was caught up and re-echoed by their adherents as they passed. Preceded by a Crucifix, about two hundred of these black and white "hounds of the Lord" entered the field of battle, followed by Fra Domenico in a rich cope, and then

Savonarola in full vestments with the Blessed Sacrament, attended by deacon and sub-deacon. A band of devout republican laymen, with candles and red crosses, brought up the rear. Savonarola entered the Loggia, set the Sacrament on the altar, and solemnly knelt in adoration.

Then, while Fra Girolamo stood firm as a column, delay after delay commenced. The Dominican's cope might be enchanted, or his robe too for the matter of that, so Domenico was hurried into the Palace and his garments changed. The two Franciscan stalwarts remained in the Priors' chapel. In the meanwhile a storm passed over the city. A rush of the Compagnacci and populace towards the Loggia was driven back by Salviati's guard. Domenico returned with changed garments, and stood among the Franciscans; stones hurtled about him; he would enter the fire with the Crucifix–this was objected to; then with the Sacrament–this was worse. Domenico was convinced that he would pass through the ordeal scathless, and that the Sacrament would not protect him if his cause were not just; but he was equally convinced that it was God's will that he should not enter the fire without it. Evening fell in the midst of the wrangling, and at last the Signoria ordered both parties to go home. Only the efforts of Salviati and his soldiery saved Savonarola and Domenico from being torn to pieces at the hands of the infuriated mob, who apparently concluded that they had been trifled with. "As the Father Fra Girolamo issued from the Loggia with the

Most Holy Sacrament in his hands," says Simone Filipepi, who was present, "and Fra Domenico with his Crucifix, the signal was given from the Palace to Doffo Spini to carry out his design; but he, as it pleased God, would do nothing." The Franciscans of Santa Croce were promised an annual subsidy of sixty pieces of silver for their share in the day's work: "Here, take the price of the innocent blood you have betrayed," was their greeting when they came to demand it.

In after years, Doffo Spini was fond of gossiping with Botticelli and his brother, Simone Filipepi, and made no secret of his intention of killing Savonarola on this occasion. Yet, of all the Friar's persecutors, he was the only one that showed any signs of penitence for what he had done. "On the ninth day of April, 1503," writes Simone in his Chronicle, "as I, Simone di Mariano Filipepi, was leaving my house to go to vespers in San Marco, Doffo Spini, who was in the company of Bartolommeo di Lorenzo Carducci, saluted me. Bartolommeo turned to me, and said that Fra Girolamo and the Piagnoni had spoilt and undone the city; whereupon many words passed between him and me, which I will not set down here. But Doffo interposed, and said that he had never had any dealings with Fra Girolamo, until the time when, as a member of the Eight, he had to examine him in prison; and that, if he had heard Fra Girolamo earlier and had been intimate with him, 'even as Simone here'–turning to me–'I would have been a more ardent partisan of his than even Simone, for nothing save good was ever seen in him even unto his death.'"

THE UFFIZI

Beyond the Palazzo Vecchio, between the Piazza and the Arno, stands the Palazzo degli Uffizi, which Giorgio Vasari reared in the third quarter of the sixteenth century, for Cosimo I. It contains the Archives, the Biblioteca Nazionale (which includes the Palatine and Magliabecchian Libraries, and, like all similar institutions in Italy, is generously thrown open to all comers without reserve), and, above all, the great picture gallery commenced by the Grand Dukes, usually simply known as the Uffizi and now officially the Galleria Reale degli Uffizi, which, together with its continuation in the Pitti Palace across the river, is undoubtedly the finest collection of pictures in the world.

LOOKING THROUGH VASARI'S LOGGIA, UFFIZI

Leaving the double lines of illustrious Florentines, men great in the arts of war and peace, in their marble niches watching over the pigeons who throng the Portico, we ascend to the picture gallery by the second door to the left.[29]

RITRATTI DEI PITTORI–PRIMO CORRIDORE.

On the way up, four rooms on the right contain the Portraits of the Painters, many of them painted by themselves. In the further room, Filippino Lippi by himself, fragment of a fresco (286). Raphael (288) at the age of twenty-three, with his spiritual, almost feminine beauty, painted by himself at Urbino during his Florentine period, about 1506. This is Raphael before the worldly influence of Rome had fallen upon him, the youth who came from Urbino and Perugia to the City of the Lilies with the letter of recommendation from Urbino's Duchess to Piero Soderini, to sit at the feet of Leonardo and Michelangelo, and wander with Fra Bartolommeo through the cloisters of San Marco. Titian (384), "in which he appears, painted by himself, on the confines of old age, vigorous and ardent still, fully conscious, moreover, though without affectation, of pre-eminent genius and supreme artistic rank" (Mr C. Phillips). Tintoretto, by himself (378); Andrea del Sarto, by himself (1176); a genuine portrait of Michelangelo (290), but of course not by himself; Rubens, by himself (228). An imaginary portrait of Leonardo da Vinci (292), of a much later period, may possibly preserve some tradition of the "magician's" appearance; the Dosso Dossi is doubtful; those of Giorgione and Bellini are certainly apocryphal. In the second room are two portraits of Rembrandt by himself. In the third room Angelica Kauffmann and Vigée Le Brun are charming in their way. In the fourth room, English visitors cannot fail to welcome several of their own painters of the nineteenth century, including Mr Watts.

Passing the Medicean busts at the head of the stairs, the famous Wild Boar and the two Molossian Hounds, we enter the first or eastern corridor, containing paintings of the earlier masters, mingled with ancient busts and sarcophagi. The best specimens of the Giotteschi are an Agony in the Garden (8), wrongly ascribed to Giotto himself; an Entombment (27), ascribed to a Giotto di Stefano, called Giottino, a painter of whom hardly anything but the nickname is known; an Annunciation (28), ascribed to Agnolo Gaddi; and an altar-piece by Giovanni da Milano (32). There are some excellent early Sienese paintings; a Madonna and Child with Angels, by Pietro Lorenzetti, 1340 (15); the Annunciation, by Simone Martini and Lippo Memmi (23); and a very curious picture of the Hermits of the Thebaid (16), a kind of devout fairy-land painted possibly by one of the Lorenzetti, in the spirit of those delightfully naïve *Vite del Santi Padri*. Lorenzo Monaco, or Don Lorenzo, a master who occupies an intermediate position between the Giotteschi and the Quattrocento, is represented by the Mystery of the Passion (40), a symbolical picture painted in 1404, of a type that Angelico brought to perfection in a fresco in San Marco; the Adoration of the Magi (39, the scenes in the frame by a later hand), and Madonna and Saints (41). The portrait of Giovanni dei Medici (43) is by an unknown hand of the Quattrocento. Paolo Uccello's Battle (52) is mainly a study in perspective. The Annunciation (53), by Neri di Bicci di Lorenzo, is a fair example of one of the least progressive painters of the Quattrocento. The pictures by Alessio Baldovinetti (56 and 60) and Cosimo Rosselli (63 and 65) are tolerable examples of very uninteresting fifteenth century masters. The allegorical figures of the Virtues (69-73), ascribed to Piero Pollaiuolo, are second-rate; and the same may be said of an Annunciation (such is the real subject of 81) and the Perseus and Andromeda pictures (85, 86, 87) by Piero di Cosimo. But the real gem of this corridor is the Madonna and Child (74), which Luca Signorelli painted for Lorenzo dei Medici, a picture which profoundly influenced Michelangelo; the splendidly modelled nude figures of men in the background transport us into the golden age.

TRIBUNA.

The famous Tribuna is supposed to contain the masterpieces of the whole collection, though the lover of the Quattrocento will naturally seek his best-loved favourites elsewhere. Of the five ancient sculptures in the centre of the hall the best is that of the crouching barbarian slave, who is preparing his knife to flay Marsyas. It is a fine work of the Pergamene school. The celebrated Venus dei Medici is a typical Græco-Roman work, the inscription at its base being a comparatively modern forgery. It was formerly absurdly overpraised, and is in consequence perhaps too much depreciated at the present day. The remaining three–the Satyr, the Wrestlers, and the young Apollo–have each been largely and freely restored.

Turning to the pictures, we have first the Madonna del Cardellino (1129), painted by Raphael during his Florentine period when under the influence of Fra Bartolommeo, in 1506 or thereabouts, and afterwards much damaged and restored: still one of the most beautiful of his early Madonnas. The St. John the Baptist (1127), ascribed to Raphael, is only a school piece, though from a design of the master's. The Madonna del Pozzo (1125), in spite of its hard and over-smooth colouring, was at one time attributed to Raphael; its ascription to Francia Bigio is somewhat conjectural. The portrait of a Lady wearing a wreath (1123), and popularly called the Fornarina, originally ascribed to Giorgione and later to Raphael, is believed to be by Sebastiano del Piombo. Then come a lady's portrait, ascribed to Raphael (1120); another by a Veronese master, erroneously ascribed to Mantegna, and erroneously said to represent the Duchess Elizabeth of Urbino (1121); Bernardino Luini's Daughter of Herodias (1135), a fine study of a female Italian criminal of the Renaissance; Perugino's portrait of Francesco delle

Opere, holding a scroll inscribed *Timete Deum*, an admirable picture painted in oils about the year 1494, and formerly supposed to be a portrait of Perugino by himself (287); portrait of Evangelista Scappa, ascribed to Francia (1124); and a portrait of a man, by Sebastiano del Piombo (3458). Raphael's Pope Julius II. (1131) is a grand and terrible portrait of the tremendous warrior Pontiff, whom the Romans called a second Mars. Vasari says that in this picture he looks so exactly like himself that "one trembles before him as if he were still alive." Albert Dürer's Adoration of the Magi (1141) and Lucas van Leyden's Mystery of the Passion (1143) are powerful examples of the religious painting of the North, that loved beauty less for its own sake than did the Italians. The latter should be compared with similar pictures by Don Lorenzo and Fra Angelico. Titian's portrait of the Papal Nuncio Beccadelli (1116), painted in 1552, although a decidedly fine work, has been rather overpraised.

Michelangelo's Holy Family (1139) is the only existing easel picture that the master completed. It was painted for the rich merchant, Angelo Doni (who haggled in a miserly fashion over the price and was in consequence forced to pay double the sum agreed upon), about 1504, in the days of the Gonfaloniere Soderini, when Michelangelo was engaged upon the famous cartoon for the Sala del Maggior Consiglio. Like Luca Signorelli, Michelangelo has introduced naked figures, apparently shepherds, into his background. "In the Doni

Madonna of the Uffizi," writes Walter Pater, "Michelangelo actually brings the pagan religion, and with it the unveiled human form, the sleepy-looking fauns of a Dionysiac revel, into the presence of the Madonna, as simpler painters had introduced other products of the earth, birds or flowers; and he has given to that Madonna herself much of the uncouth energy of the older and more primitive 'Mighty Mother.'" The painters introduced into their pictures what they loved best, in earth or sky, as votive offerings to the Queen of Heaven; and what Signorelli and Michelangelo best loved was the human form. This is reflected in the latter's own lines:–

> Nè Dio, sua grazia, mi si mostra altrove,
> più che'n alcun leggiadro e mortal velo,
> e quel sol amo, perchè'n quel si specchia.

"Nor does God vouchsafe to reveal Himself to me anywhere more than in some lovely mortal veil, and that alone I love, because He is mirrored therein."

In the strongest possible contrast to Michelangelo's picture are the two examples of the softest master of the Renaissance–Correggio's Repose on the Flight to Egypt (1118), and his Madonna adoring the Divine Child (1134). The former, with its rather out of place St. Francis of Assisi, is a work of what is known as Correggio's transition period,

1515-1518, after he had painted his earlier easel pictures and before commencing his great fresco work at Parma; the latter, a more characteristic picture, is slightly later and was given by the Duke of Mantua to Cosimo II. The figures of Prophets by Fra Bartolommeo (1130 and 1126), the side-wings of a picture now in the Pitti Gallery, are not remarkable in any way. The Madonna and Child with the Baptist and St. Sebastian (1122) is a work of Perugino's better period.

There remain the two famous Venuses of Titian. The so-called Urbino Venus (1117)–a motive to some extent borrowed, and slightly coarsened in the borrowing, from Giorgione's picture at Dresden–is much the finer of the two. It was painted for Francesco Maria della Rovere, Duke of Urbino, and, although not a portrait of Eleonora Gonzaga, who was then a middle-aged woman, it was certainly intended to conjure up the beauty of her youth. What Eleonora really looked like at this time, you can see in the first of the two Venetian rooms, where Titian's portrait of her, painted at about the same date, hangs. The Venus and Cupid (1108) is a later work; the goddess is the likeness of a model who very frequently appears in the works of Titian and Palma.

SCUOLA TOSCANA.

On the left we pass out of the Tribuna to three rooms devoted to the Tuscan school.

The first contains the smaller pictures, including several priceless Angelicos and Botticellis. Fra Angelico's Naming of St. John (1162), Marriage of the Blessed Virgin to St. Joseph (1178), and her Death (1184), are excellent examples of his delicate execution and spiritual expression in his smaller, miniature-like works. Antonio Pollaiuolo's Labours of Hercules (1153) is one of the masterpieces of this most uncompromising realist of the Quattrocento. Either by Antonio or his brother Piero, is also the portrait of that monster of iniquity, Galeazzo Maria Sforza, Duke of Milan (30). Sandro Botticelli's Calumny (1182) is supposed to have been painted as a thankoffering to a friend who had defended him from the assaults of slanderous tongues; it is a splendid example of his dramatic intensity, the very statues in their niches taking part in the action. The subject–taken from Lucian's description of a picture by Apelles of Ephesus–was frequently painted by artists of the Renaissance, and there is a most magnificent drawing of the same by Andrea Mantegna at the British Museum, which was copied by Rembrandt. On the judgment-seat sits a man with ears like those of Midas, into which Ignorance and Suspicion on either side ever whisper. Before him stands Envy,–a hideous, pale, and haggard man, seeming wasted by some slow disease. He is making the accusation and leading Calumny, a scornful Botticellian beauty, who holds in one hand a torch and with the other drags her victim by the hair to the judge's feet. Calumny is tended and adorned by two female figures, Artifice and Deceit. But Repentance slowly follows, in black mourning habit; while naked Truth–the Botticellian Venus in another form–raises her hand in appeal to the heavens.

The rather striking portrait of a painter (1163) is usually supposed to be Andrea Verrocchio, by Lorenzo di Credi, his pupil and successor; Mr Berenson, however, considers that it is Perugino and by Domenico Ghirlandaio. On the opposite wall are two very early Botticellis, Judith returning from the camp of the Assyrians (1156) and the finding of the body of Holofernes (1158), in a scale of colouring differing from that of his later works. The former is one of those pictures which have been illumined for us by Ruskin, who regards it as the only picture that is true to Judith; "The triumph of Miriam over a fallen host, the fire of exulting mortal life in an immortal hour, the purity and severity of a guardian angel–all are here; and as her servant follows, carrying indeed the head, but invisible–(a mere thing to be carried–no more to be so much as thought of)–she looks only at her mistress, with intense, servile, watchful love. Faithful, not in these days of fear only, but hitherto in all her life, and afterwards for ever." Walter Pater has read the picture in a different sense, and sees in it Judith "returning home across the hill country, when the great deed is over, and the moment of revulsion come, and the olive branch in her hand is becoming a burden."

The portrait of Andrea del Sarto by himself (280) represents him in the latter days of his life, and was painted on a tile in 1529, about a year before his death, with some colours that remained over after he had finished the portrait of one of the Vallombrosan monks; his wife kept it by her until her death. The very powerful likeness of an old man in white cap and gown (1167), a fresco ascribed to Masaccio, is more probably the work of Filippino Lippi. The famous Head of Medusa (1159) must be seen with grateful reverence by all lovers of English poetry, for it was admired by Shelley and inspired him with certain familiar and exceedingly beautiful stanzas; but as for its being a work of Leonardo da Vinci, it is now almost universally admitted to be a comparatively late forgery, to supply the place of the lost Medusa of which Vasari speaks. The portrait (1157), also ascribed to Leonardo, is better, but probably no more authentic. Here is a most dainty little example of Fra Bartolommeo's work on a small scale (1161), representing the Circumcision and the Nativity, with the Annunciation in grisaille on the back. Botticelli's St. Augustine (1179) is an early work, and, like the Judith, shows his artistic derivation from Fra Lippo Lippi, to whom indeed it was formerly ascribed. His portrait of Piero di Lorenzo dei Medici (1154), a splendid young man in red cap and flowing dark hair, has been already referred to in chapter iii.; it was formerly supposed to be a likeness of Pico della Mirandola. It was painted before Piero's expulsion from Florence, probably during the life-time of the Magnificent, and represents him before he degenerated into the low tyrannical blackguard of later years; he apparently wishes to appeal to the memory of his great-grandfather Cosimo, whose medallion he holds, to find favour with his unwilling subjects. The portraits of Duke Cosimo's son and grandchild, Don Garzia and Donna Maria (1155 and 1164), by Bronzino, should be noted. Finally we have the famous picture of Perseus freeing Andromeda, by Piero di Cosimo (1312). It is about the best specimen of his fantastic conceptions to be seen in Florence, and the monster itself is certainly a triumph of a somewhat unhealthy imagination nourished in solitude on an odd diet.

In the second room are larger works of the great Tuscans. The Adoration of the Magi (1252) is one of the very few authentic works of Leonardo; it was one of his earliest productions, commenced in 1478, and, like so many other things of his, never finished. The St. Sebastian (1279) is one of the masterpieces of that wayward Lombard or rather Piedmontese–although we now associate him with Siena–who approached nearest of all to the art of Leonardo, Giovanni Antonio Bazzi, known still as Sodoma. Ridolfo Ghirlandaio's Miracles of Zenobius (1277 and 1275) are excellent works by a usually second-rate master. The Visitation with its predella, by Mariotto Albertinelli (1259), painted in 1503, is incomparably the greatest picture that Fra

Bartolommeo's wild friend and fellow student ever produced, and one in which he most nearly approaches the best works of Bartolommeo himself. "The figures, however," Morelli points out, "are less refined and noble than those of the Frate, and the foliage of the trees is executed with miniature-like precision, which is never the case in the landscapes of the latter." Andrea del Sarto's genial and kindly St. James with the orphans (1254), is one of his last works; it was painted to serve as a standard in processions, and has consequently suffered considerably. Bronzino's Descent of Christ into Hades (1271), that "heap of cumbrous nothingnesses and sickening offensivenesses," as Ruskin pleasantly called it, need only be seen to be loathed. The so-called Madonna delle Arpie, or our Lady of the Harpies, from the figures on the pedestal beneath her feet (1112), is perhaps the finest of all Andrea del Sarto's pictures; the Madonna is a highly idealised likeness of his own wife Lucrezia, and some have tried to recognise the features of the painter himself in the St. John:–

> "You loved me quite enough, it seems to-night.
> This must suffice me here. What would one have?
> In heaven, perhaps, new chances, one more chance–
> Four great walls in the New Jerusalem
> Meted on each side by the Angel's reed,
> For Leonard, Rafael, Agnolo and me

To cover–the three first without a wife,
While I have mine! So–still they overcome
Because there's still Lucrezia,–as I choose."

The full-length portrait of Cosimo the Elder (1267), the Pater Patriae (so the flattery of the age hailed the man who said that a city destroyed was better than a city lost), was painted by Pontormo from some fifteenth century source, as a companion piece to his portrait here of Duke Cosimo I. (1270). The admirable portrait of Lorenzo the Magnificent by Vasari (1269) is similarly constructed from contemporary materials, and is probably the most valuable thing that Vasari has left to us in the way of painting. The unfinished picture by Fra Bartolommeo (1265), representing our Lady enthroned with St. Anne, the guardian of the Republic, watching over her and interceding for Florence, while the patrons of the city gather round for her defence, was intended for the altar in the Sala del Maggior Consiglio of the Palazzo Vecchio; it is conceived in something of the same spirit that made the last inheritors of Savonarola's tradition and teaching fondly believe that Angels would man the walls of Florence, rather than that she should again fall into the hands of her former tyrants, the Medici. The great Madonna and Child with four Saints and two Angels scattering flowers, by Filippino Lippi (1268), was painted in 1485 for the room in the Palazzo Vecchio in which the Otto di Pratica held their meetings.

The Adoration of the Magi (1257), also by Filippino Lippi, painted in 1496, apart from its great value as a work of art, has a curious historical significance; the Magi and their principal attendants, who are thus pushing forwards to display their devotion to Our Lady of Florence and the Child whom the Florentines were to elect their King, are the members of the younger branch of the Medici, who have returned to the city now that Piero has been expelled, and are waiting their chance. See how they have already replaced the family of the elder Cosimo, who occupy this same position in a similar picture painted some eighteen years before by Sandro Botticelli, Filippino's master. At this epoch they had ostentatiously altered their name of Medici and called themselves Popolani, but were certainly intriguing against Fra Girolamo. The old astronomer kneeling to our extreme left is the elder Piero Francesco, watching the adventurous game for a throne that his children are preparing; the most prominent figure in the picture, from whose head a page is lifting the crown, is Pier Francesco's son, Giovanni, who will soon woo Caterina Sforza, the lady of Forlì, and make her the mother of Giovanni delle Bande Nere; and the precious vessel which he is to offer to the divine Child is handed to him by the younger Pier Francesco, the father of Lorenzaccio, that "Tuscan Brutus" whose dagger was to make Giovanni's grandson, Cosimo, the sole lord of Florence and her empire. [30]

Granacci's Madonna of the Girdle (1280), over the door, formerly in San Piero Maggiore, is a good example of a painter who imitated most of his contemporaries and had little individuality. On easels in the middle of the room are (3452) Venus, by Lorenzo di Credi, a conscientious attempt to follow the fashion of the age and handle a subject quite alien to his natural sympathies–for Lorenzo di Credi was one of those who sacrificed their studies of the nude on Savonarola's pyre of the Vanities; and (3436) an Adoration of the Magi, a cartoon of Sandro Botticelli's, coloured by a later hand, marvellously full of life in movement, intense and passionate, in which–as though the painter anticipated the Reformation–the followers of the Magi are fighting furiously with each other in their desire to find the right way to the Stable of Bethlehem!

The third room of the Tuscan School contains some of the truest masterpieces of the whole collection. The Epiphany, by Domenico Ghirlandaio (1295), painted in 1487, is one of that prosaic master's best easel pictures. The wonderful Annunciation (1288), in which the Archangel has alighted upon the flowers in the silence of an Italian twilight, with a mystical landscape of mountains and rivers, and far-off cities in the background, may possibly be an early work of Leonardo da Vinci, to whom it is officially assigned, but is ascribed by contemporary critics to Leonardo's master, Andrea Verrocchio. The least satisfactory passage is the rather wooden face and inappropriate action of the Madonna; Leonardo would surely not have made her, on receiving the angelic salutation, put her finger into her book to keep the place. After Three Saints by one of the Pollaiuoli (1301) and two smaller pictures by Lorenzo di Credi (1311 and 1313), we come to Piero della Francesca's grand portraits of Federigo of Montefeltro, Duke of Urbino, and his wife, Battista Sforza (1300); on the reverse, the Duke and Duchess are seen in triumphal cars surrounded with allegorical pageantry. Federigo is always, as here, represented in profile, because he lost his right eye and had the bridge of his nose broken in a tournament. The three predella scenes (1298) are characteristic examples of the minor works of Piero's great pupil, Luca Signorelli of Cortona.

On the opposite wall are four Botticellian pictures. The Magnificat (1267 *bis*)–Sandro's most famous and familiar tondo–in which the Madonna rather sadly writes the Magnificat, while Angels cluster round to crown their Queen, to offer ink and book, or look into the thing that she has written, while the Dove hovers above her, is full of the haunting charm, the elusive mystery, the vague yearning, which makes the fascination of Botticelli to-day. She already seems to be anticipating the Passion of that Child–so unmistakably divine–who is guiding her hand. The Madonna of the Pomegranate (1289) is a somewhat similar, but less beautiful tondo; the Angel faces, who are said to be idealised portraits of the Medicean children, have partially lost their angelic look. The Fortitude (1299) is one of Sandro's earliest paintings, and its authenticity has been questioned; she seems to be dreading, almost shrinking from some great battle at hand, of which no man can foretell the end. The Annunciation (1316) is rather Botticellian in conception; but the colouring and execution generally do not suggest the master himself. Antonio Pollaiuolo's Prudence (1306) is a harsh companion to Sandro's Fortitude. The tondo (1291) of the Holy Family, by Luca Signorelli, is one of his best works in this kind; the colouring is less heavy than is usual with him, and the Child is more divine. Of the two carefully finished Annunciations by Lorenzo di Credi (1314, 1160), the latter is the earlier and finer. Fra Filippo's little Madonna of the Sea (1307), with her happy boy-like Angel attendants, is one of the monk's most attractive and characteristic works; perhaps the best of all his smaller pictures. And we have left to the last Fra Angelico's divinest dream of the Coronation of the Madonna in the Empyrean Heaven of Heavens (1290), amidst exultant throngs of Saints and Angels absorbed in the Beatific Vision of Paradise. It is the pictorial equivalent of Bernard's most ardent sermons on the Assumption of Mary and of the mystic musings of John of Damascus. Here are "the Angel choirs of Angelico, with the flames on their white foreheads waving brighter as they move, and the sparkles streaming from their purple wings like the glitter of many suns upon a sounding sea, listening in the pauses of alternate song, for the prolonging of the trumpet blast, and the answering of psaltery and cymbal, throughout the endless deep, and from all the star shores of heaven."[31]

SALA DI MAESTRI DIVERSI ITALIANI.

In the small room which opens out of the Tribune, on the opposite side to these three Tuscan rooms, are two perfect little gems of more northern Italian painting. Mantegna's Madonna of the Quarries (1025), apart from its nobility of conception and grand austerity of sentiment, is a positive marvel of minute drawing with the point of the *pennello*. Every detail in the landscape, with the winding road up to the city on the hill, the field labourers in the meadow, the shepherds and travellers, on the left, and the stone-cutterss among the caverns on the right, preparing stone for the sculptors and architects of Florence and Rome, is elaborately rendered with exquisite delicacy and finish. It was painted at Rome in 1488, while Mantegna was working on his frescoes (now destroyed) for Pope Innocent VIII. in a chapel of the Vatican. The other is a little Madonna and Child with two Angels playing musical instruments, by Correggio (1002), a most exquisite little picture in an almost perfect state of preservation, formerly ascribed to Titian, but entirely characteristic of Correggio's earliest period when he was influenced by Mantegna and the Ferrarese.

Beyond are the Dutch, Flemish, German, and French pictures which do not come into our present scope–though they include several excellent works as, notably, a little Madonna by Hans Memlinc and two Apostles by Albert Dürer. The cabinet of the gems contains some of the treasures left by the Medicean Grand Dukes, including work by Cellini and Giovanni da Bologna.

SCUOLA VENETA.

Crossing the short southern corridor, with some noteworthy ancient sculptury, we pass down the long western corridor. Out of this open first the two rooms devoted to the Venetian school. In the first, to seek the best only, are Titian's portraits of Francesco Maria della Rovere, third Duke of Urbino, and Eleonora Gonzaga, his duchess (605 and 599), painted in 1537. A triptych by Mantegna (1111)– the Adoration of the Kings, between the Circumcision and the Ascension–is one of the earlier works of the great Paduan master; the face of the Divine Child in the Circumcision is marvellously painted. The Madonna by the Lake by Giovanni Bellini (631), also called the Allegory of the Tree of Life, is an exceedingly beautiful picture, one of Bellini's later works. Titian's Flora (626), an early work of the master, charming in its way, has been damaged and rather overpraised. In the second room, are three works by Giorgione; the Judgment of Solomon and the Ordeal of Moses (630 and 621), with their fantastic costumes and poetically conceived landscapes, are very youthful works indeed; the portrait of a Knight of Malta (622) is more mature, and one of the noblest of Venetian portraits. Florence thus possesses more authentic works of this wonderful, almost mythical, Venetian than does Venice herself. Here, too, is usually–except when it is in request elsewhere for the copyist–Titian's Madonna and Child with the boy John Baptist, and the old Antony Abbot, leaning on his staff and watching the flower play (633)–the most beautiful of Titian's early Giorgionesque Madonnas.

VENUS
By Sandro Botticelli

SALA DI LORENZO MONACO.

The following passage leads to the Sala di Lorenzo Monaco, the room which bears the name of the austere monk of Camaldoli, and, hallowed by the presence of Fra Angelico's Madonna, seems at times almost to re-echo still with the music of the Angel choir; but to which the modern worshipper turns to adore the Venus of the Renaissance rising from the Sea. For here is Sandro Botticelli's famous Birth of Venus (39), the most typical picture of the Quattrocento, painted for Lorenzo dei Medici and in part inspired by certain lines of Angelo Poliziano. But let all description be left to the golden words of Walter Pater in his *Renaissance*:–

"At first, perhaps, you are attracted only by a quaintness of design, which seems to recall all at once whatever you have read of Florence in the fifteenth century; afterwards you may think that this quaintness must be incongruous with the subject, and that the colour is cadaverous or at least cold. And yet, the more you come to understand what imaginative colouring really is, that all colour is no mere delightful quality of natural things, but a spirit upon them by which they become expressive to the spirit, the better you will like this peculiar quality of colour; and you will find that quaint design of Botticelli's a more direct inlet into the Greek temper than the works of the Greeks themselves, even of the finest period. Of the Greeks as they really were, of their difference from ourselves, of the aspects of their outward life, we know far more than Botticelli, or his most learned contemporaries; but for us long familiarity has taken off the edge of the lesson, and we are hardly conscious of what we owe to the Hellenic spirit. But in pictures like this of Botticelli's you have a record of the first impression made by it on minds turned back towards it, in almost painful aspiration, from a world in which it had been ignored so long; and in the passion, the energy, the industry of realisation, with which Botticelli carries out his intention, is the exact measure of the legitimate influence over the human mind of the imaginative system of which this is the central myth. The light is indeed cold—mere sunless dawn; but a later painter would have cloyed you with sunshine; and you can see the better for that quietness in the morning air each long promontory, as it slopes down to the water's edge. Men go forth to their labours until the evening; but she is awake before them, and you might think that the sorrow in her face was at the thought of the whole long day of love yet to come. An emblematical figure of the wind blows hard across the grey water, moving forward the dainty-lipped shell on which she sails, the sea 'showing his teeth' as it moves in thin lines of foam, and sucking in, one by one, the falling roses, each severe in outline, plucked off short at the stalk, but embrowned a little, as Botticelli's flowers always are. Botticelli meant all that imagery to be altogether pleasurable;

and it was partly an incompleteness of resources, inseparable from the art of that time, that subdued and chilled it; but his predilection for minor tones counts also; and what is unmistakable is the sadness with which he has conceived the goddess of pleasure, as the depositary of a great power over the lives of men."

In this same room are five other masterpieces of early Tuscan painting. Don Lorenzo's Coronation of the Madonna (1309), though signed and dated 1413, may be regarded as the last great altar-piece of the school of Giotto and his followers. It has been terribly repainted. The presence in the most prominent position of St. Benedict and St. Romuald in their white robes shows that it was painted for a convent of Camaldolese monks. The predella, representing the Adoration of the Magi and scenes from the life of St. Benedict, includes a very sweet little picture of the last interview of the saint with his sister Scholastica, when, in answer to her prayers, God sent such a storm that her brother, although unwilling to break his monastic rule, was forced to spend the night with her. "I asked you a favour," she told him, "and you refused it me; I asked it of Almighty God, and He has granted it to me." In Browning's poem, Don Lorenzo is one of the models specially recommended to Lippo Lippi by his superiors:–

"You're not of the true painters, great and old;
Brother Angelico's the man, you'll find;

Brother Lorenzo stands his single peer;
Fag on at flesh, you'll never make the third."

The Madonna and Child with St. Francis and St. John Baptist, St. Zenobius and St. Lucy (1305), is one of the very few authentic works by Domenico Veneziano, one of the great innovators in the painting of the fifteenth century.

Sandro Botticelli's Adoration of the Magi (1286), painted for Santa Maria Novella, is enthusiastically praised by Vasari. It is not a very characteristic work of the painter's, but contains admirable portraits of the Medici and their court. The first king, kneeling up alone before the Divine Child, is Cosimo the Elder himself, according to Vasari, "the most faithful and animated likeness of all now known to exist of him"; the other two kings are his two sons, Piero il Gottoso in the centre, Giovanni di Cosimo on the right. The black-haired youth with folded hands, standing behind Giovanni, is Giuliano, who fell in the Pazzi conspiracy. On the extreme left, standing with his hands resting upon the hilt of his sword, is Lorenzo the Magnificent, who avenged Giuliano's death; behind Lorenzo, apparently clinging to him as though in anticipation or recollection of the conspiracy, is Angelo Poliziano. The rather sullen-looking personage, with a certain dash of sensuality about him, on our extreme right, gazing out of the picture, is Sandro himself. This picture, which was probably painted slightly before or shortly after the murder of Giuliano, has been called "the Apotheosis of the Medici"; it should be contrasted with the very different Nativity, now in the National Gallery, which Sandro painted many years later, in 1500, and which is full of the mystical aspirations of the disciples of Savonarola.

The Madonna and Child with Angels, two Archangels standing guard and two Bishops kneeling in adoration (1297), is a rich and attractive work by Domenico Ghirlandaio. Fra Angelico's Tabernacle (17), Madonna and Child with the Baptist and St. Mark, and the famous series of much-copied Angels, was painted for the Guild of Flax-merchants, whose patron was St. Mark. The admirable Predella (1294) represents St. Mark reporting St. Peter's sermons, and St. Mark's martyrdom, together with the Adoration of the Magi.

Passing down the corridor, we come to the entrance to the passage which leads across the Ponte Vecchio to the Pitti Palace. There are some fine Italian engravings on the way down. The halls of the Inscriptions and Cameos contain ancient statues as well, including the so-called dying Alexander, and some of those so over-praised by Shelley. Among the pictures in the Sala del Baroccio, is a very genial lady with a volume of Petrarch's sonnets, by Andrea del Sarto (188). Here, too, are some excellent portraits by Bronzino; a lady with a missal (198); a rather pathetic picture of Eleonora of Toledo, the wife of Cosimo I., with Don Garzia–the boy with whom Cellini used to romp (172); Bartolommeo Panciatichi (159); Lucrezia Panciatichi (154), a peculiarly sympathetic rendering of an attractive personality. Sustermans' Galileo (163) is also worth notice. The Duchess Eleonora died almost simultaneously with her sons, Giovanni and Garzia, in 1562, and there arose in consequence a legend that Garzia had murdered Giovanni, and had, in his turn, been killed by his own father, and that Eleonora had either also been murdered by the Duke or died of grief. Like many similar stories of the Medicean princes, this appears to be entirely fictitious.

The Hall of Niobe contains the famous series of statues representing the destruction of Niobe and her children at the hands of Apollo and Artemis. They are Roman or Græco-Roman copies of a group assigned by tradition to the fourth century b.c., and which was brought from Asia Minor to Rome in the year 35 b.c. The finest of these statues is that of Niobe's son, the young man who is raising his cloak upon his arm as a shield; he was originally protecting a sister, who, already pierced by the fatal arrow, leaned against his knee as she died.

In a room further on there is an interesting series of miniature portraits of the Medici, from Giovanni di Averardo to the family of Duke Cosimo. Six of the later ones are by Bronzino.

At the end of the corridor, by Baccio Bandinelli's copy of the Laocoön, are three rooms containing the drawings and sketches of the Old Masters. It would take a book as long as the present to deal adequately with them. Many of the Florentine painters, who were always better draughtsmen than they were colourists, are seen to much greater advantage in their drawings than in their finished pictures. Besides a most rich collection of the early men and their successors, from Angelico to Bartolommeo, there are here several of Raphael's cartoons for Madonnas and two for his St. George and the Dragon; many of the most famous and characteristic drawings of Leonardo da Vinci (and it is from his drawings alone that we can now get any real notion of this "Magician of the Renaissance"); and some important specimens of Michelangelo. Here, too, is Andrea Mantegna's terrible Judith, conceived in the spirit of some Roman heroine, which once belonged to Vasari and was highly valued by him. It is dated 1491, and should be compared with Botticelli's rendering of the same theme.

CHAPTER VI.

OR SAN MICHELE AND THE SESTO DI SAN PIERO

"Una figura della Donna mia
s'adora, Guido, a San Michele in Orto,
che di bella sembianza, onesta e pia,
de' peccatori è gran rifugio e porto."
(*Guido Cavalcanti* to *Guido Orlandi*.)

AT the end of the bustling noisy Via Calzaioli, the Street of the Stocking-makers, rises the Oratory of Our Lady, known as San Michele in Orto, "St. Michael in the Garden." Around its outer walls, enshrined in little temples of their own, stand great statues of saints in marble and bronze by the hands of the greatest sculptors of Florence—the canonised patrons of the Arts or Guilds, keeping guard over the thronging crowds that pass below. This is the grand monument of the wealth and taste, devotion and charity, of the commercial democracy of the Middle Ages.

ORCAGNA'S TABERNACLE, OR SAN MICHELE

The ancient church of San Michele in Orto was demolished by order of the Commune in the thirteenth century, to make way for a piazza for the grain and corn market, in the centre of which Arnolfo di Cambio built a loggia in 1280. Upon one of the pilasters of this loggia there was painted a picture of the Madonna, held in highest reverence by the frequenters of the market; a special company or sodality of laymen was formed, the *Laudesi* of Our Lady of Or San Michele, who met here every evening to sing *laudi* in her honour, and who were distinguished even in mediæval Florence, where charity was always on a heroic scale, by their munificence towards the poor. "On July 3rd, 1292," so Giovanni Villani writes, "great and manifest miracles began to be shown forth in the city of Florence by a figure of Holy Mary which was painted on a pilaster of the loggia of San Michele in Orto, where the grain was sold; the sick were healed, the deformed made straight, and the possessed visibly delivered in great numbers. But the preaching friars, and the friars minor likewise, through envy or some other cause, would put no faith in it, whereby they fell into much infamy with the Florentines. And so greatly grew the fame of these miracles and merits of Our Lady that folk flocked hither in pilgrimage from all parts of Tuscany at her feasts, bringing divers waxen images for the wonders worked, wherewith a great part of the loggia in front of and around the said figure was filled." In spite of ecclesiastical scepticism, this popular devotion ever increased; the company of the Laudesi, amongst whom, says Villani, was a good part of the best folk in Florence, had their hands always full of offerings and legacies, which they faithfully distributed to the poor.

The wonderful tidings roused even Guido Cavalcanti from his melancholy musings among the tombs. As a sceptical philosopher, he had little faith in miracles, but an *esprit fort* of the period could not allow himself to be on the same side as the friars. A delightful *via media* presented itself; the features of the Madonna in the picture bore a certain resemblance to his lady, and everything was at once made clear. So he took up his pen, and wrote a very beautiful sonnet to his friend, Guido Orlandi. It begins: "A figure of my Lady is adored, Guido, in San Michele in Orto, which, with her fair semblance, pure and tender, is the great refuge and harbour of sinners." And after describing (with evident devotional feeling, in spite of the obvious suggestion that it is the likeness of his lady that gives the picture its miraculous powers) the devotion of the people and the wonders worked on souls and bodies alike, he concludes: "Her fame goeth through far off lands: but the friars minor say it is idolatry, for envy that she is not their neighbour." But Orlandi professed himself much shocked at his friend's levity. "If thou hadst said, my friend, of Mary," so runs the double sonnet of his answer, "Loving and full of grace, thou art a red rose planted in the garden; thou wouldst have written fittingly. For she is the Truth and the Way, she was the mansion of our Lord, and is the port of our salvation." And he bids the greater Guido imitate the publican; cast the beam out of his own eye and let the mote alone in those of the friars: "The friars minor know the divine Latin scripture, and the good preachers are the defenders of the faith; their preaching is our medicine."

One of the most terrible faction fights in Florentine history raged round the loggia and oratory on June 10th, 1304. The Cavalcanti and their allies were heroically holding their own, here and in Mercato Vecchio, against the overwhelming forces of the Neri headed by the Della Tosa, Sinibaldo Donati and Boccaccio Adimari, when Neri Abati fired the houses round Or San Michele; the wax images in Our Lady's oratory flared up, the loggia was burned to the ground, and all the houses along Calimara and Mercato Nuovo and beyond down to the Ponte Vecchio were utterly destroyed. The young nobles of the Neri faction galloped about with flaming torches to assail the houses of their foes; the Podestà with his troops came into Mercato Nuovo, stared at the blaze, but did nothing but block the way. In this part of the town was all the richest merchandise of Florence, and the loss was enormous. The Cavalcanti, against whom the iniquitous plot was specially aimed, were absolutely ruined, and left the city without further resistance.

The pilaster with Madonna's picture had survived the fire, and the *Laudesi* still met round it to sing her praises.

But in 1336 the Signoria proposed to erect a grand new building on the site of the old loggia, which should serve at once for corn exchange and provide a fitting oratory for this new and growing cult of the Madonna di Orsanmichele. The present edifice, half palace and half church, was commenced in 1337, and finished at the opening of the fifteenth century. The actual building was in the hands of the Commune, who delegated their powers to the Arte di Por Sta. Maria or Arte della Seta. The Parte Guelfa and the Greater Guilds were to see to the external decoration of the pilasters, upon each of which tabernacles were made to receive the images of the Saints before which each of the Arts should come in state, to make offerings on the feasts of their proper patrons; while the shrine itself, and the internal decorations of the loggia (as it was still called), were left in the charge and care of the *Laudesi* themselves, the Compagnia of Orsanmichele, which was thoroughly organised under its special captains. It is uncertain whom the Arte della Seta employed as architect; Vasari says that Taddeo Gaddi gave the design, others say Orcagna (who worked for the Laudesi inside), and more recently Francesco Talenti has been suggested. Benci di Cione and Simone di Francesco Talenti, who also worked at the same epoch upon the Duomo, were among the architects employed later. The closing in of the arcades, for the better protection of the tabernacle, took away the last remnants of its original appearance as an open loggia; and, shortly before, the corn market itself was removed to the present Piazza del Grano, and thus the "Palatium" became the present church. The extremely beautifully sculptured windows are the work of Simone di Francesco Talenti.

There are fourteen of these little temples or niches, partly belonging to the Greater and partly to the Lesser Arts. It will be seen that, while the seven Greater Arts have each their niche, only six out of the fourteen Minor Arts are represented. Over the niches are *tondi* with the insignia of each Art. The statues were set up at different epochs, and are not always those that originally stood here–altered in one case from significant political motives, in others from the desire of the guilds to have something more thoroughly up to date–the rejected images being made over to the authorities of the Duomo for their unfinished façade, or sent into exile among the friars of Santa Croce. In 1404 the Signoria decreed that, within ten years from that date, the Arts who had secured their pilasters should have their statues in position, on pain of losing the right. But this does not seem to have been rigidly enforced.

WINDOW OF OR SAN MICHELE

The Story of Florence

Beginning at the corner of the northern side, facing towards the Duomo, we have the minor Art of the Butchers represented by Donatello's St. Peter in marble, an early and not very excellent work of the master, about 1412 (in a tabernacle of the previous century); the *tondo* above containing their arms, a black goat on a gold field, is modern. Next comes the marble St. Philip, the patron saint of the minor Art of the Shoemakers, by Nanni di Banco, of 1408, a beautiful and characteristic work of this too often neglected sculptor. Then, also by Nanni di Banco, the *Quattro incoronati*, the "four crowned martyrs," who, being carvers by profession, were put to death under Diocletian for refusing to make idols, and are the patrons of the masters in stone and wood, a minor Art which included sculptors, architects, bricklayers, carpenters, and masons; the bas-relief under the shrine, also by Nanni, is a priceless masterpiece of realistic Florentine democratic art, and shows us the mediæval craftsmen at their work, the every-day life of the men who made Florence the dream of beauty which she became; above it are the arms of the Guild, in an ornate and beautiful medallion, by Luca della Robbia. The following shrine, that of the Art of makers of swords and armour, had originally Donatello's famous St. George in marble, of 1415, which is now in the Bargello; the present bronze (inappropriate for a minor Art, according to the precedent of the others) is a modern copy; the bas-relief below, of St. George slaying the dragon, is still Donato's.

On the western wall, opposite the old tower of the Guild of Wool, comes first a bronze St. Matthew, made together with its tabernacle by Ghiberti and Michelozzo for the greater Guild of Money-changers and Bankers (Arte del Cambio), and finished in 1422. The Annunciation above is by Niccolò of Arezzo, at the close of the Trecento. The very beautiful bronze statue of St. Stephen, by Ghiberti, represents the great Guild of Wool, Arte della Lana; originally they had a marble St. Stephen, but, seeing what excellent statues had been made for the Cambio and the Calimala Guilds, they declared that since the Arte della Lana claimed to be always mistress of the other Arts, she must excel in this also; so sent their St. Stephen away to the Cathedral, and assigned the new work to Ghiberti (1425). Then comes the marble St. Eligius, by Nanni di Banco (1415), for the minor Art of the Maniscalchi, which included farriers, iron-smiths, knife-makers, and the like; the bas-relief below, also by Nanni, represents the Saint (San Lò he is more familiarly called, or St. Eloy in French) engaged in shoeing a demoniacal horse.

On the southern façade, we have St. Mark in marble for the minor Art of Linaioli and Rigattieri, flax merchants and hucksters, by Donatello, (about 1412).[32] The Arte dei Vaiai e Pellicciai, furriers, although a greater Guild, seems to have been contented with the rather insignificant marble St. James, which follows, of uncertain authorship, and dating from the end of the Trecento; the bas-relief seems later.

The next shrine, that of the Doctors and Apothecaries, the great Guild to which Dante belonged and which included painters and booksellers, is empty; the Madonna herself is their patroness, but their statue is now inside the church; the Madonna and Child in the medallion above are by Luca della Robbia. The next niche is that of the great Arte della Seta or Arte di Por Santa Maria, the Guild of the Silk-merchants, to which embroiderers, goldsmiths and silversmiths were attached; the bronze statue of their patron, St. John the Evangelist, is by Baccio da Montelupo (1515), and replaces an earlier marble now in the Bargello; the medallion above with their arms, a gate on a shield supported by two cherubs, is by Luca della Robbia.

Finally, on the façade in the Via Calzaioli, the first shrine is that of the Arte di Calimala or Arte dei Mercatanti, who carried on the great commerce in foreign cloth, the chief democratic guild of the latter half of the thirteenth century, but which, together with the Arte della Lana, began somewhat to decline towards the middle of the Quattrocento; their bronze St. John Baptist is Ghiberti's, but hardly one of his better works (1415). The large central tabernacle was originally assigned to the Parte Guelfa, the only organisation outside of the Guilds that was allowed to share in this work; for them, Donatello made a bronze statue of their patron, St. Louis of Toulouse, and either Donatello himself or Michelozzo prepared, in 1423, the beautiful niche for him which is still here. But, owing to the great unpopularity of the Parte Guelfa and their complete loss of authority under the new Medicean regime, this tabernacle was taken from them in 1459 and made over to the Università dei Mercanti or Magistrato della Mercanzia, a board of magistrates who presided over all the Guilds; the arms of this magistracy were set up in the present medallion by Luca della Robbia in 1462; Donatello's St. Louis was sent to the friars minor; and, some years later, Verrocchio cast the present masterly group of Christ and St. Thomas. Landucci, in his diary for 1483, tells us how it was set up, and that the bronze figure of the Saviour seemed to him the most beautiful that had ever been made. Last of all, the bronze statue of St. Luke was set up by Giovanni da Bologna in 1601, for the Judges and Notaries, who, like the silk-merchants, discarded an earlier marble. It must be observed that the substitution of the Commercial Tribunal for the tyrannical Parte Guelfa completes the purely democratic character of the whole monument.

Entering the interior, we pass from the domains of the great commercial guilds and their patrons to those of the *Laudesi* of Santa Maria. It is rich and subdued in colour, the vaults and pilasters covered with faded frescoes. It is divided into two parts, the one ending in the Shrine of the Blessed Virgin, the other in the chapel and altar of St. Anne, her mother and the deliveress of the Republic. These two record the two great events of fourteenth century Florentine history—the expulsion of the Duke of Athens and the Black Death. It was after this great plague that, in consequence of the Compagnia having had great riches left to them, "to the honour of the Holy Virgin Mary and for the benefit of the poor," the Captains of Orsanmichele, as the heads of these Laudesi were called, summoned Orcagna, in 1349, to the "work of the pilaster," as it was officially styled, to enclose what remained of the miraculous picture in a glorious tabernacle. He took ten years over it, finishing it in 1359, while the railing by Pietro di Migliore was completed in 1366. It was approximately at this epoch that it was decided to find another place for the market, and to close the arcades of the loggia, *per adornamento e salvezza del tabernacolo di Nostra Donna.*

It is goldsmith's work on a gigantic scale, this marble reliquary of the archangelic painter. "A miracle of loveliness," wrote Lord Lindsay, "and though clustered all over with pillars and pinnacles, inlaid with the richest marbles, lapis-lazuli, and mosaic work, it is chaste in its luxuriance as an Arctic iceberg—worthy of her who was spotless among women." The whole is crowned with a statue of St. Michael, and the miraculous picture is enclosed in an infinite wealth and profusion of statues and arabesques, angels and prophets, precious stones and lions' heads. Scenes in bas-relief from Our Lady's life alternate with prophets and allegorical representations of the virtues, some of these latter being single figures of great beauty and some psychological insight in the rendering—for instance, Docilitas, Solertia, Justitia, Fortitudo—while marble Angels cluster round their Queen's tabernacle in eager service and loving worship. At the back is the great scene beneath which, to right and left, the series begins and ends—the death of Madonna and her Assumption, or rather, Our Lady of the Girdle, the giving of that celestial gift to the Thomas who had doubted, the mystical treasure which Tuscan Prato still fondly believes that her Duomo holds. This is perhaps the first representation of this mystery in Italian sculpture, and is signed and dated: *Andreas Cionis pictor Florentinus oratorii archimagister extitit hujus, 1359.* The figure with a small divided beard, talking with a man in a big hat and long beard, is Orcagna's own portrait. The miraculous painting itself is within the tabernacle. The picture in front, the Madonna and Child with goldfinch, adored by eight Angels, is believed to be either by Orcagna himself or Bernardo Daddi[33]; it is decidedly more primitive than their authenticated works, probably because it is a comparatively close rendering of the original composition.

On the side altar on the right is the venerated Crucifix before which St. Antoninus used to pray. At one time the Dominicans were wont to come hither in procession on the anniversary of his death. In his Chronicle of Florence, Antoninus defends the friars from the accusations of Villani with respect to their scepticism about the miraculous picture. On the opposite side altar is the marble statue of Mother and Child from the tabernacle of the Medici e Speziali. It was executed about the year 1399; Vasari ascribes it to a Simone di Firenze, who may possibly be Simone di Francesco Talenti.

The altar of St. Anne at the east end of the left half of the nave is one of the Republic's thank-offerings for their deliverance from the tyranny of Walter de Brienne. Public thanksgiving had been held here, before Our Lady's picture, as early as 1343, while the "Palatium" was still in building; but in the following year, 1344, at the instance of the captains of Or San Michele and others, the Signoria decreed that "for the perpetual memory of the grace conceded by God to the Commune and People of Florence, on the day of blessed Anne, Mother of the glorious Virgin, by the liberation of the city and the citizens, and by the destruction of the pernicious and tyrannical yoke," solemn offerings should be made on St. Anne's feast day by the Signoria and the consuls of the Arts, before her statue in Or San Michele, and that on that day all offices and shops should be closed, and no one be subject to arrest for debt. The present statue on this votive altar, representing the Madonna (here perhaps symbolising her faithful city of Florence) seated on the lap of St. Anne, who is thus protecting her and her Divine Child, was executed by Francesco da Sangallo in 1526, and replaces an older group in wood; although highly praised by Vasari, it will strike most people as not quite worthy of the place or the occasion. The powerful and expressive head of St. Anne is the best part of the group.

The beneficent energies of these Laudesi and their captains spread far beyond the limits of this church and shrine. The great and still existing company of the Misericordia was originally connected with them; and the Bigallo for the foundling children was raised by them at the same time as their Tabernacle here. They contributed generously to the construction of the Duomo, and decorated chapels in Santa Croce and the Carmine. Sacchetti and Giovanni Boccaccio were among their officers; and it was while Boccaccio was serving as one of their captains in 1350 that they sent a sum of money by his hands to Dante's daughter Beatrice, in her distant convent at Ravenna. They appear to have spent all they had in the defence of Florentine liberty during the great siege of 1529.

The imposing old tower that rises opposite San Michele in the Calimala is the Torrione of the Arte della Lana, copiously adorned with their arms—the Lamb bearing the Baptist's cross. It was erected at the end of the thirteenth or beginning of the fourteenth century, and in it the consuls of the Guild had their meetings. It was stormed and sacked by the Ciompi in 1378. The heavy arch that connects the tower with the upper storey of Or San Michele, and rather disfigures the building, is the work of Buontalenti in the latter half of the sixteenth century. The large vaulted hall into which it leads, intended originally for the storage of grain and the like, is now known as the Sala di Dante, and witnesses the brilliant gatherings of Florentines and foreigners to listen to the readings of the *Divina Commedia* given under the auspices of the *Società Dantesca Italiana*.

This is the part of the city where the Arts had their wealth and strength; the very names of the streets show it; Calimala and Pellicceria, for instance, which run from the Mercato Vecchio to the Via Porta Rossa. The Mercato Vecchio, the centre of the city both in Roman and mediæval times, around which the houses and towers of the oldest families clustered–Elisei, Caponsacchi, Nerli, Vecchietti, and the rest of whom Dante's *Paradiso* tells–is now a painfully unsightly modern square, with what appears to be a triumphal arch bearing the inscription: *L'antico centro della città da secolare squallore a vita nuova restituita*(!). Passing down the Calimala to the Via Porta Rossa and the Mercato Nuovo, near where the former enters the Via Calzaioli, the site is still indicated of the Calimala Bottega where the government of the Arts was first organised, as told in chapter i. Near here and in the Mercato Nuovo, the Cavalcanti had their palaces. In the Via Porta Rossa the Arte della Seta had their warehouses; the gate from which they took their second name, and which is represented on their shield, is of course the Por Santa Maria,

Our Lady's Gate of the old walls or Cerchia Antica, which was somewhere about the middle of the present Via Por Santa Maria. The Church of Santa Maria sopra la Porta, between the Mercato Nuovo and the Via delle Terme, is the present San Biagio (now used by the firemen); adjoining it is the fine old palace of the dreaded captains of the Parte Guelfa. The Via Porta Rossa contains some mediæval houses and the lower portions of a few grand old towers still standing; as already said, in the first circle of walls there was a postern gate, at the end of the present street, opposite Santa Trinità. In the Mercato Nuovo, where a copy of the ancient boar–which figures in Hans Andersen's familiar story–seems to watch the flower market, the arcades were built by Battista del Tasso for Cosimo I. Here, too, modernisation has destroyed much. Hardly can we conjure up now that day of the great fire in 1304, when the nobles of the "black" faction galloped through the crowd of plunderers, with their blazing torches throwing a lurid glow on the steel-clad Podestà with his soldiers drawn up here idly to gaze upon the flames! A house that once belonged to the Cavalcanti is still standing in Mercato Nuovo, marked by the Cross of the People; the branch of the family who lived here left the magnates and joined the people, as the Cross indicates, changing their name from Cavalcanti to Cavallereschi.

TOWER OF THE ARTE DELLA LANA

The little fourteenth century church of St. Michael, now called San Carlo, which stands opposite San Michele in Orto on the other side of the Via Calzaioli, was originally a votive chapel to Saint Anne, built at the expense of the captains of the Laudesi on a site purchased by the Commune. It was begun in 1349 by Fioraventi and Benci di Cione, simultaneously with Orcagna's tabernacle, continued by Simone di Francesco Talenti, and completed at the opening of the fifteenth century. The captains intended to have the ceremonial offerings made here instead of in the Loggia; but the thing fell through owing to a disagreement with the Arte di Por Santa Maria, and the votive altar remained in the Loggia.

Between San Carlo and the Duomo the street has been completely modernised. Of old it was the Corso degli Adimari, surrounded by the houses and towers of this fierce Guelf clan, who were at deadly feud with the Donati. Cacciaguida in the *Paradiso* (canto xvi.) describes them as "the outrageous tribe that playeth dragon after whoso fleeth, and to whoso showeth tooth—or purse—is quiet as a lamb." One of their towers still stands on the left. On the right the place is marked where the famous loggia, called the Neghittosa, once stood, which belonged to the branch of the Adimari called the Cavicciuli, who, in spite of their hatred to the Donati, joined the Black Guelfs. One of them, Boccaccio or Boccaccino Adimari, seized upon Dante's goods when he was exiled, and exerted his influence to prevent his being recalled. In this loggia, too, Filippo Argenti used to sit, the *Fiorentino spirito bizzarro* whom Dante saw rise before him covered with mire out of the marshy lake of Styx. He is supposed to have ridden a horse shod with silver, and there is a rare story in the *Decameron* of a mad outburst of bestial fury on his part in this very loggia, on account of a mild practical joke on the part of Ciacco, a bon vivant of the period whom Dante has sternly flung into the hell of gluttons. On this occasion Filippo, who was an enormously big, strong, and sinewy man, beat a poor little dandy called Biondello within an inch of his life. In this same loggia, on August 4th, 1397, a party of young Florentine exiles, who had come secretly from Bologna with the intention of killing Maso degli Albizzi, took refuge, after a vain attempt to call the people to arms. From the highest part of the loggia, seeing a great crowd assembling round them, they harangued the mob, imploring them not stupidly to wait to see their would-be deliverers killed and themselves thrust back into still more grievous servitude. When not a soul moved, "finding out too late how dangerous it is to wish to set free a people that desires, happen what may, to be enslaved," as Machiavelli cynically puts it, they escaped into the Duomo, where, after a vain attempt at defending themselves, they were captured by the Captain, put to the question and executed. There were about ten of them in all, including three of the Cavicciuli and Antonio dei Medici.

On November 9th, 1494, when the Florentines rose against Piero dei Medici and his brothers, the young Cardinal Giovanni rode down this street with retainers and a few citizens shouting, *Popolo e libertà*, pretending that he was going to join the insurgents. But when he got to San Michele in Orto, the people turned upon him from the piazza with their pikes and lances, with loud shouts of "Traitor!" upon which he fled back in great dread. Landucci saw him at the windows of his palace, on his knees with clasped hand, commending himself to God. "When I saw him," he says, "I grew very sorry for him (*m'inteneri assai*); and I judged that he was a good and sensible youth."

To the east of the Via Calzaioli lies the Sesto di San Piero Maggiore, which, at the end of the thirteenth century, received the pleasant name of the Sesto di Scandali. It lies on either side of the Via del Corso, which with its continuations ran from east to west through the old city. In the Via della Condotta, at the corner of the Vicolo dei Cerchi, still stands the palace which belonged to a section of this family (the section known as the White Cerchi to distinguish them from Messer Vieri's branch, the Black Cerchi, who were even more "white" in politics, in spite of their name); in this palace the Priors sat before Arnolfo built the Palazzo Vecchio, which became the seat of government in 1299.

It was there, not here, that Dante and his colleagues, on June 15th, 1300, entered upon office, and the same day confirmed the sentences which had been passed under their predecessors against the three traitors who had conspired to betray Florence to Pope Boniface; and then, a few days later, passed the decree by which Corso Donati and Guido Cavalcanti were sent into exile. Later the vicars of Robert of Anjou for a time resided here, and the administrators appointed to assess the confiscated goods of "rebels." At the corner of the Via dei Cerchi, where it joins the Via dei Cimatori, are traces of the loggia of the Cerchi; the same corner affords a picturesque glimpse of the belfrey of the Badia and the tower of the Podesta's palace.

There was another great palace of the Cerchi, referred to in the *Paradiso*, which had formerly belonged to the Ravignani and the Conti Guidi, the acquisition of which by Messer Vieri had excited the envy of the Donati. This palace is described by Dante (*Parad.* xvi.) as being *sopra la porta*, that is, over the inner gate of St. Peter, the gate of the first circuit in Cacciaguida's day. No trace of it remains, but it was apparently on the north side of the Corso where it now joins the Via del Proconsolo. "Over the gate," says Cacciaguida, "which is now laden with new felony of such weight that there will soon be a wrecking of the ship, were the Ravignani, whence is descended the Count Guido, and whoever has since taken the name of the noble Bellincione."

Here the daughter of Bellincione Berti, the *alto Bellincion*, lived,—the beautiful and good Gualdrada, whom we can dimly discern as a sweet and gracious presence in that far-off early Florence of which the *Paradiso* sings; she was the ancestress of the great lords of the Casentino, the Conti Guidi. The principal houses of the Donati appear to have been on the Duomo side of the Corso, just before the Via dello Studio now joins it; but they had possessions on the other side as well. Giano della Bella had his house almost opposite to them, on the southern side. A little further on, at the corner where the Corso joins the Via del Proconsolo, Folco Portinari lived, the father, according to tradition, of Dante's Beatrice: "he who had been the father of so great a marvel, as this most noble Beatrice was manifestly seen to be." Folco's sons joined the Bianchi; one of them, Pigello, was poisoned during Dante's priorate; an elder son, Manetto Portinari (the friend of Dante and Cavalcanti), afterwards ratted and made his peace with the Neri. All the family are included, together with the Giuochi who lived opposite to them, in a sentence passed against Dante and his sons in 1315, from which Manetto Portinari is excepted by name. The building which now occupies the site of the Casa Portinari was once the Salviati Palace.

HOUSE OF DANTE

In the little Piazza di San Martino is shown the Casa di Dante, which undoubtedly belonged to the Alighieri, and in which Dante is said to have been born. It has been completely modernised. The Alighieri had also a house in the Via Santa Margherita, which runs from the Piazza San Martino to the Corso, opposite the little church of Santa Margherita. Hard by, in the Piazza dei Donati a section of that family had a house and garden; and here Dante saw and wooed Gemma, the daughter of Manetto Donati. The old tower which seems to watch over Dante's house from the other side of the Piazza San Martino, the Torre della Castagna, belonged in Dante's days to the monks of the Badia; in it, in 1282, the Priors of the Arts held their first meeting, when the government of the Republic was placed in their hands. At the corner of the Piazza, opposite Dante's house, lived the Sacchetti, the family from which the novelist, Franco, sprang. They were in deadly feud with Geri del Bello, the cousin of Dante's father, who lived in the house next to Dante's; and, shortly before the year of Dante's vision, the Sacchetti murdered Geri. He seems to have deserved his fate, and Dante places him among the sowers of discord in Hell, where he points at Dante and threatens him vehemently. "His violent death," says the poet in *Inferno* xxix, "which is not yet avenged for him, by any that is a partner of his shame, made him indignant; therefore, as I suppose, he went away without speaking to me; and in that he has made me pity him the more." Thirty years after the murder, Geri's nephews broke into the house of the Sacchetti and stabbed one of the family to death; and the two families were finally reconciled in 1342, on which occasion Dante's half-brother, Francesco Alighieri, was the representative of the Alighieri. Many years later, Dante's great-grandson, Leonardo Alighieri, came from Verona to Florence. "He paid me a visit," writes Leonardo Bruni, "as a friend of the memory of his great-grandfather, Dante. And I showed him Dante's house, and that of his forebears, and I pointed out to him many particulars with which he was not acquainted, because he and his family had been estranged from their fatherland. And so does Fortune roll this world around, and change its inhabitants up and down as she turns her wheel."

Beyond the Via del Proconsolo the Borgo, now called of the Albizzi, was originally the Borgo di San Piero–a suburb of the old city, but included in the second walls of the twelfth century. The present name records the brief, but not inglorious period of the rule of the oligarchy or Ottimati, before Cosimo dei Medici obtained complete possession of the State. It was formerly called the Corso di Por San Piero. The first palace on the right (De Rast or Quaratesi) was built for the Pazzi by Brunelleschi, and still shows their armorial bearings by Donatello. They had another palace further on, on the left, opposite the Via dell'Acqua. Still further on (past the Altoviti palace, with its caricatures) is the palace of the

Albizzi family, on the left, as you approach the Piazza. Here Maso degli Albizzi, and then Rinaldo, lived and practically ruled the state. Giuliano dei Medici alighted here in 1512. At the end of the Borgo degli Albizzi is now the busy, rather picturesque little Piazza di San Piero Maggiore, usually full of stalls and trucks. St. Peter's Gate in Dante's time lay just beyond the church, to the left. In this Piazza also the Donati had houses; and it was through this gate that Corso Donati burst into Florence with his followers on the morning of November 5th, 1301; "and he entered into the city like a daring and bold cavalier," as Dino Compagni–who loves a strong personality even on the opposite side to his own– puts it. The Bianchi in the Sesto largely outnumbered his forces, but did not venture to attack him, while the populace bawled *Viva il Barone* to their hearts' content. He incontinently seized that tall tower of the Corbizzi that still rises opposite to the façade of the church, at the southern corner of the Piazza in the Via del Mercatino, and hung out his banner from it. Seven years later he made his last stand in this square and round this tower, as we have told in chapter ii. Of the church of San Piero Maggiore, only the seventeenth century façade remains; but of old it ranked as the third of the Florentine temples. According to the legend, it was on his way to this church that San Zenobio raised the French child to life in the Borgo degli Albizzi, opposite the spot where the Palazzo Altoviti now stands. It is said to have been the only church in Florence free from the taint of simony in the days of St. Giovanni Gualberto, and of old had the privilege of first receiving the new Archbishops when they entered Florence. The Archbishop went through a curious and beautiful ceremony of mystic marriage with the Abbess of the Benedictine convent attached to the church, who apparently personified the diocese of Florence. Every year on Easter Monday the canons of the Duomo came here in procession; and on St. Peter's day the captains of the Parte Guelfa entered the Piazza in state to make a solemn offering, and had a race run in the Piazza Santa Croce after the ceremony. The artists, Lorenzo di Credi, Mariotto Albertinelli, Piero di Cosimo and Luca della Robbia were buried here. Two of the best pictures that the church contained–a Coronation of the Madonna ascribed to Orcagna and the famous Assumption said by Vasari to have been painted by Botticelli for Matteo Palmieri (which was supposed to inculcate heretical neoplatonic doctrines concerning the human soul and the Angels in the spheres), are now in the National Gallery of London.

It was in this Piazza that the conspirators resolved to assassinate Maso degli Albizzi. Their spies watched him leave his palace, walk leisurely towards the church and then enter an apothecary's shop, close to San Piero. They hurried off to tell their associates, but when the would-be assassins arrived on the scene, they found that Maso had given them the slip and left the shop.

Turning down the Via del Mercatino and back to the Badia along the Via Pandolfini, we pass the palace which once belonged to Francesco Valori, Savonarola's formidable adherent. Here it was on that terrible Palm Sunday, 1498, when Hell broke loose, as Landucci puts it, that Valori's wife was shot dead at a window, while her husband in the street below, on his way to answer the summons of the Signoria, was murdered near San Procolo by the kinsmen of the men whom he had sent to the scaffold.

The Badia shares with the Baptistery and San Miniato the distinction of being the only Florentine churches mentioned by Dante. In Cacciaguida's days it was close to the old Roman wall; from its campanile even in Dante's time, Florence still "took tierce and nones "; and, at the sound of its bells, the craftsmen of the Arts went to and from their work. Originally founded by the Countess Willa in the tenth century, the Badia di San Stefano (as it was called) that Dante and Boccaccio knew was the work of Arnolfo di Cambio; but it was entirely rebuilt in the seventeenth century, with consequent destruction of priceless frescoes by Giotto and Masaccio. The present graceful campanile is of the fourteenth century. The relief in the lunette over the chief door, rather in the manner of Andrea della Robbia, is by Benedetto Buglione. In the left transept is the monument by

Mino da Fiesole of Willa's son Hugo, Margrave of Tuscany, who died on St. Thomas' day, 1006. Dante calls him the great baron; his anniversary was solemnly celebrated here, and he was supposed to have conferred knighthood and nobility upon the Della Bella and other Florentine families. "Each one," says Cacciaguida, "who beareth aught of the fair arms of the great baron, whose name and worth the festival of Thomas keepeth living, from him derived knighthood and privilege" (*Paradiso* xvi.). In a chapel to the left of this monument is Filippino Lippi's picture of the Madonna appearing to St. Bernard, painted in 1480, one of the most beautiful renderings of an exceedingly poetical subject. For Dante, Bernard is *colui ch'abbelliva di Maria, come del sole stella mattutina*, "he who drew light from Mary, as the morning star from the sun." Filippino has introduced the portrait of the donor, on the right, Francesco di Pugliese. The church contains two other works by Mino da Fiesole, a Madonna and (in the right transept) the sepulchral monument of Bernardo Giugni, who served the State as ambassador to Milan and Venice in the days of Cosimo and Piero dei Medici. At the entrance to the cloisters Francesco Valori is buried.

It was in the Badia (and not in the Church of San Stefano, near the Via Por Santa Maria, as usually stated) that Boccaccio lectured upon the *Divina Commedia* in 1373. Benvenuto da Imola came over from Bologna to attend his beloved master's readings, and was much edified. But the audience were not equally pleased, and Boccaccio had to defend himself in verse. One of the sonnets he wrote on this occasion, *Se Dante piange, dove ch'el si sia*, has been admirably translated by Dante Rossetti:–

> If Dante mourns, there wheresoe'er he be,
> That such high fancies of a soul so proud
> Should be laid open to the vulgar crowd,
> (As, touching my Discourse, I'm told by thee),
>
> This were my grievous pain; and certainly
> My proper blame should not be disavow'd;
> Though hereof somewhat, I declare aloud
> Were due to others, not alone to me.
>
> False hopes, true poverty, and therewithal
> The blinded judgment of a host of friends,
> And their entreaties, made that I did thus.
>
> But of all this there is no gain at all
> Unto the thankless souls with whose base ends
> Nothing agrees that's great or generous.

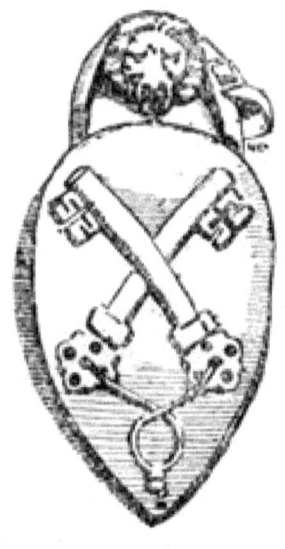

ARMS OF THE SESTO DI SAN PIERO

CHAPTER VII.

FROM THE BARGELLO PAST SANTA CROCE

"Non ha l'ottimo artista alcun concetto,
ch'un marmo solo in sé non circonscriva
col suo soverchio; e solo a quello arriva
la man che ubbidisce all'intelletto."
–*Michelangelo Buonarroti.*

EVEN as the Palazzo Vecchio or Palace of the Priors is essentially the monument of the *Secondo Popolo*, so the Palazzo del Podestà or Palace of the Commune belongs to the *Primo Popolo*; it was commenced in 1255, in that first great triumph of the democracy, although mainly finished towards the middle of the following century. Here sat the Podestà, with his assessors and retainers, whom he brought with him to Florence–himself always an alien noble. Originally he was the chief officer of the Republic, for the six months during which he held office, led the burgher forces in war, and acted as chief justice in peace; but he gradually sunk in popular estimation before the more democratic Captain of the People (who was himself, it will be remembered, normally an alien Guelf noble). A little later, both Podestà and Captain were eclipsed by the Gonfaloniere of Justice. In the fifteenth century the Podestà was still the president of the chief civil and criminal court of the city, and his office was only finally abolished during the Gonfalonierate of Piero Soderini at the beginning of the Cinquecento. Under the Medicean grand dukes the Bargello, or chief of police, resided here–hence the present name of the palace; and it is well to repeat, once for all, that when the Bargello, or Court of the Bargello, is mentioned in Florentine history–in grim tales of torture and executions and the like–it is not this building, but the residence of the Executore of Justice, now incorporated into the Palazzo Vecchio, that is usually meant.

It was in this Palace of the Podestà, however, that Guido Novello resided and ruled the city in the name of King Manfred, during the short period of Ghibelline tyranny that followed Montaperti, 1260-1266, and which the Via Ghibellina, first opened by him, recalls. The Palace was broken into by the populace in 1295, just before the fall of Giano della Bella, because a Lombard Podestà had unjustly acquitted Corso Donati for the death of a burgher at the hands of his riotous retainers. Here, too, was Cante dei Gabbrielli of Gubbio installed by Charles of Valois, in November 1301, and from its gates issued the Crier of the Republic that summoned Dante Alighieri and his companions in misfortune to appear before the Podestà's court. In one of those dark vaulted rooms on the ground floor, now full of a choice collection of mediæval arms and armour, Cante's successor, Fulcieri da Calvoli, tortured those of the Bianchi who fell into his cruel hands. "He sells their flesh while it is still alive," says Dante in the *Purgatorio*, "then slayeth them like a worn out brute: many doth he deprive of life, and himself of honour." Some died under the torments, others were beheaded.

"Messer Donato Alberti," writes Dino Compagni, "mounted vilely upon an ass, in a peasant's smock, was brought before the Podestà. And when he saw him, he asked him: 'Are you Messer Donato Alberti?' He replied: 'I am Donato. Would that Andrea da Cerreto were here before us, and Niccola Acciaioli, and Baldo d'Aguglione, and Jacopo da Certaldo, who have destroyed Florence.'[34] Then he was fastened to the rope and the cord adjusted to the pulley, and so they let him stay; and the windows and doors of the Palace were opened, and many citizens called in under other pretexts, that they might see him tortured and derided."

In the rising of the Ciompi, July 1378, the palace was forced to surrender to the insurgents after an assault of two hours. They let the Podestà escape, but burnt all books and papers, especially those of the hated Arte della Lana. At night as many as the palace could hold quartered themselves here.

BARGELLO COURTYARD AND STAIRCASE

The beautiful court and stairway, surrounded by statues and armorial bearings, the ascent guarded by the symbolical lion of Florence and leading to an open loggia, is the work of Benci di Cione and Neri di Fioraventi, 1333-1345. The palace is now the National Museum of Sculpture and kindred arts and crafts. Keeping to the left, round the court itself, we see a marble St. Luke by Niccolò di Piero Lamberti, of the end of the fourteenth century, from the niche of the Judges and Notaries at Or San Michele; a magnificent sixteenth century portalantern in beaten iron; the old marble St. John Evangelist, contemporaneous with the St. Luke, and probably by Piero di Giovanni Tedesco, from the niche of the Arte della Seta at Or San Michele; some allegorical statues by Giovanni da Bologna and Vincenzo Danti, in rather unsuccessful imitation of Michelangelo; a dying Adonis, questionably ascribed to Michelangelo. And, finally (numbered 18), there stands Michelangelo's so-called "Victory," the triumph of the ideal over outworn tyranny and superstition; a radiant youth, but worn and exhausted by the struggle, rising triumphantly over a shape of gigantic eld, so roughly hewn as to seem lost in the mist from which the young hero has gloriously freed himself.[35]

Also on the ground floor, to the left, are two rooms full of statuary. The first contains nothing important, save perhaps the Madonna and Child with St. Peter and St. Paul, formerly above the Porta Romana. In the second room, a series of bas-reliefs by Benedetto da Rovezzano, begun in 1511 and terribly mutilated by the imperial soldiery during the siege, represent scenes connected with the life and miracles of St. Giovanni Gualberto, including the famous trial of Peter Igneus, who, in order to convict the Bishop of Florence of simony, passed unharmed through the ordeal of fire. Here is the unfinished bust of Brutus (111) by Michelangelo, one of his latest works, and a significant expression of the state of the man's heart, when he was forced to rear sumptuous monuments for the new tyrants who had overthrown his beloved Republic. Then a chimney-piece by Benedetto da Rovezzano from the Casa Borgherini, one of the most sumptuous pieces of domestic furniture of the Renaissance; a very beautiful tondo of the Madonna and Child with the little St. John (123) by Michelangelo, made for Bartolommeo Pitti early in the Cinquecento; the mask of a grinning faun with gap-teeth, traditionally shown as the head struck out by the boy Michelangelo in his first visit to the Medici Gardens, when he attracted the attention of Lorenzo the Magnificent—but probably a comparatively modern work suggested by Vasari's story; a sketch in marble for the martyrdom of St. Andrew, supposed to be a juvenile work of Michelangelo's, but also doubtful. Here too is Michelangelo's drunken Bacchus (128), an exquisitely-modelled intoxicated vine-crowned youth, behind whom a sly little satyr lurks, nibbling grapes. It is one of the master's earliest works, very carefully and delicately finished, executed during his first visit to Rome, for Messer Jacopo Galli, probably about 1497. Of this statue Ruskin wrote, while it was still in the Uffizi: "The white lassitude of joyous limbs, panther-like, yet passive, fainting with their own delight, that gleam among the Pagan formalisms of the Uffizi, far away, separating themselves in their lustrous lightness as the waves of an Alpine torrent do by their dancing from the dead stones, though the stones be as white as they." Shelley, on the contrary, found it "most revolting," "the idea of the deity of Bacchus in the conception of a Catholic." Near it is a tondo of the Virgin and Child with the Baptist, by Andrea Ferrucci.

At the top of the picturesque and richly ornamented staircase, to the right of the loggia on the first floor, opens a great vaulted hall, where the works of Donatello, casts and originals, surround a cast of his great equestrian monument to Gattamelata at Padua–a hall of such noble proportions that even Gattamelata looks insignificant, where he sits his war-horse between the Cross of the People and the Lily of the Commune. Here the general council of the Commune met–the only council (besides the special council of the Podestà) in which the magnates could sit and vote, and it was here, on July 6th, 1295, that Dante Alighieri first entered public life; he spoke in support of the modifications of the Ordinances of Justice–which may have very probably been a few months before he definitely associated himself with the People by matriculating in the Arte dei Medici e Speziali. Among the casts and copies that fill this room, there are several original and splendid works of Donatello; the Marzocco, or symbolical lion of Florence protecting the shield of the Commune, which was formerly in front of the Palace of the Priors; the bronze David, full of Donatello's delight in the exuberance of youthful manhood just budding; the San Giovannino or little St. John; the marble David, inferior to the bronze, but heralding Michelangelo; the bronze bust of a youth, called the son of Gattamelata; Love trampling upon a snake (bronze); St. George in marble from Or San Michele, an idealised condottiere of the Quattrocento; St. John the Baptist from the Baptistery; and a bronze relief of the Crucifixion. The coloured bust is now believed by many critics to be neither the portrait of Niccolò da Uzzano nor by Donatello; it is possibly a Roman hero by some sculptor of the Seicento.

The next room is the audience chamber of the Podestà. Besides the Cross and the Lilies on the windows, its walls and roof are covered with the gold lion on azure ground, the arms of the Duke of Athens. They were cancelled by decree of the Republic in 1343, and renewed in 1861; as a patriotically worded tablet on the left, under the window, explains. Opening out of this is the famous Chapel of the Podestà–famous for the frescoes on its walls–once a prison.

From out of these terribly ruined frescoes stands the figure of Dante (stands out, alas, because completely repainted–a mere *rifacimento* with hardly a trace of the original work left) in what was once a *Paradiso*; the dim figures on either side are said to represent Brunette Latini and either Corso Donati or Guido Cavalcanti. In spite of a very pleasant fable, it is absolutely certain that this is not a contemporaneous portrait of Dante (although it may be regarded as an authentic likeness, to some extent) and was not painted by Giotto; the frescoes were executed by some later follower of Giotto (possibly by Taddeo Gaddi, who painted the lost portraits of Dante and Guido in Santa Croce) after 1345. The two paintings below on either side, Madonna and Child and St. Jerome, are votive pictures commissioned by pious Podestàs in 1490 and 1491, the former by Sebastiano Mainardi, the brother-in-law of Domenico Ghirlandaio.

The third room contains small bronze works by Tuscan masters of the Quattrocento. In the centre, Verrocchio's David (22), cast for Lorenzo dei Medici, one of the masterpieces of the fifteenth century. Here are the famous trial plates for the great competition for the second bronze gates of the Baptistery, announced in 1401, the Sacrifice of Abraham, by Brunelleschi and Ghiberti respectively; the grace and harmony of Ghiberti's composition (12) contrast strongly with the force, almost violence, the dramatic action and movement of Brunelleschi's (13). Ghiberti's, unlike his rival's, is in one single piece; but, until lately, there has been a tendency to underrate the excellence of Brunelleschi's relief. Here, too, are Ghiberti's reliquary of St. Hyacinth, executed in 1428, with two beautiful floating Angels (21); several bas-reliefs by Bertoldo, Donatello's pupil and successor; the effigy of Marino Soccino, a lawyer of Siena, by the Sienese sculptor Il Vecchietta (16); and, in a glass case, Orpheus by Bertoldo, Hercules and Antæus by Antonio Pollaiuolo, and Love on a Scallop Shell by Donatello. The following room contains mostly bronzes by later masters, especially Cellini, Giovanni da Bologna, Vincenzo Danti. The most noteworthy of its contents are Daniele Ricciarelli's striking bust of Michelangelo (37); Cellini's bronze sketch for Perseus (38), his bronze bust of Duke Cosimo I. (39), his wax model for Perseus (40), the liberation of Andromeda, from the pedestal of the statue in the Loggia dei Lanzi (42); and above all, Giovanni da Bologna's flying Mercury (82), showing what exceedingly beautiful mythological work could still be produced when the golden days of the Renaissance were over. It was cast in 1565, and, like many of the best bronzes of this epoch, was originally placed on a fountain in one of the Medicean villas.

On the second floor, first a long room with seals, etc., guarded by Rosso's frescoed Justice. Here, and in the room on the left, is a most wonderful array of the works in enamelled terra cotta of the Della Robbias—Luca and Andrea, followed by Giovanni and their imitators. In the best work of Luca and Andrea—and there is much of their very best and most perfect work in these two rooms—religious devotion received its highest and most perfect expression in sculpture. Their Madonnas, Annunciations, Nativities and the like, are the sculptural counterpart to Angelico's divinest paintings, though never quite attaining to his spiritual insight and supra-sensible gaze upon life. Andrea's work is more pictorial in treatment than Luca's, has less vigour and even at times a perceptible trace of sentimentality; but in sheer beauty his very best creations do not yield to those of his great master and uncle. Both Luca and Andrea kept to the simple blue and white—in the best part of their work—and surrounded their Madonnas with exquisite festoons of fruit and leaves: "wrought them," in Pater's words, "into all sorts of marvellous frames and garlands, giving them their natural colours, only subdued a little, a little paler than nature."

To the right of the first Della Robbia room, are two more rooms full of statuary, and one with a collection of medals, including that commemorating Savonarola's Vision of the Sword of the Lord. In the first room—taking merely the more important—we may see Music, wrongly ascribed to Orcagna, probably earlier (139); bust of Charles VIII. of France (164), author uncertain; bust in terra cotta of a young warrior, by Antonio Pollaiuolo (161), as grandly insolent and confident as any of Signorelli's savage youths in the Orvieto frescoes. Also, bust of Matteo Palmieri, the humanist and suspected heretic, by Antonio Rossellino (160); bust of Pietro Mellini by Benedetto da Maiano (153); portrait of a young lady, by Matteo Civitali of Lucca (142); a long relief (146) ascribed to Verrocchio and representing the death of a lady of the Tornabuoni family in child-birth, which Shelley greatly admired and described at length, under the impression that he was studying a genuine antique: "It is altogether an admirable piece," he says, "quite in the spirit of Terence." The uncompromising realism of the male portraiture of the fifteenth and early sixteenth centuries is fully illustrated in this room, and there is at the same time a peculiar tenderness and winsomeness in representing young girls, which is exceedingly attractive.

In the next room there are many excellent portraits of this kind, named and unnamed. Of more important works, we should notice the San Giovannino by Antonio Rossellino, and a tondo by the same master representing the Adoration of the Shepherds; Andrea Verrocchio's Madonna and Child; Verrocchio's Lady with the Bouquet (181), with those exquisite hands of which Gabriele D'Annunzio has almost wearied the readers of his *Gioconda*; by Matteo Civitali of Lucca, Faith gazing ecstatically upon the Sacrament. By Mino da Fiesole are a Madonna and Child, and several portrait busts—of the elder Piero dei Medici (234) and his brother Giovanni di Cosimo (236), and of Rinaldo della

Luna. We should also notice the statues of Christ and three Apostles, of the school of Andrea Pisano; portrait of a girl by Desiderio da Settignano; two bas-reliefs by Luca della Robbia, representing the Liberation and Crucifixion of St. Peter, early works executed for a chapel in the Duomo; two sixteenth century busts, representing the younger Giuliano dei Medici and Giovanni delle Bande Nere; and, also, a curious fourteenth century group (222) apparently representing the coronation of an emperor by the Pope's legate.

In the centre of the room are St. John Baptist by Benedetto da Maiano; Bacchus, by Jacopo Sansovino; and Michelangelo's second David (224), frequently miscalled Apollo, made for Baccio Valori after the siege of Florence, and pathetically different from the gigantic David of his youth, which had been chiselled more than a quarter of a century before, in all the passing glory of the Republican restoration.

When the Duke of Athens made himself tyrant of Florence, King Robert urged him to take up his abode in this palace, as Charles of Calabria had done, and leave the Palace of the People to the Priors. The advice was not taken, and, when the rising broke out, the palace was easily captured, before the Duke and his adherents in the Palazzo Vecchio were forced to surrender. Passing along the Via Ghibellina, we presently come on the right to what was originally the *Stinche*, a prison for nobles, *in qua carcerentur et custodiantur magnates*, so called from a castle of the Cavalcanti captured by the Neri in 1304, from which the prisoners were imprisoned here: it is now a part of the Teatro Pagliano. Later it became the place of captivity of the lowest criminals, and a first point of attack in risings of the populace. It contains, in a lunette on the stairs, a contemporary fresco representing the expulsion of the Duke of Athens on St. Anne's Day, 1343. St. Anne is giving the banners of the People and of the Commune to a group of stern Republican warriors, while with one hand she indicates the Palace of the Priors, fortified with the tyrant's towers and battlements. By its side rises a great throne, from which the Duke is shrinking in terror from the Angel of the wrath of God; a broken sword lies at his feet; the banner of Brienne lies dishonoured in the dust, with the scales of justice that he profaned and the book of the law that he outraged. In so solemn and chastened a spirit could the artists of the Trecento conceive of their Republic's deliverance. The fresco was probably painted by either Giottino or Maso di Banco; it was once wrongly ascribed to Cennino Cennini, who wrote the *Treatise on Painting*, which was the approved text-book in the studios and workshops of the earlier masters.

Further down the Via Ghibellina is the Casa Buonarroti, which once belonged to Michelangelo, and was bequeathed by his family to the city. It is entirely got up as a museum now, and not in the least suggestive of the great artist's life, though a tiny little study and a few letters and other relics are shown. There are, however, a certain number of his drawings here, including a design for the façade of San Lorenzo, which is of very questionable authenticity, and a Madonna. Two of his earliest works in marble are preserved here, executed at that epoch of his youth when he frequented the house and garden of Lorenzo the Magnificent. One is a bas-relief of the Madonna and Child–somewhat in the manner of Donatello–with two Angels at the top of a ladder. The other is a struggle of the Centaurs and Lapithae, a subject suggested to the boy by Angelo Poliziano, full of motion and vigour and wonderfully modelled. Vasari says, "To whoso considers this work, it does not seem from the hand of a youth, but from that of an accomplished and past master in these studies, and experienced in the art." The former is in the fifth room, the latter in the antechamber. There are also two models for the great David; a bust of the master in bronze by Ricciarelli, and his portrait by his pupil, Marcello Venusti. A predella representing the legend of St. Nicholas is by Francesco Pesellino, whose works are rare. In the third room (among the later allegories and scenes from the master's life) is a large picture supposed to have been painted by Jacopo da Empoli from a cartoon by Michelangelo, representing the Holy Family with the four Evangelists; it is a peculiarly unattractive work. The cartoon, ascribed to Michelangelo, is in the British Museum; and I would suggest that it was originally not a religious picture at all, but an allegory of Charity. The cross in the little Baptist's hand does not occur in the cartoon.

Almost at the end of the Via Ghibellina are the Prisons which occupy the site of the famous convent of *Le Murate*. In this convent Caterina Sforza, the dethroned Lady of Forlì and mother of Giovanni delle Bande Nere, ended her days in 1509. Here the Duchessina, or "Little Duchess," as Caterina dei Medici was called, was placed by the Signoria after the expulsion of the Medici in 1527, in order to prevent Pope Clement VII. from using her for the purpose of a political marriage which might endanger the city. They seem to have feared especially the Prince of Orange. The result was that the convent became a centre of Medicean intrigue; and the Signoria, when the siege commenced, sent Salvestro Aldobrandini to take her away. When Salvestro arrived, after he had been kept waiting for some time, the little Duchess came to the grill of the parlour, dressed as a nun, and said that she intended to take the habit and stay for ever "with these my reverend mothers." According to Varchi, the poor little girl–she was barely eleven years old, had lost both parents in the year of her birth, and was practically alone in the city where the cruellest threats had been uttered against her—was terribly frightened and cried bitterly, "not knowing to what glory and felicity her life had been reserved by God and the Heavens." But Messer Salvestro and Messer Antonio de' Nerli did all they could to comfort and reassure her, and took her to the convent of Santa Lucia in the Via di San Gallo; "in which monastery," says Nardi, "she was received and treated with the same maternal love by those nuns, until the end of the war."

In the centre of the oblong Piazza di Santa Croce rises the statue and monument of Dante Alighieri, erected on the occasion of the sixth centenary of his birth, in those glowing early days of the first completion of Italian unity; at its back stand the great Gothic church and convent, which Arnolfo di Cambio commenced for the Franciscans in 1294, while Dante was still in Florence—the year before he entered political life.

The great Piazza was a centre of festivities and stirring Florentine life, and has witnessed many historical scenes, in old times and in new, from the tournaments and jousts of the Middle Ages and early Renaissance to the penitential processions of the victims of the Inquisition in the days of the Medicean Grand Dukes, from the preaching of San Bernardino of Siena to the missionary labours of the Jesuit Segneri. On Christmas Day, 1301, Niccolò dei Cerchi was passing through this Piazza with a few friends on horseback on his way to his farm and mill–for that was hardly a happy Christmas for Guelfs of the white faction in Florence–while a friar was preaching in the open air, announcing the birth of Christ to the crowd; when Simone Donati with a band of mounted retainers gave chase, and, when he overtook him, killed him. In the scuffle Simone himself received a mortal wound, of which he died the same night. "Although it was a just judgment," writes Villani, "yet was it held a great loss, for the said Simone was the most accomplished and virtuous squire in Florence, and of the greatest promise, and he was all the hope of his father, Messer Corso." It was in the convent of Santa Croce that the Duke of Athens took up his abode in 1342, with much parade of religious simplicity, when about to seize upon the lordship of Florence; here, on that fateful September 8th, he assembled his followers and adherents in the Piazza, whence they marched to the Parliament at the Palazzo Vecchio, where he was proclaimed Signor of Florence for life. But in the following year, when he attempted to celebrate Easter with great pomp and luxury, and held grand jousts in this same Piazza for many days, the people sullenly held aloof and very few citizens entered the lists.

Most gorgeous and altogether successful was the tournament given here by Lorenzo dei Medici in 1467, to celebrate his approaching marriage with Clarice Orsini, when he jousted against all comers in honour of the lady of his sonnets and odes, Lucrezia Donati. There was not much serious tilting about it, but a magnificent display of rich costumes and precious jewelled caps and helmets, and a glorious procession which must have been a positive feast of colour. "To follow the custom," writes Lorenzo himself, "and do like others, I gave a tournament on the Piazza Santa Croce at great cost and with much magnificence; I find that about 10,000 ducats were spent on it. Although I was not a very vigorous warrior, nor a hard hitter, the first prize was adjudged to me, a helmet inlaid with silver and a figure of Mars as the crest."[36] He sent a long account of the proceedings to his future bride, who answered: "I am glad that you are successful in what gives you pleasure, and that my prayer is heard, for I have no other wish than to see you happy." Luca Pulci, the luckless brother of Luigi, wrote a dull poem on the not very inspiring theme. A few years later, at the end of January 1478, a less sumptuous entertainment of the same sort was given by Giuliano dei Medici; and it was apparently on this occasion that Poliziano commenced his famous stanzas in honour of Giuliano and his lady love, Simonetta,–stanzas which were interrupted by the daggers of the Pazzi and their accomplices. It was no longer time for soft song or courtly sport when prelates and nobles were hanging from the palace windows, and the thunders of the Papal interdict were about to burst over the city and her rulers.

Entering the Church through the unpleasing modern façade (which is, however, said to have followed the design of Cronaca himself, the architect of the exceedingly graceful convent of San Salvadore al Monte on the other side of the river), we catch a glow of colour from the east end, from the stained glass and frescoes in the choir. The vast and spacious nave of Arnolfo–like his Palazzo Vecchio, partly spoiled by Vasari–ends rather abruptly in the line of ten chapels with, in the midst of them, one very high recess which represents the apse and choir, thus giving the whole the T shape which we find in the Italian Gothic churches which were reared for the friars preachers and friars minor. The somewhat unsightly appearance, which many churches of this kind present in Italy, is due to the fact that Arnolfo and his school intended every inch of wall to be covered with significant fresco paintings, and this coloured decoration was seldom completely carried out, or has perished in the course of time. Fergusson remarks that "an Italian Church without its coloured decoration is only a framed canvas without harmony or meaning."

Santa Croce is, in the words of the late Dean of Westminster, "the recognised shrine of Italian genius." On the pavement beneath our feet, outstretched on their tombstones, lie effigies of grave Florentine citizens, friars of note, prelates, scholars, warriors; in their robes of state or of daily life, in the Franciscan garb or in armour, with arms folded across their breasts, or still clasping the books they loved and wrote (in this way the humanists, such as Leonardo Bruni, were laid out in state after death); the knights have their swords by their sides, which they had wielded in defence of the Republic, and their hands clasped in prayer. Here they lie, waiting the resurrection. Has any echo of the Risorgimento reached them? In their long sleep, have they dreamed aught of the movement that has led Florence to raise tablets to the names of Cavour and Mazzini upon these walls? The tombs on the floor of the nave are mostly of the fourteenth and fifteenth centuries; the second from the central door is that of Galileo dei Galilei, like the other scholars lying with his hands folded across the book on his breast, the ancestor of the immortal astronomer: "This Galileo of the Galilei was, in his time, the head of philosophy and medicine; who also in the highest magistracy loved the Republic marvellously." About the middle of the nave is the tomb of John Catrick, Bishop of Exeter, who had come to Florence on an embassy from Henry V. of England to Pope Martin V., in 1419. But those on the floor at the end of the right aisle and in the short right transept are the earliest and most interesting to the lover of early Florentine history; notice, for instance, the knightly tomb of a warrior of the great Ghibelline house of the Ubaldini, dated 1358, at the foot of the steps to the chapel at the end of the right transept; and there is a similar one, only less fine, on the opposite side. Larger and more pretentious tombs and monuments of more recent date, to the heroes of Italian life and thought, pass in series along the side walls of the whole church, between the altars of the south and north (right and left) aisles.

The Story of Florence

SANTA CROCE

Over the central door, below the window whose stained glass is said to have been designed by Ghiberti, is Donatello's bronze statue of King Robert's canonised brother, the Franciscan Bishop St. Louis of Toulouse. This St. Louis, the patron saint of the Parte Guelfa, had been ordered by the captains of the Party for their niche at San Michele in Orto, from which he was irreverently banished shortly after the restoration of Cosimo dei Medici, when the Parte Guelfa was forced to surrender its niche. On the left of the entrance should be noticed with gratitude the tomb of the historian of the Florentine Republic, the Italian patriot, Gino Capponi.

In the right aisle are the tomb and monument of Michelangelo, designed by Giorgio Vasari; on the pillar opposite to it, over the holy water stoop, a beautiful Madonna and Child in marble by Bernardo Rossellino, beneath which lies Francesco Nori, who was murdered whilst defending Lorenzo dei Medici in the Pazzi conspiracy; the comparatively modern monument to Dante, whose bones rest at Ravenna and for whom Michelangelo had offered in vain to raise a worthy sepulchre. Two sonnets by the great sculptor supply to some extent in verse what he was not suffered to do in marble: I quote the finer of the two, from Addington Symonds' excellent translation:–

From Heaven his spirit came, and, robed in clay,
The realms of justice and of mercy trod:

> Then rose a living man to gaze on God,
> That he might make the truth as clear as day.
> For that pure star, that brightened with its ray
> The undeserving nest where I was born,
> The whole wide world would be a prize to scorn:
> None but his Maker can due guerdon pay.
> I speak of Dante, whose high work remains
> Unknown, unhonoured by that thankless brood
> Who only to just men deny their wage.
> Were I but he! Born for like lingering pains,
> Against his exile coupled with his good
> I'd gladly change the world's best heritage.

Then comes Canova's monument to Vittorio Alfieri, the great tragic dramatist of Italy (died 1803); followed by an eighteenth century monument to Machiavelli (died 1527), and the tomb of Padre Lanzi, the Jesuit historian of Italian art. The pulpit by a pillar in the nave is considered the most beautiful pulpit in Italy, and is, perhaps, Benedetto da Maiano's finest work; the bas-reliefs in marble represent scenes from the life of St. Francis and the martyrdom of some of his friars, with figures of the virtues below. Beyond Padre Lanzi's grave, over the tomb of the learned Franciscan Fra Benedetto Cavalcanti, are two exceedingly powerful figures of saints in fresco, the Baptist and St. Francis; they have been ascribed to various painters, but are almost certainly the work of Domenico Veneziano, and closely resemble the figures of the same saints in his undoubtedly genuine picture in the Sala di Lorenzo Monaco in the Uffizi. The adjacent Annunciation by Donatello, in *pietra serena*, was also made for the Cavalcanti; its fine Renaissance architectural setting is likewise Donatello's work. Above it are four lovely wooden Putti, who seem embracing each other for fear of tumbling off from their height; originally there were six, and the other two are preserved in the convent. M. Reymond has shown that this Annunciation is not an early work of the master's, as Vasari and others state, but is of the same style and period as the Cantoria of the Duomo, about 1435. Lastly, at the end of the right aisle is the splendid tomb of Leonardo Bruni (died 1444), secretary of the Republic, translator of Plato, historian of Florence, biographer of Dante,–the outstretched recumbent figure of the grand old humanist, watched over by Mary and her Babe with the Angels, by Bernardo Rossellino. A worthy monument to a noble soul, whose memory is dear to every lover of Dante. Yet we may, not without advantage, contrast it with the simpler Gothic sepulchres on the floor of the transepts,–the marble slabs that cover the bones of the old Florentines who, in war and peace, did the deeds of which Leonardo and his kind wrote.

The tombs and monuments in the left aisle are less interesting. Opposite Leonardo Bruni's tomb is that of his successor, Carlo Marsuppini, called Carlo Aretino (died 1453), by Desiderio da Settignano; he was a good Greek scholar, a fluent orator and a professed Pagan, but accomplished no literary work of any value; utterly inferior as a man and as an author to Leonardo, he has an even more gorgeous tomb. In this aisle there are modern monuments to Vespasiano Bisticci and Donatello; and, opposite to Michelangelo's tomb, that of Galileo himself (died 1642), with traces of old fourteenth century frescoes round it, which may, perhaps, symbolise for us the fleeting phantoms of mediæval thought fading away before the advance of science.

In the central chapel of the left or northern transept is the famous wooden Crucifix by Donatello, which gave rise to the fraternal contest between him and Brunelleschi. Brunelleschi told his friend that he had put upon his cross a contadino and not a figure like that of Christ. "Take some wood then," answered the nettled sculptor, "and try to make one thyself." Filippo did so; and when it was finished Donatello was so stupefied with admiration, that he let drop all the eggs and other things that he was carrying for their dinner. "I have had all I want for to-day," he exclaimed; "if you want your share, take it: to thee is it given to carve Christs and to me to make contadini." The rival piece may still be seen in Santa Maria Novella, and there is not much to choose between them. Donatello's is, perhaps, somewhat more realistic and less refined.

The first two chapels of the left transept (fifth and fourth from the choir, respectively,) contain fourteenth century frescoes; a warrior of the Bardi family rising to judgment, the healing of Constantine's leprosy and other miracles of St. Sylvester, ascribed to Maso di Banco; the martyrdom of St. Lawrence and the martyrdom of St. Stephen, by Bernardo Daddi (the painter to whom it is attempted to ascribe the famous Last Judgment and Triumph of Death in the Pisan Campo Santo). All these imply a certain Dantesque selection; these subjects are among the examples quoted for purposes of meditation or admonition in the *Divina Commedia*. The coloured terracotta relief is by Giovanni della Robbia. The frescoes of the choir, by Agnolo Gaddi, are among the finest works of Giotto's school. They set forth the history of the wood of the True Cross, which, according to the legend, was a shoot of the tree of Eden planted by Seth on Adam's grave; the Queen of Sheba prophetically adored it, when she came to visit Solomon during the building of the Temple; cast into the pool of Bethsaida, the Jews dragged it out to make the Cross for Christ; then, after it had been buried on Mount Calvary for three centuries, St. Helen discovered it by its power of raising the dead to life. These subjects are set forth on the right wall; on the left, we have the taking of the relic of the Cross by the Persians under Chosroes, and its recovery by the Emperor Heraclius. In the scene where the Emperor barefooted carries the Cross into Jerusalem, the painter has introduced his own portrait, near one of the gates of the city, with a small beard and a red hood. Vasari thinks poorly of these frescoes; but the legend of the True Cross is of some importance to the student of Dante, whose profound allegory of the Church and Empire in the Earthly Paradise, at the close of the *Purgatorio*, is to some extent based upon it.

The two Gothic chapels to the right of the choir contain Giotto's frescoes—both chapels were originally entirely painted by him—rescued from the whitewash under which they were discovered, and, in part at least, most terribly "restored." The frescoes in the first, the Bardi Chapel, illustrating the life of St. Francis, have suffered most; all the peculiar Giottesque charm of face has disappeared, and, instead, the restorer has given us monotonous countenances, almost deadly in their uniformity and utter lack of expression. Like all mediæval frescoes dealing with St. Francis, they should be read with the *Fioretti* or with Dante's *Paradiso*, or with one of the old lives of the Seraphic Father in our hands. On the left (beginning at the top) we have his renunciation of the world in the presence of his father and the Bishop of Assisi—*innanzi alla sua spirital corte, et coram patre*, as Dante puts it; on the right, the confirmation of the order by Pope Honorius; on the left, the apparition of St. Francis to St. Antony of Padua; on the right, St. Francis and his followers before the Soldan—*nella presenza del Soldan superba*—in the ordeal of fire; and, below it, St. Francis on his death-bed, with the apparition to the sleeping bishop to assure him of the truth of the Stigmata. Opposite, left, the body is surrounded by weeping friars, the incredulous judge touching the wound in the side, while the simplest of the friars, at the saint's head, sees his soul carried up to heaven in a little cloud. This conception of saintly death was, perhaps, originally derived from Dante's dream of Beatrice in the *Vita Nuova*: "I seemed to look towards heaven, and to behold a multitude of Angels who were returning upwards, having before them an exceedingly white cloud; and these Angels were singing together gloriously." It became traditional in early Italian painting. On the window wall are four great Franciscans. St. Louis the King (one whom Dante does not seem to have held in honour), a splendid figure, calm and noble, in one hand the sceptre and in the other the Franciscan cord, his royal robe besprinkled with the golden lily of France over the armour of the warrior of the Cross; his face absorbed in celestial contemplation. He is the Christian realisation of the Platonic philosopher king; "St. Louis," says Walter Pater, "precisely because his whole being was full of heavenly vision, in self banishment from it for a while, led and ruled the French people so magnanimously alike in peace and war." Opposite him is St. Louis of Toulouse, with the royal crown at his feet; below are St. Elizabeth of Hungary, with her lap full of flowers; and, opposite to her, St. Clare, of whom Dante's Piccarda tells so sweetly in the

Paradiso–that lady on high whom "perfected life and lofty merit doth enheaven." On the vaulted roof of the chapel are the glory of St. Francis and symbolical representations of the three vows–Poverty, Chastity, Obedience; not rendered as in Giotto's great allegories at Assisi, of which these are, as it were, his own later simplifications, but merely as the three mystical Angels that met Francis and his friars on the road to Siena, crying "Welcome, Lady Poverty." The picture of St. Francis on the altar, ascribed by Vasari to Cimabue, is probably by some unknown painter at the close of the thirteenth century.

The frescoes in the following, the Chapel of the Peruzzi, are very much better preserved, especially in the scene of Herod's feast. Like all Giotto's genuine work, they are eloquent in their pictorial simplicity of diction; there are no useless crowds of spectators, as in the later work of Ghirlandaio and his contemporaries. On the left is the life of St. John the Baptist–the Angel appearing to Zacharias, the birth and naming of the Precursor, the dance of the daughter of Herodias at Herod's feast. This last has suffered less from restoration than any other work of Giotto's in Florence; both the rhythmically moving figure of the girl herself and that of the musician are very beautiful, and the expression on Herod's face is worthy of the psychological insight of the author of the Vices and Virtues in the Madonna's chapel at Padua. Ruskin talks of "the striped curtain behind the table being wrought with a variety and fantasy of playing colour which Paul Veronese could not better at his best." On the right wall is the life of the Evangelist, John the Divine, or rather its closing scenes; the mystical vision at Patmos, the seer *dormendo con la faccia arguta*, like the solitary elder who brought up the rear of the triumphal pageant in Dante's Earthly Paradise; the raising of Drusiana from the dead; the assumption of St. John. The curious legend represented in this last fresco–that St. John was taken up body and soul, *con le due stole*, into Heaven after death, and that his disciples found his tomb full of manna–was, of course, based upon the saying that went abroad among the brethren, "that that disciple should not die"; it is mentioned as a pious belief by St. Thomas, but is very forcibly repudiated by Giotto's great friend, Dante; in the *Paradiso* St. John admonishes him to tell the world that only Christ and the Blessed Virgin rose from the dead. "In the earth my body is earth, and shall be there with the others, until our number be equalled with the eternal design."

In the last chapel of the south transept, there are two curious frescoes apparently of the beginning of the fourteenth century, in honour of St. Michael; they represent his leading the Angelic hosts against the forces of Lucifer, and the legend of his apparition at Monte Gargano. The frescoes in the chapel at the end of the transept, the Baroncelli chapel, representing scenes in the life of the Blessed Virgin, are by

Giotto's pupil, Taddeo Gaddi; they are similar to his work at Assisi. The Assumption opposite was painted by Sebastiano Mainardi from a cartoon by Domenico Ghirlandaio. In the Chapel of the Blessed Sacrament there are more frescoed lives of saints by Taddeo's son, Agnolo Gaddi, less admirable than his work in the choir; and statues of two Franciscans, of the Della Robbia school. The monument of the Countess of Albany may interest English admirers of the Stuarts, but hardly concerns the story of Florence.

From the right transept a corridor leads off to the chapel of the Noviciate and the Sacristy. The former, built by Michelozzo for Cosimo, contains some beautiful terracotta work of the school of the Della Robbia, a tabernacle by Mino da Fiesole, and a Coronation of the Blessed Virgin ascribed to Giotto. This Coronation was originally the altar piece of the Baroncelli chapel, and is an excellent picture, although its authenticity is not above suspicion; the signature is almost certainly a forgery; this title of *Magister* was Giotto's pet aversion, as we know from Boccaccio, and he never used it. Opening out of the Sacristy is a chapel, decorated with beautiful frescoes of the life of the Blessed Virgin and St. Mary Magdalene, now held to be the work of Taddeo Gaddi's Lombard pupil, Giovanni da Milano. There is, as has already been said, very little individuality in the work of Giotto's followers, but these frescoes are among the best of their kind.

The first Gothic cloisters belong to the epoch of the foundation of the church, and were probably designed by Arnolfo himself; the second, early Renaissance, are Brunelleschi's. The Refectory, which is entered from the first cloisters, contains a fresco of the Last Supper—one of the earliest renderings of this theme for monastic dining-rooms—which used to be assigned to Giotto, and is probably by one of his scholars. This room had the invidious honour of being the seat of the Inquisition, which in Florence had always—save for a very brief period in the thirteenth century—been in the hands of the Franciscans, and not the Dominicans. It never had any real power in Florence—the *bel viver fiorentino*, which, even in the days of tyranny, was always characteristic of the city, was opposed to its influence. The beautiful chapel of the Pazzi was built by Brunelleschi; its frieze of Angels' heads is by Donatello and Desiderio; within are Luca della Robbia's Apostles and Evangelists. Jacopo Pazzi had headed the conspiracy against the Medici in 1478, and, after attempting to raise the people, had been captured in his escape, tortured and hanged. It was said that he had cried in dying that he gave his soul to the devil; he was certainly a notorious gambler and blasphemer. When buried here, the peasants believed that he brought a curse upon their crops; so the rabble dug him up, dragged the body through the streets, and finally with every conceivable indignity threw it into the Arno.

Behind Santa Croce two streets of very opposite names and traditions meet, the *Via Borgo Allegri* (which also intersects the Via Ghibellina) and the *Via dei Malcontenti*; the former records the legendary birthday of Italian painting, the latter the mournful processions of poor wretches condemned to death.

According to the tradition, Giovanni Cimabue had his studio in the former street, and it was here that, in Dante's words, he thought to hold the field in painting: *Credette Cimabue nella pittura tener lo campo.* Here, according to Vasari, he was visited by Charles the Elder of Anjou, and his great Madonna carried hence in procession with music and lighted candles, ringing of bells and waving of banners, to Santa Maria Novella; while the street that had witnessed such a miracle was ever after called *Borgo Allegri*, "the happy suburb:" "named the Glad Borgo from that beauteous face," as Elizabeth Barrett Browning puts it. Unfortunately there are several little things that show that this story needs revision of some kind. When Charles of Anjou came to Florence, the first stone of Santa Maria Novella had not yet been laid, and the picture now shown there as Cimabue's appears to be a Sienese work. The legend, however, is very precious, and should be devoutly held. The king in question was probably another Angevin Charles–Carlo Martello, grandson of the elder Charles and titular King of Hungary, Dante's friend, who was certainly in Florence for nearly a month in the spring of 1295, and made himself exceedingly pleasant. Vasari has made a similar confusion in the case of two emperors of the name of Frederick. The picture has doubtless perished, but the Joyous Borgo has not changed its name.

The Via dei Malcontenti leads out into the broad Viale Carlo Alberto, which marks the site of Arnolfo's wall. It formerly ended in a postern gate, known as the Porta della Giustizia, beyond which was a little chapel–of which no trace is left–and the place where the gallows stood. The condemned were first brought to a chapel which stood in the Via dei Malcontenti, near the present San Giuseppe, and then taken out to the chapel beyond the gate, where the prayers for the dying were said over them by the friars, after which they were delivered to the executioner.[37] In May 1503, as Simone Filipepi tells us, a man was beheaded here, whom the people apparently regarded as innocent; when he was dead, they rose up and stoned the executioner to death. And this was the same executioner who, five years before, had hanged Savonarola and his companions in the Piazza, and had insulted their dead bodies to please the dregs of the populace. The tower, of which the mutilated remains still stand here, the *Torre della Zecca Vecchia*, formerly called the *Torre Reale*, was originally a part of the defences of a bridge which it was intended to build here in honour of King Robert of Naples in 1317, and guarded the Arno at this point. After the siege, during which the Porta della Giustizia was walled up, Duke Alessandro incorporated the then lofty Torre Reale into a strong fortress which he constructed here, the Fortezza Vecchia. In later days, offices connected with the Arte del Cambio and the Mint were established in its place, whence the present name of the Torre della Zecca Vecchia.

OLD HOUSES ON THE ARNO

CHAPTER VIII.

THE BAPTISTERY, THE CAMPANILE, AND THE DUOMO

"There the traditions of faith and hope, of both the Gentile and Jewish races, met for their beautiful labour: the Baptistery of Florence is the last building raised on the earth by the descendants of the workmen taught by Dædalus: and the Tower of Giotto is the loveliest of those raised on earth under the inspiration of the men who lifted up the tabernacle in the wilderness. Of living Greek work there is none after the Florentine Baptistery; of living Christian work, none so perfect as the Tower of Giotto."–*Ruskin.*

"Il non mai abbastanza lodato tempio di Santa Maria del Fiore."–*Vasari.*

TO the west of the Piazza del Duomo stands the octagonal building of black and white marble–"*l'antico vostro Batisteo*" as Cacciaguida calls it to Dante–which, in one shape or another, may be said to have watched over the history of Florence from the beginning. "It is," says Ruskin, "the central building of Etrurian Christianity–of European Christianity." Here, in old pagan times, stood the Temple of Mars, with the shrine and sanctuary of the God of War. This was the Cathedral of Florence during a portion at least of the early history of the Republic, before the great Gothic building rose that now overshadows it to the east.

Villani and other early writers all suppose that this present building really was the original Temple of Mars, converted into a church for St. John the Baptist. Villani tells us that, after the founding of Florence by Julius Cæsar and other noble Romans, the citizens of this new Rome decided to erect a marvellous temple to the honour of Mars, in thanksgiving for the victory which the Romans had won over the city of Fiesole; and for this purpose the Senate sent them the best and most subtle masters that there were in Rome. Black and white marble was brought by sea and then up the Arno, with columns of various sizes; stone and other columns were taken from Fiesole, and the temple was erected in the place where the Etruscans of Fiesole had once held their market:–

"Right noble and beauteous did they make it with eight faces, and when they had done it with great diligence, they consecrated it to their god Mars, who was the god of the Romans; and they had him carved in marble, in the shape of a knight armed on horseback. They set him upon a marble column in the midst of that temple, and him did they hold in great reverence and adored as their god, what time Paganism lasted in Florence. And we find that the said temple was commenced at the time that Octavian Augustus reigned, and that it was erected under the ascendency of such a constellation that it will last well nigh to eternity."

There is much difference of opinion as to the real date of construction of the present building. While some authorities have assigned it to the eleventh or even to the twelfth century, others have supposed that it is either a Christian temple constructed in the sixth century on the site of the old Temple of Mars, or the original Temple converted into Christian use. It has indeed been recently urged that it is essentially a genuine Roman work of the fourth century, very analogous in structure to the Pantheon at Rome, on the model of which it was probably built. The little apse to the south-west–the part which contains the choir and altar–is certainly of the twelfth century. There was originally a round opening at the centre of the dome–like the Pantheon–and under this opening, according to Villani, the statue of Mars stood. It was closed in the twelfth century. The dome served Brunelleschi as a model for the cupola of Santa Maria del Fiore. The lantern was added in the sixteenth century. Although this building, so sacrosanct to the Florentines, had been spared by the Goths and Lombards, it narrowly escaped destruction at the hands of the Tuscan Ghibellines. In 1249, when the Ghibellines, with the aid of the Emperor Frederick II., had expelled the Guelfs, the conquerors endeavoured to destroy the Baptistery by means of the tower called the Guardamorto, which stood in the Piazza towards the entrance of the Corso degli Adimari, and watched over the tombs of the dead citizens who were buried round San Giovanni. This device of making the tower fall upon the church failed. "As it pleased God," writes Villani, "through the reverence and miraculous power of the blessed John, the tower, when it fell, manifestly avoided the holy Church, and turned back and fell across the Piazza; whereat all the Florentines wondered, and the People greatly rejoiced."

At the close of the thirteenth century, in those golden days of Dante's youth and early manhood, there were steps leading up to the church, and it was surrounded by these tombs. Many of the latter seem to have been old pagan sarcophagi adopted for use by the Florentine aristocracy. Here Guido Cavalcanti used to wander in his solitary musings and speculations–trying to find out that there was no God, as his friends charitably suggested–and Boccaccio tells a most delightful story of a friendly encounter between him and some young Florentine nobles, who objected to his unsociable habits. In 1293, Arnolfo di Cambio levelled the Piazza, removed the tombs, and plastered the pilasters in the angles of the octagonal with slabs of black and white marble of Prato, as now we see. The similar decoration of the eight faces of the church is much earlier.

The interior is very dark indeed–so dark that the mosaics, which Dante must in part have looked upon, would need a very bright day to be visible. At present they are almost completely concealed by the scaffolding of the restorers.[38] Over the whole church preside the two Saints whom an earlier Florentine worshipper of Mars could least have comprehended–the Baptist and the Magdalene. And the spirit of Dante haunts it as he does no other Florentine building–*il mio bel San Giovanni*, he lovingly calls it. "In your ancient Baptistery," his ancestor tells him in the fifteenth Canto of the *Paradiso*, "I became at once a Christian and Cacciaguida." And, indeed, the same holds true of countless generations of Florentines–among them the keenest intellects and most subtle hands that the world has known– all baptised here. But it has memories of another kind. The shameful penance of oblation to St. John–if Boccaccio's tale be true, and if the letter ascribed to Dante is authentic–was rejected by him; but many another Florentine, with bare feet and lighted candle, has entered here as a prisoner in penitential garb. The present font–although of early date– was placed here in the seventeenth century, to replace the very famous one which played so large a part in Dante's thoughts. Here had he been baptised–here, in one of the most pathetic passages of the *Paradiso*, did he yearn, before death came, to take the laurel crown:–

> Se mai continga che il poema sacro,
> al quale ha posto mano e cielo e terra,
> sì che m'ha fatto per più anni macro,

> vinca la crudeltà, che fuor mi serra
> del bello ovil, dov'io dormii agnello,
> nimico ai lupi che gli danno guerra;
> con altra voce omai, con altro vello
> ritornerò poeta, ed in sul fonte
> del mio battesmo prenderò il cappello;
> però che nella Fede, che fa conte
> l'anime a Dio, quivi entra' io.[39]

This ancient font, which stood in the centre of the church, appears to have had round holes or *pozzetti* in its outer wall, in which the priests stood to baptise; and Dante tells us in the *Inferno* that he broke one of these *pozzetti*, to save a boy from being drowned or suffocated. The boy saved was apparently not being baptised, but was playing about with others, and had either tumbled into the font itself or climbed head foremost into one of the *pozzetti*. When the divine poet was exiled, charitable people said that he had done this from heretical motives—just as they had looked with suspicion upon his friend Guido's spiritual wanderings in the same locality.

THE BAPTISTERY

Though the old font has gone, St. John, to the left of the high altar, still keeps watch over all the Florentine children brought to be baptised–to be made *conti*, known to God, and to himself in God. Opposite to him is the great type of repentance after baptism, St. Mary Magdalene, a wooden statue by Donatello. What a contrast is here with those pagan Magdalenes of the Renaissance–such as Titian and Correggio painted! Fearfully wasted and haggard, this terrible figure of asceticism–when once the first shock of repulsion is got over–is unmistakably a masterpiece of the sculptor; it is as though one of the Penitential Psalms had taken bodily shape.

On the other side of the church stands the tomb of the dethroned Pope, John XXIII., Baldassarre Cossa, one of the earliest works in the Renaissance style, reared by Michelozzo and Donatello, 1424-1427, for Cosimo dei Medici. The fallen Pontiff rests at last in peace in the city which had witnessed his submission to his successful rival, Martin V., and which had given a home to his closing days; here he lies, forgetful of councils and cardinals:–

"After life's fitful fever he sleeps well."

The recumbent figure in bronze is the work of Donatello, as also the Madonna and Child that guard his last slumber. Below, are Faith, Hope, and Charity–the former by Michelozzo (to whom also the architectural part of the monument is due), the two latter by Donatello. It is said that Pope Martin V. objected to the inscription, "quondam papa," and was answered in the words of Pilate: *quod scripsi, scripsi.*

But the glory of the Baptistery is in its three bronze gates, the finest triumph of bronze casting. On November 6th, 1329, the consuls of the Arte di Calimala, who had charge of the works of San Giovanni, ordained that their doors should be of metal and as beautiful as possible. The first of the three, now the southern gate opposite the Bigallo (but originally the *porta di mezzo* opposite the Duomo), was assigned by them to Andrea Pisano on January 9th, 1330; he made the models in the same year, as the inscription on the gate itself shows; the casting was finished in 1336. Vasari's statement that Giotto furnished the designs for Andrea is now entirely discredited. These gates set before us, in twenty-eight reliefs, twenty scenes from the life of the Baptist with eight symbolical virtues below–all set round with lions' heads. Those who know the work of the earlier Pisan masters, Niccolò and Giovanni, will at once perceive how completely Andrea has freed himself from the traditions of the school of Pisa; instead of filling the whole available space with figures on different planes and telling several stories at once, Andrea composes his relief of a few figures on the same plane, and leaves the background free. There are never any unnecessary figures or mere spectators; the bare essentials of the episode are set before us as simply as possible, whether it be Zacharias writing the name of John or the dance of the daughter of Herodias, which may well be compared with Giotto's frescoes in Santa Croce. Most perfect of all are the eight figures of the Virtues in the eight lower panels, and they should be compared with Giotto's allegories at Padua. We have Hope winged and straining upwards towards a crown, Faith with cross and sacramental cup, Charity and Prudence, above; Fortitude, Temperance and Justice below; and then, to complete the eight, Dante's favourite virtue, the maiden Humility. The Temperance, with Giotto and Andrea Pisano, is not the mere opposite of Gluttony, with pitcher of water and cup (as we may see her presently in Santa Maria Novella); but it is the cardinal virtue which, St. Thomas says, includes "any virtue whatsoever that puts in practice moderation in any matter, and restrains appetite in its tendency in any direction." Andrea Pisano's Temperance sits next to his Justice, with the sword and scales; she too has a sword, even as Justice has, but she is either sheathing it or drawing it with reluctance.

The lovely and luxuriant decorative frieze that runs round this portal was executed by Ghiberti's pupils in the middle of the fifteenth century. Over the gate is the beheading of St. John the Baptist—two second-rate figures by Vincenzo Danti.

The second or northern gate is more than three-quarters of a century later, and it is the result of that famous competition which opened the Quattrocento. It was assigned to Lorenzo Ghiberti in 1403, and he had with him his stepfather Bartolo di Michele, and other assistants (including possibly Donatello). It was finished and set up gilded in April 1424, at the main entry between the two porphyry columns, opposite the Duomo, whence Andrea's gate was removed. It will be observed that each new gate was first put in this place of honour, and then translated to make room for its better. The plan of Ghiberti's is similar to that of Andrea's gate—in fact it is his style of work brought to its ultimate perfection. Twenty-eight reliefs represent scenes from the New Testament, from the Annunciation to the Descent of the Holy Spirit, while in eight lower compartments are the four Evangelists and the four great Latin Doctors. The scene of the Temptation of the Saviour is particularly striking, and the figure of the Evangelist John, the Eagle of Christ, has the utmost grandeur. Over the door are three finely modelled figures representing St. John the Baptist disputing with a Levite and a Pharisee—or, perhaps, the Baptist between two Prophets—by Giovanni Francesco Rustici (1506-1511), a pupil of Verrocchio's, who appears to have been influenced by Leonardo da Vinci.

But in the third or eastern gate, opposite the Duomo, Ghiberti was to crown the whole achievement of his life. Mr Perkins remarks: "Had he never lived to make the second gates, which to the world in general are far superior to the first, he would have been known in history as a continuator of the school of Andrea Pisano, enriched with all those added graces which belonged to his own style, and those refinements of technique which the progress made in bronze casting had rendered perfect."[40] In the meantime the laws of perspective had been understood, and their science set forth by Brunelleschi; and when Ghiberti, on the completion of his first gates, was in January 1425 invited by the consuls of the Guild (amongst whom was the great anti-Medicean politician, Niccolò da Uzzano) to model the third doors, he was full of this new knowledge. "I strove," he says in his commentaries, "to imitate nature to the uttermost." The subjects were selected for him by Leonardo Bruni–ten stories from the Old Testament which, says Leonardo in his letter to Niccolò da Uzzano and his colleagues, "should have two things: first and chiefly, they must be illustrious; and secondly, they must be significant. Illustrious, I call those which can satisfy the eye with variety of design; significant, those which have importance worthy of memory." For the rest, their main instructions to him were that he should make the whole the richest, most perfect and most beauteous work imaginable, regardless of time and cost.

The work took more than twenty-five years. The stories were all modelled in wax by 1440, when the casting of the bronze commenced; the whole was finished in 1447, gilded in 1452–the gilding has happily worn off from all the gates– and finally set up in June 1452, in the place where Ghiberti's other gate had been. Among his numerous assistants were again his stepfather Bartolo, his son Vittorio, and, among the less important, the painters Paolo Uccello and Benozzo Gozzoli.

The result is a series of most magnificent pictures in bronze. Ghiberti worked upon his reliefs like a painter, and lavished all the newly-discovered scientific resources of the painter's art upon them. Whether legitimate sculpture or not, it is, beyond a doubt, one of the most beautiful things in the world. "I sought to understand," he says in his second commentary, that book which excited Vasari's scorn, "how forms strike upon the eye, and how the theoretic part of graphic and pictorial art should be managed. Working with the utmost diligence and care, I introduced into some of my compositions as many as a hundred figures, which I modelled upon different planes, so that those nearest the eye might appear larger, and those more remote smaller in proportion." It is a triumph of science wedded to the most exquisite sense of beauty. Each of the ten bas-reliefs contains several motives and an enormous number of these figures on different planes; which is, in a sense, going back from the simplicity of Andrea Pisano to glorify the old manner of Niccolò and Giovanni. In the first, the creation of man, the creation of woman, and the expulsion from Eden are seen; in the second, the sacrifice of Abel, in which the ploughing of Cain's oxen especially pleased Vasari; in the third, the story of Noah; in the fourth, the story of Abraham, a return to the theme in which Ghiberti had won his first laurels,–the three Angels appearing to Abraham have incomparable grace and loveliness, and the landscape in bronze is a marvel of skill. In the fifth and sixth, we have the stories of Jacob and Joseph, respectively; in the seventh and eighth, of Moses and Joshua; in the ninth and tenth, of David and Solomon. The latter is supposed to have been imitated by Raphael, in his famous fresco of the School of Athens in the Vatican. The architectural backgrounds–dream palaces endowed with permanent life in bronze–are as marvellous as the figures and landscapes. Hardly less beautiful are the minor ornaments that surround these masterpieces,–the wonderful decorative frieze of fruits and birds and beasts that frames the whole, the statuettes alternating with busts in the double border round the bas-reliefs. It is the ultimate perfection of decorative art. Among the statuettes a figure of Miriam, recalling an Angel of Angelico, is of peculiar loveliness. In the middle of the whole, in the centre at the lower corners of the Jacob and Joseph respectively, are portrait busts of

Lorenzo Ghiberti himself and Bartolo di Michele. Vasari has said the last word:–

"And in very truth can it be said that this work hath its perfection in all things, and that it is the most beautiful work of the world, or that ever was seen amongst ancients or moderns. And verily ought Lorenzo to be truly praised, seeing that one day Michelangelo Buonarroti, when he stopped to look at this work, being asked what he thought of it and if these gates were beautiful, replied: 'They are so beautiful that they would do well for the Gates of Paradise.' Praise verily proper, and spoken by one who could judge them."

The Baptism of Christ over the portal is an unattractive work by Andrea Sansovino (circa 1505), finished by Vincenzo Danti. The Angel is a seventeenth century addition. More interesting far, are the scorched porphyry columns on either side of the gate; these were part of the booty carried off by the Pisan galleys from Majorca in 1117, and presented to the Florentines in gratitude for their having guarded Pisa during the absence of the troops. Villani says that the Pisans offered their allies the choice between these porphyry columns and some metal gates, and that, on their choosing the columns, they sent them to Florence covered with scarlet, but that some said that they scorched them first for envy. It was between these columns that Cavalcanti was lingering and musing when the gay cavalcade of Betto Brunelleschi and his friends, in Boccaccio's novel, swooped down upon him through the Piazza di Santa Reparata: "Thou, Guido, wilt none of our fellowship; but lo now! when thou shalt have found that there is no God, what wilt thou have done?"

From the gate which might have stood at the doors of Paradise, or at least have guarded that sacred threshold by which Virgil and Dante entered Purgatory, we cross to the tower which might fittingly have sounded tierce and nones to the valley of the Princes. This "Shepherd's Tower," according to Ruskin, is "the model and mirror of perfect architecture." The characteristics of Power and Beauty, he writes in the *Seven Lamps of Architecture*, "occur more or less in different buildings, some in one and some in another. But all together, and all in their highest possible relative degrees, they exist, as far as I know, only in one building in the world, the Campanile of Giotto."

Like Ghiberti's bronze gates, this exquisitely lovely tower of marble has beauty beyond words: "That bright, smooth, sunny surface of glowing jasper, those spiral shafts and fairy traceries, so white, so faint, so crystalline, that their slight shapes are hardly traced in darkness on the pallor of the eastern sky, that serene height of mountain alabaster, coloured like a morning cloud, and chased like a sea-shell." It was commenced by Giotto himself in 1334, when the first stone was solemnly laid. When Giotto died in 1336, the work had probably not risen above the stage of the lower series of reliefs. Andrea Pisano was chosen to succeed him, and he carried it on from 1337 to 1342, finishing the first story and bringing it up to the first of the three stories of windows; it will be observed that Andrea, who was primarily a sculptor, unlike Giotto, made provision for the presence of large monumental statues as well as reliefs in his decorative scheme. Through some misunderstanding, Andrea was then deprived of the work, which was intrusted to Francesco Talenti. Francesco Talenti carried it on until 1387, making a general modification in the architecture and decoration; the three most beautiful windows, increasing in size as we ascend, with their beautiful Gothic tracery, are his work. According to Giotto's original plan, the whole was to have been crowned with a pyramidical steeple or spire; Vasari says that it was abandoned "because it was a German thing, and of antiquated fashion."

All around the base of the tower runs a wonderful series of bas-reliefs on a very small scale, setting forth the whole history of human skill under divine guidance, from the creation of man to the reign of art, science, and letters, in twenty-seven exquisitely "inlaid jewels of Giotto's." At each corner of the tower are three shields, the red Cross of the People between the red lilies of the Commune. "This smallness of scale," says Ruskin of these reliefs "enabled the master workmen of the tower to execute them with their own hands; and for the rest, in the very finest architecture, the decoration of the most precious kind is usually thought of as a jewel, and set with space round it—as the jewels of a crown, or the clasp of a girdle." These twenty-seven subjects, with the possible exception of the last five on the northern side, were designed by Giotto himself; and are, together with the first bronze door, the greatest Florentine work in sculpture of the first half of the fourteenth century. The execution is, in the main, Andrea Pisano's; but there is a constant tradition that some of the reliefs are from Giotto's own hand. Antonio Pucci, in the eighty-fifth canto of his *Centiloquio*, distinctly states that Giotto carved the earlier ones, *i primi intagli fe con bello stile*, and Pucci was almost Giotto's contemporary. "Pastoral life," "Jubal," "Tubal Cain," "Sculpture," "Painting," are the special subjects which it is most plausible, or perhaps most attractive, to ascribe to him.

On the western side we have the creation of Man, the creation of Woman; and then, thirdly, Adam and Eve toiling, or you may call it the dignity of labour, if you will—Giotto's rendering of the thought which John Ball was to give deadly meaning to, or ever the fourteenth century closed—

When Adam delved and Evë span,
Who was then the gentleman?

Then come pastoral life, Jabal with his tent, his flock and dog; Jubal, the maker of stringed and wind instruments;

Tubal Cain, the first worker in metal; the first vintage, represented by the story of Noah. On the southern side comes first Astronomy, represented by either Zoroaster or Ptolemy. Then follow Building, Pottery, Riding, Weaving, and (according to Ruskin) the Giving of Law. Lastly Daedalus, symbolising, according to Ruskin, "the conquest of the element of air"; or, more probably, here as in Dante (*Paradiso* viii.), the typical mechanician. Next, on the eastern side, comes Rowing, symbolising, according to Ruskin, "the conquest of the sea"–very possibly intended for Jason and the Argo, a type adopted in several places by Dante. The next relief, "the conquest of the earth," probably represents the slaying of Antæus by Hercules, and symbolises the "beneficent strength of civilisation, crushing the savageness of inhumanity." Giotto uses his mythology much as Dante does–as something only a little less sacred, and of barely less authority than theology–and the conquest of Antæus by Hercules was a solemn subject with Dante too; besides a reference in the *Inferno*, he mentions it twice in the *De Monarchia* as a special revelation of God's judgment by way of ordeal, and touches upon it again in the *Convivio, secondo le testimonianze delle scritture*. Here Hercules immediately follows the "conquest of the sea," as having, by his columns, set sacred limits to warn men that they must pass no further (*Inferno* xxvi.). Brutality being thus overthrown, we are shown agriculture and trade,–represented by a splendid team of ploughing bulls and a horse-chariot, respectively. Then, over the door of the tower, the Lamb with the symbol of Resurrection, perhaps, as Ruskin thinks, to "express the law of Sacrifice and door of ascent to Heaven"; or, perhaps, merely as being the emblem of the great Guild of wool merchants, the Arte della Lana, who had charge of the cathedral works. Then follow the representations of the arts, commencing with the relief at the corner: Geometry, regarded as the foundation of the others to follow, as being *senza macula d'errore e certissima*. Turning the corner, the first and second, on the northern side, represent Sculpture and Painting, and were possibly carved by Giotto himself. The remaining five are all later, and from the hand of Luca della Robbia, who perhaps worked from designs left by Giotto–Grammar, which may be taken to represent Literature in general, Arithmetic, the science of numbers (in its great mediæval sense), Dialectics; closing with Music, in some respects the most beautiful of the series, symbolised in Orpheus charming beasts and birds by his strains, and Harmony. "Harmony of song," writes Ruskin, "in the full power of it, meaning perfect education in all art of the Muses and of civilised life; the mystery of its concord is taken for the symbol of that of a perfect state; one day, doubtless, of the perfect world."

Above this fundamental series of bas-reliefs, there runs a second series of four groups of seven. They were probably executed by pupils of Andrea Pisano, and are altogether inferior to those below–the seven Sacraments on the northern side being the best. Above are a series of heroic statues in marble. Of these the oldest are those less easily visible, on the north opposite the Duomo, representing David and Solomon, with two Sibyls; M. Reymond ascribes them to Andrea Pisano. Those opposite the Misericordia are also of the fourteenth century. On the east are Habakkuk and Abraham, by Donatello (the latter in part by a pupil), between two Patriarchs probably by Niccolò d'Arezzo, the chief sculptor of the Florentine school at the end of the Trecento. Three of the four statues opposite the Baptistery are by Donatello; figures of marvellous strength and vigour. It is quite uncertain whom they are intended to represent (the "Solomon" and "David," below the two in the centre, refer to the older statues which once stood here), but the two younger are said to be the Baptist and Jeremiah. The old bald-headed prophet, irreverently called the *Zuccone* or "Bald-head," is one of Donatello's masterpieces, and is said to have been the sculptor's own favourite creation. Vasari tells us that, while working upon it, Donatello used to bid it talk to him, and, when he wanted to be particularly believed, he used to swear by it: "By the faith that I bear to my Zuccone."

THE BIGALLO

At the end of the Via Calzaioli, opposite the Baptistery, is that little Gothic gem, the Loggia called the *Bigallo*, erected between 1352 and 1358, for the "Captains of Our Lady of Mercy," while Orcagna was rearing his more gorgeous tabernacle for the "Captains of Our Lady of Or San Michele." Its architect is unknown; his manner resembles Orcagna's, to whom the work has been erroneously ascribed. The Madonna is by Alberto Arnoldi (1361). The Bigallo was intended for the public functions of charity of the foundling hospital, which was founded under the auspices of the Confraternity of the Misericordia, whose oratory is on the other side of the way. These Brothers of Mercy, in their mysterious black robes hiding their faces, are familiar enough even to the most casual visitor to Florence; and their work of succour to the sick and injured has gone on uninterruptedly throughout the whole of Florentine history.

In the last decade of the thirteenth century, when the People and Commune of Florence were in an unusually peaceful state, after the tumults caused by the reforms and expulsion of Giano della Bella had subsided, the new Cathedral was commenced on the site of the older church of Santa Reparata. The first stones and foundations were blessed with great solemnity in 1296; and, in this golden age of the democracy, the work proceeded apace, until in a document of April 1299, concerning the exemption of Arnolfo di Cambio from all taxation, it is stated that "by reason of his industry, experience and genius, the Commune and People of Florence from the magnificent and visible beginning of the said work of the said church, commenced by the same Master Arnolphus, hope to have a more beautiful and more honourable temple than any other which there is in the regions of Tuscany."

But although the original design and beginning were undoubtedly Arnolfo's, the troublous times that fell upon Florence appear to have interrupted the work; and it was almost abandoned for lack of funds until 1334, when Giotto was appointed capo-maestro of the Commune and of the work of Santa Reparata, as it was still called. The Cathedral was now in charge of the Arte della Lana, as the Baptistery was in that of the Arte di Calimala. It is not precisely known what Giotto did with it; but the work languished again after his death, until Francesco Talenti was appointed capo-maestro, and, in July 1357, the foundations were laid of the present church of Santa Maria del Fiore, on a larger and more magnificent scale. Arnolfo's work appears to have been partly destroyed, partly enlarged and extended. Other capo-maestri carried on what Francesco Talenti had commenced, until, in 1378, just at the end of mediæval Florence, the fourth and last great vault was closed, and the main work finished.

The completion of the Cathedral belongs to that intermediate epoch which saw the decline of the great democracy and the dawn of the Renaissance, and ran from 1378 to 1421, in which latter year the third tribune was finished. Filippo Brunelleschi's dome or cupola, raised upon a frieze or drum high above the three great semi-domes, with a large window in each of the eight sides, was commenced in 1420 and finished in 1434, the year which witnessed the establishment of the Medicean regime in Florence. Vasari waxes most enthusiastic over this work. "Heaven willed," he writes, "after the earth had been for so many years without an excellent soul or a divine spirit, that Filippo should leave to the world from himself the greatest, the most lofty and the most beauteous construction of all others made in the time of the moderns and even in that of the ancients." And Michelangelo imitated it in St Peter's at Rome, turning back, as he rode away from Florence, to gaze upon Filippo's work, and declaring that he could not do anything more beautiful. Some modern writers have passed a very different judgment. Fergusson says:–"The plain, heavy, simple outlined dome of Brunelleschi acts like an extinguisher, crushing all the lower part of the composition, and both internally and externally destroying all harmony between the parts." Brunelleschi also designed the Lantern, which was commenced shortly before his death (1446) and finished in 1461. The palla or ball, which crowns the whole, was added by Andrea Verrocchio. In the fresco in the Spanish Chapel of Santa Maria Novella, you shall see the Catholic Church symbolised by the earlier church of Santa Reparata; and, as the fresco was executed before the middle of the fourteenth century, it apparently represents the designs of Arnolfo and Giotto. Vasari, indeed, states that it was taken from Arnolfo's model in wood. "From this painting," he says, "it is obvious that Arnolfo had proposed to raise the dome immediately over the piers and above the first cornice, at that point namely where Filippo di Ser Brunellesco, desiring to render the building less heavy, interposed the whole space wherein we now see the windows, before adding the dome."[41]

PORTA DELLA MANDORLA, DUOMO

The Duomo has had three façades. Of the first façade, the façade of Arnolfo's church before 1357, only two statues remain which probably formed part of it; one of Boniface VIII. within the Cathedral, of which more presently, and a statue of a Bishop in the sacristy. The second façade, commenced in 1357, and still in progress in 1420, was left unfinished, and barbarously destroyed towards the end of the sixteenth century. A fresco by Poccetti in the first cloister of San Marco, the fifth to the right of the entrance, representing the entrance of St. Antoninus into Florence to take possession of his see, shows this second façade. Some of the statues that once decorated it still exist. The Boniface reappeared upon it from the first façade, between St. Peter and St. Paul; over the principal gate was Our Lady of the Flower herself, presenting her Child to give His blessing to the Florentines–and this is still preserved in the Opera del Duomo–by an unknown artist of the latter half of the fourteenth century; she was formerly attended by Zenobius and Reparata, while Angels held a canopy over her–these are lost. Four Doctors of the Church, now mutilated and transformed into poets, are still to be seen on the way to Poggio Imperiale–by Niccolò d'Arezzo and Piero di Giovanni Tedesco (1396); some Apostles, probably by the latter, and very fine works, are in the court of the Riccardi Palace. The last statues made for the façade, the four Evangelists, of the first fifteen years of the Quattrocento, are now within the present church, in the chapels of the Tribune of St. Zenobius. There is a curious tradition that Donatello placed Farinata degli Uberti on the façade; and few men would have deserved the honour better. After the sixteenth century the façade remained a desolate waste down to our own times. The present façade, gorgeous but admirable in its way, was designed by De Fabris, and finished between 1875 and 1887; the first stone was laid by Victor Emmanuel in 1860. Thus has the United Italy of to-day completed the work of the great Republic of the Middle Ages.

STATUE OF BONIFACE VIII.

The four side gates of the Duomo are among the chief artistic monuments of Florentine sculpture in the epoch that intervened between the setting of Andrea Pisano and Orcagna, and the rising of Donatello and Ghiberti. Nearer the façade, south and north, the two plainer and earlier portals are always closed; the two more ornate and later, the gate of the canons on the south and the gate of the Mandorla on the north, are the ordinary entrances into the aisles of the cathedral.

Earliest of the four is the minor southern portal near the Campanile, over which the pigeons cluster and coo. Our Lady of the Pigeons, in the tympanum, is an excellent work of the school of Nino Pisano (Andrea's son), rather later than the middle of the Trecento. The northern minor portal is similar in style, with sculpture subordinated to polychromatic decoration, but with beautiful twisted columns, of which the two outermost rest upon grand mediæval lions, who are helped to bear them by delicious little winged *putti*. Third in order of construction comes the chief southern portal, the Porta dei Canonici, belonging to the last decade of the fourteenth century. The pilasters are richly decorated with sculptured foliage and figures of animals in the intervals between the leaves. In the tympanum above, the Madonna and Child with two adoring Angels–statues of great grace and beauty–are by Lorenzo di Giovanni d'Ambrogio, 1402. Above are Angels bearing a tondo of the Pietà.

The Porta della Mandorla is one of the most perfect examples of Florentine decorative sculpture that exists. M. Reymond calls it "le produit le plus pur du génie florentin dans toute l'indépendance de sa pensée." It was commenced by Giovanni di Ambrogio, the chief master of the canons' gate; and finished by Niccolò da Arezzo, in the early years of the fifteenth century. The decorations of its pilasters, with nude figures amidst the conventional foliage between the angels with their wings and scrolls, are already almost in the spirit of the Renaissance. The mosaic over the door, representing the Annunciation, was executed by Domenico Ghirlandaio in 1490. "Amongst modern masters of mosaic," says Vasari, "nothing has yet been seen better than this. Domenico was wont to say that painting is mere design, and that the true painting for eternity is mosaic." The two small statues of Prophets are the earliest works of Donatello, 1405-1406. Above is the famous relief which crowns the whole, and from which the door takes its name—the glorified Madonna of the Mandorla. Formerly ascribed to Jacopo della Quercia, it is now recognised as the work of Nanni di Banco, whose father Antonio collaborated with Niccolò da Arezzo on the door. It represents the Madonna borne up in the Mandorla surrounded by Angels, three of whom above are hymning her triumph. With a singularly sweet yet majestic maternal gesture, she consigns her girdle to the kneeling Thomas on the left; on the right among the rocks, a bear is either shaking or climbing a tree. This work, executed slightly before 1420, is the best example of the noble manner of the fourteenth century united to the technical mastery of the fifteenth. Though matured late, it is the most perfect fruit of the school of Orcagna. Nanni died before it was quite completed. The precise symbolism of the bear is not easy to determine; it occurs also in Andrea Pisano's relief of Adam and Eve labouring, on the Campanile. According to St. Buonaventura, the bear is an emblem of Lust; according to the Bestiaries, of Violence. The probability is that here it merely represents the evil one, symbolising the Fall in the Adam and Eve relief, and now implying that Mary healed the wound that Eve had dealt the human race—*la piaga che Maria richiuse ed unse.*

The interior is somewhat bare, and the aisles and vaults are so proportioned and constructed as to destroy much of the effect of the vast size both of the whole and of the parts. The nave and aisles lead to a great octagonal space beneath the dome, where the choir is placed, extending into three polygonal apses, those to right and left representing the transepts.

Over the central door is a fine but restored mosaic of the Coronation of Madonna, by Giotto's friend and contemporary, Gaddo Gaddi, which is highly praised by Vasari. On either side stand two great equestrian portraits in fresco of condottieri, who served the Republic in critical times; by Andrea del Castagno is Niccolò da Tolentino, who fought in the Florentine pay with average success and more than average fidelity, and died in 1435, a prisoner in the hands of Filippo Maria Visconti; by Paolo Uccello is Giovanni Aguto, or John Hawkwood, a greater captain, but of more dubious character, who died in 1394. Let it stand to Hawkwood's credit that St Catherine of Siena once wrote to him, *O carissimo e dolcissimo fratello in Cristo Gesù*. By the side of the entrance is the famous statue, mutilated but extraordinarily impressive, of Boniface VIII., ascribed by Vasari to Andrea Pisano, but which is certainly earlier, and may possibly, according to M. Reymond, be assigned to Arnolfo di Cambio himself. It represents the terrible Pontiff in the flower of his age; hardly a portrait, but an idealised rendering of a Papal politician, a *papa re* of the Middle Ages. Even so might he have looked when he received Dante and his fellow-ambassadors alone, and addressed to them the words recorded by Dino Compagni: "Why are ye so obstinate? Humble yourselves before me. I tell you in very truth that I have no other intention, save for your peace. Let two of you go back, and they shall have my benediction if they bring it about that my will be obeyed."

As though in contrast with this worldly Pope, on the first pillars in the aisles are pictures of two ideal pastors; on the left, St Zenobius enthroned with Eugenius and Crescentius, by an unknown painter of the school of Orcagna; on the right, a similar but comparatively modern picture of St Antoninus giving his blessing. In the middle of the nave, is the original resting-place of the body of Zenobius; here the picturesque blessing of the roses takes place on his feast-day. The right and left aisles contain some striking statues and interesting monuments. First on the right is a statue of a Prophet (sometimes called Joshua), an early Donatello, said to be the portrait of Giannozzo Manetti, between the monuments of Brunelleschi and Giotto; the bust of the latter is by Benedetto da Maiano, and the inscription by Poliziano. Opposite these, in the left aisle, is a most life-like and realistic statue of a Prophet by Donatello, said to be the portrait of Poggio Bracciolini, between modern medallions of De Fabris and Arnolfo. Further on, on the right, are Hezekiah by Nanni di Banco, and a fine portrait bust of Marsilio Ficino by Andrea Ferrucci (1520)–the mystic dreamer caught in a rare moment of inspiration, as on that wonderful day when he closed his finished Plato, and saw young Pico della Mirandola before him. Opposite them, on the left, are David by Ciuffagni, and a bust of the musician Squarcialupi by Benedetto da Maiano. On the last pillars of the nave, right and left, stand later statues of the Apostles–St Matthew by Vincenzo de' Rossi, and St James by Jacopo Sansovino.

Under Brunelleschi's vast dome–the effect of which is terribly marred by miserable frescoes by Vasari and

Zuccheri—are the choir and the high altar. The stained glass in the windows in the drum is from designs of Ghiberti, Donatello (the Coronation), and Paolo Uccello. Behind the high altar is one of the most solemn and pathetic works of art in existence—Michelangelo's last effort in sculpture, the unfinished Deposition from the Cross; "the strange spectral wreath of the Florence Pietà, casting its pyramidal, distorted shadow, full of pain and death, among the faint purple lights that cross and perish under the obscure dome of Santa Maria del Fiore."[42] It is a group of four figures more than life-size; the body of Christ is received in the arms of His mother, who sustains Him with the aid of St Mary Magdalene and the standing Nicodemus, who bends over the group at the back with a countenance full of unutterable love and sorrow. Although, in a fit of impatience, Michelangelo damaged the work and allowed it to be patched up by others, he had intended it for his own sepulchre, and there is no doubt that the Nicodemus—whose features to some extent are modelled from his own—represents his own attitude as death approached. His sonnet to Giorgio Vasari is an expression of the same temper, and the most precious commentary upon his work:–

> Now hath my life across a stormy sea,
> Like a frail bark reached that wide port where all
> Are bidden, ere the final reckoning fall

Of good and evil for eternity.
Now know I well how that fond phantasy,
Which made my soul the worshipper and thrall
Of earthly art, is vain; how criminal
Is that which all men seek unwillingly.
Those amorous thoughts which were so lightly dressed,
What are they when the double death is nigh?
The one I know for sure, the other dread.
Painting nor sculpture now can lull to rest
My soul that turns to His great Love on high,
Whose arms, to clasp us, on the Cross were spread.
(*Addington Symonds' translation.*)

The apse at the east end, or tribuna di San Zenobio, ends in the altar of the Blessed Sacrament, which is also the shrine of Saint Zenobius. The reliquary which contains his remains is the work of Lorenzo Ghiberti, and was finished in 1446; the bronze reliefs set forth his principal miracles, and there is a most exquisite group of those flying Angels which Ghiberti realises so wonderfully. Some of the glass in the windows is also from his design. The seated statues in the four chapels, representing the four Evangelists, were originally on the façade; the St. Luke, by Nanni di Banco, in the first chapel on the right, is the best of the four; then follow St. John, a very early Donatello, and, on the other side, St. Matthew by Ciuffagni and St. Mark by Niccolò da Arezzo (slightly earlier than the others). The two Apostles standing on guard at the entrance of the tribune, St. John and St. Peter, are by Benedetto da Rovezzano. To right and left are the southern and northern sacristies. Over the door of the southern sacristy is a very beautiful bas-relief by Luca della Robbia, representing the Ascension (1446), like a Fra Angelico in enamelled terracotta; within the sacristy are two kneeling Angels also by Luca (1448), practically his only isolated statues, of the greatest beauty and harmony; and also a rather indifferent St. Michael, a late work of Lorenzo di Credi. Over the door of the northern sacristy is the Resurrection by Luca della Robbia (1443), perhaps his earliest extant work in this enamelled terracotta. The bronze doors of this northern sacristy are by Michelozzo and Luca della Robbia, assisted by Maso and Giovanni di Bartolommeo, and were executed between 1446 and 1467. They are composed of ten reliefs with decorative heads at the corners of each, as in Lorenzo Ghiberti's work. Above are Madonna and Child with two Angels; the Baptist with two Angels; in the centre the four Evangelists, each with two Angels; and below, the four Doctors, each with two Angels. M. Reymond has shown that the four latter are the work of Michelozzo. Of Luca's work, the four Evangelists are later than the two topmost reliefs, and are most beautiful; the Angels are especially lovely, and there are admirable decorative heads between. Within, are some characteristic *putti* by Donatello.

The side apses, which represent the right and left transepts, guarded by sixteenth century Apostles, and with frescoed Saints and Prophets in the chapels by Bicci di Lorenzo, are quite uninteresting.

By the door that leads out of the northern aisle into the street, is a wonderful picture, painted in honour of Dante by order of the State in 1465, by Domenico di Michelino, a pupil of Fra Angelico, whose works, with this exception, are hardly identified. At the time that this was painted, the authentic portrait of Dante still existed in the (now lost) fresco at Santa Croce, so we may take this as a fairly probable likeness; it is, at the same time, one of the earliest efforts to give pictorial treatment to the *Purgatorio*. Outside the gates of Florence stands Dante in spirit, clothed in the simple red robe of a Florentine citizen, and wearing the laurel wreath which was denied to him in life; in his left hand he holds the open volume of the *Divina Commedia*, from which rays of burning light proceed and illumine all the city. But it is not the mediæval Florence that the divine singer had known, which his ghost now revisits, but the Florence of the Quattrocento–with the completed Cathedral and the cupola of Brunelleschi rising over it, with the Campanile and the great tower of the Palazzo della Signoria completed–the Florence which has just lost Cosimo dei Medici, Pater Patriae, and may need fresh guidance, now that great mutations are at hand in Italy. With his right hand he indicates the gate of Hell and its antechamber; but it is not the torments of its true inmates that he would bid the Florentines mark, but the shameful and degrading lot of the cowards and neutrals, the trimmers, who would follow no standard upon earth, and are now rejected by Heaven and Hell alike; "the crew of caitiffs hateful to God and to his enemies," who now are compelled, goaded on by hornets and wasps, to rush for ever after a devil-carried ensign, "which whirling ran so quickly that it seemed to scorn all pause." Behind, among the rocks and precipices of Hell, the monstrous fiends of schism, treason and anarchy glare through the gate, preparing to sweep down upon the City of the Lily, if she heeds not the lesson. In the centre of the picture, in the distance, the Mountain of Purgation rises over the shore of the lonely ocean, on the little island where rushes alone grow above the soft mud. The Angel at the gate, seated upon the rock of diamond, above the three steps of contrition, confession, and satisfaction, marks the brows of the penitent souls with his dazzling sword, and admits them into the terraces of the mountain, where Pride, Anger, Envy, Sloth, Avarice, Gluttony, and Lust (the latter, in the purifying fire of the seventh terrace, merely indicated by the flames on the right) are purged away. On the top of the mountain Adam and Eve stand in the Earthly Paradise, which symbolises blessedness of this life, the end to which an ideal ruler is to lead the human race, and the state of innocence to which the purgatorial pains restore man. Above and around sweep the spheres of the planets, the lower moving heavens, from which the angelic influences are poured down upon the Universe beneath their sway.

Thirteen years after this picture was painted, the Duomo saw Giuliano dei Medici fall beneath the daggers of the Pazzi and their confederates on Sunday, April 26th, 1478. The bell that rang for the Elevation of the Host was the signal. Giuliano had been moving round about the choir, and was standing not far from the picture of Dante, when Bernardo Baroncelli and Francesco Pazzi struck the first blows. Lorenzo, who was on the opposite side of the choir, beat off his assailants with his sword and then fled across into the northern sacristy, through the bronze gates of Michelozzo and Luca della Robbia, which Poliziano and the Cavalcanti now closed against the conspirators. The boy cardinal, Raffaello Sansoni, whose visit to the Medicean brothers had furnished the Pazzi with their chance, fled in abject terror into the other sacristy. Francesco Nori, a faithful friend of the Medici, was murdered by Baroncelli in defending his masters' lives; he is very probably the bare-headed figure kneeling behind Giuliano in Botticelli's Adoration of the Magi in the Uffizi.[43]

But of all the scenes that have passed beneath Brunelleschi's cupola, the most in accordance with the spirit of Dante's picture are those connected with Savonarola. It was here that his most famous and most terrible sermons were delivered; here, on that fateful September morning when the French host was sweeping down through Italy, he gazed in silence upon the expectant multitude that thronged the building, and then, stretching forth his hands, cried aloud in a terrible voice the ominous text of Genesis: "Behold I, even I, do bring a flood of waters upon the earth;" and here, too, the fatal riot commenced which ended with the storming of the convent. And here, in a gentler vein, the children of Florence were wont to await the coming of their father and prophet. "The children," writes Simone Filipepi, "were placed all together upon certain steps made on purpose for them, and there were about three thousand of them; they came an hour or two before the sermon; and, in the meanwhile, some read psalms and others said the rosary, and often choir by choir they sang lauds and psalms most devoutly; and when the Father appeared, to mount up into the pulpit, the said children sang the *Ave Maris Stella*, and likewise the people answered back, in such wise that all that time, from early morning even to the end of the sermon, one seemed to be verily in Paradise."

The Opera del Duomo or Cathedral Museum contains, besides several works of minor importance (including the Madonna from the second façade), three of the great achievements of Florentine sculpture during the fifteenth century; the two *cantorie*, or organ galleries, of Donatello and Luca della Robbia; the silver altar for the Baptistery, with the statue of the Baptist by Michelozzo, and reliefs in silver by Antonio Pollaiuolo and Andrea Verrocchio, representing the Nativity of the Baptist by the former, the dance of the daughter of Herodias and the Decollation of the Saint by the latter.

The two organ galleries, facing each other and finished almost simultaneously (about 1440), are an utter contrast both in spirit and in execution. There is nothing specially angelic or devotional about Donatello's wonderful frieze of dancing genii, winged boys that might well have danced round Venus at Psyche's wedding-feast, but would have been out of place among the Angels who, as the old mystic puts it, "rejoiced exceedingly when the most Blessed Virgin entered the Heavenly City." The beauty of rhythmic movement, the joy of living and of being young, exultancy, *baldanza*–these are what they express for us. Luca della Robbia's boys and girls, singing together and playing musical instruments, have less exuberance and motion, but more grace and repose; they illustrate in ten high reliefs the verses of the psalm, *Laudate Dominum in sanctis ejus*, which is inscribed upon the Cantoria; and those that dance are more chastened in their joy, more in the spirit of David before the Ark. But all are as wrapt and absorbed in their music, as are Donatello's in their wild yet harmonious romp.

In detail and considered separately, Luca's more perfectly finished groups, with their exquisite purity of line, are decidedly more lovely than Donatello's more roughly sketched, lower and flatter bas-reliefs; but, seen from a distance and raised from the ground, as they were originally intended, Donatello's are decidedly more effective as a whole. It is only of late years that the reliefs have been remounted and set up in the way we now see; and it is not quite certain whether their present arrangement, in all respects, exactly corresponds to what was originally intended by the masters. It was in this building, the Opera del Duomo, that Donatello at one time had his school and studio; and it was here, in the early years of the Cinquecento, that Michelangelo worked upon the shapeless mass of marble which became the gigantic David.

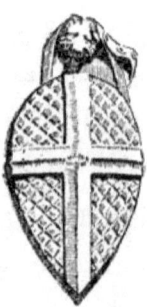

CROSS OF THE FLORENTINE PEOPLE
(FROM OLD HOUSE ON NORTH SIDE OF DUOMO)

ARMS OF THE MEDICI FROM
THE BADIA AT FIESOLE.

CHAPTER IX.

THE PALAZZO RICCARDI–SAN LORENZO SAN MARCO.

Per molti, donna, anzi per mille amanti,
creata fusti, e d'angelica forma.
Or par che'n ciel si dorma,
s'un sol s'appropria quel ch'è dato a tanti.
(*Michelangelo Buonarroti*).

THE Via dei Martelli leads from the Baptistery into the Via Cavour, formerly the historical Via Larga. Here stands the great Palace of the Medici, now called the Palazzo Riccardi from the name of the family to whom the Grand Duke Ferdinand II. sold it in the seventeenth century.

The palace was begun by Michelozzo for Cosimo the Elder shortly before his exile, and completed after his return, when it became in reality the seat of government of the city, although the Signoria still kept up the pretence of a republic in the Palazzo Vecchio. Here Lorenzo the Magnificent was born on January 1st, 1449, and here the most brilliant and cultured society of artists and scholars that the world had seen gathered round him and his family.[44] Here, too, after the expulsion of Lorenzo's mad son, Piero, in 1494, Charles VIII. of France was splendidly lodged; here Piero Capponi tore the dishonourable treaty and saved the Republic, and here Fra Girolamo a few days later admonished the fickle king. On the return of the Medici, the Cardinal Giovanni, the younger Lorenzo, and the Cardinal Giulio successively governed the city here; until in 1527 the people drove out the young pretenders, Alessandro and Ippolito, with their guardian, the Cardinal Passerini. It was on this latter occasion that Piero's daughter, Madonna Clarice, the wife of the younger Filippo Strozzi, was carried hither in her litter, and literally slanged these boys and the Cardinal out of Florence. She is reported, with more vehemence than delicacy, to have told her young kinsmen that the house of Lorenzo dei Medici was not a stable for mules. During the siege, the people wished to entirely destroy the palace and rename the place the Piazza dei Muli.

After the restoration Alessandro carried on his abominable career here, until, on January 5th, 1537, the dagger of another Lorenzo freed the world from an infamous monster. Some months before, Benvenuto Cellini came to the palace, as he tells us in his autobiography, to show the Duke the wax models for his medals which he was making. Alessandro was lying on his bed, indisposed, and with him was only this Lorenzino or Lorenzaccio, *quel pazzo malinconico filosafo di Lorenzino*, as Benvenuto calls him elsewhere. "The Duke," writes Benvenuto, "several times signed to him that he too should urge me to stop; upon which Lorenzino never said anything else, but: 'Benvenuto, you would do best for yourself to stay.' To which I said that I wanted by all means to return to Rome. He said nothing more, and kept continually staring at the Duke with a most evil eye. Having finished the medal and shut it up in its case, I said to the Duke: 'My Lord, be content, for I will make you a much more beautiful medal than I made for Pope Clement; for reason wills that I should do better, since that was the first that ever I made; and Messer Lorenzo here will give me some splendid subject for a reverse, like the learned person and magnificent genius that he is.' To these words the said Lorenzo promptly answered: 'I was thinking of nothing else, save how to give thee a reverse that should be worthy of his Excellency.' The Duke grinned, and, looking at Lorenzo, said: 'Lorenzo, you shall give him the reverse, and he shall make it here, and shall not go away.' Lorenzo replied hastily, saying: 'I will do it as quickly as I possibly can, and I hope to do a thing that will astonish the world.' The Duke, who sometimes thought him a madman and sometimes a coward, turned over in his bed, and laughed at the words which he had said to him. I went away without other ceremonies of leave-taking, and left them alone together."

On the fatal night Lorenzino lured the Duke into his own rooms, in what was afterwards called the Strada del

Traditore, which was incorporated into the palace by the Riccardi. Alessandro, tired out with the excesses of the day, threw himself upon a bed; Lorenzino went out of the room, ostensibly to fetch his kinswoman, Caterina Ginori, whose beauty had been the bait; and he returned with the bravo Scoroncocolo, with whose assistance he assassinated him. Those who saw Sarah Bernhardt in the part of "Lorenzaccio," will not easily forget her rendering of this scene. Lorenzino published an Apologia, in which he enumerates Alessandro's crimes, declares that he was no true offspring of the Medici, and that his own single motive was the liberation of Florence from tyranny. He fled first to Constantinople, and then to Venice, where he was murdered in 1547 by the agents of Alessandro's successor, Cosimo I., who transferred the ducal residence from the present palace first to the Palazzo Vecchio, and then across the river to the Pitti Palace.

With the exception of the chapel, the interior of the Palazzo Riccardi is not very suggestive of the old Medicean glories of the days of Lorenzo the Magnificent. There is a fine court, surrounded with sarcophagi and statues, including some of the old tombs which stood round the Baptistery and among which Guido Cavalcanti used to linger, and some statues of Apostles from the second façade of the Duomo. Above the arcades are eight fine classical medallions by Donatello, copied and enlarged from antique gems. The rooms above have been entirely altered since the days when

Capponi defied King Charles, and Madonna Clarice taunted Alessandro and Ippolito; the large gallery, which witnessed these scenes, is covered with frescoes by Luca Giordano, executed in the early part of the seventeenth century. The Chapel–still entirely reminiscent of the better Medici–was painted by Benozzo Gozzoli shortly before the death of Cosimo the Elder, with frescoes representing the Procession of the Magi, in a delightfully impossible landscape. The two older kings are the Patriarch Joseph of Constantinople, and John Paleologus, Emperor of the East, who had visited Florence twenty years before on the occasion of the Council (Benozzo, it must be observed, was painting them in 1459, after the fall of Constantinople); the third is Lorenzo dei Medici himself, as a boy. Behind follow the rest of the Medicean court, Cosimo himself and his son, Piero, content apparently to be led forward by this mere lad; and in their train is Benozzo Gozzoli himself, marked by the signature on his hat. The picture of the Nativity itself, round which Benozzo's lovely Angels–though very earthly compared with Angelico's–seem still to linger in attendance, is believed to have been one by Lippo Lippi, now at Berlin.

In the chapter *Of the Superhuman Ideal*, in the second volume of *Modern Painters*, Ruskin refers to these frescoes as the most beautiful instance of the supernatural landscapes of the early religious painters:–

"Behind the adoring angel groups, the landscape is governed by the most absolute symmetry; roses, and pomegranates, their leaves drawn to the last rib and vein, twine themselves in fair and perfect order about delicate trellises; broad stone pines and tall cypresses overshadow them, bright birds hover here and there in the serene sky, and groups of angels, hand joined with hand, and wing with wing, glide and float through the glades of the unentangled forest. But behind the human figures, behind the pomp and turbulence of the kingly procession descending from the distant hills, the spirit of the landscape is changed. Severer mountains rise in the distance, ruder prominences and less flowery vary the nearer ground, and gloomy shadows remain unbroken beneath the forest branches."

Among the manuscripts in the *Biblioteca Riccardiana*, which is entered from the Via Ginori at the back of the palace, is the most striking and plausible of all existing portraits of Dante. It is at the beginning of a codex of the Canzoni (numbered 1040), and appears to have been painted about 1436.

From the palace where the elder Medici lived, we turn to the church where they, and their successors of the younger line, lie in death. In the Piazza San Lorenzo there is an inane statue of the father of Cosimo I., Giovanni delle Bande Nere, by Baccio Bandinelli. Here, in June 1865, Robert Browning picked up at a stall the "square old yellow Book" with "the crumpled vellum covers," which gave him the story of *The Ring and the Book*:–

> "I found this book,
> Gave a lira for it, eightpence English just,
> (Mark the predestination!) when a Hand,
> Always above my shoulder, pushed me once,
> One day still fierce 'mid many a day struck calm,
> Across a square in Florence, crammed with booths,
> Buzzing and blaze, noon-tide and market-time,
> Toward Baccio's marble–ay, the basement ledge
> O' the pedestal where sits and menaces
> John of the Black Bands with the upright spear,
> 'Twixt palace and church–Riccardi where they lived,
> His race, and San Lorenzo where they lie.
>
> "That memorable day,
> (June was the month, Lorenzo named the Square)
> I leaned a little and overlooked my prize
> By the low railing round the fountain-source
> Close to the statue, where a step descends:
> While clinked the cans of copper, as stooped and rose
> Thick-ankled girls who brimmed them, and made place
> For market men glad to pitch basket down,

Dip a broad melon-leaf that holds the wet,
And whisk their faded fresh."

THE TOMB OF GIOVANNI AND PIERO DEI MEDICI
By Andrea Verrocchio
(In San Lorenzo)

The Story of Florence

The unsightly bare front of San Lorenzo represents several fruitless and miserable years of Michelangelo's life. Pope Leo X. and the Cardinal Giulio dei Medici commissioned him to make a new façade, in 1516, and for some years he consumed his time labouring among the quarries of Carrara and Pietrasanta, getting the marble for it and for the statues with which it was to be adorned. In one of his letters he says: "I am perfectly disposed (*a me basta l'animo*) to make this work of the façade of San Lorenzo so that, both in architecture and in sculpture, it shall be the mirror of all Italy; but the Pope and the Cardinal must decide quickly, if they want me to do it or not"; and again, some time later: "What I have promised to do, I shall do by all means, and I shall make the most beautiful work that was ever made in Italy, if God helps me." But nothing came of it all; and in after years Michelangelo bitterly declared that Leo had only pretended that he wanted the façade finished, in order to prevent him working upon the tomb of Pope Julius.

"The ancient Ambrosian Basilica of St. Lawrence," founded according to tradition by a Florentine widow named Giuliana, and consecrated by St. Ambrose in the days of Zenobius, was entirely destroyed by fire early in the fifteenth century, during a solemn service ordered by the Signoria to invoke the protection of St. Ambrose for the Florentines in their war against Filippo Maria Visconti. Practically the only relic of this Basilica is the miraculous image of the Madonna in the right transept. The present church was erected from the designs of Filippo Brunelleschi, at the cost of the Medici (especially Giovanni di Averardo, who may be regarded as its chief founder) and seven other Florentine families. It is simple and harmonious in structure; the cupola, which is so visible in distant views of Florence, looking like a smaller edition of the Duomo, unlike the latter, rests directly upon the cross. This appears to be one of the modifications from what Brunelleschi had intended.

The two pulpits with their bronze reliefs, right and left, are the last works of Donatello; they were executed in part and finished by his pupil, Bertoldo. The marble singing gallery in the left aisle (near a fresco of the martyrdom of St. Lawrence, by Bronzino) is also the joint work of Donatello and Bertoldo. In the right transept is a marble tabernacle by Donatello's great pupil, Desiderio da Settignano. Beneath a porphyry slab in front of the choir, Cosimo the Elder, the Pater Patriae, lies; Donatello is buried in the same vault as his great patron and friend. In the Martelli Chapel, on the left, is an exceedingly beautiful Annunciation by Fra Filippo Lippi, a fine example of his colouring (in which he is decidedly the best of all the early Florentines); Gabriel is attended by two minor Angels, squires waiting upon this great Prince of the Archangelic order, who are full of that peculiar mixture of boyish high spirits and religious sentiment which gives a special charm of its own to all that Lippo does.

The *Sagrestia Vecchia*, founded by Giovanni di Averardo, was erected by Brunelleschi and decorated by Donatello for Cosimo the Elder. In the centre is the marble sarcophagus, adorned with *putti* and festoons, containing the remains of Giovanni and his wife Piccarda, Cosimo's father and mother, by Donatello. The bronze doors (hardly among his best works), the marble balustrade before the altar, the stucco medallions of the Evangelists, the reliefs of patron saints of the Medici and the frieze of Angels' heads are all Donatello's; also an exceedingly beautiful terracotta bust of St. Lawrence, which is one of his most attractive creations. In the niche on the left of the entrance is the simple but very beautiful tomb of the two sons of Cosimo, Piero and Giovanni–who are united also in Botticelli's Adoration of the Magi as the two kings–and it serves also as a monument to Cosimo himself; it was made by Andrea Verrocchio for Lorenzo and Giuliano, Piero's sons. The remains of Lorenzo and Giuliano rested together in this sacristy until they were translated in the sixteenth century. In spite of a misleading modern inscription, they were apparently not buried in their father's grave, and the actual site of their former tomb is unknown. They now lie together in the *Sagrestia Nuova*. The simplicity of these funereal monuments and the *pietàs* which united the members of the family so closely, in death and in life alike, are very characteristic of these earlier Medicean rulers of Florence.

The cloisters of San Lorenzo, haunted by needy and destitute cats, were also designed by Brunelleschi. To the right, after passing Francesco da San Gallo's statue of Paolo Giovio, the historian, who died in 1559, is the entrance to the famous Biblioteca Laurenziana. The nucleus of this library was the collection of codices formed by Niccolò Niccoli, which were afterwards purchased by Cosimo the Elder, and still more largely increased by Lorenzo the Magnificent; after the expulsion of Piero the younger, they were bought by the Friars of San Marco, and then from them by the Cardinal Giovanni, who transferred them to the Medicean villa at Rome. In accordance with Pope Leo's wish, Clement VII. (then the Cardinal Giulio) brought them back to Florence, and, when Pope, commissioned Michelangelo to design the building that was to house them. The portico, vestibule and staircase were designed by him, and, in judging of their effect, it must be remembered that Michelangelo professed that architecture was not his business, and also that the vestibule and staircase were intended to have been adorned with bronzes and statues. It was commenced in 1524, before the siege. Of the numberless precious manuscripts which this collection contains, we will mention only two classical and one mediæval; the famous Pandects of Justinian which the Pisans took from Amalfi, and the Medicean Virgil of the fourth or fifth century; and Boccaccio's autograph manuscript of Dante's Eclogues and Epistles. This latter codex, shown under the glass at the entrance to the Rotunda, is the only manuscript in existence which contains Dante's Epistles to the Italian Cardinals and to a Florentine Friend. In the first, he defines his attitude towards the Church, and declares that he is not touching the Ark, but merely turning to the kicking oxen who are dragging it out of the right path; in the second, he proudly proclaims his innocence, rejects the amnesty, and refuses to return to Florence under dishonourable conditions. Although undoubtedly in Boccaccio's handwriting, it has been much disputed of late years as to whether these two letters are really by Dante. There is not a single autograph manuscript, nor a single scrap of Dante's handwriting extant at the present day.

From the Piazza Madonna, at the back of San Lorenzo, we enter a chilly vestibule, the burial vault of less important members of the families of the Medicean Grand Dukes, and ascend to the *Sagrestia Nuova*, where the last male descendants of Cosimo the Elder and Lorenzo the Magnificent lie. Although the idea of adding some such mausoleum to San Lorenzo appears to have originated with Leo X., this New Sacristy was built by Michelangelo for Clement VII., commenced while he was still the Cardinal Giulio and finished in 1524, before the Library was constructed. Its form was intended to correspond with that of Brunelleschi's Old Sacristy, and it was to contain four sepulchral monuments. Two of these, the only two that were actually constructed, were for the younger Lorenzo, titular Duke of Urbino (who died in 1519, the son of Piero and nephew of Pope Leo), and the younger Giuliano, Duke of Nemours (who died in 1516, the third son of the Magnificent and younger brother of Leo). It is not quite certain for whom the other two monuments were to have been, but it is most probable that they were for the fathers of the two Medicean Popes, Lorenzo the Magnificent and his brother the elder Giuliano, whose remains were translated hither by Duke Cosimo I. and rediscovered a few years ago. Michelangelo commenced the statues before the third expulsion of the Medici, worked on them in secret while he was fortifying Florence against Pope Clement before the siege, and returned to them, after the downfall of the Republic, as the condition of obtaining the Pope's pardon. He resumed work, full of bitterness at the treacherous overthrow of the Republic, tormented by the heirs of Pope Julius II., whose tomb he had been forced to abandon, suffering from insomnia and shattered health, threatened with death by the tyrant Alessandro. When he left Florence finally in 1534, just before the death of Clement, the statues had not even been put into their places.

Neither of the ducal statues is a portrait, but they appear to represent the active and contemplative lives, like the Leah and Rachel on the tomb of Pope Julius II. at Rome. On the right sits Giuliano, holding the baton of command as Gonfaloniere of the Church. His handsome sensual features to some extent recall those of the victorious youth in the allegory in the Bargello. He holds his baton somewhat loosely, as though he half realised the baseness of the historical part he was doomed to play, and had not got his heart in it. Opposite is Lorenzo, immersed in profound thought, "ghastly as a tyrant's dream." What visions are haunting him of the sack of Prato, of the atrocities of the barbarian hordes in the Eternal City, of the doom his house has brought upon Florence? Does he already smell the blood that his daughter will shed, fifty years later, on St. Bartholomew's day? Here he sits, as Elizabeth Barrett Browning puts it:–

> "With everlasting shadow on his face,
> While the slow dawns and twilights disapprove
> The ashes of his long extinguished race,
> Which never more shall clog the feet of men."

"It fascinates and is intolerable," as Rogers wrote of this statue. It is, probably, not due to Michelangelo that the niches in which the dukes sit are too narrow for them; but the result is to make the tyrants seem as helpless as their victims, in the fetters of destiny. Beneath them are four tremendous and terrible allegorical figures: "those four ineffable types," writes Ruskin, "not of darkness nor of day–not of morning nor evening, but of the departure and the resurrection, the twilight and the dawn of the souls of men." Beneath Lorenzo are Dawn and Twilight; Dawn awakes in agony, but her most horrible dreams are better than the reality which she must face; Twilight has worked all day in vain, and, like a helpless Titan, is sinking now into a slumber where is no repose. Beneath Giuliano are Day and Night: Day is captive and unable to rise, his mighty powers are uselessly wasted and he glares defiance; Night is buried in torturing dreams, but Michelangelo has forbidden us to wake her:–

"Grato mi è il sonno, e più l'esser di sasso;
mentre che il danno e la vergogna dura,
non veder, non sentir, m'è gran ventura;
però non mi destar; deh, parla basso!" [45]

It will be remembered that it was for these two young men, to whom Michelangelo has thus reared the noblest sepulchral monuments of the modern world, that Leo X. desired to build kingdoms and that Machiavelli wrote one of the masterpieces of Italian prose–the *Principe*. Giuliano was the most respectable of the elder Medicean line; in Castiglione's *Cortigiano* he is an attractive figure, the chivalrous champion of women. It is not easy to get a definite idea of the character of Lorenzo, who, as we saw in chapter iv., was virtually tyrant of Florence during his uncle's pontificate. The Venetian ambassador once wrote of him that he was fitted for great deeds, and only a little inferior to Cæsar Borgia–which was intended for very high praise; but there was nothing in him to deserve either Michelangelo's monument or Machiavelli's dedication. He usurped the Duchy of Urbino, and spent his last days in fooling with a jester. His reputed son, the foul Duke Alessandro, lies buried with him here in the same coffin.

Opposite the altar is the Madonna and Child, by Michelangelo. The Madonna is one of the noblest and most beautiful of all the master's works, but the Child, whom Florence had once chosen for her King, has turned His face away from the city. A few years later, and Cosimo I. will alter the inscription which Niccolò Capponi had set up on the Palazzo Vecchio. The patron saints of the Medici on either side, Sts. Cosmas and Damian, are by Michelangelo's pupils and assistants, Fra Giovanni Angiolo da Montorsoli and Raffaello da Montelupo. Beneath these statues lie Lorenzo the Magnificent and his brother, the elder Giuliano. Their bodies were removed hither from the Old Sacristy in 1559, and the question as to their place of burial was finally set at rest, in October 1895, by the discovery of their bodies. It is probable that Michelangelo had originally intended the Madonna for the tomb of his first patron, Lorenzo.

In judging of the general effect of this *Sagrestia Nuova*, which is certainly somewhat cold, it must be remembered that Michelangelo intended it to be full of statues and that the walls were to have been covered with paintings. "Its justification," says Addington Symonds, "lies in the fact that it demanded statuary and colour for its completion." The vault was frescoed by Giovanni da Udine, but is now whitewashed. In 1562, Vasari wrote to Michelangelo at Rome on behalf of Duke Cosimo, telling him that "the place is being now used for religious services by day and night, according to the intentions of Pope Clement," and that the Duke was anxious that all the best sculptors and painters of the newly instituted Academy should work upon the Sacristy and finish it from Michelangelo's designs. "He intends," writes Vasari, "that the new Academicians shall complete the whole imperfect scheme, in order that the world may see that, while so many men of genius still exist among us, the noblest work which was ever yet conceived on earth has not been left unfinished." And the Duke wants to know what Michelangelo's own idea is about the statues and paintings; "He is particularly anxious that you should be assured of his determination to alter nothing you have already done or planned, but, on the contrary, to carry out the whole work according to your conception. The Academicians, too, are unanimous in their hearty desire to abide by this decision."[46]

In the *Cappella dei Principi*, gorgeous with its marbles and mosaics, lie the sovereigns of the younger line, the Medicean Grand Dukes of Tuscany, the descendants of the great captain Giovanni delle Bande Nere. Here are the sepulchral monuments of Cosimo I. (1537-1574); of his sons, Francesco (1574-1587) and Ferdinand I. (1587-1609); and of Ferdinand's son, grandson and great-grandson, Cosimo II. (1609-1621), Ferdinand II. (1627-1670), Cosimo III. (1670-1723). The statues are those of Ferdinand I. and Cosimo II.

Cosimo I. finally transformed the republic into a monarchy, created a new aristocracy and established a small standing army, though he mainly relied upon Spanish and German mercenaries. He conquered Siena in 1553, and in 1570 was invested with the grand ducal crown by Pius V.–a title which the Emperor confirmed to his successor. Although the tragedy which tradition has hung round the end of the Duchess Eleonora and her two sons has not stood the test of historical criticism, there are plenty of bloody deeds to be laid to Duke Cosimo's account during his able and ruthless reign. Towards the close of his life he married his mistress, Cammilla Martelli, and made over the government to his son. This son, Francesco, the founder of the Uffizi Gallery and of the modern city of Leghorn, had more than his father's vices and hardly any of his ability; his intrigue with the beautiful Venetian, Bianca Cappello, whom he afterwards married, and who died with him, has excited more interest than it deserves. The Cardinal Ferdinand, who succeeded him and renounced the cardinalate, was incomparably the best of the house–a man of magnanimous character and an enlightened ruler. He shook off the influence of Spain, and built an excellent navy to make war upon the Turks and Barbary corsairs. Cosimo II. and Ferdinand II. reigned quietly and benevolently, with no ability but with plenty of good intentions. Chiabrera sings their praises with rather unnecessary fervour. But the wealth and prosperity of Tuscany was waning, and Cosimo III., a luxurious and selfish bigot, could do nothing to arrest the decay. On the death of his miserable and contemptible successor, Gian Gastone dei Medici in 1737, the Medicean dynasty was at an end.

Stretching along a portion of the Via Larga, and near the Piazza di San Marco, were the famous gardens of the Medici, which the people sacked in 1494 on the expulsion of Piero. The Casino Mediceo, built by Buontalenti in 1576, marks the site. Here were placed some of Lorenzo's antique statues and curios; and here Bertoldo had his great art school, where the most famous painters and sculptors came to bask in the sun of Medicean patronage, and to copy the antique. Here the boy Michelangelo came with his friend Granacci, and here Andrea Verrocchio first trained the young Leonardo. In this garden, too, Angelo Poliziano walked with his pupils, and initiated Michelangelo into the newly revived Hellenic culture. There is nothing now to recall these past glories.

THE WELL OF S. MARCO

The church of San Marco has been frequently altered and modernised, and there is little now to remind us that it was here on August 1, 1489, that Savonarola began to expound the Apocalypse. Over the entrance is a Crucifix ascribed by Vasari to Giotto. On the second altar to the right is a much-damaged but authentic Madonna and Saints by Fra Bartolommeo; that on the opposite altar, on the left, is a copy of the original now in the Pitti Palace. There are some picturesque bits of old fourteenth century frescoes on the left wall, and beneath them, between the second and third altars, lie Pico della Mirandola and his friend Girolamo Benivieni, and Angelo Poliziano. The left transept contains the tomb and shrine of St Antoninus, the good Dominican Archbishop of Florence, with statues by Giovanni da Bologna and his followers, and later frescoes. In the sacristy, which was designed by Brunelleschi, there is a fine bronze recumbent statue of him. Antoninus was Prior of San Marco in the days of Angelico, and Vasari tells us that when Angelico went to Rome, to paint for Pope Eugenius, the Pope wished to make the painter Archbishop of Florence: "When the said friar heard this, he besought his Holiness to find somebody else, because he did not feel himself apt to govern people; but that since his Order had a friar who loved the poor, who was most learned and fit for rule, and who feared God, this dignity would be much better conferred upon him than on himself. The Pope, hearing this, and bethinking him that what he said was true, granted his request freely; and so Fra Antonino was made Archbishop of Florence, of the Order of Preachers, a man truly most illustrious for sanctity and learning."

It was in the church of San Marco that Savonarola celebrated Mass on the day of the Ordeal; here the women waited and prayed, while the procession set forth; and hither the Dominicans returned at evening, amidst the howls and derision of the crowd. Here, on the next evening, the fiercest of the fighting took place. The attempt of the enemy to break into the church by the sacristy door was repulsed. One of the Panciatichi, a mere boy, mortally wounded, joyfully received the last sacraments from Fra Domenico on the steps of the altar, and died in such bliss, that the rest envied him. Finally the great door of the church was broken down; Fra Enrico, a German, mounted the pulpit and fired again and again into the midst of the Compagnacci, shouting with each shot, *Salvum fac populum tuum, Domine*. Driven from the pulpit, he and other friars planted their arquebusses beneath the Crucifix on the high altar, and continued to fire. The church was now so full of smoke that the friars could hardly continue the defence, until Fra Giovacchino della Robbia broke one of the windows with a lance. At last, when the Signoria threatened to destroy the whole convent with artillery, Savonarola ordered the friars to go in procession from the church to the dormitory, and himself, taking the Blessed Sacrament from the altar, slowly followed them.

The convent itself, now officially the *Museo di San Marco*, originally a house of Silvestrine monks, was made over to the Dominicans by Pope Eugenius IV., at the instance of Cosimo dei Medici and his brother Lorenzo. They solemnly took possession in 1436, and Michelozzo entirely rebuilt the whole convent for them, mainly at the cost of Cosimo, between 1437 and 1452. "It is believed," says Vasari, "to be the best conceived and the most beautiful and commodious convent of any in Italy, thanks to the virtue and industry of Michelozzo." Fra Giovanni da Fiesole, as the Beato Angelico was called, came from his Fiesolan convent, and worked simultaneously with Michelozzo for about eight or nine years (until the Pope summoned him to Rome in 1445 to paint in the Vatican), covering with his mystical dreams the walls that his friend designed. That other artistic glory of the Dominicans, Fra Bartolommeo, took the habit here in 1500, though there are now only a few unimportant works of his remaining in the convent. Never was there such a visible outpouring of the praying heart in painting, as in the work of these two friars. And Antoninus and Savonarola strove to make the spirit world that they painted a living reality, for Florence and for the Church.

The first cloister is surrounded by later frescoes, scenes from the life of St. Antoninus, partly by Bernardino Poccetti and Matteo Rosselli, at the beginning of the seventeenth century. They are not of great artistic value, but one, the fifth on the right of the entrance, representing the entry of St. Antoninus into Florence, shows the old façade of the Duomo. Like gems in this rather indifferent setting, are five exquisite frescoes by Angelico in lunettes over the doors; St. Thomas Aquinas, Christ as a pilgrim received by two Dominican friars, Christ in the tomb, St. Dominic (spoilt), St. Peter Martyr; also a larger fresco of St. Dominic at the foot of the Cross. The second of these, symbolising the hospitality of the convent rule, is one of Angelico's masterpieces; beneath it is the entrance to the Foresteria, the guest-chambers. Under the third lunette we pass into the great Refectory, with its customary pulpit for the novice reader: here, instead of the usual Last Supper, is a striking fresco of St. Dominic and his friars miraculously fed by Angels, painted in 1536 by Giovanni Antonio Sogliani (a pupil of Lorenzo di Credi); the Crucifixion above, with St. Catherine of Siena and St. Antoninus, is said to be by Fra Bartolommeo. Here, too, on the right is the original framework by Jacopo di Bartolommeo da Sete and Simone da Fiesole, executed in 1433, for Angelico's great tabernacle now in the Uffizi.

Angelico's St. Dominic appropriately watches over the Chapter House, which contains the largest of Fra Giovanni's frescoes and one of the greatest masterpieces of religious art: the Crucifixion with the patron saints of Florence, of the convent, and of the Medici, the founders of the religious orders, the representatives of the zeal and learning of the Dominicans, all gathered and united in contemplation around the Cross of Christ. It was ordered by Cosimo dei Medici, and painted about 1441. On our left are the Madonna, supported by the Magdalene, the other Mary, and the beloved Disciple; the Baptist and St. Mark, representing the city and the convent; St. Lawrence and St. Cosmas (said by Vasari to be a portrait of Nanni di Banco, who died twenty years before), and St. Damian. On our right, kneeling at the foot of the Cross, is St. Dominic, a masterpiece of expression and sentiment; behind him St. Augustine and St. Albert of Jerusalem represent Augustinians and Carmelites; St. Jerome, St. Francis, St. Bernard, St. John Gualbert kneel; St. Benedict and St. Romuald stand behind them, while at the end are St. Peter Martyr and St. Thomas Aquinas. All the male heads are admirably characterised and discriminated, unlike Angelico's women, who are usually either merely conventionally done or idealised into Angels. Round the picture is a frieze of prophets, culminating in the mystical Pelican; below is the great tree of the Dominican order, spreading out from St. Dominic himself in the centre, with Popes Innocent V. and Benedict XI. on either hand. The St. Antoninus was added later. Vasari tells us that, in this tree, the brothers of the order assisted Angelico by obtaining portraits of the various personages represented from different places; and they may therefore be regarded as the real, or traditional, likenesses of the great Dominicans. The same probably applies to the wonderful figure of Aquinas in the picture itself.

Beyond is a second and larger cloister, surrounded by very inferior frescoes of the life of St. Dominic, full of old armorial bearings and architectural fragments arranged rather incongruously. Some of the lunettes over the cells contain frescoes of the school of Fra Bartolommeo. The Academy of the Crusca is established here, in what was once the dormitory of the Novices. Connected with this cloister was the convent garden. "In the summer time," writes Simone Filipepi, "in the evening after supper, the Father Fra Girolamo used to walk with his friars in the garden, and he would make them all sit round him with the Bible in his hand, and here he expounded to them some fair passage of the Scriptures, sometimes questioning some novice or other, as occasion arose. At these meetings there gathered also some fifty or sixty learned laymen, for their edification. When, by reason of rain or other cause, it was not possible in the garden, they went into the *hospitium* to do the same; and for an hour or two one seemed verily to be in Paradise, such charity and devotion and simplicity appeared in all. Blessed was he who could be there." Shortly before the Ordeal of Fire, Fra Girolamo was walking in the garden with Fra Placido Cinozzi, when an exceedingly beautiful boy of noble family came to him with a ticket upon which was written his name, offering himself to pass through the flames. And thinking that this might not be sufficient, he fell upon his knees, begging the Friar that he might be allowed to undergo the ordeal for him. "Rise up, my son," said Savonarola, "for this thy good will is wondrously pleasing unto God"; and, when the boy had gone, he turned to Fra Placido and said: "From many persons have I had these applications, but from none have I received so much joy as from this child, for which may God be praised."

To the left of the staircase to the upper floor, is the smaller refectory with a fresco of the Last Supper by Domenico Ghirlandaio, not by any means one of the painter's best works.

On the top of the stairs we are initiated into the spirit of the place by Angelico's most beautiful Annunciation, with its inscription, *Virginis intacte cum veneris ante figuram, pretereundo cave ne sileatur Ave*, "When thou shalt have come before the image of the spotless Virgin, beware lest by negligence the Ave be silent."

On the left of the stairway a double series of cells on either side of the corridor leads us to Savonarola's room. At the head of the corridor is one of those representations that Angelico repeated so often, usually with modifications, of St. Dominic at the foot of the Cross. Each of the cells has a painted lyric of the life of Christ and His mother, from Angelico's hand; almost each scene with Dominican witnesses and auditors introduced,–Dominic, Aquinas,

Peter Martyr, as the case may be. In these frescoes Angelico was undoubtedly assisted by pupils, from whom a few of the less excellent scenes may come; there is an interesting, but altogether untrustworthy tradition that some were executed by his brother, Fra Benedetto da Mugello, who took the Dominican habit simultaneously with him and was Prior of the convent at Fiesole. Taking the cells on the left first, we see the *Noli me tangere* (1), the Entombment (2), the Annunciation (3), the Crucifixion (4), the Nativity (5), the Transfiguration (6), a most wonderful picture. Opposite the Transfiguration, on the right wall of the corridor, is a Madonna and Saints, painted by the Friar somewhat later than the frescoes in the cells (which, it should be observed, appear to have been painted on the walls before the cells were actually partitioned off)–St. John Evangelist and St. Mark, the three great Dominicans and the patrons of the Medici. Then, on the left, the following cells contain the Mocking of Christ (7), the Resurrection with the Maries at the tomb (8), the Coronation of the Madonna (9), one of the grandest of the whole series, with St. Dominic and St. Francis kneeling below, and behind them St. Benedict and St. Thomas Aquinas, St. Peter Martyr and St. Paul the Hermit. The Presentation in the Temple (10), and the Madonna and Child with Aquinas and Augustine (11), are inferior to the rest.

The shorter passage now turns to the cells occupied by Fra Girolamo Savonarola; one large cell leading into two smaller ones (12-14). In the larger are placed three frescoes by Fra Bartolommeo; Christ and the two disciples at Emmaus, formerly over the doorway of the refectory, and two Madonnas–one from the Dominican convent in the Mugnone being especially beautiful. Here are also modern busts of Savonarola by Dupré and Benivieni by Bastianini. In the first inner cell are Savonarola's portrait, apparently copied from a medal and wrongly ascribed to Bartolommeo, his Crucifix and his relics, his manuscripts and books of devotion, and, in another case, his hair shirt and rosary, his beloved Dominican garb which he gave up on the day of his martyrdom. In the inmost cell are the Cross which he is said to have carried, and a copy of the old (but not contemporary) picture of his death, of which the original is in the Corsini Palace.

The seven small cells on the right (15-21) were assigned to the Juniors, the younger friars who had just passed through the Noviciate. Each contains a fresco by Angelico of St. Dominic at the foot of the Cross, now scourging himself, now absorbed in contemplation, now covering his face with his hands, but in no two cases identical. Into one of these cells a divine apparition was said to have come to one of these youths, after hearing Savonarola's "most fervent and most wondrous discourse" upon the mystery of the Incarnation. The story is told by Simone Filipepi:–

"On the night of the most Holy Nativity, to a young friar in the convent, who had not yet sung Mass, had appeared visibly in his cell on the little altar, whilst he was engaged in prayer, Our Lord in the form of a little infant even as when He was born in the stable. And when the hour came to go into the choir for matins, the said friar commenced to debate in his mind whether he ought to go and leave here the Holy Child, and deprive himself of such sweetness, or not. At last he resolved to go and to bear It with him; so, having wrapped It up in his arms and under his cowl as best he could, all trembling with joy and with fear, he went down into the choir without telling anyone. But, when it came to his turn to sing a lesson, whilst he approached the reading-desk, the Infant vanished from his arms; and when the friar was aware of this, he remained so overwhelmed and almost beside himself that he commenced to wander through the choir, like one who seeks a thing lost, so that it was necessary that another should read that lesson."

Passing back again down the corridor, we see in the cells two more Crucifixions (22 and 23); the Baptism of Christ with Madonna as witness (24), the Crucifixion (25); then, passing the great Madonna fresco, the Mystery of the Passion (26), in one of those symbolical representations which seem to have originated with the Camaldolese painter,

Don Lorenzo; Christ bound to the pillar, with St. Dominic scourging himself and the Madonna appealing to us (27, perhaps by a pupil); Christ bearing the Cross (28); two more Crucifixions (29 and 30), apparently not executed by Angelico himself.

At the side of Angelico's Annunciation opposite the stairs, we enter the cell of St. Antoninus (31). Here is one of Angelico's most beautiful and characteristic frescoes, Christ's descent into Hades: "the intense, fixed, statue-like silence of ineffable adoration upon the spirits in prison at the feet of Christ, side by side, the hands lifted and the knees bowed, and the lips trembling together," as Ruskin describes it. Here, too, is the death mask of Antoninus, his portrait perhaps drawn from the death mask by Bartolommeo, his manuscripts and relics; also a tree of saintly Dominicans, Savonarola being on the main trunk, the third from the root.

The next cell on the right (32) has the Sermon on the Mount and the Temptation in the Wilderness. In the following (33), also double, besides the frescoed Kiss of Judas, are two minute pictures by Fra Angelico, belonging to an earlier stage of his art than the frescoes, intended for reliquaries and formerly in Santa Maria Novella. One of them, the *Madonna della Stella*, is a very perfect and typical example of the Friar's smaller works, in their "purity of colour almost shadowless." The other, the Coronation of the

Madonna, is less excellent and has suffered from retouching. The Agony in the Garden (in cell 34) contains a curious piece of mediæval symbolism in the presence of Mary and Martha, contemplation and action, the Mary being here the Blessed Virgin. In the same cell is another of the reliquaries from Santa Maria Novella, the Annunciation over the Adoration of the Magi, with Madonna and Child, the Virgin Martyrs, the Magdalene and St. Catherine of Siena below; the drawing is rather faulty. In the following cells are the Last Supper (35), conceived mystically as the institution of the Blessed Sacrament of the Altar, with the Madonna alone as witness; the Deposition from the Cross (36); and the Crucifixion (37), in which Dominic stands with out-stretched arms.

Opposite on the right (38-39) is the great cell where Pope Eugenius stayed on the occasion of the consecration of San Marco in 1442; here Cosimo the Elder, Pater Patriae, spent long hours of his closing days, in spiritual intercourse with St. Antoninus and after the latter's death. In the outer compartment the Medicean saint, Cosmas, joins Madonna and Peter Martyr at the foot of the Cross. Within are the Adoration of the Magi and a Pietà, both from Angelico's hand, and the former, one of his latest masterpieces, probably painted with reference to the fact that the convent had been consecrated on the Feast of the Epiphany. Here, too, is an old terracotta bust of Antoninus, and a splendid but damaged picture of Cosimo himself by Jacopo da Pontormo, incomparably finer than that artist's similarly constructed work in the Uffizi. Between two smaller cells containing Crucifixions, both apparently by Angelico himself (42-43– the former with the Mary and Martha motive at the foot of the Cross), is the great Greek Library, built by Michelozzo for Cosimo. Here Cosimo deposited a portion of the manuscripts which had been collected by Niccolò Niccoli, with additions of his own, and it became the first public library in Italy. Its shelves are now empty and bare, but it contains a fine collection of illuminated ritual books from suppressed convents, several of which are, rather doubtfully, ascribed to Angelico's brother, Fra Benedetto da Mugello.

It was in this library that Savonarola exercised for the last time his functions of Prior of San Marco, and surrendered to the commissioners of the Signoria, on the night of Palm Sunday, 1498. What happened had best be told in the words of the Padre Pacifico Burlamacchi of the same convent, Savonarola's contemporary and follower. After several fictitious summonses had come:–

"They returned at last with the decree of the Signoria in writing, but with the open promise that Fra Girolamo should be restored safe and sound, together with his companions. When he heard this, he told them that he would obey. But first he retired with his friars into the Greek Library, where he made them in Latin a most beautiful sermon, exhorting them to follow onwards in the way of God with faith, prayer, and patience; telling them that it was necessary to go to heaven by the way of tribulations, and that therefore they ought not in any way to be terrified; alleging many old examples of the ingratitude of the city of Florence in return for the benefits received from their Order. As that of St. Peter Martyr who, after doing so many marvellous things in Florence, was slain, the Florentines paying the price of his blood. And of St. Catherine of Siena, whom many had sought to kill, after she had borne so many labours for them, going personally to Avignon to plead their cause before the Pope. Nor had less happened to St. Antoninus, their Archbishop and excellent Pastor, whom they had once wished to throw from the windows. And that it was no marvel, if he also, after such sorrows and labourings, was paid at the end in the same coin. But that he was ready to receive everything with desire and happiness for the love of his Lord, knowing that in nought else consisted the Christian life, save in doing good and suffering evil. And thus, while all the bye-standers wept, he finished his sermon. Then, issuing forth from the library, he said to those laymen who awaited him: 'I will say to you what Jeremiah said: This thing I expected, but not so soon nor so suddenly.' He exhorted them further to live well and to be fervent in prayer. And having confessed to the Father Fra Domenico da Pescia, he took the Communion in the first library. And the same did Fra Domenico. After eating a little, he was somewhat refreshed; and he spoke the last words to his friars, exhorting them to persevere in religion, and kissing them all, he took his last departure from them. In the parting one of his children said to him: 'Father, why dost thou abandon us and leave us so desolate?' To which he replied: 'Son, have patience, God will help you'; and he added that he would either see them again alive, or that after death he would appear to them without fail. Also, as he departed, he gave up the common keys to the brethren, with so great humility and charity, that the friars could not keep themselves from tears; and many of them wished by all means to go with him. At last, recommending himself to their prayers, he made his way towards the door of the library, where the first Commissioners all armed were awaiting him; to whom, giving himself into their hands like a most meek lamb, he said: 'I recommend to you this my flock and all these other citizens.' And when he was in the corridor of the library, he said: 'My friars, doubt not, for God will not fail to perfect His work; and although I be put to death, I shall help you more than I have done in life, and I will return without fail to console you, either dead or alive.' Arrived at the holy water, which is at the exit of the choir, Fra Domenico said to him: 'Fain would I too come to these nuptials.' Certain of the laymen, his friends, were arrested at the command of the Signoria. When the Father Fra Girolamo was in the first cloister, Fra Benedetto, the miniaturist, strove ardently to go with him; and, when the officers thrust him back, he still insisted that he would go. But the Father Fra Girolamo turned to him, and said: 'Fra Benedetto, on your obedience come not, for I and Fra Domenico have to die for the love of Christ.' And thus he was torn away from the eyes of his children."

CHAPTER X.

THE ACCADEMIA DELLE BELLE ARTI–THE SANTISSIMA ANNUNZIATA–AND OTHER BUILDINGS

"In Firenze, più che altrove, venivano gli uomini perfetti in tutte l'arti, e specialmente nella pittura."–*Vasari*.

TURNING southwards from the Piazza di San Marco into the Via Ricasoli, we come to the *Accademia delle Belle Arti*, with its collection of Tuscan and Umbrian pictures, mostly gathered from suppressed churches and convents.

In the central hall, the Tribune of the David, Michelangelo's gigantic marble youth stands under the cupola, surrounded by casts of the master's other works. The young hero has just caught sight of the approaching enemy, and is all braced up for the immortal moment. Commenced in 1501 and finished at the beginning of 1504, out of a block of marble over which an earlier sculptor had bungled, it was originally set up in front of the Palazzo Vecchio on the Ringhiera, as though to defend the great Palace of the People. It is supposed to have taken five days to move the statue from the Opera del Duomo, where Michelangelo had chiselled it out, to the Palace. When the simple-minded Gonfaloniere, Piero Soderini, saw it, he told the artist that the nose appeared to him to be too large; whereupon Michelangelo mounted a ladder, pretended to work upon it for a few moments, dropping a little marble dust all the time, which he had taken up with him, and then turned round for approval to the Gonfaloniere, who assured him that he had now given the statue life. This *gigante di Fiorenza*, as it was called, was considerably damaged during the third expulsion of the Medici in 1527, but retained its proud position before the Palace until 1873.

On the right, as we approach the giant, is the *Sala del Beato Angelico*, containing a lovely array of Fra Angelico's smaller paintings. Were we to attempt to sum up Angelico's chief characteristics in one word, that word would be *onestà*, in its early mediaeval sense as Dante uses it in the *Vita Nuova*, signifying not merely purity or chastity, as it came later to mean, but the outward manifestation of spiritual beauty,– the *honestas* of which Aquinas speaks. A supreme expression of this may be found in the Paradise of his Last Judgment (266), the mystical dance of saints and Angels in the celestial garden that blossoms under the rays of the Sun of Divine Love, and on all the faces of the blessed beneath the Queen of Mercy on the Judge's right. The Hell is, naturally, almost a failure. In many of the small scenes from the lives of Christ and His Mother, of which there are several complete series here, some of the heads are absolute miracles of expression; notice, for instance, the Judas receiving the thirty pieces of silver, and all the faces in the Betrayal (237), and, above all perhaps, the Peter in the Entry into Jerusalem (252), on every line of whose face seems written: "Lord, why can I not follow thee now? I will lay down my life for thy sake." The Deposition from the Cross (246), contemplated by St. Dominic, the Beata Villana and St. Catherine of Alexandria, appears to be an earlier work of Angelico's. Here, also, are three great Madonnas painted by the Friar as altar pieces for convent churches; the Madonna and Child surrounded by Angels and saints, while Cosmas and Damian, the patrons of the Medici, kneel at her feet (281), was executed in 1438 for the high altar of San Marco, and, though now terribly injured, was originally one of his best pictures; the Madonna and Child, with two Angels and six saints, Peter Martyr, Cosmas and Damian, Francis, Antony of Padua, and Louis of Toulouse (265), was painted for the convent of the Osservanza near Mugello,–hence the group of Franciscans on the left; the third (227), in which Cosmas and Damian stand with St. Dominic on the right of the Madonna, and St. Francis with Lawrence and John the Divine on her left, is an inferior work from his hand.

Also in this room are four delicious little panels by Lippo Lippi (264 and 263), representing the Annunciation divided into two compartments, St. Antony Abbot and the Baptist; two Monks of the Vallombrosa, by Perugino (241, 242), almost worthy of Raphael; and two charming scenes of mediaeval university life, the School of Albertus Magnus (231) and the School of St. Thomas Aquinas (247). These two latter appear to be by some pupil of Fra Angelico, and may possibly be very early works of Benozzo Gozzoli. In the first, Albert is lecturing to an audience, partly lay and partly clerical, amongst whom is St. Thomas, then a youthful novice but already distinguished by the halo and the sun upon his breast; in the second, Thomas himself is now holding the professorial chair, surrounded by pupils listening or taking notes, while Dominicans throng the cloisters behind. On his right sits the King of France; below his seat the discomforted Averrhoes humbly places himself on the lowest step, between the heretics–William of St. Amour and Sabellius.

From the left of the David's tribune, we turn into three rooms containing masterpieces of the Quattrocento (with a few later works), and appropriately named after Botticelli and Perugino.

In the *Sala prima del Botticelli* is Sandro's famous *Primavera*, the Allegory of Spring or the Kingdom of Venus (80). Inspired in part by Poliziano's *stanze* in honour of Giuliano dei Medici and his Bella Simonetta, Botticelli nevertheless has given to his strange–not altogether decipherable–allegory, a vague mysterious poetry far beyond anything that Messer Angelo could have suggested to him. Through this weirdly coloured garden of the Queen of Love, in "the light that never was on sea or land," blind Cupid darts upon his little wings, shooting, apparently at random, a flame-tipped arrow which will surely pierce the heart of the central maiden of those three, who, in their thin clinging white raiment, personify the Graces. The eyes of Simonetta–for it is clearly she–rest for a moment in the dance upon the stalwart Hermes, an idealised Giuliano, who has turned away carelessly from the scene. Flora, "pranked and pied for birth," advances from our right, scattering flowers rapidly as she approaches; while behind her a wanton Zephyr, borne on his strong wings, breaks through the wood to clasp Fertility, from whose mouth the flowers are starting. Venus herself, the mistress of nature, for whom and by whom all these things are done, stands somewhat sadly apart in the centre of the picture; this is only one more of the numberless springs that have passed over her since she first rose from the sea, and she is somewhat weary of it all:–

"Te, dea, te fugiunt venti, te nubila caeli
Adventumque tuum, tibi suavis daedala tellus
Summittit flores, tibi rident aequora ponti
Placatumque nitet diffuso lumine caelum."[47]

This was one of the pictures painted for Lorenzo the Magnificent. Botticelli's other picture in this room, the large Coronation of the Madonna (73) with its predella (74), was commissioned by the Arte di Por Sta. Maria, the Guild of

Silk-merchants, for an altar in San Marco; the ring of festive Angels, encircling their King and Queen, is in one of the master's most characteristic moods. On either side of the Primavera are two early works by Lippo Lippi; Madonna adoring the Divine Child in a rocky landscape, with the little St. John and an old hermit (79), and the Nativity (82), with Angels and shepherds, Jerome, Magdalene and Hilarion. Other important pictures in this room are Andrea del Sarto's Four Saints (76), one of his latest works painted for the monks of Vallombrosa in 1528; Andrea Verrocchio's Baptism of Christ (71), in which the two Angels were possibly painted by Verrocchio's great pupil, Leonardo, in his youth; Masaccio's Madonna and Child watched over by St. Anne (70), an early and damaged work, the only authentic easel picture of his in Florence. The three small predella pictures (72), the Nativity, the martyrdom of Sts. Cosmas and Damian, St. Anthony of Padua finding a stone in the place of the dead miser's heart, by Francesco Pesellino, 1422-1457, the pupil of Lippo Lippi, are fine examples of a painter who normally only worked on this small scale and whose works are very rare indeed. Francesco Granacci, who painted the Assumption (68), is chiefly interesting as having been Michelangelo's friend and fellow pupil under Ghirlandaio.

The *Sala del Perugino* takes its name from three works of that master which it contains; the great Vallombrosa

Assumption (57), signed and dated 1500, one of the painter's finest altar pieces, with a very characteristic St. Michael–the Archangel who was by tradition the genius of the Assumption, as Gabriel had been of the Annunciation; the Deposition from the Cross (56); and the Agony in the Garden (53). But the gem of the whole room is Lippo Lippi's Coronation of the Madonna (62), one of the masterpieces of the early Florentine school, which he commenced for the nuns of Sant' Ambrogio in 1441. The throngs of boys and girls, bearing lilies and playing at being Angels, are altogether delightful, and the two little orphans, that are being petted by the pretty Florentine lady on our right, are characteristic of Fra Filippo's never failing sympathy with child life. On the left two admirably characterised monks are patronised by St. Ambrose, and in the right corner the jolly Carmelite himself, under the wing of the Baptist, is welcomed by a little Angel with the scroll, *Is perfecit opus*. It will be observed that "poor brother Lippo" has dressed himself with greater care for his celestial visit, than he announced his intention of doing in Robert Browning's poem:–

> "Well, all these
> Secured at their devotion, up shall come
> Out of a corner when you least expect,
> As one by a dark stair into a great light,
> Music and talking, who but Lippo! I!–

Mazed, motionless and moon-struck–I'm the man!
Back I shrink–what is this I see and hear?
I, caught up with my monk's things by mistake,
My old serge gown and rope that goes all round,
I, in this presence, this pure company!
Where's a hole, where's a corner for escape?
Then steps a sweet angelic slip of a thing
Forward, puts out a soft palm–'Not so fast!'
Addresses the celestial presence, 'Nay–
'He made you and devised you, after all,
'Though he's none of you! Could Saint John there draw–
'His camel-hair make up a painting-brush?
'We come to brother Lippo for all that,
'*Iste perfecit opus!*'"

Fra Filippo's Madonna and Child, with Sts. Cosmas and Damian, Francis and Antony, painted for the Medicean chapel in Santa Croce (55), is an earlier and less characteristic work. Over the door is St. Vincent preaching, by Fra Bartolommeo (58), originally painted to go over the entrance to the sacristy in San Marco–a striking representation of a Dominican preacher of repentance and renovation, conceived in the spirit of Savonarola, but terribly "restored." The Trinità (63) is one of Mariotto Albertinelli's best works, but sadly damaged. The two child Angels (61) by Andrea del

Sarto, originally belonged to his picture of the Four Saints, in the last room; the Crucifixion, with the wonderful figure of the Magdalene at the foot of the Cross (65), ascribed to Luca Signorelli, does not appear to be from the master's own hand; Ghirlandaio's predella (67), with scenes from the lives of Sts. Dionysius, Clement, Dominic, and Thomas Aquinas, belongs to a great picture which we shall see presently.

The *Sala seconda del Botticelli* contains three pictures ascribed to the master, but only one is authentic–the Madonna and Child enthroned with six Saints, while Angels raise the curtain over her throne or hold up emblems of the Passion (85); it is inscribed with Dante's line–

"Vergine Madre, Figlia del tuo Figlio."

The familiar Three Archangels (84), though attributed to Sandro, is not even a work of his school. There is a charming little predella picture by Fra Filippo (86), representing a miracle of San Frediano, St. Michael announcing her death to the Blessed Virgin, and a friar contemplating the mystery of the Blessed Trinity–pierced by the "three arrows of the three stringed bow," to adopt Dante's phrase. The Deposition from the Cross (98), was commenced by Filippino Lippi for the Annunziata, and finished after his death in 1504 by Perugino, who added the group of Maries with the Magdalene and the figure on our right. The Vision of St. Bernard (97), by Fra Bartolommeo, is the first picture that the Friar undertook on resuming his brush, after Raphael's visit to Florence had stirred him up to new efforts; commenced in 1506, it was left unfinished, and has been injured by renovations. Here are two excellent paintings by Lorenzo di Credi (92 and 94), the former, the Adoration of the Shepherds, being his very best and most perfectly finished work. High up are two figures in niches by Filippino Lippi, the Baptist and the Magdalene (93 and 89), hardly pleasing. The Resurrection (90), by Raffaellino del Garbo, is the only authentic work in Florence of a pupil of Filippino's, who gave great promise which was never fulfilled.

At the end of the hall are three Sale *dei Maestri Toscani*, from the earliest Primitives down to the eighteenth century. Only a few need concern us much.

The first room contains the works of the earlier masters, from a pseudo-Cimabue (102), to Luca Signorelli, whose Madonna and Child with Archangels and Doctors (164), painted for a church in Cortona, has suffered from restoration. There are four genuine, very tiny pictures by Botticelli (157, 158, 161, 162). The Adoration of the Kings (165), by Gentile da Fabriano, is one of the most delightful old pictures in Florence; Gentile da Fabriano, an Umbrian master who, through Jacopo Bellini, had a considerable influence upon the early Venetian school, settled in Florence in 1422, and finished this picture in the following year for Santa Trinità, near which he kept a much frequented bottega. Michelangelo said that Gentile had a hand similar to his name; and this picture, with its rich and varied poetry, is his masterpiece. The man wearing a turban, seen full face behind the third king, is the painter himself. Kugler remarks: "Fra Angelico and Gentile are like two brothers, both highly gifted by nature, both full of the most refined and amiable feelings; but the one became a monk, the other a knight." The smaller pictures surrounding it are almost equally charming in their way–especially, perhaps, the Flight into Egypt in the predella. The Deposition from the Cross (166), by Fra Angelico, also comes from Santa Trinità, for which it was finished in 1445; originally one of Angelico's masterpieces, it has been badly repainted; the saints in the frame are extremely beautiful, especially a most wonderful St. Michael at the top, on our left; the man standing on the ladder, wearing a black hood, is the architect, Michelozzo, who was the Friar's friend, and may be recognised in several of his paintings. The lunettes in the three Gothic arches above Angelico's picture, and which, perhaps, did not originally belong to it, are by the Camaldolese Don Lorenzo, by whom are also the Annunciation with four Saints (143), and the three predella scenes (144, 145, 146).

Of the earlier pictures, the Madonna and Child adored by Angels (103) is now believed to be the only authentic easel picture of Giotto's that remains to us–though this is, possibly, an excess of scepticism. Besides several works ascribed to Taddeo Gaddi and his son Agnolo, by the former of whom are probably the small panels from Santa Croce, formerly attributed to Giotto, we should notice the Pietà by Giovanni da Milano (131); the Presentation in the Temple by Ambrogio Lorenzetti (134), signed and dated 1342; and a large altarpiece ascribed to Pietro Cavallini (157). The so-called Marriage of Boccaccio Adimari with Lisa Ricasoli (147) is an odd picture of the social customs of old Florence.

In the second room are chiefly works by Fra Bartolommeo and Mariotto Albertinelli. By the Frate, are the series of heads of Christ and Saints (168), excepting the Baptist on the right; they are frescoes taken from San Marco, excepting the Christ on the left, inscribed "Orate pro pictore 1514," which is in oil on canvas. Also by him are the two frescoes of Madonna and Child (171, 173), and the splendid portrait of Savonarola in the character of St. Peter Martyr (172), the great religious persecutor of the Middle Ages, to whom Fra Girolamo had a special devotion. By Albertinelli, are the Madonna and Saints (167), and the Annunciation (169), signed and dated 1510. This room also contains several pictures by Fra Paolino da Pistoia and the Dominican nun, Plautilla Nelli, two pious but insipid artists, who inherited Fra Bartolommeo's drawings and tried to carry on his traditions. On a stand in the middle of the room, is Domenico Ghirlandaio's Adoration of the Shepherds (195), from Santa Trinità, a splendid work with–as Vasari puts it–"certain heads of shepherds which are held a divine thing."

On the walls of the third room are later pictures of no importance or significance. But in the middle of the room is another masterpiece by Ghirlandaio (66); the Madonna and Child with two Angels, Thomas Aquinas and Dionysius standing on either side of the throne, Dominic and Clement kneeling. It is seldom, indeed, that this prosaic painter succeeded in creating such a thinker as this Thomas, such a mystic as this Dionysius; in the head of the latter we see indeed the image of the man who, according to the pleasant mediæval fable eternalised by Dante, "in the flesh below, saw deepest into the Angelic nature and its ministry."

In the Via Cavour, beyond San Marco, is the *Chiostro dello Scalzo*, a cloister belonging to a brotherhood dedicated to St. John, which was suppressed in the eighteenth century. Here are a series of frescoes painted in grisaille by Andrea del Sarto and his partner, Francia Bigio, representing scenes from the life of the Precursor, with allegorical figures of the Virtues. The Baptism of Christ is the earliest, and was painted by the two artists in collaboration, in 1509 or 1510. After some work for the Servites, which we shall see presently, Andrea returned to this cloister; and painted, from 1515 to 1517, the Justice, St. John preaching, St. John baptising the people, and his imprisonment. Some of the figures in these frescoes show the influence of Albert Dürer's engravings. Towards the end of 1518, Andrea went off to France to work for King Francis I.; and, while he was away, Francia Bigio painted St. John leaving his parents, and St. John's first meeting with Christ. On Andrea's return, he set to work here again and painted, at intervals from 1520 to 1526, Charity, Faith and Hope, the dance of the daughter of Herodias, the decollation of St. John, and the presentation of his head, the Angel appearing to Zacharias, the Visitation, and, last of all, the Birth of the Baptist. The Charity is Andrea's own wife, Lucrezia, who at this very time, if Vasari's story is true, was persuading him to break his promise to the French King and to squander the money which had been intrusted to him for the purchase of works of art.

The Via della Sapienza leads from San Marco into the *Piazza della Santissima Annunziata*. In one of the houses on the left, now incorporated into the Reale Istituto di Studi Superiori, Andrea del Sarto and Francia Bigio lodged with other painters, before Andrea's marriage; and here, usually under the presidency of the sculptor Rustici, the "Compagnia del Paiuolo," an artists' club of twelve members, met for feasting and disport.[48]

This Piazza was a great place for processions in old Florence. Here stand the church of the *Santissima Annunziata* and the convent of the Servites, while the Piazza itself is flanked to right and left by arcades originally designed by

Brunelleschi. The equestrian statue of the Grand Duke Ferdinand I. was cast by Giovanni da Bologna out of metal from captured Turkish guns. The arcade on the right, as we face the church, with its charming medallions of babies in swaddling clothes by Andrea della Robbia, is a part of the Spedale degli Innocenti or Hospital for Foundlings, which was commenced from Brunelleschi's designs in 1421, during the Gonfalonierate of Giovanni dei Medici; the work, which was eloquently supported in the Council of the People by Leonardo Bruni, was raised by the Silk-merchants Guild, the Arte di Por Santa Maria. On its steps the Compagnacci murdered their first victim in the attack on San Marco. There is a picturesque court, designed by Brunelleschi, with an Annunciation by Andrea della Robbia over the door of the chapel, and a small picture gallery, which contains nothing of much importance, save a Holy Family with Saints by Piero di Cosimo. In the chapel, or church of Santa Maria degli Innocenti, there is a masterpiece by Domenico Ghirlandaio, painted in 1488, an Adoration of the Magi (the fourth head on the left is the painter himself), in which the Massacre of the Innocents is seen in the background, and two of these glorified infant martyrs, under the protection of the two St. Johns, are kneeling most sweetly in front of the Madonna and her Child, for whom they have died, joining in the adoration of the kings and the *gloria* of the angelic choir.

The church of the Santissima Annunziata was founded in the thirteenth century, but has been completely altered and modernised since at different epochs. In summer mornings lilies and other flowers lie in heaps in its portico and beneath Ghirlandaio's mosaic of the Annunciation, to be offered at Madonna's shrine within. The entrance court was built in the fifteenth century, at the expense of the elder Piero dei Medici. The fresco to the left of the entrance, the Nativity of Christ, is by Alessio Baldovinetti. Within the glass, to the left, are six frescoes representing the life and miracles of the great Servite, Filippo Benizzi; that of his receiving the habit of the order is by Cosimo Rosselli (1476); the remaining five are early works by Andrea del Sarto, painted in 1509 and 1510, for which he received a mere trifle; in the midst of them is an indifferent seventeenth century bust of their painter. The frescoes on the right, representing the life of the Madonna, of whom this order claims to be the special servants, are slightly later. The approach of the Magi and the Nativity of the Blessed Virgin, the latter dated 1514, are among the finest works of Andrea del Sarto; in the former he has introduced himself and the sculptor Sansovino, and among the ladies in the latter is his wife. Fifty years afterwards the painter Jacopo da Empoli was copying this picture, when a very old lady, who was going into the church to hear mass, stopped to look at his work, and then, pointing to the portrait of Lucrezia, told him that it was herself. The Sposalizio, by

Francia Bigio, painted in 1513, was damaged by the painter himself in a fit of passion at the meddling of the monks. The Visitation, by Jacopo da Pontormo, painted in 1516, shows what admirable work this artist could do in his youth, before he fell into his mannered imitations of Michelangelo; the Assumption, painted slightly later by another of Andrea's pupils, Rosso Fiorentino, is less excellent.

Inside the church itself, on the left, is the sanctuary of Our Lady of the Annunciation, one of the most highly revered shrines in Tuscany; it was constructed from the designs of Michelozzo at the cost of the elder Piero dei Medici to enclose the miraculous picture of the Annunciation, and lavishly decorated and adorned by the Medicean Grand Dukes. After the Pazzi conspiracy, Piero's son Lorenzo had a waxen image of himself suspended here in thanksgiving for his escape. Over the altar there is usually a beautiful little head of the Saviour, by Andrea del Sarto. The little oratory beyond, with the Madonna's mystical emblems on its walls, was constructed in the seventeenth century.

In the second chapel from the shrine is a fresco by Andrea del Castagno, which was discovered in the summer of 1899 under a copy of Michelangelo's Last Judgment. It represents St. Jerome and two women saints adoring the Blessed Trinity, and is characteristic of the *modo terribile* in which this painter conceived his subjects; the heads of the Jerome and the older saint to our right are particularly powerful. For the rest, the interior of this church is more gorgeous than tasteful; and the other works which it contains, including the two Peruginos, and some tolerable monuments, are third rate. The rotunda of the choir was designed by Leo Battista Alberti and erected at the cost of the Marquis of Mantua, whose descendant, San Luigi Gonzaga, had a special devotion to the miraculous picture.

From the north transept, the cloisters are entered. Here, over the door, is the Madonna del Sacco, an exceedingly beautiful fresco by Andrea del Sarto, painted in 1525. St. Joseph, leaning upon the sack which gives the picture its name, is reading aloud the Prophecies to the Mother and Child whom they concern. In this cloister–which was built by Cronaca–is the monument of the French knight slain at Campaldino in 1289 (*see* chapter ii.), which should be contrasted with the later monuments of condottieri in the Duomo. Here also is the chapel of St. Luke, where the Academy of Artists, founded under Cosimo I., used to meet.

A good view of the exterior of the rotunda can be obtained from the Via Gino Capponi. At the corner of this street and the Via del Mandorlo is the house which Andrea del Sarto bought for himself and his Lucrezia, after his return from France, and here he died in 1531, "full of glory and of domestic sorrows." Lucrezia survived him for nearly forty years, and died in 1570. Perhaps, if she had not made herself so unpleasant to her husband's pupils and assistants, good Giorgio Vasari–the youngest of them–might not have left us so dark a picture of this beautiful Florentine.

The rather picturesque bit of ruin in the Via degli Alfani, at the corner of the Via del Castellaccio, is merely a part of an oratory in connection with Santa Maria degli Angioli, which Brunelleschi commenced for Filippo Scolari, but which was abandoned. *Santa Maria degli Angioli* itself, a suppressed Camaldolese house, was of old one of the most important convents in Florence. The famous poet, Fra Guittone d'Arezzo, of whom Dante speaks disparagingly in the *Commedia* and in the *De Vulgari Eloquentia*, was instrumental in its foundation in 1293. It was sacked in 1378 during the rising of the Ciompi. This convent in the earlier portion of the fifteenth century was a centre of Hellenic studies and humanistic culture, under Father Ambrogio Traversari, who died at the close of the Council of Florence. In the cloister there is still a powerful fresco by Andrea del Castagno representing Christ on the Cross, with Madonna and the Magdalene, the Baptist, St. Benedict and St. Romuald. The Romuald especially, the founder of the order, is a fine life-like figure.

The *Spedale di Santa Maria Nuova* was originally founded by Messer Folco Portinari, the father of the girl who may have been Dante's "Giver of Blessing," in 1287. Folco died in 1289, and is buried within the church, which contains one of Andrea della Robbia's Madonnas. Over the portal is a terracotta Coronation of the Madonna by Bicci di Lorenzo, erected in 1424. The two frescoes, representing scenes in the history of the hospital, are of the early part of the fifteenth century; the one on the right was painted in 1424 by Bicci di Lorenzo. In the Via Bufalini, Ghiberti had his workshop; in what was once his house is now the picture gallery of the hospital. Here is the fresco of the Last Judgment, commenced by Fra Bartolommeo in 1499, before he abandoned the world, and finished by Mariotto Albertinelli. Among its contents are an Annunciation by Albertinelli, Madonnas by Cosimo Rosselli and Rosso Fiorentino, and a terracotta Madonna by Verrocchio. The two pictures ascribed to Angelico and Botticelli are not authentic. But in some respects more interesting than these Florentine works is the triptych by the Fleming, Hugo Van der Goes, painted between 1470 and 1475 for Tommaso Portinari, Messer Folco's descendant; in the centre is the "Adoration of the Shepherds," with deliciously quaint little Angels; in the side wings, Tommaso Portinari with his two boys, his wife and their little girl, are guarded by their patron saints. Tommaso Portinari was agent for the Medici in Bruges; and, on the occasion of the wedding of Charles the Bold of Burgundy with Margaret of York in 1468, he made a fine show riding in the procession at the head of the Florentines.

THE CLOISTER OF THE INNOCENTI

A little more to the east are the church and suppressed convent of Santa Maria Maddalena de' Pazzi. In the church, which has a fine court designed by Giuliano da San Gallo, is a Coronation of the Madonna by Cosimo Rosselli; in the chapter-house of the convent is a Crucifixion by Perugino, painted in the closing years of the Quattrocento, perhaps the grandest of all his frescoes. In Ruskin's chapter on the *Superhuman Ideal*, in the second volume of *Modern Painters*, he cites the background of this fresco (together with Benozzo Gozzoli's in the Palazzo Riccardi) as one of the most perfect examples of those ideal landscapes of the religious painters, in which Perugino is supreme: "In the landscape of the fresco in Sta. Maria Maddalena at Florence there is more variety than is usual with him: a gentle river winds round the bases of rocky hills, a river like our own Wye or Tees in their loveliest reaches; level meadows stretch away on its opposite side; mounds set with slender-stemmed foliage occupy the nearer ground, and a small village with its simple spire peeps from the forest at the bend of the valley."

Beyond is the church of Sant' Ambrogio, once belonging to the convent of Benedictine nuns for whom Fra Lippo Lippi painted his great Coronation of Madonna. The church is hardly interesting at present, but contains an Assumption by Cosimo Rosselli, and, in the chapel of the Blessed Sacrament, a marble tabernacle by Mino da Fiesole and a fresco by Cosimo Rosselli painted in 1486, representing the legend of a miraculous chalice with some fine Florentine portrait heads, altogether above the usual level of Cosimo's work.

The Borgo la Croce leads hence to the Porta alla Croce, in the very prosaic and modern Piazza Beccaria. This Porta alla Croce, the eastern gate of Florence in the third walls, was commenced by Arnolfo di Cambio in 1284; the frescoed Madonna in the lunette is by one of the later followers of Ghirlandaio. Through this gate, on October 6th 1308, Corso Donati fled from Florence, after his desperate attempt to hold the Piazza di San Piero Maggiore against the forces of the Signoria. Following the Via Aretina towards Rovezzano, we soon reach the remains of the Badia di San Salvi, where he was slain by his captors—as Dante makes his brother Forese darkly prophesy in the twenty-fourth canto of the *Purgatorio*. Four year later, in October 1312, the Emperor Henry VII. lay sick in the Abbey, while his army ineffectually besieged Florence. Nothing remains to remind us of that epoch, although the district is still called the Campo di Marte or Campo di Arrigo. We know from Leonardo Bruni that Dante, although he had urged the Emperor on to attack the city, did not join the imperial army like many of his fellow exiles had done: "so much reverence did he yet retain for his fatherland." In the old refectory of the Abbey is Andrea del Sarto's Last Supper, one of his most admirable frescoes, painted between 1525 and 1527, equally excellent in colour and design. "I know not," writes Vasari, "what to say of this *Cenacolo* that would not be too little, seeing it to be such that all who behold it are struck with astonishment." When the siege was expected in 1529, and the defenders of the city were destroying everything in the suburbs which could give aid or cover to the enemy, a party of them broke down a wall in the convent and found themselves face to face with this picture. Lost in admiration, they built up a portion of what they had destroyed, in order that this last triumph of Florentine painting might be secure from the hand of war.

On this side of the river, those walls of Florence which Lapo Gianni would fain have seen *inargentate*—the third circle reared by Arnolfo and his successors—have been almost entirely destroyed, and their site marked by the broad utterly prosaic Viali. Besides the Porta alla Croce, the Porta San Gallo and the Porta al Prato still stand, on the north and west respectively. The Porta San Gallo was begun from Arnolfo's design in 1284, but not finished until 1327; the fresco in the lunette is by Michele di Ridolfo Ghirlandaio, Ridolfo's adopted son. On July 21, 1304, the exiled Bianchi and Ghibellines made a desperate attempt to surprise Florence through this gate, led by the heroic young Baschiera della

Tosa. In 1494, Piero dei Medici and his brother Giuliano fled from the people through it; and in 1738 the first Austrian Grand Duke, Francis II., entered by it. The triumphant arch beyond, at which the lions of the Republic, to right and left of the gate, appear to gaze with little favour, marked this latter event.

These Austrian Grand Dukes were decidedly better rulers than the Medici, to whom, by an imperial usurpation, they succeeded on the death of Gian Gastone. Leopold I., Ferdinand III., Leopold II., were tolerant and liberal-minded sovereigns, and under them Tuscany became the most prosperous state in Italy: "a Garden of Paradise without the tree of knowledge and without the tree of life." But, when the Risorgimento came, their sway was found incompatible with the aspirations of the Italians towards national unification; the last Grand Duke, after wavering between Austria and young Italy, threw in his lot with the former, and after having brought the Austrians into Tuscany, was forced to abdicate. Thus Florence became the first capital of Victor Emmanuel's kingdom.

In the Via di San Gallo is the very graceful Palazzo Pandolfini, commenced in 1520 from Raphael's designs, on the left as we move inwards from the gate. From the Via 27 Aprile, which joins the Via di San Gallo, we enter the former convent of Sta. Appollonia. In what was once its refectory is a fresco of the Last Supper by Andrea del Castagno, with the Crucifixion, Entombment, and Resurrection. Andrea del Castagno impressed his contemporaries by his furious passions and savage intractability of temper, his quality of *terribilità*; although we now know that Vasari's story that Andrea obtained the secret of using oil as a vehicle in painting from his friend, Domenico Veneziano, and then murdered him, must be a mere fable, since Domenico survived Andrea by nearly five years. Rugged unadorned strength, with considerable power of characterisation and great technical dexterity, mark his extant works, which are very few in number. This *Cenacolo* in the finest of them all; the figures are full of life and character, although the Saviour is unpleasing and the Judas inclines to caricature. The nine figures from the Villa Pandolfini, frescoes transferred to canvas, are also his; Filippo Scolari, known as Pippo Spano (a Florentine connected with the Buondelmonti, but Ghibelline, who became Count of Temesvar and a great Hungarian captain), Farinata degli Uberti, Niccolò Acciaiuoli (a Florentine who became Grand Seneschal of the kingdom of Naples and founded the Certosa), the Cumæan Sibyl, Esther, Queen Tomyris, Dante, Petrarch, and Boccaccio. The two poets and Boccaccio are the least successful, since they were altogether out of Andrea's line, but there must have been something noble in the man to enable him so to realise Farinata degli Uberti, as he stood alone at Empoli when all others agreed to destroy Florence, to defend her to the last: *Colui che la difese a viso aperto.*

A *Cenacolo* of a very different character may be seen in the refectory of the suppressed convent of Sant' Onofrio in the Via di Faenza. Though showing Florentine influence in its composition, this fresco is mainly Umbrian in character; from a half deciphered inscription on the robe of one of the Apostles (which appears to have been altered), it was once attempted to ascribe it to Raphael. It is now believed to be partly the work of Perugino, partly that of some pupil or pupils of his–perhaps Gerino da Pistoia or Giannicola Manni. It has also been ascribed to Giovanni Lo Spagna and to Raffaellino del Garbo. Morelli supposed it to be the work of a pupil of Perugino who was inspired by a Florentine engraving of the fifteenth century, and suggested Giannicola Manni. In the same street is the picturesque little Gothic church of San Jacopo in Campo Corbolini.

A FLORENTINE SUBURB

At the end of the Via Faenza—where once stood one of Arnolfo's gates—we are out again upon the Viale, here named after Filippo Strozzi. Opposite rises what was the great Medicean citadel, the Fortezza da Basso, built by Alessandro dei Medici to overawe the city. Michelangelo steadfastly refused, at the risk of his life, to have anything to do with it. Filippo Strozzi is said to have aided Alessandro in carrying out this design, and even to have urged it upon him, although he was warned that he was digging his own grave. After the unsuccessful attempt of the exiles to overthrow the newly-established government of Duke Cosimo, while Baccio Valori and the other prisoners were sent to be beheaded or hanged in the Bargello, Filippo Strozzi was imprisoned here and cruelly tortured, in spite of the devoted attempts of his children to obtain his release. Here at length, in 1538, he was found dead in his cell. He was said to have left a paper declaring that, lest he should be more terribly tortured and forced to say things to prejudice his own honour and inculpate innocent persons, he had resolved to take his own life, and that he commended his soul to God, humbly praying Him, if He would grant it no other good, at least to give it a place with that of Cato of Utica. It is not improbable that the paper was a fabrication, and that Filippo had been murdered by orders of the Duke.

CHAPTER XI.

THE BRIDGES–THE QUARTER OF SANTA MARIA NOVELLA

"Sopra il bel fiume d'Arno alla gran villa."
–*Dante*.

OUTSIDE the portico of the Uffizi four Florentine heroes–Farinata degli Uberti, Piero Capponi, Giovanni delle Bande Nere, Francesco Ferrucci–from their marble niches keep watch and ward over the river. This Arno, which Lapo Gianni dreamed of as *balsamo fino*, is spanned by four ancient and famous bridges, and bordered on both banks by the Lungarno.

To the east is the Ponte Rubaconte–so called after the Milanese Podestà, during whose term of office it was made–or Ponte alle Grazie, built in 1237; it is mentioned by Dante in Canto xii. of the *Purgatorio*, and is the only existing Florentine bridge which could have actually felt the footsteps of the man who was afterwards to tread scathless through the ways of Hell, "unbitten by its whirring sulphur-spume." It has, however, been completely altered at various periods. On this bridge a solemn reconciliation was effected between Guelfs and Ghibellines on July 2, 1273, by Pope Gregory X. The Pope in state, between Charles of Anjou and the Emperor Baldwin of Constantinople, blessed his "reconciled" people from the bridge, and afterwards laid the first stone of a church called San Gregorio della Pace in the Piazza dei Mozzi, now destroyed. As soon as the Pope's back was turned, Charles contrived that his work should be undone, and the Ghibellines hounded again out of the city. [49]

Below the Ponte alle Grazie comes the Ponte Vecchio, the Bridge *par excellence*; *il ponte*, or *il passo d'Arno*, as Dante calls it. More than a mere bridge over a river, this Ponte Vecchio is a link in the chain binding Florence to the Eternal City. A Roman bridge stood here of old, and a Roman road may be said to have run across it; it heard the tramp of Roman legionaries, and shook beneath the horses of Totila's Gothic chivalry. This Roman bridge possibly lasted down to the great inundation of 1333. The present structure, erected by Taddeo Gaddi after 1360, with its exquisite framed pictures of the river and city in the centre, is one of the most characteristic bits of old Florence still remaining. The shops of goldsmiths and jewellers were originally established here in the days of Cosimo I., for whom Giorgio Vasari built the gallery that runs above to connect the two Grand Ducal Palaces. Connecting the Porta Romana with the heart of the city, the bridge has witnessed most of the great pageants and processions in Florentine history. Popes and Emperors have crossed it in state; Florentine generals, or hireling condottieri, at the head of their victorious troops; the Piagnoni, bearing the miraculous Madonna of the Impruneta to save the city from famine and pestilence; and Savonarola's new Cyrus, Charles VIII., as conqueror, with lance levelled. Across it, in 1515, was Pope Leo X. borne in his litter, blessing the people to right and left, amidst the exultant cries of *Palle, Palle!* from the crowd, who had forgotten for the time all the crimes of his house in their delight at seeing their countryman, the son of Lorenzo the Magnificent, raised to the papal throne.

In Dante's day, what remained of the famous statue supposed of Mars, *quella pietra scema che guarda il ponte*, "that mutilated stone which guardeth the bridge," still stood here at the corner, probably at the beginning of the present Lungarno Acciaiuoli. "I was of that city that changed its first patron for the Baptist," says an unknown suicide in the seventh circle of Hell, probably one of the Mozzi: "on which account he with his art will ever make it sorrowful. And were it not that at the passage of the Arno there yet remains some semblance of him, those citizens, who afterwards rebuilt it on the ashes left by Attila, would have laboured in vain." Here, as we saw in chapter i., young Buondelmonte was murdered in 1215, a sacrifice to Mars in the city's "last time of peace," *nella sua pace postrema.*

THE PONTE VECCHIO

Lower down comes the Ponte Santa Trinità, originally built in 1252; and still lower the Ponte alla Carraia, built between 1218 and 1220 in the days of Frederick II., for the sake of the growing commerce of the Borgo Ognissanti. This latter bridge was originally called the Ponte Nuovo, as at that time the only other bridge over the Arno was the Ponte Vecchio. It was here that a terrible disaster took place on May 1st, 1304–a strange piece of grim mediæval jesting by the irony of fate turned to still grimmer earnest. After a cruel period of disasters and faction fights, there had come a momentary gleam of peace, and it was determined to renew the pageants and festivities that had been held in better days on May-day, "in the good time passed, of the tranquil and good state of Florence," each contrada trying to rival the other. What followed had best be told in the words of Giovanni Villani, an eye-witness:–

"Amongst the others, the folk of the Borgo San Frediano, who had been wont of yore to devise the newest and most diverse pastimes, sent out a proclamation, that those who wished to know news of the other world should be upon the Ponte alla Carraia and around the Arno on the day of the calends of May. And they arranged scaffolds on the Arno upon boats and ships, and made thereon the likeness and figure of Hell with fires and other pains and torments, with men arrayed like demons, horrible to behold, and others who bore the semblance of naked souls, that seemed real persons; and they hurled them into those divers torments with loud cries and shrieks and uproar, the which seemed hateful and appalling to hear and to behold. Many were the citizens that gathered here to witness this new sport; and the Ponte alla Carraia, the which was then of wood from pile to pile, was so laden with folk that it broke down in several places, and fell with the people who were upon it, whereby many persons died there and were drowned, and many were grieviously injured; so that the game was changed from jest to earnest, and, as the proclamation had run, so indeed did many depart in death to hear news of the other world, with great mourning and lamentation to all the city, for each one thought that he had lost son or brother."

The famous inundation of November 1333 swept away all the bridges, excepting the Ponte Rubaconte. The present Ponte Santa Trinità and Ponte alla Carraia were erected for Duke Cosimo I. by Bartolommeo Ammanati, shortly after the middle of the sixteenth century.

Turning from the river at the Ponte Vecchio by the Via Por Sta. Maria, we see on the right the old church of San Stefano, with a completely modernised interior. Here in 1426 Rinaldo degli Albizzi and Niccolò da Uzzano held a meeting of some seventy citizens, and Rinaldo proposed to check the growing power of the populace by admitting the magnates into the government and reducing the number of Arti Minori. Their plan failed through the opposition of Giovanni dei Medici, who acquired much popularity thereby. It should be remembered that it was not here, as usually stated, but in the Badia, which was also dedicated to St. Stephen, that Boccaccio lectured on Dante.

Right and left two very old streets diverge, the Via Lambertesca and the Borgo Santissimi Apostoli, with splendid mediæval towers. In the former, at the angle of the Via di Por Santa Maria, are the towers of the Girolami and Gherardini, round which there was fierce fighting in the expulsion of the Ghibellines in 1266. Opposite, at the opening of the Borgo Santissimi Apostoli, are the towers of the Baldovinetti (the tower of San Zenobio) and of the Amidei—*la casa di che nacque il vostro fleto*, as Cacciaguida puts it to Dante:

"the house from which your wailing sprang," whose feud with the Buondelmonti was supposed to have originated the Guelf and Ghibelline factions in Florence. And further down the Borgo Santissimi Apostoli, at the opening of the Chiasso delle Misure, is the tall and stately tower of these Buondelmonti themselves, who also had a palace on the opposite side of the street.

The old church of the Santissimi Apostoli, in the Piazza del Limbo, has an inscription on its façade stating that it was founded by Charlemagne, and consecrated by Archbishop Turpin, with Roland and Oliver as witnesses. It appears to have been built in the eleventh century, and is the oldest church on this side of the Arno, with the exception of the Baptistery. Its interior, which is well preserved, is said to have been taken by Filippo Brunelleschi as the model for San Lorenzo and Santo Spirito. In it is a beautiful Ciborium by Andrea della Robbia, with monuments of some of the Altoviti family.

The Story of Florence

THE TOWER OF S. ZANOBI

The Piazza Santa Trinità was a great place for social and other gatherings in mediæval and renaissance Florence. Here on the first of May 1300, a dance of girls was being held to greet the calends of May in the old Florentine fashion, when a band of mounted youths of the Donati, Pazzi and Spini came to blows with a rival company of the Cerchi and their allies; and thus the first blood was shed in the disastrous struggle between the Bianchi and Neri. A few days later a similar faction fight took place on the other side of the bridge, in the Piazza Frescobaldi, on the occasion of a lady's funeral. The great Palazzo Spini, opposite the church, was built at the end of the thirteenth and beginning of the fourteenth century by Geri Spini, the rich papal banker and one of the leaders of the "black" faction. Here he received the Pope's ambassadors and made a great display of his wealth and magnificence, as we gather from Boccaccio's *Decameron*, which gives us an amusing story of his friendship with Cisti the baker, and another of the witty repartees of Madonna Oretta, Geri's wife, a lady of the Malaspina. When Charles of Valois entered Florence in November 1301, Messer Geri entertained a portion of the French barons here, while the Prince himself took up his quarters with the Frescobaldi over the river; during that tumultuous period of Florentine history that followed the expulsion of the Bianchi, Geri was one of the most prominent politicians in the State.

Savonarola's processions of friars and children used to pass through this piazza and over the bridge, returning by way of the Ponte Vecchio. On the Feast of Corpus Christi, 1497, as the Blessed Sacrament was being borne along, with many children carrying red crosses, they were set upon by some of the Compagnacci. The story is quaintly told by Landucci: "As the said procession was passing over the Bridge of Santa Trinità, certain youths were standing to see it pass, by the side of a little church which is on the bridge on the right hand going towards Santo Spirito. Seeing those children with the crosses, they said: 'Here are the children of Fra Girolamo.' And one of them coming up to them, took one of these crosses and, snatching it out of the hand of that child, broke it and threw it into the Arno, as though he had been an infidel; and all this he did for hatred of the Friar."

The column in the Piazza–taken from the Baths of Caracalla at Rome–was set here by Duke Cosimo I., to celebrate his victory over the heroic Piero Strozzi, *il maravigliosissimo bravo Piero Strozzi* as Benvenuto Cellini calls him, in 1563. The porphyry statue of Justice was set high up on this pedestal by the most unjust of all rulers of Florence, the Grand Duke Francesco I., Cosimo's son. This same piazza witnessed a not over friendly meeting of Leonardo da Vinci and Michelangelo. Leonardo, at the time that he was engaged upon his cartoon for the Sala del Maggior Consiglio, was walking in the square, dressed in his usual sumptuous fashion, with a rose coloured tunic reaching down to his knees; when a group of citizens, who were discussing Dante, called him and asked him the meaning of a passage in question. At that moment Michelangelo passed by, and Leonardo courteously referred them to him. "Explain it yourself," said the great sculptor, "you, who made the model of a horse to cast in bronze, and could not cast it, and to your shame left it in the lurch."[50] And he abruptly turned his back on the group, leaving Leonardo red with either shame or anger.

The church of Santa Trinità was originally built in the Gothic style by Niccolò Pisano, shortly after 1250, in the days of the Primo Popolo and contemporaneously with the Palazzo del Podestà. It was largely altered by Buontalenti in the last part of the sixteenth century, and has been recently completely restored. It is a fine example of Italian Gothic. In the interior, are a Mary Magdalene by Desiderio da Settignano and a marble altar by Benedetto da Rovezzano; and also, in one of the chapels of the right aisle, an Annunciation by Don Lorenzo, one of his best works, with some frescoes, partly obliterated and much "restored," by the same good Camaldolese monk.

But the great attraction of this church is the Sassetti Chapel next to the sacristy, which contains a splendid series of frescoes painted in 1485 by Domenico Ghirlandaio. The altar piece is only a copy of the original, now in the Accademia.

The frescoes represent scenes from the life of St. Francis, and should be compared with Giotto's simpler handling of the same theme in the Bardi Chapel at Santa Croce. We have the Saint renouncing the world, the confirmation of his rule by Honorius, his preaching to the Soldan, his reception of the Stigmata, his death and funeral (in which the life-like spectacled bishop aroused Vasari's enthusiastic admiration), and the raising to life of a child of the Sassetti family by an apparition of St. Francis in the Piazza outside the church. The last is especially interesting as giving us a picture of the Piazza in its former state, such as it might have been in the Mayday faction fight, with the Spini Palace, the older bridge, and the houses of the Frescobaldi beyond the river. Each fresco is full of interesting portraits; among the spectators in the consistory is Lorenzo the Magnificent; Ghirlandaio himself appears in the death scene; and, perhaps, most interesting of all, if Vasari's identification can be trusted, are the three who stand on the right near the church in the scene of the resuscitation of the child. These three are said to be Maso degli Albizzi, the founder of the party of the Ottimati, those *nobili popolani* who held the State before they were eclipsed by the Medici; Agnolo Acciaiuoli, who was ruined by adhering to Luca Pitti against Piero dei Medici; and that noblest of all the Medicean victims, Palla Strozzi (*see* chapter iii.). It should, however, be remembered that Maso degli Albizzi had died nearly seventy years before, and that not even Palla Strozzi can be regarded as a contemporary portrait. The sacristy of this church was founded by the Strozzi, and one of the house, Onofrio, lies buried within it. Extremely fine, too, are the portraits of Francesco Sassetti himself and his wife, kneeling below near the altar, also by Ghirlandaio, who likewise painted the sibyls on the ceiling and the fresco representing the sibyl prophesying of the Incarnation to Augustus, over the entrance to the chapel. The sepulchral monuments of Francesco and his wife are by Giuliano da San Gallo.

The famous Crucifix of San Miniato, which bowed its head to San Giovanni Gualberto when he spared the murderer of his brother, was transferred to Santa Trinità in 1671 with great pomp and ceremony, and is still preserved here.

In June 1301 a council was held in the church by the leaders of the Neri, nominally to bring about a concord with the rival faction, in reality to entrap the Cerchi and pave the way for their expulsion by foreign aid. Among the Bianchi present was the chronicler, Dino Compagni; "desirous of unity and peace among citizens," and, before the council broke up, he made a strong appeal to the more factious members. "Signors," he said, "why would you confound and undo so good a city? Against whom would you fight? Against your own brothers? What victory shall ye have? Nought else but lamentation." The Neri answered that the object of their council was merely to stop scandal and establish peace; but it soon became known that there was a conspiracy between them and the Conte Simone da Battifolle of the Casentino, who was sending his son with a strong force towards Florence. Simone dei Bardi (who had been the husband of Beatrice Portinari) appears to have been the connecting link of the conspiracy, which the prompt action of the Signoria checked for the present. The evil day, however, was postponed, not averted.

Following the Via di Parione we reach the back of the Palazzo Corsini–a large seventeenth century palace whose front is on the Lungarno. Here is a large picture gallery, in which a good many of the pictures are erroneously ascribed, but which contains a few more important works. The two gems of the collection are Botticelli's portrait of a Goldsmith (210), formerly ascribed to one of the Pollaiuoli; and Luca Signorelli's tondo (157), of Madonna and Child with St. Jerome and St. Bernard. A Madonna and Child with Angels and the Baptist (162) by Filippino Lippi, or ascribed to him, is a charming and poetical picture; but is not admitted by Mr Berenson into his list of genuine works by this painter. The supposed cartoon for Raphael's Julius II. is of very doubtful authenticity. The picture of the martyrdom of Savonarola (292) is interesting and valuable as affording a view of the Piazza at that epoch, but cannot be regarded as an accurate historical representation of the event. That seventeenth century reincarnation of Lorenzo di Credi, Carlo Dolci, is represented here by several pictures which are above his usual level; for instance, Poetry (179) is a really beautiful thing of its kind. Among the other pictures is a little Apollo and Daphne (241), probably an early work of Andrea del Sarto. The Raffaellino di Carlo who painted the Madonna and Saints (200), is not to be confused with Filippino's pupil, Raffaellino del Garbo.

In the Via Tornabuoni, the continuation of the Piazza Santa Trinità, stands the finest of all Florentine palaces of the Renaissance, the Palazzo Strozzi. It was begun in 1489 for the elder Filippo Strozzi, with the advice and encouragement of Lorenzo the Magnificent, by Benedetto da Maiano, and continued by Simone del Pollaiuolo (called "Cronaca" from his yarning propensities), to whom the cornice and court are due. It was finished for the younger Filippo Strozzi, the husband of Clarice dei Medici, shortly before his fall, in the days of Duke Alessandro. The works in iron on the exterior—lanterns, torch-holders and the like, especially a wonderful *fanale* at the corner—are by Niccolò Grosso (called "Caparra" from his habit of demanding payment in advance), and the finest things of their kind imaginable. Filippo Strozzi played a curiously inconstant part in the history of the closing days of the Republic. After having been the most intimate associate of his brother-in-law, the younger Lorenzo, he was instrumental first in the expulsion of Ippolito and Alessandro, then in the establishment of Alessandro's tyranny; and finally, finding himself cast by the irony of fate for the part of the last Republican hero, he took the field against Duke Cosimo, only to find a miserable end in a dungeon. One of his daughters, Luisa Capponi, was believed to have been poisoned by order of Alessandro; his son, Piero, became the bravest Italian captain of the sixteenth century and carried on a heroic contest with Cosimo's mercenary troops.

ARMS OF THE STROZZI

Down the Via della Vigna Nuova is another of these Renaissance palaces, built for a similar noble family associated with the Medici,–the Palazzo Rucellai. Bernardo Rucellai–who was not originally of noble origin, but whose family had acquired what in Florence was the real title to nobility, vast wealth in commerce–married Nannina, the younger sister of Lorenzo the Magnificent, and had this palace begun for him in 1460 by Bernardo Rossellino from the design of Leo Battista Alberti,–to whom also the Rucellai loggia opposite is due. More of Alberti's work for the Rucellai may be seen at the back of the palace, in the Via della Spada, where in the former church of San Pancrazio (which gave its name to a *sesto* in old Florence) is the chapel which he built for Bernardo Rucellai in imitation of the Holy Sepulchre of Jerusalem.

The Via delle Belle Donne–most poetically named of Florentine streets–leads hence into the Piazza di Santa Maria Novella. On the way, where five roads meet, is the Croce al Trebbio, with symbols of the four Evangelists below the Crucifix. It marks the site of one of St Peter Martyr's fiercest triumphs over the Paterini, one of those "marvellous works" for which Savonarola, in his last address to his friars, complains that the Florentines had been so ungrateful towards his Order. But the story of the Dominicans of Santa Maria Novella is not one of persecution, but of peace-making. They played at times as noble a part in mediæval Florence as their brethren of San Marco were to do in the early Renaissance; and later, during the great siege, they took up the work of Fra Girolamo, and inspired the people to their last heroic defence of the Republic.

Opposite Santa Maria Novella is the Loggia di San Paolo, designed by Brunelleschi, and erected in 1451, shortly after his death. The coloured terracotta reliefs, by Andrea della Robbia, include two fine portraits of governors of the hospital (not of the Della Robbia themselves, as frequently stated). The relief in a lunette over the door on the right, representing the meeting of St Francis and St Dominic, is one of Andrea's best works:–

"L'un fu tutto serafico in ardore,
l'altro per sapienza in terra fue
di cherubica luce uno splendore.
Dell'un dirò, però che d'ambedue
si dice l'un pregiando, qual ch'uom prende,
perchè ad un fine fur l'opere sue."[51]

In 1212, three years before the murder of Buondelmonte, the first band of Franciscans had come to Florence, sent thither by St Francis himself from Assisi. A few years later, at the invitation of a Florentine merchant Diodato, who had built a chapel and house as an act of restitution, St Dominic, from Bologna, sent the Blessed John of Salerno with twelve friars to occupy this mission at Ripoli, about three miles beyond where now stands the Gate of S. Niccolò. Thence they extended their apostolic labours into the city, and when St Dominic came, at the end of 1219, they had already made progress. Finally they moved into the city–first to San Pancrazio, and at length settled at Santa Maria tra le Vigne, a little church then outside the walls, where B.

Giovanni was installed by the Pope's legate and the bishop in 1221. Before the church, in the present piazza, St Peter Martyr, the "hammer of the heretics," fought the Paterini with both spiritual and material arms. At last, the growth of the order requiring larger room, on St Luke's day, 1278, Cardinal Latino de' Frangipani laid here the first stone of Santa Maria Novella.

Where once the little church of Our Lady among the Vines stood outside the second circuit of the city's walls, rises now the finest Italian Gothic church in Florence. Less than a year after it had been commenced, the same Dominican cardinal who had laid the first stone summoned a mass meeting in the Piazza, and succeeded in patching up a temporary peace between Guelfs and Ghibellines, and among the Guelf magnates themselves, 1279. This Cardinal Latino left a memory revered in Florence, and Fra Angelico, in the picture now in our National Gallery, placed him among the glorified saints attending upon the resurrection of Our Lord. Some twenty years later, in November 1301, a parliament was held within the still unfinished church, at which another Papal peacemaker, the infamous Charles of Valois, in the presence of the Priors of the Republic, the Podestà and the Captain, the bishop and chief citizens, received the *balìa* to guard Florence and pacify the Guelfs, and swore on the faith of the son of a king to preserve the city in peace and prosperity. We have seen how he kept his word. Santa Maria

Novella, in 1304, was the centre of the sincere and devoted attempts made by Boniface's successor, the sainted Benedict XI., to heal the wounds of Florence; attempts in which, throughout Italy, the Dominicans were his "angels of peace," as he called his missioners. When the Republic finally fell into the hands of Cosimo dei Medici in 1434, the exiled Pope Eugenius IV. was staying in the adjoining monastery; it was here that he made his unsuccessful attempt to mediate, and heard the bitter farewell words of Rinaldo degli Albizzi: "I blame myself most of all, because I believed that you, who had been hunted out of your own country, could keep me in mine."

IN THE GREEN CLOISTERS, S. MARIA NOVELLA

The church itself, striped tiger-like in black and white marble, was constructed from the designs of three Dominican friars, Fra Ristoro da Campi, Fra Sisto, and Fra Giovanni da Campi. Fra Giovanni was a scholar or imitator of Arnolfo di Cambio, and the two former were the architects who restored the Ponte alla Carraia and the Ponte Santa Trinità after their destruction in 1269. The façade (with the exception of the lower part, which belongs to the fourteenth century) was designed by Leo Battista Alberti, whose friends the Rucellai were the chief benefactors of this church; the lovely but completely restored pointed arcades on the right, with niches for tombs and armorial bearings, were designed by Brunelleschi. On the left, though in part reduced to vile usage, there is a bit comparatively less altered. The interior was completed soon after the middle of the fourteenth century, when Fra Jacopo Passavanti–the author of that model of pure Tuscan prose, *Lo Specchio della vera Penitenza*–was Prior of the convent. The campanile is said to have been designed by another Dominican, Fra Jacopo Talenti, the probable architect of the so-called Spanish Chapel in the cloisters on the left of the church, of which more presently.

During the great siege of Florence the mantle of Savonarola seemed to have fallen upon the heroic Prior of Santa Maria Novella, Fra Benedetto da Foiano. When the news of the alliance between Pope and Emperor came to

The Story of Florence

Florence, while all Bologna was in festa for the coronation of the Emperor, Varchi tells us that Fra Benedetto delivered a great sermon in the Sala del Maggior Consiglio, which was thrown open to all who would come to hear; in which sermon he proved from passages in the Old and New Testaments that Florence would be delivered from all dangers, and then enjoy perpetual perfect felicity in the liberty she so desired. With such grace and eloquence did he speak, that the vast audience was moved to tears and to joy by turns. At the end, "with ineffable gestures and words," he gave to the Gonfaloniere, Raffaello Girolami, a standard upon one side of which was a Christ victorious over the hostile soldiery, and upon the other the red Cross of the Florentine Commune, saying: *Cum hoc et in hoc vinces*. After the capitulation Malatesta Baglioni seized the friar and sent him to Rome, where he was slowly starved to death in the dungeon of Sant' Angelo.

The interior was thus not quite finished, when Boccaccio's seven maidens met here on a Wednesday morning in early spring in that terrible year of pestilence, 1348; yet we may readily picture to ourselves the scene described in the introduction to the *Decameron*; the empty church; the girls in their dark mourning garb, after hearing Mass, seated together in a side chapel and gradually passing from telling their beads to discussing more mundane matters; and then, no sooner do three members of the other sex appear upon the scenes than a sudden gleam of gladness lights up their faces, and even the plague itself is forgotten. One of them, indeed, blushed; "she became all crimson in the face through modesty," says Boccaccio, "because there was one of their number who was beloved by one of these youths;" but afterwards found no difficulty in rivalling the others in the impropriety of her talk.

Entering the western portal, we find ourselves in a nave of rather large proportions, somewhat dark but not without a glow from the stained glass windows–adapted above all for preaching. As in Santa Croce, it is cut across by a line of chapels, thus giving the whole a T shape, and what represents the apse is merely a deeper and taller recess behind the high altar. There is nothing much to interest us here in the nave or aisles, save, by the side of the central door, one of the very few extant works of Masaccio, a fresco representing the Blessed Trinity adored by the Madonna and St. John, with two kneeling donors–portraits of which no amount of restoration can altogether destroy the truth and grandeur. The Annunciation, on the opposite side of the door, is a mediocre fresco of the fourteenth century. The Crucifix above is one of several works of the kind ascribed to Giotto.

It will be best to take the chapels at the end of the nave and in the transepts in the order into which they fall, as illustrating the development of Florentine art.

On the right a flight of steps leads up into the Rucellai chapel where, half concealed in darkness, hangs the famous picture once supposed to mark the very birthday of Florentine painting. That Cimabue really painted a glorious Madonna for this church, which was worshipped by a king and hailed with acclamation by a rejoicing people, is to be most firmly and devoutly held. Unfortunately, it seems highly probable that this picture is not Cimabue's Madonna. It is decidedly Sienese in character, and, as there is documentary evidence that Duccio of Siena painted a Madonna for Santa Maria Novella, and as the attendant Angels are in all respects similar to those in Duccio's authenticated works, the picture is probably his. It deserves all veneration, nevertheless, for it is a noble picture in the truest sense of the word. In the same chapel is the monument of the Dominican nun, the Beata Villana, by Bernardo Rossellino.

Crossing the church to the chapel in the left transept, the Strozzi Chapel, we mount into the true atmosphere of the Middle Ages–into one of those pictured theatres which set before us in part what Dante gave in full in his *Commedia*. The whole chapel is dedicated to St. Thomas Aquinas, the glory of the philosophy of the mediæval world and, above all, of the Dominican order, whose cardinal virtues are extolled in allegorical fashion on the ceiling; but the frescoes are drawn from the work of his greatest Florentine disciple, Dante Alighieri, in whose poem Thomas mainly lives for the non-Catholic world. It contains all Orcagna's extant work in painting. The altar piece, executed by Andrea Orcagna in 1357, is the grandest of its kind belonging to the Giottesque period. Its central motive, of the Saviour delivering the keys to St. Peter and the Summa to St. Thomas, the spiritual and philosophical regimens of the mediæval world, is very finely rendered; while the angelic choir is a foretaste of Angelico. Madonna presents St. Thomas; the Baptist, St. Peter; Michael and Catherine are in attendance upon the Queen of Heaven, Lawrence and Paul upon the Precursor. The predella represents St. Peter walking upon the waves, with on either side an episode in the life of St. Thomas and a miracle of St. Lawrence. The frescoes are best seen on a very bright morning, shortly before noon. The Last Judgment, by Andrea, shows the traditional representation of the Angels with trumpets and with the emblems of the Passion, wheeling round the Judge; and the dead rising to judgment, impelled irresistibly to right or left even before the sentence is pronounced. Above the one band, kneels the white-robed Madonna in intercession–type of the Divine Mercy as in Dante; over the others, at the head of the Apostles, is the Baptist who seems appealing for judgment–type of the Divine Justice. This placing Mary and St John opposite to each other, as in Dante's Rose of Paradise, is typical of Florentine art; Santa Maria del Fiore and San Giovanni are, as it were, inseparable. Among the blessed is Dante, gazing up in fixed adoration at the Madonna, as when following St Bernard's prayer at the close of his Vision; on the other side some of the faces of the lost are a miracle of expression. The Hell on the right wall, by Andrea's brother Leonardo, is more immediately taken from the *Commedia*. The Paradise on the left, or, rather, the Empyrean Heaven–with the faces *suadi di carità*, Angels and Saints absorbed in vision and love of God–is by Andrea himself, and is more directly pictorial than Dante's *Paradiso* could admit. Christ and the Madonna are enthroned side by side, whereas we do not actually see Him in human form in the *Commedia*,–perhaps in accordance with that reverence which impels the divine poet to make the name *Cristo* rhyme with nothing but itself. For sheer loveliness in detail, no other fourteenth century master produced anything to compare with this fresco; it may be said to mark the advent of a new element in Italian art.

Thence we pass into the early Renaissance with Brunelleschi and Ghiberti, with Ghirlandaio and Filippino Lippi. In the chapel to the left of the choir hangs Filippo Brunelleschi's famous wooden Crucifix, carved in friendly rivalry with Donatello. The rival piece, Donatello's share in this sculptured *tenzone*, has been seen in Santa Croce.

In the choir are frescoes by Domenico Ghirlandaio, and a fine brass by Lorenzo Ghiberti. These frescoes were begun in 1486, immediately after the completion of the Santa Trinità series, and finished in 1490; and, though devoid of the highest artistic qualities, are eminently characteristic of their epoch. Though representing scenes from the life of the Madonna and the Baptist, this is entirely subordinated to the portrait groups of noble Florentines and their ladies, introduced as usually utterly uninterested spectators of the sacred events. As religious pictures they are naught; but as representations of contemporary Florentine life, most valuable. Hardly elsewhere shall you see so fine a series of portraits of the men and women of the early Renaissance; but they have other things to think of than the Gospel history. Look at the scene of the Angel appearing to Zacharias. The actual event is hardly noticed; hidden in the throng of citizens, too busily living the life of the Renaissance to attend to such trifles; besides, it would not improve their style to read St. Luke. In the Visitation, the Nativity of the Baptist, the Nativity of the Blessed Virgin, a fashionable beauty of the period sweeps in with her attendants—and it is hardly uncharitable to suppose that, if not herself, at least her painter thought more of her fine clothes than of her devotional aspect. The portraits of the donors, Giovanni Tornabuoni and his wife, are on the window wall. In the scene of the expulsion of Joachim from the Temple, a group of painters stands together (towards the window); the old cleanly-shaven man in a red hat is Alessio Baldovinetti, Ghirlandaio's master; next to him, with a lot of dark hair, dressed in a red mantle and blue vest, is Domenico

Ghirlandaio himself; his pupil and brother-in-law, Sebastiano Mainardi, and his brother, David Ghirlandaio, are with him—the latter being the figure with shoulder turned and hat on head. In the apparition to Zacharias, among the numerous portraits, a group of four half figures discussing at the foot of the history is of special interest; three of them are said to represent Marsilio Ficino, Cristoforo Landini, and Angelo Poliziano (in the middle, slightly raising his hand); the fourth, turned to speak to Landini, is said by Vasari to be a famous teacher of Greek, Demetrius, but now supposed to be Gentile Becchi, a learned bishop of Arezzo. The stained glass was designed by Filippino Lippi. Under the high altar rests the body of the Blessed John of Salerno, the "Apostle of Florence," who brought the first band of Dominicans to the city.

Less admired, but in some respects more admirable, are the frescoes by Filippino Lippi in the chapel on the right of the choir, almost his last works, painted about 1502, and very much injured by restoration. The window is also from his design. The frescoes represent scenes from the lives of St. John and St. Philip, and are remarkable for their lavish display of Roman antiquities, in which they challenge comparison with Andrea Mantegna. The scene of St. Philip exorcising the dragon is especially fine. Observe how the characteristic intensity of the school of Botticelli is shown in the way in which the very statues take part in the action.

Mars flourishes his broken spear, his wolves and kites cower to him for protection from the emissaries of the new faith, whose triumph is further symbolised in the two figures above of ancient deities conquered by Angels. An analogous instance will be found in Botticelli's famous Calumny in the Uffizi. In this statue of Mars is seen the last rendering of the old Florentine tradition of their *primo padrone*. Thus, perhaps, did the new pagans of the Renaissance lovingly idealise "that mutilated stone which guards the bridge."

The monument of the elder Filippo Strozzi, in the same chapel, is a fine piece of work by Benedetto da Maiano, with a lovely tondo of the Madonna and Child attended by Angels. And we should also notice Giovanni della Robbia's fountain in the sacristy, before passing into the cloisters.

Here in the cloisters we pass back again into more purely mediæval thought. Passing some early frescoes of the life of the Madonna–the dream of Joachim, his meeting St. Anne, the Birth and Presentation of the Blessed Virgin–which Ruskin believed to be by Giotto himself–we enter to the left the delicious Green Cloisters; a pleasant lounging place in summer. In the lunettes along the walls are frescoed scenes from Genesis in *terra verde*, of which the most notable are by Paolo Uccello–the Flood and the Sacrifice of Noah. Uccello's interests were scientific rather than artistic. These frescoes are amazingly clever exercises in the new art of perspective, the *dolce cosa* as he called it when his wife complained of his absorption; but are more curious than beautiful, and hardly inspire us with more than mild admiration at the painter's cleverness in poising the figure—which, we regret to say, he intends for the Almighty—so ingeniously in mid air.

But out of these cloisters, on the right, opens the so-called Spanish Chapel—the Cappella degli Spagnuoli—one of the rarest buildings in Italy for the student of mediæval doctrine. Here, as in the Strozzi Chapel, we are in the grasp of the same mighty spirit that inspired the *Divina Commedia* and the *De Monarchia*, although the actual execution falls far below the design. The chapel—designed by Fra Jacopo Talenti in 1320—was formerly the chapter-house of the convent; it seems to have acquired the title of Spanish Chapel in the days of Duke Cosimo I., when Spaniards swarmed in Florence and were wont to hold solemn festival here on St. James' day. The frescoes that cover its ceiling and walls were executed about the middle of the fourteenth century—according to Vasari by Simone Martini and Taddeo Gaddi, though this seems highly doubtful. Their general design is possibly due to Fra Jacopo Passavanti. They set forth the Dominican ideal, the Church and the world as the Friars Preachers conceived of them, even as Giotto's famous allegories at Assisi show us the same through Franciscan glasses. While Orcagna painted the world beyond the grave in honour of the Angelical Doctor, these artists set forth the present world as it should be under his direction and that of his brothers, the "hounds of the Lord," *domini canes*, who defended the *orto cattolico*.

The vaulted roof is divided into four segments; and the picture in each segment corresponds to a great fresco on the wall below. On the wall opposite, as we enter, is represented the supreme event of the world's history, from which all the rest starts and upon which the whole hinges, the Passion of Christ, leading up to the Resurrection on the roof above it. On the segment of the roof over the door is the Ascension, and on the wall below was shown (now much damaged) how the Dominicans received and carried out Christ's last injunction to His disciples. In the left segment of the roof is the Descent of the Holy Spirit; and beneath it, on the wall, the result of this outpouring upon the world of intellect is shown in the triumph of Philosophy in the person of Aquinas, its supreme mediæval exponent. In the right segment is the Ship of Peter; and, on the wall below, is seen how Peter becomes a fisher of men, the triumph of his Church under the guidance of the Dominicans. These two great allegorical frescoes–the triumph of St. Thomas and the *civil briga* of the Church–are thus a more complete working out of the scheme set forth more simply by Orcagna in his altar piece in the Strozzi Chapel above–the functions delegated by Christ to Peter and St. Thomas–the power of the Keys and the doctrine of the *Summa Theologica*.

In the centre of the philosophical allegory, St. Thomas Aquinas is seated on a Gothic throne, with an open book in his hands bearing the text from the Book of Wisdom with which the Church begins her lesson in his honour: *Optavi, et datus est mihi sensus. Invocavi, et venit in me spiritus sapientiae; et praeposui illam regnis et sedibus.*[52] Over his head hover seven Angels, invested with the emblems of the three theological and four cardinal virtues; around him are seated the Apostles and Prophets, in support of his doctrine; beneath his feet heresiarchs are humbled–Sabellius and Arius, to wit–and even Averrhoes, who "made the great comment," seems subdued. Below, in fourteen little shrines, are allegorical figures of the fourteen sciences which meet and are given ultimate form in his work, and at the feet of each maiden sits some great exponent of the science. From right to left, the seven liberal arts of the Trivium and Quadrivium lead up to the Science of Numbers, represented on earth by Pythagoras; from left to right, the earthly and celestial sciences lead up to Dogmatic Theology, represented by Augustine.[53]

On the opposite wall is the Church militant and triumphant. Before Santa Maria del Fiore, here symbolising the Church militant, sit the two ideal guides of man, according to the dual scheme of Dante's *De Monarchia*–the Pope and the Emperor. On either side are seated in a descending line the great dignitaries of the Church and the Empire; Cardinal and Abbot, King and Baron; while all around are gathered the clergy and the laity, religious of every order, judges and nobles, merchants and scholars, with a few ladies kneeling on the right, one of whom is said to be Petrarch's Laura. Many of these figures are apparently portraits, but the attempts at identification–such as that of the Pope with Benedict XI., the Emperor with Henry VII.–are entirely untrustworthy. The Bishop, however, standing at the head of the clergy, is apparently Agnolo Acciaiuoli, Bishop of Florence; and the French cavalier, in short tunic and hood, standing opposite to him at the head of the laity (formerly called Cimabue), is said–very questionably–to be the Duke of Athens. At the feet of the successors of Peter and Cæsar are gathered the sheep and lambs of Christ's fold, watched over by the black and white hounds that symbolise the Dominicans. On the right, Dominic urges on his watchdogs against the heretical wolves who are carrying off the lambs of the flock; Peter Martyr hammers the unbelievers with the weapon of argument alone; Aquinas convinces them with the light of his philosophic doctrine. But beyond is Acrasia's Bower of Bliss, a mediaeval rendering of what Spenser hereafter so divinely sung in the second book of the *Faerie Queene*. Figures of vice sit enthroned; while seven damsels, Acrasia's handmaidens, dance before them; and youth sports in the shade of the forbidden myrtles. Then come repentance and the confessional; a Dominican friar (not one of the great

Saints, but any humble priest of the order) absolves the penitents; St Dominic appears again, and shows them the way to Paradise; and then, becoming as little children, they are crowned by the Angels, and St. Peter lets them through the gate to join the Church Triumphant. Above in the Empyrean is the Throne of the Lord, with the Lamb and the four mystical Beasts, and the Madonna herself standing up at the head of the Angelic Hierarchies.

In the great cloisters beyond, the Ciompi made their headquarters in 1378, under their Eight of Santa Maria Novella; and, at the request of their leaders, the prior of the convent sent some of his preachers to furnish them with spiritual consolation and advice.

Passing through the Piazza—where marble obelisks resting on tortoises mark the goals of the chariot races held here under Cosimo I. and his successors, on the Eve of St. John—and down the Via della Scala, we come to the former Spezeria of the convent, still a flourishing manufactory of perfumes, liqueurs and the like, though no longer in the hands of the friars. In what was once its chapel, are frescoes by Spinello Aretino and his pupils, painted at the end of the Trecento, and representing the Passion of Christ. They are inferior to Spinello's work at Siena and on San Miniato, but the Christ bearing the Cross has much majesty, and, in the scene of the washing of the feet, the nervous action of Judas as he starts up is finely conceived.

The famous Orti Oricellari, the gardens of the Rucellai, lie further down the Via della Scala. Here in the early days of the Cinquecento the most brilliant literary circles of Florentine society met; and there was a sort of revival of the old Platonic Academy, which had died out with Marsilio Ficino. Machiavelli wrote for these gatherings his discourses on Livy and his Art of War. Although their meetings were mainly frequented by Mediceans, some of the younger members were ardent Republicans; and it was here that a conspiracy was hatched against the life of the Cardinal Giulio dei Medici, for which Jacopo da Diacceto and one of the Alamanni died upon the scaffold. In later days these Orti belonged to Bianca Cappello. At the corner of the adjoining palace is a little Madonna by Luca della Robbia; and further on, in a lunette on the right of the former church of San Jacopo in Ripoli, there is a group of Madonna and Child with St. James and St. Dominic, probably by Andrea della Robbia. In the Via di Palazzuolo, the little church of San Francesco dei Vanchetoni contains two small marble busts of children, exceedingly delicately modelled, supposed to represent the Gesù Bambino and the boy Baptist; they are ascribed to Donatello, but recent writers attribute them to Desiderio or Rossellino.

In the Borgo Ognissanti, where the Swiss of Charles VIII. in 1494, forcing their way into the city from the Porta al Prato, were driven back by the inhabitants, are the

The Story of Florence

church of Ognissanti and the Franciscan convent of San Salvadore. The church and convent originally belonged to the Frati Umiliati, who settled here in 1251, were largely influential in promoting the Florentine wool trade, and exceedingly democratic in their sympathies. Their convent was a great place for political meetings in the days of Giano della Bella, who used to walk in their garden taking counsel with his friends. After the siege they were expelled from Florence, and the church and convent made over to the Franciscans of the Osservanza, who are said to have brought hither the habit which St. Francis wore when he received the Stigmata. The present church was built in the second half of the sixteenth century, but contains some excellent pictures and frescoes belonging to the older edifice. Over the second altar to the right is a frescoed Pietà, one of the earliest works of Domenico Ghirlandaio, with above it the Madonna taking the Vespucci family under her protection—among them Amerigo, who was to give his name to the new continent of America. Further on, over a confessional, is Sandro Botticelli's St. Augustine, the only fresco of his still remaining in Florence; opposite to it, over a confessional on the left, is St. Jerome by Domenico Ghirlandaio; both apparently painted in 1480. In the left transept is a Crucifix ascribed to Giotto; Vasari tells us that it was the original of the numerous works of this kind which Puccio Capanna and others of his pupils multiplied through Italy. In the sacristy is a much restored fresco of the Crucifixion, belonging to the Trecento. Sandro Botticelli was buried in this church in 1510, and, two years later, Amerigo Vespucci in 1512. In the former Refectory of the convent is a fresco of the Last Supper, painted by Domenico Ghirlandaio in 1480, and very much finer than his similar work in San Marco. In the lunette over the portal of the church is represented the Coronation of the Blessed Virgin, by Giovanni della Robbia.

The Borgo Ognissanti leads hence westward into the Via del Prato, and through the Porta al Prato, one of the four gates of the third wall of the city, begun by Arnolfo in 1284; now merely a mutilated torso of Arnolfo's stately structure, left stranded in the prosaic wilderness of the modern Viale. The fresco in the lunette is by Michele di Ridolfo Ghirlandaio. Down towards the Arno a single tower remains from the old walls, mutilated, solitary and degraded so as to look a mere modern bit of masonry.

Beyond are the Cascine Gardens, stretching for some two miles between the Arno and the Mugnone, delicious to linger in, and a sacred place to all lovers of English poetry. For here, towards the close of 1819, "in a wood that skirts the Arno, near Florence, and on a day when that tempestuous wind, whose temperature is at once mild and animating, was collecting the vapours which pour down the autumnal rains," Shelley wrote the divinest of all English lyrics: the *Ode to the West Wind.*

The Story of Florence

"Make me thy lyre, even as the forest is:
What if my leaves are falling like its own!
The tumult of thy mighty harmonies

Will take from both a deep, autumnal tone,
Sweet though in sadness. Be thou, spirit fierce,
My spirit! Be thou me, impetuous one!

Drive my dead thoughts over the universe
Like withered leaves to quicken a new birth!
And, by the incantation of this verse,

Scatter, as from an unextinguished hearth
Ashes and sparks, my words among mankind!
Be through my lips to unawakened earth

The trumpet of a prophecy! O, wind,
If Winter comes, can Spring be far behind?"

IN THE BOBOLI GARDENS

CHAPTER XII.

ACROSS THE ARNO

"Come a man destra, per salire al monte,
dove siede la Chiesa che soggioga
la ben guidata sopra Rubaconte,
si rompe del montar l'ardita foga.
per le scalee che si fero ad etade
ch'era sicuro il quaderno e la doga."
–*Dante.*

ACROSS the river, partly lying along its bank and partly climbing up St. George's hill to the south, lies what was the Sesto d'Oltrarno in the days when old Florence was divided into sextaries, and became the Quartiere di Santo Spirito when the city was reorganised in quarters after the expulsion of the Duke of Athens. It was not originally a part of the city itself. At the time of building the second walls in the twelfth century (*see* chapter i.), there were merely three *borghi* or suburbs beyond the Arno, inhabited by the poorest classes, each of the three beginning at the head of the Ponte Vecchio; the Borgo Pidiglioso to the east, towards the present Via dei Bardi and Santa Lucia, where the road went on to Rome by way of Figline and Arezzo; the Borgo di

Santa Felicità, to the south, ending in a gate at the present Piazza San Felice, where the road to Siena commenced; and the Borgo San Jacopo to the west, with a gate in the present Piazza Frescobaldi, on the way to Pisa. A few rich and noble families began to settle here towards the beginning of the thirteenth century. When the dissensions between Guelfs and Ghibellines came to a head in 1215, the Nerli and Rossi were Guelfs, the Gangalandi, Ubbriachi and Mannelli, Ghibellines; and these were then the only nobles of the Oltrarno, although Villani tells us that "the Frescobaldi and the Bardi and the Mozzi were already beginning to become powerful." The *Primo Popolo* commenced to wall it in, in 1250, with the stones from dismantled feudal towers; and it was finally included in the third circle of the walls at the beginning of the fourteenth century–a point to which we shall return.

As we saw in chapter iii., it was in the Oltrarno that the nobles made their last stand against the People in 1343, when the Nerli held the Ponte alla Carraia, the Frescobaldi and Mannelli the Ponte di Santa Trinità, and the Rossi and Bardi defended the Ponte Vecchio and the Ponte Rubaconte, with the narrow streets between. In the following century it was the headquarters of the faction opposed to the Medici, the Party of the Mountain, as it was called, from the lofty position of Luca Pitti's great palace. A century more, and it became the seat of government under the Medicean Grand

Dukes, and the whole was crowned by the fortress of the Belvedere which Buontalenti built in 1590 for Ferdinand I.

At the head of the Ponte Vecchio, to right and left, the Borgo San Jacopo and the Via dei Bardi still retain something of their old characteristics and mediæval appearance. In the former especially are some fine towers remaining of the Rossi, Nerli, Barbadori, and other families; particularly one which belonged to the Marsili, opposite the church of San Jacopo. A side street, the Via dei Giudei, once inhabited by Jews, is still very picturesque. The little church of San Jacopo, originally built in the eleventh century, but entirely reconstructed in more recent times, still possesses an old Romanesque portico. In this church some of the more bitter spirits among the nobles held a council in 1294, and unanimously decided to murder Giano della Bella. "The dogs of the people," said Messer Berto Frescobaldi, who was the spokesman, "have robbed us of honour and office, and we cannot enter the Palace. If we beat one of our own servants, we are undone. Wherefore, my lords, it is my rede that we should come forth from this servitude. Let us take up arms and assemble in the piazza; let us slay the plebeians, friends and foes alike, so that never again shall we or our children be subjected to them." His plan, however, seemed too dangerous to the other nobles. "If our design failed," said Messer Baldo della Tosa, "we should all be killed"; and it was decided to proceed by more prudent means, and to disorganise the People and undermine Giano's credit with them, before taking further action.

At the end of the Borgo San Jacopo, the Frescobaldi had their palaces in the piazza which still bears their name, at the head of the Ponte Santa Trinità. Here Charles of Valois took up his headquarters in November 1301, with the intention of keeping this portion of the city in case he lost his hold of the rest. Opposite the bridge the Capponi had their palace; the heroic Piero Capponi lived here; and then the Gonfaloniere Niccolò, who, accused of favouring the Medici, was deprived of his office, and died broken-hearted just before the siege.

On the left of the Ponte Vecchio the Via dei Bardi, where the nobles and retainers of that fierce old house made their last stand against the People after the Frescobaldi had been forced to surrender, has been much spoilt of recent years, though a few fine palaces remain, and some towers, especially two, of the Mannelli and Ridolfi, at the beginning of the street. In the Via dei Bardi, the fine Capponi Palace was built for Niccolò da Uzzano at the beginning of the Quattrocento. The church of Santa Lucia has a Della Robbia relief over the entrance, and a picture of the school of Fra Filippo in the interior. The street ends in the Piazza dei Mozzi, opposite the Ponte alle Grazie or Ponte Rubaconte, where stands the Torrigiani Palace, built by Baccio d'Agnolo in the sixteenth century.

The Story of Florence

From the Ponte Vecchio the Via Guicciardini leads to the Pitti Palace, and onwards to the Via Romana and great Porta Romana. In the Piazza Santa Felicità a column marks the site of one of St. Peter Martyr's triumphs over the Paterini; the loggia is by Vasari; the historian Guicciardini is buried in the church, which contains some second-rate pictures. Further on, on the right, is the house where Machiavelli died, a disappointed and misunderstood patriot, in 1527; on the left is Guicciardini's palace.

The magnificent Palazzo Pitti was commenced shortly after 1440 by Brunelleschi and Michelozzo, for Luca Pitti, that vain and incompetent old noble who hoped to eclipse the Medici during the closing days of the elder Cosimo. Messer Luca grew so confident, Machiavelli tells us, that "he began two buildings, one in Florence and the other at Ruciano, a place about a mile from the city; both were in right royal style, but that in the city was altogether greater than any other that had ever been built by a private citizen until that day. And to complete them he shrank from no measures, however extraordinary; for not only did citizens and private persons contribute and aid him with things necessary for the building, but communes and corporations lent him help. Besides this, all who were under ban, and whosoever had committed murder or theft or anything else for which he feared public punishment, provided that he were a person useful for the work, found secure refuge within these buildings." After the triumph of Piero dei Medici in 1466, Luca Pitti was pardoned, but ruined. "Straightway," writes Machiavelli, "he learned what difference there is between success and failure, between dishonour and honour. A great solitude reigned in his houses, which before had been frequented by vast throngs of citizens. In the street his friends and relations feared not merely to accompany him, but even to salute him, since from some of them the honours had been taken, from others their property, and all alike were menaced. The superb edifices which he had commenced were abandoned by the builders; the benefits which had been heaped upon him in the past were changed into injuries, honours into insults. Many of those who had freely given him something of great value, now demanded it back from him as having been merely lent, and those others, who had been wont to praise him to the skies, now blamed him for an ungrateful and violent man. Wherefore too late did he repent that he had not trusted Niccolò Soderini, and sought rather to die with honour with arms in hand, than live on in dishonour among his victorious enemies."

In 1549 the unfinished palace was sold by Luca Pitti's descendants to Eleonora of Toledo, Duke Cosimo's wife, and it was finished by Ammanati during the latter half of the sixteenth century; the wings are a later addition. The whole building, with its huge dimensions and boldly rusticated masonry, is one of the most monumental and grandiose of

European palaces. It was first the residence of the Medicean Grand Dukes, then of their Austrian successors, and is now one of the royal palaces of the King of Italy.

In one of the royal apartments there is a famous picture of Botticelli's, Pallas taming a Centaur, which probably refers to the return of Lorenzo the Magnificent to Florence after his diplomatic victory over the King of Naples and the League, in 1480. The beautiful and stately Medicean Pallas is wreathed all over with olive branches; her mantle is green, like that of Dante's Beatrice in the Earthly Paradise; her white dress is copiously besprinkled with Lorenzo's crest, the three rings. The Centaur himself is splendidly conceived and realised–a characteristic Botticellian modification of those terrible beings who hunt the damned souls of tyrants and robbers through the river of blood in Dante's Hell. Opposite the Pallas there is a small tondo, in which the Madonna and four Angels are adoring the divine Child in a garden of roses and wild strawberries. The latter was discovered in 1899 and ascribed to Botticelli, but appears to be only a school piece.

The great glory of the Pitti Palace is its picture gallery, a magnificent array of masterpieces, hung in sumptuously decorated rooms with allegorical ceiling-paintings in the overblown and superficial style of the artists of the decadence–Pietro da Cortona and others of his kind:–

"Both in Florence and in Rome
The elder race so make themselves at home
That scarce we give a glance to ceilingfuls
Of such like as Francesco."

So Robert Browning writes of one of Pietro's pupils. The Quattrocento is, with a few noteworthy exceptions, scarcely represented; but no collection is richer in the works of the great Italians of the Cinquecento at the culmination of the Renaissance. We can here, as in the Uffizi, merely indicate the more important pictures in each room. At the top of the staircase is a marble fountain ascribed to Donatello. The names of the rooms are usually derived from the subjects painted on the ceilings; we take the six principal saloons first.

In the **Sala dell' Iliade**.

First, the three masterpieces of this room. Fra Bartolommeo's great altar-piece painted in 1512 for San Marco (208), representing Madonna and Child surrounded by Saints, with a group of Dominicans attending upon the mystic marriage of St. Catherine of Siena, is a splendid picture, but darkened and injured; the two *putti*, making melody at the foot of Madonna's throne, are quite Venetian in character.

Titian's Cardinal Ippolito dei Medici (201) is one of the master's grandest portraits; the Cardinal is represented in Hungarian military costume. Ippolito, like his reputed father the younger Giuliano, was one of the more respectable members of the elder branch of the Medici; he was brought up with Alessandro, but the two youths hated each other mortally from their boyhood. Young and handsome, cultured and lavishly generous, Ippolito was exceedingly popular and ambitious, and felt bitterly the injustice of Pope Clement in making Alessandro lord of Florence instead of him. Clement conferred an archbishopric and other things upon him, but could by no means keep him quiet. "Aspiring to temporal greatness," writes Varchi, "and having set his heart upon things of war rather than affairs of the Church, he hardly knew himself what he wanted, and was never content." The Pope, towards whom Ippolito openly showed his contempt, complained that he could not exert any control over so eccentric and headstrong a character, *un cervello eteroclito e così balzano*. After the Pope's death, the Cardinal intrigued with the Florentine exiles in order to supplant Alessandro, upon which the Duke had him poisoned in 1535, in the twenty-fifth year of his age. Titian painted him in 1533.

The famous Concert (185), representing a passionate-faced monk of the Augustinian order at the harpsichord, while an older and more prosaic ecclesiastic stands behind him with a viol, and a youthful worldling half carelessly listens, was formerly taken as the standard of Giorgione's work; it is now usually regarded as an early Titian. Although much damaged and repainted, it remains one of the most beautiful of Venetian painted lyrics.

Andrea del Sarto's two Assumptions, one (225) painted before 1526 for a church at Cortona, the other (191) left unfinished in 1531, show the artist ineffectually striving after the sublime, and helplessly pulled down to earth by the draperies of the Apostles round the tomb. Of smaller works should be noticed: an early Titian, the Saviour (228); two portraits by Ridolfo Ghirlandaio (224, 207), of which the latter, a goldsmith, has been ascribed to Leonardo; a lady known as *La Gravida* (229), probably by Raphael early in his Florentine period; Daniele Barbaro by Paolo Veronese (216); Titian's Philip II. of Spain (200); a male portrait by Andrea del Sarto (184), said, with little plausibility, to represent himself; a Holy Family (235) by Rubens.

In the **Sala di Saturno**.

Here are some of the choicest pictures in the collection, including a whole series of Raphael's. Raphael's Madonna del Gran Duca (178)–so called from its modern purchaser, Ferdinand III.–was painted in 1504 or 1505, either before leaving Urbino or shortly after his arrival in Florence; it is the sweetest and most purely devotional of all his Madonnas. Morelli points out that it is strongly reminiscent of Raphael's first master, Timoteo Viti. The portraits of Angelo Doni and Maddalena Doni (61 and 59) also belong to the beginning of Raphael's Florentine epoch, about 1505 or 1506, and show

how much he felt the influence of Leonardo; Angelo Doni, it will be remembered, was the parsimonious merchant for whom Michelangelo painted the Madonna of the Tribuna. The Madonna del Baldacchino (165) was commenced by Raphael in 1508, the last picture of his Florentine period, ordered by the Dei for Santo Spirito; it shows the influence of Fra Bartolommeo in its composition, and was left unfinished when Pope Julius summoned the painter to Rome; in its present state, there is hardly anything of Raphael's about it. The beautiful Madonna della Seggiola (151) is a work of Raphael's Roman period, painted in 1513 or 1514. The Vision of Ezekiel (174) is slightly later, painted in 1517 or thereabout, and shows that Raphael had felt the influence of Michelangelo; one of the smallest and most sublime of all his pictures; the landscape is less conventional than we often see in his later works. Neither of the two portraits ascribed to Raphael in this room (171, 158) can any longer be accepted as a genuine work of the master.

Andrea del Sarto and Fra Bartolommeo are likewise represented by masterpieces. The Friar's Risen Christ with Four Evangelists (159), beneath whom two beautiful *putti* hold the orb of the world, was painted in 1516, the year before the painter's death; it is one of the noblest and most divine representations of the Saviour in the whole history of art. Andrea's so-called *Disputa* (172), in which a group of Saints is discussing the mystery of the Blessed Trinity, painted in 1518, is as superbly coloured as any of the greatest Venetian triumphs; the Magdalene is again the painter's own wife. Perugino's Deposition from the Cross (164), painted in 1495, shows the great Umbrian also at his best.

Among the minor pictures in this room may be noted a pretty little trifle of the school of Raphael, so often copied, Apollo and the Muses (167), questionably ascribed to Giulio Romano; and a Nymph pursued by a Satyr (147), supposed by Morelli to be by Giorgione, now assigned to Dosso Dossi of Ferrara.

In the **Sala di Giove**.

The treasure of this room is the *Velata* (245), Raphael's own portrait of the woman that he loved, to whom he wrote his sonnets, and whom he afterwards idealised as the Madonna di San Sisto; her personality remains a mystery. Titian's *Bella* (18), a rather stolid rejuvenation of Eleonora Gonzaga, is chiefly valuable for its magnificent representation of a wonderful Venetian costume. Here are three works of Andrea del Sarto–the Annunciation (124), the Madonna in Glory, with four Saints (123), and St John the Baptist (272); the first is one of his most beautiful paintings. The picture supposed to represent Andrea and his wife (118) is not by the master himself. Bartolommeo's St Mark (125) was painted by him in 1514, to show that he could do large figures, whereas he had been told that he had a *maniera minuta*; it is not altogether successful. His Deposition from the Cross (64) is one of his latest and most earnest religious works. The Three Fates (113) by Rosso Fiorentino is an undeniably powerful and impressive picture; it was formerly ascribed to Michelangelo. The Three Ages (110), ascribed to Lorenzo Lotto here, was by Morelli attributed to Giorgione, and is now assigned by highly competent critics to a certain Morto da Feltre, of whom little is known save that he is said to have been Giorgione's successful rival for the favours of a ripe Venetian beauty; the picture itself, though injured by restoration, belongs to the same category as the Concert. "In such favourite incidents of Giorgione's school," writes Walter Pater, "music or music-like intervals in our existence, life itself is conceived as a sort of listening–listening to music, to the reading of Bandello's novels, to the sound of water, to time as it flies."

In the **Sala di Marte**.

The most important pictures of this room are: Titian's portrait of a young man with a glove (92); the Holy Family, called of the *Impannata* or "covered window" (94) a work of Raphael's Roman period, painted by his scholars, perhaps by Giulio Romano; Cristofano Allori's Judith (96), a splendid and justly celebrated picture, showing what exceedingly fine works could be produced by Florentines even in the decadence (Allori died in 1621); Andrea del Sarto's scenes from the history of Joseph (87, 88), panels for cassoni or bridal chests, painted for the marriage of Francesco Borgherini and Margherita Acciaiuoli; a Rubens, the so-called Four Philosophers (85), representing himself with his brother, and the scholars Lipsius and Grotius; Andrea del Sarto's Holy Family (81), one of his last works, painted in 1529 for Ottaviano dei Medici and said to have been finished during the siege; Van Dyck's Cardinal Giulio Bentivoglio (82). It is uncertain whether this Julius II. (79) or that in the Tribuna of the Uffizi is Raphael's original, but the present picture appears to be the favourite; both are magnificent portraits of this terrible old warrior pontiff, who, for all his fierceness, was the noblest and most enlightened patron that Raphael and Michelangelo had. It was probably at his bidding that Raphael painted Savonarola among the Church's doctors and theologians in the Vatican.

In the **Sala di Apollo** and **Sala di Venere**.

Here, first of all, is Raphael's celebrated portrait of Pope Julius' unworthy successor, Leo X. (40), the son of Lorenzo the Magnificent; on the left–that is, the Pope's right hand–is the Cardinal Giulio dei Medici, afterwards Pope Clement VII.; behind the chair is the Cardinal Luigi dei Rossi, the descendant of a daughter of Piero il Gottoso. One of Raphael's most consummate works.

Andrea del Sarto's Pietà (58) was painted in 1523 or 1524 for a convent of nuns in the Mugello, whither Andrea had taken his wife and household while the plague raged in Florence; it is one of his finest works. Titian's Magdalene

(67) has been called by Ruskin a "disgusting" picture; as a pseudo-religious work, it would be hard to find anything more offensive; but it has undeniably great technical qualities. His Pietro Aretino (54), on the other hand, is a noble portrait of an infamous blackguard. Noteworthy are also Andrea del Sarto's portrait (66), apparently one of his many representations of himself, and Murillo's Mother and Child (63).

In the *Sala di Venere*, are a superb landscape by Rubens (14), sometimes called the Hay Harvest and sometimes the Return of the Contadini; also a fine female portrait, wrongly ascribed to Leonardo (140); the Triumph of David by Matteo Rosselli (13). It should be observed that the gems of the collection are frequently shifted from room to room for the benefit of the copyist.

The **Sala dell' Educazione di Giove** and following rooms.

A series of smaller rooms, no less gorgeously decorated, adjoins the Sala dell' Iliade. In the *Sala dell' Educazione di Giove* are: Fra Bartolommeo's Holy Family with St. Elizabeth (256), over the door; the Zingarella or Gipsy Girl (246), a charming little idyllic picture by Boccaccino of Cremona, formerly ascribed to Garofalo; Philip IV. of Spain (243) by Velasquez. Carlo Dolci's St Andrew (266) is above his usual level; but it is rather hard to understand how Guido Reni's Cleopatra (270) could ever be admired.

In the *Sala di Prometeo* are some earlier paintings; but those ascribed to Botticelli, Filippino Lippi, and Ghirlandaio are merely school-pieces. Fra Filippo Lippi's Madonna and Child with the Pomegranate (343) is a genuine and excellent work; in the background are seen the meeting of Joachim and Anne, with the Nativity of the Blessed Virgin. Crowe and Cavalcasella observe that "this group of the Virgin and Child reminds one forcibly of those by Donatello or Desiderio da Settignano," and it shows how much the painters of the Quattrocento were influenced by the sculptors; the Madonna's face, for no obvious reason, is said to be that of Lucrezia Buti, the girl whom Lippo carried off from a convent at Prato. A curious little allegory (336) is ascribed by Morelli to Filippino Lippi. We should also notice the beautiful Madonna with Angels adoring the Divine Child in a rose garden (347), a characteristic Florentine work of the latter part of the Quattrocento, once erroneously ascribed to Filippino Lippi; an Ecce Homo in fresco by Fra Bartolommeo (377); a Holy Family by Mariotto Albertinelli (365); and a tondo by Luca Signorelli (355), in which St. Catherine is apparently writing at the dictation of the Divine Child. But the two gems of this room are the head of a Saint (370) and the portrait of a man in red dress and hat (375) by one of the earlier painters of the Quattrocento, probably Domenico Veneziano; "perhaps," writes Mr Berenson, "the first great achievements in this kind of the Renaissance." Here, too, is a fine portrait by Lorenzo Costa (376) of Giovanni Bentivoglio.

In the *Sala del Poccetti, Sala della Giustizia, Sala di Flora, Sala dei Putti*, the pictures are, for the most part, unimportant. The so-called portrait of the *bella Simonetta*, the innamorata of Giuliano dei Medici (353), is not authentic and should not be ascribed to Sandro Botticelli. There are some fairly good portraits; a Titian (495), a Sebastiano del Piombo (409), Duke Cosimo I. by Bronzino (403), Oliver Cromwell by Lely (408). Calumny by Francia Bigio (427) is curious as a later rendering of a theme that attracted the greatest masters of the Quattrocento (Botticelli, Mantegna, Luca Signorelli all tried it). Lovers of Browning will be glad to have their attention called to the Judith of Artemisia Gentileschi (444): "a wonder of a woman painting too."

A passage leads down two flights of steps, with occasional glimpses of the Boboli Gardens, through corridors of Medicean portraits, Florentine celebrities, old pictures of processions in piazza, and the like. Then over the Ponte Vecchio, with views of the Arno on either hand as we cross, to the Uffizi.

Behind the Pitti Palace are the delicious Boboli Gardens, commenced for Duke Cosimo I., with shady walks and exquisitely framed views of Florence. In a grotto near the entrance are four unfinished statues by Michelangelo; they are usually supposed to have been intended for the tomb of Julius II., but may possibly have been connected with the projected façade of San Lorenzo.

Nearly opposite the Palazzo Pitti is the Casa Guidi, where the Brownings lived and wrote. Here Elizabeth Barrett Browning died in June 1861, she who "made of her verse a golden ring linking England to Italy"; these were the famous "Casa Guidi windows" from which she watched the liberation and unification of Italy:–

"I heard last night a little child go singing
'Neath Casa Guidi windows, by the church,
O bella libertà, O bella!–stringing
The same words still on notes he went in search
So high for, you concluded the upspringing
Of such a nimble bird to sky from perch
Must leave the whole bush in a tremble green,
And that the heart of Italy must beat,
While such a voice had leave to rise serene
'Twixt church and palace of a Florence street."

The church in question, San Felice, contains a good picture of St. Anthony, St. Rock and St. Catherine by some follower of Botticelli and Filippino Lippi; also a Crucifixion of the school of Giotto. Thence the Via Mazzetta leads into the Piazza Santo Spirito, at the corner of which is the Palazzo Guadagni, built by Cronaca at the end of the Quattrocento; with fine iron work, lantern holders and the like, on the exterior.

The present church of Santo Spirito–the finest Early Renaissance church in Florence–was built between 1471 and 1487, after Brunelleschi's designs, to replace his earlier building which had been burned down in 1471 on the occasion of the visit of Galeazzo Maria Sforza to Lorenzo the Magnificent and his brother. It is a fine example of Brunelleschi's adaptation of the early basilican type, is borne upon graceful Corinthian columns and nobly proportioned. The octagonal sacristy is by Giuliano da San Gallo and Cronaca, finished in 1497, and the campanile by Baccio d'Agnolo at the beginning of the sixteenth century.

The stained glass window over the entrance was designed by Perugino. In the right transept is an excellent picture by Filippino Lippi; Madonna and Child with the little St. John, St. Catherine and St. Nicholas, with the donor, Tanai de' Nerli, and his wife. Also in the right transept is the tomb of the Capponi; Gino, the conqueror of Pisa and historian of the Ciompi; Neri, the conqueror of the Casentino; and that great republican soldier and hero, Piero Capponi, who had saved Florence from Charles of France and fell in the Pisan war. The vision of St. Bernard is an old copy from Perugino.

None of the other pictures in the church are more than school pieces; there are two in the left transept ascribed to Filippino's disappointing pupil, Raffaellino del Garbo–the Trinità with St. Mary of Egypt and St. Catherine, and the Madonna with Sts. Lawrence, Stephen, John and Bernard. The latter picture is by Raffaellino di Carlo.

During the last quarter of the fourteenth century the convent of Santo Spirito–which is an Augustinian house–was the centre of a circle of scholars, who represent an epoch intermediate between the great writers of the Trecento and the humanists of the early Quattrocento. Prominent among them was Coluccio Salutati, who for many years served the Republic as Chancellor and died in 1406. He was influential in founding the first chair of Greek, and his letters on behalf of Florence were so eloquent and powerful that the "great viper," Giovanni Galeazzo Visconti, declared that he dreaded one of them more than many swords. Also Filippo Villani, the nephew of the great chroniclers, Giovanni and Matteo, who had succeeded Boccaccio as lecturer on Dante. They met here with other kindred spirits in the cell of Fra Luigi Marsili, a learned monk and impassioned worshipper of Petrarch, upon whose great crusading canzone–*O aspettata in ciel, beata e bella*–he wrote a commentary which is still extant. Fra Luigi died in 1394. A century later, the monks of this convent took a violent part in opposition to Savonarola; and it was here, in the pulpit of the choir of the church, that

Landucci tells us that he heard the bull of excommunication read "by a Fra Leonardo, their preacher, and an adversary of the said Fra Girolamo,"–"between two lighted torches and many friars," as he rather quaintly puts it.

"The Carmine's my cloister: hunt it up," says Browning's Lippo Lippi to his captors; and the Via Mazzetta and the Via Santa Monaca will take us to it. This church of the Carmelites, Santa Maria del Carmine, was consecrated in 1422; and, almost immediately after, the mighty series of frescoes was begun in the Brancacci Chapel at the end of the right transept–frescoes which were to become the school for all future painting. In the eighteenth century the greater part of the church was destroyed by fire, but this chapel was spared by the flames, and the frescoes, though terribly damaged and grievously restored, still remain on its walls.

This Brancacci Chapel of the Carmine plays the same part in the history of painting as the bronze gates of the Baptistery in that of sculpture. It was in that same eventful year, 1401, of the famous competition between Ghiberti and Brunelleschi, that the new Giotto was born–Tommaso, the son of a notary in Castello San Giovanni di Valdarno. With him, as we saw in chapter iii., the second great epoch of Italian painting, the Quattrocento, or Epoch of Character, opens. His was a rare and piquant personality; *persona astrattissima e molto a caso*, says Vasari, "an absent-minded fellow and very casual." Intent upon his art, he took no care of himself and thought nothing of the ordinary needs and affairs of the world, though always ready to do others a good turn. From his general negligence and untidiness, he was nicknamed *Masaccio*–"hulking Tom"–which has become one of the most honourable names in the history of art. The little chapel in which we now stand and survey his handiwork, or what remains of it, is nothing less than the birthplace of modern painting. Sculpture had indeed preceded painting in its return to nature and in its direct study of the human form, and the influence of Donatello lies as strongly over all the painters of the Quattrocento. Vasari even states that Masolino da Panicale (Masolino = "dear little Tom"), Masaccio's master, had been one of Ghiberti's assistants in the casting of the bronze gates, but this is questionable; it is possible that he had been Ghiberti's pupil, though he learned the principles of painting from Gherardo Starnina, one of the last artists of the Trecento. It was shortly after 1422 that Masolino commenced this great series of frescoes setting forth the life of St. Peter; within the next few years Masaccio continued his work; and, more than half a century later, in 1484, Filippino Lippi took it up where Masaccio had left off, and completed the series.

 Masolino's contribution to the whole appears to be confined to three pictures: St. Peter preaching, with Carmelites in the background to carry his doctrines into fifteenth century Florence, on the left of the window; the upper row of scenes on the right wall, representing St. Peter and St. John raising the cripple at the Beautiful Gate of the Temple, and the healing of Tabitha (according to others, the resuscitation of Petronilla); and the narrow fresco of the Fall of Adam and Eve, on the right of the entrance. Some have also ascribed to him the striking figure of St. Peter enthroned, attended by Carmelites, while the faithful approach to kiss his feet–the picture in the corner on the left which, in a way, sets the keynote to the whole–but it is more probably the work of Masaccio (others ascribe it to Filippino). Admirable though these paintings are, they exhibit a certain immaturity as contrasted with those by Masaccio: in the Raising of Tabitha, for instance, those two youths with their odd headgear might almost have stepped out of some Giottesque fresco; and the rendering of the nude in the Adam and Eve, though wonderful at that epoch, is much inferior to Masaccio's opposite. Nevertheless, Masolino's grave and dignified figures introduced the type that Masaccio was soon to render perfect.

From the hand of Masaccio are the Expulsion from Paradise; the Tribute Money; the Raising of the Dead Youth (in part); and (probably) the St. Peter enthroned, on the left wall; St. Peter and St. John healing the sick with their shadow, under Masolino's Peter preaching (and the figure behind with a red cap, leaning on a stick, is Masaccio's pious portrait of his master Masolino himself); St. Peter baptising,

St. Peter and St. John giving alms, on the opposite side of the window. Each figure is admirably rendered, its character perfectly realised; Masaccio may indeed be said to have completed what Giotto had begun, and freed Italian art from the mannerism of the later followers of Giotto, even as Giotto himself had delivered her from Byzantine formalism. "After Giotto," writes Leonardo da Vinci, "the art of painting declined again, because every one imitated the pictures that were already done; thus it went on from century to century until Tommaso of Florence, nicknamed Masaccio, showed by his perfect works how those who take for their standard any one but Nature–the mistress of all masters–weary themselves in vain."[54] This return to nature is seen even in the landscape, notably in the noble background to the Tribute Money; but above all, in his study of man and the human form. "For the first time," says Kugler, "his aim is the study of form for itself, the study of the external conformation of man. With such an aim is identified a feeling which, in beauty, sees and preserves the expression of proportion; and in repose or motion, the expression of an harmonious development of the powers of the human frame." For sheer dignity and grandeur there is nothing to compare with it, till we come to the work of Raphael and Michelangelo in the Vatican; the composition of the Tribute Money and the Healing of the Sick initiated the method of religious illustration that reached its ultimate perfection in

Raphael–what has been called giving Greek form to Hebrew thought. The treatment of the nude especially seemed a novel thing in its day; the wonderful modelling of the naked youth shivering with the cold, in the scene of St. Peter baptising, was hailed as a marvel of art, and is cited by Vasari as one of the *cose rarissime* of painting. In the scene of the Tribute Money, the last Apostle on our right (in the central picture where our Lord and His disciples are confronted by the eager collector) whose proud bearing is hardly evangelical, is Masaccio himself, with scanty beard and untidy hair. Although less excellent than the Baptism as a study of the nude, the Expulsion of Adam and Eve from Eden is a masterpiece of which it is impossible to speak too highly. Our *primi parenti*, weighed down with the consciousness of ineffable tragedy, are impelled irresistibly onward by divine destiny; they need not see the Angel in his flaming robe on his cloud of fire, with his flashing sword and out-stretched hand; terrible in his beauty as he is to the spectator, he is as nothing to them, compared with the face of an offended God and the knowledge of the *tanto esilio*. Surely this is how Dante himself would have conceived the scene.

    Masaccio died at Rome in 1428, aged twenty-seven years. In his short life he had set modern painting on her triumphant progress, and his frescoes became the school for all subsequent painters, "All in short," says Vasari, "who have sought to acquire their art in its perfection, have constantly repaired to study it in this chapel, there imbibing the precepts and rules necessary to be followed for the command of success, and learning to labour effectually from the figures of Masaccio." If he is to rank among "the inheritors of unfulfilled renown," Masaccio may be said to stand towards Raphael as Keats towards Tennyson. Masolino outlived his great pupil for several years, and died about 1435.

The fresco of the Raising up of the dead Youth, left unfinished by Masaccio when he left Florence for Rome, was completed by Filippino Lippi (the son of that run-a-way Carmelite in whom the spirit of Masaccio was said to have lived again), in 1484. The five figures on the left appear to be from Filippino's hand (the second from the end is said to be Luigi Pulci, the poet), as also the resuscitated boy (said to be Francesco Granacci the painter, who was then about fifteen years old) and the group of eight on the right. Under Masaccio's Adam and Eve, he painted St. Paul visiting St. Peter in prison; under Masolino's Fall, the Liberation of Peter by the Angel, two exceedingly beautiful and simple compositions. And, on the right wall of the chapel, St. Peter and St. Paul before the Proconsul and the Crucifixion of St. Peter are also by Filippino. In the Crucifixion scene, which is inferior to the rest, the last of the three spectators on our right, wearing a black cap, is Filippino's master, Sandro Botticelli. In the presence of the Proconsul, the elderly man with a keen face, in a red cap to the right of the judge, is

Antonio Pollaiuolo; and, on our right, the youth whose head appears in the corner is certainly Filippino himself—a kind of signature to the whole.

Apart from the Brancacci chapel, the interest of the Carmine is mainly confined to the tomb of the noble and simple-hearted ex-Gonfaloniere, Piero Soderini (who died in 1513), in the choir; it was originally by Benedetto da Rovezzano, but has been restored. There are frescoes in the sacristy, representing the life of St. Cecilia, by one of Giotto's later followers, possibly Spinello Aretino, and, in the cloisters, a noteworthy Madonna of the same school, ascribed to Giovanni da Milano.

Beyond the Carmine, westwards, is the Borgo San Frediano, now, as in olden time, the poorest part of Florence. It was the ringing of the bell of the Carmine that gave the signal for the rising of the Ciompi in 1378. Unlike their neighbours, the Augustinians of Santo Spirito, the good fathers of Our Lady of Mount Carmel were for the most part ardent followers of Savonarola, and, on the first of October 1497, one of them preached an open-air sermon near the Porta San Frediano, in which he declared that he himself had had a special revelation from God on the subject of Fra Girolamo's sanctity, and that all who resisted the Friar would be horribly punished; even Landucci admits that he talked arrant nonsense, *pazzie*. The parish church of this district, San Frediano in Cestello, is quite uninteresting. At the end of the Via San Frediano is the great Porta San Frediano, of which more presently.

The gates and walls of Oltrarno were built between 1324 and 1327, in the days of the Republic's great struggle with Castruccio Interminelli. Unlike those on the northern bank, they are still in part standing. There are five gates on this side of the river—the Porta San Niccolò, the Porta San Miniato, the Porta San Giorgio, the Porta Romana or Por San Piero Gattolino, and the Porta San Frediano. It was all round this part of the city that the imperial army lay during the siege of 1529 and 1530.

On the east of the city, on the banks of the Arno, rises first the Porta San Niccolò—mutilated and isolated, but the only one of the gates that has retained a remnant of its ancient height and dignity. In a lunette on the inner side is a fresco of 1357—Madonna and Child with Saints, Angels and Prophets. Around are carved the lilies of the Commune. On the side facing the hill are the arms of the Parte Guelfa and of the People, with the lily of the Commune between them. Within the gate the Borgo San Niccolò leads to the church of San Niccolò, which contains a picture by Neri di Bicci and one of the Pollaiuoli, and four saints ascribed to Gentile da Fabriano. It is one of the oldest Florentine churches, though not interesting in its present state. There is an altogether untrustworthy tradition that Michelangelo was sheltered in the tower of this church after the capitulation of the city, but he seems to have been more probably in the house of a trusted friend. Pope Clement ordered that he should be sought for, but left at liberty and treated with all courtesy if he agreed to go on working at the Medicean monuments in San Lorenzo; and, hearing this, the sculptor came out from his hiding place. It may be observed that San Niccolò was a most improbable place for him to have sought refuge in, as Malatesta Baglioni had his headquarters close by.

Beyond the Porta San Niccolò is the Piano di Ripoli, where the Prince of Orange had his headquarters. Before his exile Dante possessed some land here. It was here that the first Dominican house was established in Tuscany under St Dominic's companion, Blessed John of Salerno. Up beyond the terminus of the tramway a splendid view of Florence can be obtained.

Near the Porta San Niccolò the long flight of stairs mounts up the hill of *San Francesco e San Miniato*, which commands the city from the south-east, to the Piazzale Michelangelo just below the church. A long and exceedingly beautiful drive leads also to this Piazzale from the Porta Romana–the Viale dei Colli–and passes down again to the Barriera San Niccolò by the Viale Michelangelo. This Viale dei Colli, at least, is one of those few works which even those folk who make a point of sneering at everything done in Florence since the unification of Italy are constrained to admire. It would seem that even in the thirteenth century there were steps of some kind constructed up the hill-side to the church. In that passage from the *Purgatorio* (canto xii.) which I have put at the head of this chapter, Dante compares the ascent from the first to the second circle of Purgatory to this climb: "As on the right hand, to mount the hill where stands the church which overhangs the well-guided city, above Rubaconte, the bold abruptness of the ascent is broken by the steps that were made in the age when the ledger and the stave were safe."[55]

The Piazzale, adorned with bronze copies of Michelangelo's great statues, commands one of the grandest views of Florence, with the valley of the Arno and the mountains round, that "in silence listen for the word said next," as Mrs Browning has it. Up beyond is the exceedingly graceful Franciscan church of San Salvadore al Monte–"the purest vessel of Franciscan simplicity," a modern Italian poet has called it–built by Cronaca in the last years of the fifteenth century. It contains a few works by Giovanni della Robbia. It was as he descended this hill with a few armed followers that Giovanni Gualberto met and pardoned the murderer of his brother; a small chapel or tabernacle, on the way up from the convent to San Miniato, still marks the spot, but the Crucifix which is said to have bowed down its head towards him is now preserved in Santa Trinità.

THE FORTIFICATIONS OF MICHELANGELO

This Monte di San Francesco e di San Miniato overlooks the whole city, and Florence lay at the mercy of whoever got possession of it. Varchi in his history apologises for those architects who built the walls of the city by reminding us that, in their days, artillery was not even dreamed of, much less invented. Michelangelo armed the campanile of San Miniato, against which the fiercest fire of the imperialists was directed, and erected bastions covering the hill, enclosing it, as it were, within the walls up from the Porta San Miniato and down again to the Porta San Niccolò. It was intrusted to the guard of Stefano Colonna, who finally joined Malatesta Baglioni in betraying the city. Some bits of Michelangelo's work remain near the Basilica, which itself is one of the most venerable edifices of the kind in Tuscany; the earliest Florentine Christians are said to have met here in the woods, during the reign of Nero, and here Saint Miniatus, according to tradition the son of an Armenian king, lived in his hermitage until martyred by Decius outside the present Porta alla Croce. In the days of Gregory the Great, San Frediano of Lucca came every year with his clergy to worship the relics of Miniatus; a basilica already stood here in the time of Charlemagne; and the present edifice is said to have been begun in 1013 by the Bishop Alibrando, with the aid of the Emperor St Henry and his wife Cunegunda. It was held by the Benedictines, first the black monks and then the Olivetans who took it over from Gregory XI. in 1373. The new Bishops of Florence, the first time they set foot out of the city, came here to sing Mass. In 1553 the monastery was suppressed by Duke Cosimo I., and turned into a fortress.

San Miniato al Monte is one of the earliest and one of the finest examples of the Tuscan Romanesque style of architecture. Both interior and exterior are adorned with inlaid coloured marble, of simple design, and the fine "nearly classical" pillars within are probably taken from some ancient Roman building. Fergusson remarks that, but for the rather faulty construction of the façade, "it would be difficult to find a church in Italy containing more of classical elegance, with perfect appropriateness for the purposes of Christian worship." In the crypt beneath the altar is the tomb of San Miniato and others of the Decian martyrs. The great mosaic on the upper part of the apse was originally executed at the end of the thirteenth century. The Early Renaissance chapel in the nave was constructed by Michelozzo in 1448 for Piero dei Medici, to contain Giovanni Gualberto's miraculous Crucifix. In the left aisle is the Cappella di San Jacopo with the monument of the Cardinal James of Portugal, who "lived in the flesh as if he were freed from it, like an Angel rather than a man, and died in the odour of sanctity at the early age of twenty-six," in 1459. This tomb by Antonio Rossellino is the third of the "three finest Renaissance tombs in Tuscany," the other two being those of Leonardo Bruni (1444) by Antonio's brother Bernardo, and Carlo Marsuppini by Desiderio (1453), both of which we have seen in Santa Croce. Mr Perkins observes that the present tomb preserves the golden mean in point of ornament between the other two. The Madonna and Child with the Angels, watching over the young Cardinal's repose, are especially beautiful. The Virtues on the ceiling are by Luca della Robbia, and the Annunciation opposite the tomb by Alessio Baldovinetti. The Gothic sacristy was built for one of the great Alberti family, Benedetto di Nerozzo, in 1387, and decorated shortly after with a splendid series of frescoes by Spinello Aretino, setting forth the life of St. Benedict. These are Spinello's noblest works and the last great creation of the genuine school of Giotto. Especially fine are the scenes with the Gothic king Totila, and the death and apotheosis of the Saint, which latter may be compared with Giotto's St. Francis in Santa Croce. The whole is like a painted chapter of St. Gregory's Dialogues.

The Story of Florence

PORTA SAN GIORGIO

The Porta San Miniato, below the hill, almost at the foot of the Basilica, is little more than a gap in the wall. On both sides are the arms of the Commune and the People, the Cross of the latter outside the lily of the former. Upwards from the Porta San Miniato to the Porta San Giorgio a glorious bit of the old wall remains, clad inside and out with olives, running up the hillside of San Giorgio; even some remnants of the old towers are standing, two indeed having been only partially demolished. Beneath the former Medicean fortress and upper citadel of Belvedere stands the Porta San Giorgio. This, although small, is the most picturesque of all the gates of Florence. On its outer side is a spirited bas-relief of St. George and the Dragon in stone–of the end of the fourteenth century–over the lily of the Commune; in the lunette, on the inner side, is a fresco painted in 1330–probably by Bernardo Daddi–of Santa Maria del Fiore enthroned with the Divine Babe between St. George and St. Leonard. This was the only gate held by the nobles in the great struggle of 1343, when the banners of the people were carried across the bridge in triumph, and the Bardi and Frescobaldi fought from street to street; through it the magnates had secretly brought in banditti and retainers from the country, and through it some of the Bardi fled when the people swept down upon their palaces. Inside the gate the steep Via della Costa San Giorgio winds down past Galileo's house to Santa Felicità. Outside the gate the Via San Leonardo leads, between olive groves and vineyards, into the Viale dei Colli. In the curious little church of San Leonardo in Arcetri, on the left, is an old *ambone* or pulpit from the demolished church of San Piero Scheraggio, with ancient bas-reliefs. This pulpit is traditionally supposed to have been a part of the spoils in the destruction of Fiesole; it appears to belong to the latter part of the twelfth century.

The great Porta Romana, or Porta San Piero Gattolino, was originally erected in 1328; it is still of imposing dimensions, though its immediate surroundings are somewhat prosaic. Many a Pope and Emperor has passed through here, to or from the eternal city; the marble tablets on either side record the entrance of Leo X. in 1515, on his way from Rome to Bologna to meet Francis I. of France, and of Charles V. in 1536 to confirm the infamous Duke Alessandro on the throne–a confirmation which the dagger of Lorenzino happily annulled in the following year. It was here that Pope Leo's brother, Piero dei Medici, had made his unsuccessful attempt to surprise the city on April 28th 1497, with some thousand men or more, horse and foot. A countryman at daybreak had seen them resting and breakfasting on the way, some few miles from the city; by taking short cuts over the country, he evaded their scouts who were intercepting all persons passing northwards, and reached Florence with the news just at the morning opening of the gate. The result was that the Magnifico Piero and his braves found it closed in their faces and the forces of the Signoria guarding the walls, so, after ignominiously skulking for a few hours out of range of the artillery, they fled back towards Siena.

Near the Porta Romana the Viale dei Colli commences to the left, as the Viale Machiavelli; and, straight on, the beautifully shady Stradone del Poggio Imperiale runs up to the villa of that name, built for Maria Maddalena of Austria in 1622. The statues at the beginning of the road were once saints on the second façade of the Duomo. It was on the rising ground that divides the Strada Romana from the present Stradone that the famous convent of Monticelli stood, recorded in Dante's *Paradiso* and Petrarca's *Trionfo della Pudicizia*, in which Piccarda Donati took the habit of St. Clare, and from which she was dragged by her brother Corso to marry Rossellino della Tosa:—

"Perfetta vita ed alto merto inciela
donna più su, mi disse, alla cui norma
nel vostro mondo giù si veste e vela,

perchè in fino al morir si vegghi e dorma
con quello sposo ch'ogni voto accetta,
che caritate a suo piacer conforma.

Dal mondo, per seguirla, giovinetta
fuggi'mi, e nel suo abito mi chiusi,
e promisi la via della sua setta.

Uomini poi, a mal più ch'al bene usi,
fuor mi rapiron della dolce chiostra;
e Dio si sa qual poi mia vita fusi."[56]

It was at Poggio Imperiale, then called the Poggio dei Baroncelli, that a famous combat took place during the early days of the siege, in which Ludovico Martelli and Dante da Castiglione fought two Florentines who were serving in the imperial army, Giovanni Bandini and Bertino Aldobrandini. Both Martelli, the original challenger, and Aldobrandini were mortally wounded. Martelli's real motive in sending the challenge is said to have been that he and Bandini were rivals for the favours of a Florentine lady, Marietta de' Ricci. Among the many beautiful villas and gardens which stud the country beyond Poggio Imperiale, are Galileo's Tower, from which he made his astronomical observations, and the villa in which he was visited by Milton. Near Santa Margherita a Montici, to the east, is the villa in which the articles of capitulation were arranged by the Florentine ambassadors with Ferrante Gonzaga, commander of the Imperial troops, and Baccio Valori, commissary of the Pope. But already Malatesta had opened the Porta Romana and turned his artillery against the city which he had solemnly sworn to defend.

Beyond the Porta Romana the road to the right of Poggio Imperiale leads to the valley of the Ema, above which the great Certosa rises on the hill of Montaguto. Shortly before reaching the monastery the Ema is crossed—an insignificant stream in which Cacciaguida (in *Paradiso* xvi.) rather paradoxically regrets that Buondelmonte was not drowned on his way to Florence: "Joyous had many been who now are sad, had God committed thee unto the Ema the first time that thou camest to the city." The Certosa itself, that "huge battlemented convent-block over the little forky flashing Greve," as Browning calls it, was founded by Niccolò Acciaiuoli, the Florentine Grand Seneschal of Naples, in 1341; it is one of the finest of the later mediæval monasteries. Orcagna is said to have built one of the side chapels of the church, which contains a fine early Giottesque altarpiece; and in a kind of crypt there are noble tombs of the Acciaiuoli–one, the monument of the founder, being possibly by Orcagna, and one of the later ones ascribed (doubtfully) to Donatello. In the chapter-house are a Crucifixion by Mariotto Albertinelli, and the monument of Leonardo Buonafede by Francesco da San Gallo. From the convent and further up the valley, there are beautiful views. About three miles further on is the sanctuary and shrine of the Madonna dell' Impruneta, built for the miraculous image

The Story of Florence

of the Madonna, which was carried down in procession to Florence in times of pestilence and danger. Savonarola especially had placed great faith in the miraculous powers of this image and these processions; and during the siege it remained in Florence ceremoniously guarded in the Duomo, a kind of mystic Palladium.

Between the Porta Romana and Porta San Frediano some tracts of the city wall remain, but the whole is painfully prosaic. The Porta San Frediano itself is a massive structure, erected between 1324 and 1327, possibly by Andrea Pisano; it need hardly be repeated that we cannot judge of the original mediæval appearance of the gates of Florence, with their towers and ante-portals, even from the least mutilated of their present remnants. It was through this gate that the Florentine army passed in triumph in 1363 with their long trains of captured Pisans; and here, after Pisa had shaken off for a while the yoke, Charles of France rode in as a conqueror on November 17, 1494, Savonarola's new Cyrus, and was solemnly received at the gate by the Signoria. Within the gate a strip of wall runs down to the river, with two later towers built by Medicean grand dukes. At the end is a chapel built in 1856, and containing a Pietà from the walls of a demolished convent–ascribed without warrant to Domenico Ghirlandaio.

It was somewhere near here that S. Frediano, coming from Lucca to pay his annual visit to the shrine of San

Miniato, miraculously crossed the Arno in flood. Outside the gate, a little off the Leghorn road to the left, is the suppressed abbey of Monte Oliveto, and beyond it, to the south, the hill of Bellosguardo–both points from which splendid views of Florence and its surroundings are obtained.

These dream-like glimpses of the City of Flowers, which every coign of vantage seems to give us round Florence–might we not, sometimes, imagine that we had stumbled unawares upon the Platonic City of the Perfect? There are two lines from one of Dante's canzoni in praise of his mystical lady that rise to our mind at every turn:–

"Io non la vidi tante volte ancora,
ch'io non trovassi in lei nuova bellezza,"

CHAPTER XIII.

CONCLUSION

THE setting of Florence is in every way worthy of the gem which it encloses. On each side of the city and throughout its province beautiful walks and drives lead to churches, villas and villages full of historical interest or enriched with artistic treasures. I can here merely indicate a very few such places.

To the north of the city rises Fiesole on its hill, of which the historical connection with Florence has been briefly discussed in chapter i. At its foot stands the Dominican convent, in which Fra Giovanni, whom we know better as the Beato Angelico, took the habit of the order, and in which both his brother, Fra Benedetto, and himself were in turn priors. Savonarola's fellow martyr, Fra Domenico da Pescia, was likewise prior of this house. The church contains a Madonna by Angelico, with the background painted in by Lorenzo di Credi (its exquisitely beautiful predella is now one of the chief ornaments of the National Gallery of London), a Baptism of Christ by Lorenzo di Credi, and an Adoration of the Magi designed by Andrea del Sarto and executed by Sogliani. A little to the left is the famous Badia di Fiesole, originally of the eleventh century, but rebuilt for Cosimo the Elder by Filippo Brunelleschi. It was one of Cosimo's favourite foundations; Marsilio Ficino's Platonic Academy frequently met in the loggia with its beautiful view towards the city. In the church, Lorenzo's second son, Giovanni, was invested with the Cardinalate in 1492; and here, in 1516, his third son, Giuliano, Duke of Nemours, the best of the Medici, died. On the way up to Fiesole itself is the handsome villa Mozzi, built for Giovanni di Cosimo de' Medici by Michelozzo. It was in this villa that the Pazzi had originally intended to murder Lorenzo and the elder Giuliano, but their plan was frustrated by the illness of Giuliano, which prevented his being present.

In Fiesole itself, the remains of the Etruscan wall and the old theatre tell of the classical Faesulae; its Tuscan Romanesque Duomo (of the eleventh and twelfth centuries) recalls the days when the city seemed a rival to Florence itself and was the resort of the robber barons, who preyed upon her ever growing commerce. It contains sculptures by Mino da Fiesole and that later Fiesolan, Andrea Ferrucci (to whom we owe the bust of Marsilio Ficino), and a fine terracotta by one of the Della Robbias. From the Franciscan convent, which occupies the site of the old Roman citadel, a superb view of Florence and its valley is obtained. From Fiesole, towards the south-east, we reach Ponte a Mensola (also reached from the Porta alla Croce), the Mensola of Boccaccio's *Ninfale fiesolano*, above which is Settignano, where Desiderio was

The Story of Florence

born and Michelangelo nurtured, and where Boccaccio had a podere. The Villa Poggio Gherardo, below Settignano, shares with the Villa Palmieri below Fiesole the distinction of being traditionally one of those introduced into the *Decameron*.

Northwestwards of the Badia of Fiesole runs the road from Florence to Bologna, past the village of Trespiano, some three or four miles from the Porta San Gallo. In the twelfth century Trespiano was the northern boundary of Florentine territory, as Galluzzo–on the way towards the Certosa and about two miles from the Porta Romana–was its southern limit. Cacciaguida, in *Paradiso* xvi., refers to this as an ideal golden time when the citizenship "saw itself pure even in the lowest artizan." A little way north of Trespiano, on the old Bolognese road, is the Uccellatoio–referred to in canto xv.–the first point from which Florence is visible. Below Trespiano, at La Lastra, rather more than two miles from the city, the exiled Bianchi and Ghibellines, with auxiliaries from Bologna and Arezzo, assembled in that fatal July of 1304. The leaders of the Neri were absent at Perugia, and, at the first sight of the white standards waving from the hill, terror and consternation filled their partisans throughout the city. Had their enterprise been better organised, the exiles would undoubtedly have captured Florence. Seeing that they were discovered, and urged on by their friends within the city, without waiting for the Uberti, whose cavalry was advancing from Pistoia to their support and whose appointed day of coming they had anticipated, Baschiera della Tosa, in spite of the terrible heat, ordered an immediate advance upon the Porta San Gallo. The walls of the third circle were only in part built at that epoch, and those of the second circle still stood with their gates. The exiles, for the most part mounted, drew up round San Marco and the Annunziata, "with white standards spread, with garlands of olive and drawn swords, crying *peace*," writes Dino Compagni, who was in Florence at the time, "without doing violence or plundering anyone. A right goodly sight was it to see them, with the sign of peace thus arrayed. The heat was so great, that it seemed that the very air burned." But their friends within did not stir. They forced the Porta degli Spadai which stood at the head of the present Via dei Martelli, but were repulsed at the Piazza San Giovanni and the Duomo, and the sudden blazing up of a palace in the rear completed their rout. Many fell on the way, simply from the heat, while the Neri, becoming fierce-hearted like lions, as Compagni says, hotly pursued them, hunting out those who had hidden themselves among the vineyards and houses, hanging all they caught. In their flight, a little way from Florence, the exiles met Tolosato degli Uberti hastening up with his Ghibellines to meet them on the appointed day. Tolosato, a fierce captain and experienced in civil war, tried in vain to rally them, and, when all his efforts proved unavailing, returned to Pistoia declaring that the youthful rashness of Baschiera had lost

The Story of Florence

him the city. Dante had taken no part in the affair; he had broken with his fellow exiles in the previous year, and made a party for himself as he tells us in the *Paradiso*.

To the west and north-west of Florence are several interesting villas of the Medici. The Villa Medicea in Careggi, the most famous of all, is not always accessible. It is situated in the loveliest country, within a short walk of the tramway station of Ponte a Rifredi. Built originally by Michelozzo for Cosimo the Elder, it was almost burned down by a band of republican youths shortly before the siege. Here Cosimo died, consoling his last hours with Marsilio Ficino's Platonics; here the elder Piero lived in retirement, too shattered in health to do more than nominally succeed his father at the head of the State. On August 23rd 1466, there was an attempt made to murder Piero as he was carried into Florence from Careggi in his litter. A band of armed men, in the pay of Luca Pitti and Dietisalvi Neroni, lay in wait for the litter on the way to the Porta Faenza; but young Lorenzo, who was riding on in advance of his father's cortège, came across them first, and, without appearing to take any alarm at the meeting, secretly sent back a messenger to bid his father take another way. Under Lorenzo himself, this villa became the centre of the Neo-Platonic movement; and here on November 7th, the day supposed to be the anniversary of Plato's birth and death, the famous banquet was held at which Marsilio Ficino and the chosen spirits of the Academy discussed and expounded the *Symposium*. Here on April 8th 1492, the Magnifico died (see chap. iii.). In the same neighbourhood, a little further on in the direction of Pistoia, are the villas of Petraia and Castello (for both of which *permessi* are given at the Pitti Palace, together with that for Poggio a Caiano), both reminiscent of the Medicean grand ducal family; in the latter Cosimo I. lived with his mother, Maria Salviati, before his accession to the throne, and here he died in 1574.

Also beyond the Porta al Prato (about an hour and a half by the tramway from behind Santa Maria Novella), is the Villa Reale of Poggio a Caiano, superbly situated where the Pistoian Apennines begin to rise up from the plain. The villa was built by Giuliano da San Gallo for Lorenzo, and the Magnifico loved it best of all his country houses. It was here that he wrote his *Ambra* and his *Caccia col Falcone*; in both of these poems the beautiful scenery round plays its part. When Pope Clement VII. sent the two boys, Ippolito and Alessandro, to represent the Medici in Florence, Alessandro generally stayed here, while Ippolito resided within the city in the palace in the Via Larga. When Charles V. came to Florence in 1536 to confirm Alessandro upon the throne, he declared that this villa "was not the building for a private citizen." Here, too, the Grand Duke Francesco and Bianca Cappello died, on October 19th and 20th, 1587, after entertaining the Cardinal Ferdinando, who thus became Grand Duke; it was said that Bianca had attempted to poison the Cardinal, and that she and her husband had themselves eaten of the pasty that she had prepared for him. It appears, however, that there is no reason for supposing that their deaths were other than natural. At present the villa is a royal country house, in which reminiscences of the Re Galantuomo clash rather oddly with those of the Medicean Princes. All round runs a loggia with fine views, and there are an uninteresting park and garden. The classical portico is noteworthy, all the rest being of the utmost simplicity.

Within the palace a large room, with a remarkably fine ceiling by Giuliano da San Gallo, is decorated with a series of frescoes from Roman history intended to be typical of events in the lives of Cosimo the Elder and Lorenzo the Magnificent. Vasari says that, for a villa, this is *la più bella sala del mondo*. The frescoes, ordered by Pope Leo X. and the Cardinal Giulio, under the direction of Ottaviano dei Medici, were begun by Andrea dei Sarto, Francia Bigio and Jacopo da Pontormo, left unfinished for more than fifty years, and then completed by Alessandro Allori for the Grand Duke Francesco. The Triumph of Cicero, by Francia Bigio, is supposed to typify the return of Cosimo from exile in 1434; Caesar receiving tribute from Egypt, by Andrea del Sarto, refers to the coming of an embassy from the Soldan to Lorenzo in 1487, with magnificent gifts and treasures. Andrea's fresco is full of curious beasts and birds, including the long-eared sheep which Lorenzo naturalised in the grounds of the villa, and the famous giraffe which the Soldan sent on this occasion and which, as Mr Armstrong writes, "became the most popular character in Florence," until its death at the beginning of 1489. The Regent of France, Anne of Beaujeu, made ineffectual overtures to Lorenzo to get him to make her a present of the strange beast. This fresco was left unfinished on the death of Pope Leo in 1521, and finished by Alessandro Allori in 1582. The charming mythological decorations between the windows are by Jacopo da Pontormo. The two later frescoes by Alessandro Allori, painted about 1580, represent Scipio in the house of Syphax and Flamininus in Greece, which typify Lorenzo's visit to Ferrante of Naples, in 1480, and his presence at the Diet of Cremona in 1483, on which latter occasion, as Mr Armstrong puts it, "his good sense and powers of expression and persuasion gave him an importance which the military weakness of Florence denied to him in the field"–but the result was little more than a not very honourable league of the Italian powers against Venice. The Apples of the Hesperides, and the rest of the mythological decorations in continuation of Pontormo's lunette, are also Allori's. The whole has an air of regal triumph without needless parade.

 The road should be followed beyond the villa, in order to ascend to the left to the little church among the hills. A superb view is obtained over the plain to Florence beyond the Villa Reale lying below us. Behind, we are already among the Apennines. A beautiful glimpse of Prato can be seen to the left, four miles away.

Prato itself is about twelve miles from Florence. It was a gay little town in the fifteenth century, when it witnessed "brother Lippo's doings, up and down," and heard Messer Angelo Poliziano's musical sighings for the love of Madonna Ippolita Leoncina. A few years later it listened to the voice of Fra Girolamo Savonarola, and at last its bright day of prosperity ended in the horrible sack and carnage from the Spanish soldiery under Raimondo da Cardona in 1512. Its Duomo–dedicated to St. Stephen and the Baptist–a Tuscan Romanesque church completed in the Gothic style by Giovanni Pisano, with a fine campanile built at the beginning of the fourteenth century, claims to possess a strange and wondrous relic: nothing less than the Cintola or Girdle of the Blessed Virgin, delivered by her–according to a pious and poetical legend–to St. Thomas at her Assumption, and then won back for Christendom by a native of Prato, Michele Dagonari, in the Crusades. Be that as it may, what purports to be this relic is exhibited on occasions in the Pulpito della Cintola on the exterior of the Duomo, a magnificent work by Donatello and Michelozzo, in which the former master has carved a wonderful series of dancing genii hardly, if at all, inferior to those more famous bas-reliefs executed a little later for the cantoria of Santa Maria del Fiore. Within, over the entrance wall, is a picture by

Ridolfo Ghirlandaio of the Madonna giving the girdle to the Thomas who had doubted. And in the chapel on the left (with a most beautifully worked bronze screen, with a lovely frieze of cupids, birds and beasts–the work of Bruno Lapi and Pasquino di Matteo, 1444-1461), the Cintola is preserved amid frescoes by Agnolo Gaddi setting forth the life of Madonna, her granting of Prato's treasure to St Thomas at the Assumption, and its discovery by Michele Dagonari.

The church is rich in works of Florentine art–a pulpit by Mino da Fiesole and Antonio Rossellino; the Madonna dell' Ulivo by Giuliano da Maiano; frescoes said to be in part by Masolino's reputed master Starnina in the chapel to the right of the choir. But Prato's great artistic glory must be sought in Fra Lippo Lippi's frescoes in the choir, painted between 1452 and 1464. These are the great achievements of the Friar's life. On the left is the life of St. Stephen, on the right that of the Baptist. They show very strongly the influence of Masaccio, and make us understand why the Florentines said that the spirit of Masaccio had entered into the body of Fra Filippo. Inferior to Masaccio in most respects, Filippo had a feeling for facial beauty and spiritual expression, and for a certain type of feminine grace which we hardly find in his prototype. The wonderful figure of the dancing girl in Herod's banquet, and again her naïve bearing when she kneels before her mother with the martyr's head, oblivious of the horror of the spectators and merely bent upon showing us her own sweet face, are characteristic of Lippo, as also, in another way, his feeling for boyhood shown in the little St. John's farewell to his parents. The Burial of St. Stephen is full of fine Florentine portraits in the manner of the Carmine frescoes. The dignified ecclesiastic at the head of the clergy is Carlo dei Medici, the illegitimate son of Cosimo. On the extreme right is Lippo himself. Carlo looks rather like a younger, more refined edition of Leo X.

It was while engaged upon these frescoes that Lippo Lippi was commissioned by the nuns of Santa Margherita to paint a Madonna for them, and took the opportunity of carrying off Lucrezia Buti, a beautiful girl staying in the convent who had sat to him as the Madonna, during one of the Cintola festivities. Lippo appears to have been practically unfrocked at this time, but he refused the dispensation of the Pope who wished him to marry her legally, as he preferred to live a loose life. Between the station and the Duomo you can see the house where they lived and where Filippino Lippi was born. Opposite the convent of Santa Margherita is a tabernacle containing a wonderfully beautiful fresco by Filippino, a Madonna and Child with Angels, adored by St. Margaret and St. Catherine, St. Antony and St. Stephen. All the faces are of the utmost loveliness, and the Catherine especially is like a foretaste of Luini's famous fresco at Milan. In the town picture gallery there are four pictures ascribed to

Lippo Lippi—all four of rather questionable authenticity—and one by Filippino, a Madonna and Child with St. Stephen and the Baptist, which, although utterly ruined, appears to be genuine. The Protomartyr and the Precursor seem always inseparable throughout the faithful little city of the Cintola.

Prato can likewise boast some excellent terracotta works by Andrea della Robbia, both outside the Duomo and in the churches of Our Lady of Good Counsel and Our Lady of the Prisons. This latter church, the Madonna delle Carceri, reared by Giuliano da San Gallo between 1485 and 1491, is perhaps the most beautiful and most truly classical of all Early Renaissance buildings in Tuscany.

Ten miles beyond Prato lies Pistoia, at the very foot of the Apennines, the city of Dante's friend and correspondent, Messer Cino, the poet of the golden haired Selvaggia, he who sang the dirge of Caesar Henry; the centre of the fiercest faction struggles of Italian history. It was the Florentine traditional policy to keep Pisa by fortresses and Pistoia by factions. It lies, however, beyond the scope of the present book, with the other Tuscan cities that owned the sway of the great Republic. San Gemignano, that most wonderful of all the smaller towns of Tuscany, the city of "the fair towers," of Santa Fina and of the gayest of mediæval poets, Messer Folgore, comes into another volume of this series.

The Story of Florence

But it is impossible to conclude even the briefest study of Florence without a word upon that Tuscan Earthly Paradise, the Casentino and upper valley of the Arno, although it lies for the most part not in the province of Florence but in that of Arezzo. It is best reached by the diligence which runs from Pontassieve over the Consuma Pass–where Arnaldo of Brescia, who lies in the last horrible round of Dante's Malebolge, was burned alive for counterfeiting the golden florins of Florence–to Stia.[57] A whole chapter of Florentine history may be read among the mountains of the Casentino, writ large upon its castles and monasteries. If the towers of San Gemignano give us still the clearest extant picture of the life led by the nobles and magnates when forced to enter the cities, we can see best in the Casentino how they exercised their feudal sway and maintained for a while their independence of the burgher Commune. The Casentino was ruled by the Conti Guidi, that great clan whose four branches–the Counts of Romena, the Counts of Porciano, the Counts of Battifolle and Poppi, the Counts of Dovadola (to whom Bagno in Romagna and Pratovecchio here appear to have belonged)–sprang from the four sons of Gualdrada, Bellincion Berti's daughter. Poppi remains a superb monument of the power and taste of these "Counts Palatine of Tuscany"; its palace on a small scale resembles the Palazzo Vecchio of Florence. Romena and Porciano, higher up stream, overhanging Pratovecchio and Stia, have been immortalised by the verse and hallowed by the footsteps of Dante Alighieri. Beneath the hill upon which Poppi stands, an old bridge still spans the Arno, upon which the last of the Conti Guidi, the Count Francesco, surrendered in 1440 to the Florentine commissary, Neri Capponi. After the second expulsion of the Medici from Florence, Piero and Giuliano for some time lurked in the Casentino, with Bernardo Dovizi at Bibbiena.

Throughout the Casentino Dante himself should be our guide. There is hardly another district in Italy so intimately connected with the divine poet; save only Florence and Ravenna, there is, perhaps, none where we more frequently need to have recourse to the pages of the *Divina Commedia*. With the *Inferno* in our hands, we seek out Count Alessandro's castle of Romena and what purports to be the Fonte Branda, below the castle to the left, for whose waters—even to cool the thirst of Hell—Maestro Adamo would not have given the sight of his seducer sharing his agony. With the *Purgatorio* we trace the course of the Arno from where, a mere *fiumicello*, it takes its rise in Falterona, and runs down past Porciano and Poppi to sweep away from the Aretines, "turning aside its muzzle in disdain." There is a tradition that Dante was imprisoned in the castle of Porciano. We know that he was the guest of various members of the Conti Guidi at different times during his exile; it was from one of their castles, probably Poppi, that on March 31st and April 16th, 1311, he directed his two terrible letters to the Florentine government and to the Emperor Henry. It was in the Casentino, too, that he composed the Canzone *Amor, dacchè convien pur ch'io mi doglia*, "Love, since I needs must make complaint," one of the latest and most perplexing of his lyrics.

The battlefield of Campaldino lies beyond Poppi, on the eastern side of the river, near the old convent and church of Certomondo, founded some twenty or thirty years before by two of the Conti Guidi to commemorate the great Ghibelline victory of Montaperti, but now to witness the triumph of the Guelfs. The Aretines, under their Bishop and Buonconte da Montefeltro, had marched up the valley along the direction of the present railway to Bibbiena, to check the ravages of the Florentines who, with their French allies, had made their way through the mountains above Pratovecchio and were laying waste the country of the Conti Guidi. It was on the Feast of St. Barnabas, 1289, that the two armies stood face to face, and Dante riding in the Florentine light cavalry, if the fragment of a letter preserved to us by Leonardo Bruni be authentic, "had much dread and at the end the greatest gladness, by reason of the varying chances of that battle." There are no relics of the struggle to be found in Certomondo; only a very small portion of the cloisters remains, and the church itself contains nothing of note save an Annunciation by Neri di Bicci. But about an hour's walk from the battlefield, perhaps a mile from the foot of the hill on which Bibbiena stands, is a spot most sacred to all lovers of Dante. Here the stream of the Archiano, banked with poplars and willows, flows into the Arno; and here, at the close of that same terrible and glorious day, Buonconte da Montefeltro died of his wounds, gasping out the name of Mary. At evening the nightingales are loud around the spot, but their song is less sweet then the ineffable stanzas in the fifth canto of the *Purgatorio* in which Dante has raised an imperishable monument to the young Ghibelline warrior.

But, more famous than its castles or even its Dantesque memories, the Casentino is hallowed by its noble sanctuaries of Vallombrosa, Camaldoli, La Verna. Less noted but still very interesting is the Dominican church and convent of the Madonna del Sasso, just below Bibbiena on the way towards La Verna, hallowed with memories of Savonarola and the Piagnoni, and still a place of devout pilgrimage to Our Lady of the Rock. There is a fine Assumption in its church, painted by Fra Paolino from Bartolommeo's cartoon. Vallombrosa and Camaldoli, founded respectively by Giovanni Gualberto and Romualdus, have shared the fate of all such institutions in modern Italy.

La Verna remains undisturbed, that "harsh rock between Tiber and Arno," as Dante calls it, where Francis "received from Christ the final seal;" the sacred mountain from which, on that September morning before the dawn, so bright a light of Divine Love shone forth to rekindle the mediæval world, that all the country seemed aflame, as the crucified Seraph uttered the words of mystery—*Tu sei il mio Gonfaloniere*: "Thou art my standard-bearer." To enter the precincts of this sacred place, under the arch hewn out from between the rocks, is like a first introduction to the spirit of the *Divina Commedia*.

"Non est in toto sanctior orbe mons."

For here, at least, is one spot left in the world, where, although Renaissance and Reformation, Revolution and Risorgimento, have swept round it, the Middle Ages still reign a living reality, in their noblest aspect, with the *poverelli* of the Seraphic Father; and the mystical light, that shone out on the day of the Stigmata, still burns: "while the eternal ages watch and wait."

TABLE OF THE MEDICI

GIOVANNI DI AVERARDO (GIOVANNI BICCI) 1360-1429, m. Piccarda Bueri.

- **COSIMO** (Pater Patriae), 1389-1464, m. Contessina dei Bardi.
  - **PIERO** (il Gottoso), 1416-1469, m. Lucrezia Tornabuoni.
    - **LORENZO** (the Magnificent), 1449-1492, m. Clarice Orsini.
      - **PIERO**, 1471-1503, m. Alfonsina Orsini.
        - **LORENZO** (titular Duke of Urbino), 1492-1519, m. Madeleine de la Tour d'Auvergne.
          - **ALESSANDRO†** (Illegitimate), d. 1537, m. Margherita of Austria.
          - **CATERINA**, 1519-1589, m. Henri II. of France.
        - **CLARICE**, m. Filippo Strozzi.
      - **GIOVANNI**, 1475-1521, (Pope Leo X.)
      - **GIULIANO** (Duke of Nemours), 1479-1516, m. Filiberta of Savoy.
        - **IPPOLITO*** (Illegitimate), 1511-1535, (Cardinal).
    - **GIULIO** (Illegitimate), d. 1534, (Pope Clement VII.)
    - **MADDALENA**, m. Franceschetto Cibo.
    - **LUCREZIA**, m. Giacomo Salviati.
      - **MARIA**, m. Giovanni delle Bande Nere.
      - **FRANCESCA**, m. Ottaviano dei Medici.
        - **ALESSANDRO**, d. 1605, (Pope Leo XI.)
    - **NANNINA**, m. Bernardo Rucellai.
    - **BIANCA**, m. Guglielmo dei Pazzi.
  - **GIULIANO**, 1453-1478.
- **GIOVANNI**, 1424-1463, m. Ginevra degli Alessandri.
  - **LORENZO**, 1395-1440, m. Ginevra Cavalcanti.
    - **PIERO FRANCESCO**, d. 1467 (or 1476), m. Laudomia Acciaiuoli.
      - **LORENZO**, d. 1503, m. Semiramide Appini.
        - **PIER FRANCESCO**, d. 1525, m. Maria Soderini.
          - **LORENZO** ("LORENZINO" or "Lorenzaccio"), 1514-1547.
          - **LAUDOMIA**, m. Piero Strozzi.
          - **MADDALENA**, m. Roberto Strozzi.
      - **GIOVANNI** d. 1498, m. Caterina Sforza.
        - **GIOVANNI**, ("delle Bande Nere"), 1498-1526, m. Maria Salviati.
          - **COSIMO I.** (Grand Duke), 1519-1574, m. Eleonora of Toledo (and Cammilla Martelli).
            - **FRANCESCO I.**, 1541-1587, m. Joanna of Austria (and Bianca Cappello).
              - **MARIA**, m. Henri IV. of France.
            - **GARZIA**, d. 1562.
            - **GIOVANNI**, d. 1562.
            - **FERDINAND I.**, 1549-1609, m. Christina of Lorraine.
              - **COSIMO II.**, 1590-1621, m. Maria Maddalena of Austria.
                - **FERDINAND II.**, 1610-1670.
                  - **COSIMO III.**, 1642-1723.
                    - **GIOVANNI GASTONE**, 1671-1737.
- **CARLO** (Illegitimate), d. 1492.

* The parentage of Ippolito and Alessandro is somewhat uncertain. The former was probably Giuliano's son by a lady of Pesaro, the latter probably the son of Lorenzo by a mulatto woman.

CHRONOLOGICAL INDEX OF ARCHITECTSSCULPTORS & PAINTERS

(*Names of non-Italians in italics*)
ARCHITECTS AND SCULPTORS
Niccolò Pisano (circa 1206-1278)Fra Sisto (died 1289)
Fra Ristoro da Campi (died 1283)
Arnolfo di Cambio (1232?-1300 or 1310)
Giovanni Pisano (circa 1250-after 1328)
Giotto da Bondone See under Painters
Andrea Pisano (1270-1348)
Fra Giovanni da Campi (died 1339)
Taddeo Gaddi See under Painters
Fra Jacopo Talenti da Nipozzano (died 1362)
Nino Pisano (died 1368)
Andrea Orcagna See under Painters
Francesco Talenti (died after 1387)
Pietro di Migliore (middle of fourteenth century)196
Alberto Arnoldi (died circa 1378)
Simone di Francesco Talenti (end of fourteenth century)
Benci di Cione (latter half of fourteenth century)
Neri di Fioraventi (latter half of fourteenth century)

The Story of Florence

Giovanni di Ambrogio (last quarter of fourteenth century)
Jacopo di Piero (last quarter of fourteenth century)
Piero di Giovanni Tedesco (end of Trecento)
Niccolò di Piero Lamberti da Arezzo (1360?-1444?)
Nanni di Antonio di Banco (died in 1421)-
Jacopo della Quercia (1371-1438)
Bicci di Lorenzo See under Painters
Filippo Brunelleschi (1377-1446)
Lorenzo Ghiberti (1378-1455)--
Bernardo Ciuffagni (1381-1457)
DonatelloDonate di Betto Bardi (1386-1466)--
Michelozzo Michelozzi (1396-1472)
Luca della Robbia (1399-1482)
Leo (Leone) Battista Alberti (1405-1472)
Bernardo Rossellino (1409-1464)
Vecchietta (1410-1480)
Antonio Rossellino (1427-1478)
Desiderio da Settignano (1428-1464)
Antonio Pollaiuolo (1429-1498)
Mino da Fiesole (1431-1484)
Giuliano da Maiano (1432-1490)
Andrea Verrocchio (1435-1488)
Matteo Civitali (1435-1501)
Andrea della Robbia (1435-1525)
Benedetto da Maiano (1442-1497)

Bertoldo (died 1491)
Giuliano da San Gallo (1445-1516)
CronacaSimone del Pollaiuolo (1457-1508)
Benedetto Buglione (1461-1521)
CaparraNiccolò Grosso (worker in metallatter half of fifteenth century)
Andrea Ferrucci da Fiesole (1465-1526)
Baccio d'Agnolo (1462-1543)
Giovanni della Robbia (1469-1527)
Andrea Sansovino (circa 1460-1529)
Baccio da Montelupo (1469-1535)
Benedetto da Rovezzano (1474-1552)
Giovanni Francesco Rustici (1474-1554)
Michelangelo Buonarroti (1475-1564)----
Jacopo Sansovino (1486-1570)
Baccio Bandinelli (1487-1559)
Francesco da San Gallo (1494-1576)
Benvenuto Cellini (1500-1571)
Raffaello di Baccio da Montelupo (1505-1566)
Fra Giovanni Agnolo da Montorsoli (1506-1563)
Battista del Tasso (died 1555)
Bartolommeo Ammanati (1511-1592)
Giorgio Vasari (1512-1574)et passim
Giovanni da Bologna (1524-1608)
Vincenzo Danti(1530-1576)
Bernardo Buontalenti (1536-1608)

The Story of Florence

PAINTERS

Fra Jacopoworker in mosaic (working in 1225)
Giovanni Cimabue (1240-1302)
Andrea Tafiworker in mosaic (1250?-1320?)
Gaddo Gaddi (circa 1259-1333)
Duccio di Buoninsegna (circa 1260-1339)
Giotto da Bondone (1276?-1336)--
Simone Martini (1283-1344)
Lippo Memmi (died 1356)
Pietro and Ambrogio Lorenzetti (died circa 1348)
Taddeo Gaddi (circa 1300-1366)
Bernardo Daddi (died in 1350)
GiottinoGiotto di Stefano (died after 1369)
Puccio Capanna (flourished circa 1350)
Maso di Banco (working in middle of Trecento)
Pietro Cavallini (died circa 1360)
Giovanni da Milano (died after 1360)
Leonardo Orcagna (born before 1308)
Andrea Orcagna (1308-1368)
Agnolo Gaddi (died 1396)
Cennino Cennini (end of Trecento)
Spinello Aretino (1333-1410)
Gherardo Starnina (1354-1408)
Don Lorenzoil Monaco (1370-1425)
Gentile da Fabriano (1370-1450)
Bicci di Lorenzo (1373-1452)

The Story of Florence

Masolino (born circa 1384died after 1435)-
Masaccio (1401-1428)-
Fra Giovanni Angelico (1387-1455)--
Andrea del Castagno (1396?-1457)
Domenico Veneziano (died 1461)
Paolo Uccello (1397-1475)
Fra Filippo Lippi (1406-1469)--
Piero della Francesca (1415-1492)
Neri di Bicci (1419-1491)
Benozzo Gozzoli (1420-1498)
Domenico di Michelino (working in 1461)
Francesco Pesellino (1422-1457)
Alessio Baldovinetti (1427-1499)
Antonio Pollaiuolo See under Sculptors
Giovanni Bellini (circa 1428-1516)
Andrea Mantegna (1431-1506)
Andrea Verrocchio See under Sculptors
Hans Memlinc (circa 1435-1495)
Cosimo Rosselli (1439-1507)
Piero Pollaiuolo (1443-1496)
Luca Signorelli (1441-1523)
Hugo Van der Goes (died 1482)
Pietro VannucciPerugino (1446-1523)
Alessandro FilipepiSandro Botticelli (1447-1510)-
Domenico Ghirlandaio (1449-1494)
Francesco RaiboliniFrancia (1450-1517)

The Story of Florence

David Ghirlandaio (1452-1525)
Sebastiano Mainardi (died 1513)
Leonardo da Vinci (1452-1519)
Filippino Lippi (1457-1504)
Lorenzo di Credi (1459-1537)
Piero di Cosimo (1462-1521)
Lorenzo Costa (circa 1460-1535)
Raffaellino del Garbo (1466-1524)
Raffaellino di Carlo (1470-1516)
Boccaccino da Cremona (died 1518)
Timoteo Viti (1469-1523)
Francesco Granacci (1469-1543)
Albert Dürer (1471-1528)
Mariotto Albertinelli (1474-1515)-
Michelangelo Buonarroti See under Architects and Sculptors
Fra Bartolommeo (1475-1517)---
Bernardino Luini (1475-1533)
Morto da Feltre (1475?-1522?)
Giorgio BarbarelliGiorgione (1477-1511)
Tiziano VecelliTitian (1477-1576)-
Giovanni Antonio BazziSodoma (1477-1549)
Dosso Dossi (1479-1542)
Lorenzo Lotto (1480-1555)
Francia Bigio (1482-1525)-
Raffaello SanzioRaphael (1483-1520)-

The Story of Florence

Ridolfo Ghirlandaio (1483-1561)
Sebastiano del Piombo (1485-1547)
Andrea del Sarto (1486-1531)--
Giovanni da Udine (1487-1564)
Fra Paolino da Pistoia (1490-1547)
Giovanni Antonio Sogliani (1492-1544)
Giulio Romano (1492-1546)
Antonio Allegri da Correggio (1494-1534)
Rosso Fiorentino (1494-1541)
Jacopo da Pontormo (1494-1557)
Lucas Van Leyden (1494-1533)
Angelo Bronzino (1502-1572)
Michele di Ridolfo Ghirlandaio (1503-1577)
Daniele Ricciarellida Volterra (1509-1566)
Francesco Salviati (1510-1563)
Giorgio Vasari See under Architects and Sculptors
Jacopo RobustiTintoretto (1518-1594)
Paolo Veronese (1528-1588)
Taddeo Zuccheri (1529-1566)
Marcello Venusti (died circa 1580)
Alessandro Allori (1535-1607)
Bernardo Poccetti (1542-1612)
Jacopo da Empoli (1554-1640)
Guido Reni (1575-1642)
Cristofano Allori (1577-1621)
Peter Paul Rubens (1577-1640)

Matteo Rosselli (1578-1650)
Artemisia Gentileschi (died 1642)
Pietro da Cortona (1596-1669)
Justus Sustermans (1597-1681)
Antony Van Dyck (1599-1641)
Diego Velasquez (1599-1660)
Rembrandt Van Rijn (1606-1669)
Carlo Dolci (1616-1686)
Peter Lely (1618-1680)
Luca Giordano (1632-1705)

FOOTNOTES:

[1] The Frontispiece and the Illustrations facing pages 97, 135, 144, 178 and 288 are reproduced, by permission, from photographs by Messrs Alinari of Florence.

"Love, I demand to have my lady in fee,
Fine balm let Arno be,
The walls of Florence all of silver rear'd,
And crystal pavements in the public way;
With castles make me fear'd,
Till every Latin soul have owned my sway."
–Lapo Gianni (*Rossetti*).

[3]"For amongst the tart sorbs, it befits not the sweet fig to fructify."

[4] "Let the beasts of Fiesole make litter of themselves, and not touch the plant, if any yet springs up amid their rankness, in which the holy seed revives of those Romans who remained there when it became the nest of so much malice."

[5] "With these folk, and with others with them, did I see Florence in such full repose, she had not cause for wailing;

> With these folk I saw her people so glorious and so just, ne'er was the lily on the shaft reversed, nor yet by faction dyed vermilion."
> —Wicksteed's translation.

[6] "The house from which your wailing sprang, because of the just anger which hath slain you and placed a term upon your joyous life,

"was honoured, it and its associates. Oh Buondelmonte, how ill didst thou flee its nuptials at the prompting of another!

"Joyous had many been who now are sad, had God committed thee unto the Ema the first time that thou camest to the city.

"But to that mutilated stone which guardeth the bridge 'twas meet that Florence should give a victim in her last time of peace."

"And one who had both hands cut off, raising the stumps through the dim air so that their blood defiled his face, cried: 'Thou wilt recollect the Mosca too, ah me! who said, "A thing done has an end!" which was the seed of evil to the Tuscan people.'" (*Inf.* xxviii.)

[8] The Arte di Calimala, or of the Mercatanti di Calimala, the dressers of foreign cloth; the Arte della Lana, or wool; the Arte dei Giudici e Notai, judges and notaries, also called the Arte del Proconsolo; the Arte del Cambio or dei Cambiatori, money-changers; the Arte dei Medici e Speziali, physicians and apothecaries; the Arte della Seta, or silk, also called the Arte di Por Santa Maria; and the Arte dei Vaiai e Pellicciai, the furriers. The Minor Arts were organised later.

Some years later a new officer, the Executor of Justice, was instituted to carry out these ordinances instead of leaving them to the Gonfaloniere. This Executor of Justice was associated with the Captain, but was usually a foreign Guelf burgher; later he developed into the Bargello, head of police and governor of the gaol. It will, of course, be seen that while Podestà, Captain, Executore (the *Rettori*), were aliens, the Gonfaloniere and Priors (the *Signori*) were necessarily Florentines and popolani.

Rossetti's translation of the *ripresa* and second stanza of the Ballata *Perch'i' no spero di tornar giammai.*

[11] "Thou shall abandon everything beloved most dearly; this is the arrow which the bow of exile shall first shoot.

"Thou shalt make trial of how salt doth taste another's bread, and how hard the path to descend and mount upon another's stair."
—Wicksteed's translation.

[12] "On that great seat where thou dost fix thine eyes, for the crown's sake already placed above it, ere at this wedding feast thyself do sup,

"Shall sit the soul (on earth 'twill be imperial) of the lofty Henry, who shall come to straighten Italy ere she be ready for it."

i.e. The Nativity of the Blessed Virgin.

Purg. VI.–
"Athens and Lacedæmon, they who made
The ancient laws, and were so civilised,
Made towards living well a little sign
Compared with thee, who makest such fine-spun
Provisions, that to middle of November
Reaches not what thou in October spinnest.
How oft, within the time of thy remembrance,
Laws, money, offices and usages

Hast thou remodelled, and renewed thy members?
And if thou mind thee well, and see the light,
Thou shalt behold thyself like a sick woman,
Who cannot find repose upon her down,
But by her tossing wardeth off her pain."
—*Longfellow.*

[15] "In painting Cimabue thought that he
Should hold the field, now Giotto has the cry,
So that the other's fame is growing dim."

[16] The "Colleges" were the twelve Buonuomini and the sixteen Gonfaloniers of the Companies. Measures proposed by the Signoria had to be carried in the Colleges before being submitted to the Council of the People, and afterwards to the Council of the Commune.
From Mr Armstrong's *Lorenzo de' Medici*.
The *Palle*, it will be remembered, were the golden balls on the Medicean arms, and hence the rallying cry of their adherents.
[19] The familiar legend that Lorenzo told Savonarola that the three sins which lay heaviest on his conscience were the sack of Volterra, the robbery of the Monte delle Doti, and the vengeance he had taken for the Pazzi conspiracy, is only valuable as showing what were popularly supposed by the Florentines to be his greatest crimes.

This *Compendium of Revelations* was, like the *Triumph of the Cross*, published both in Latin and in Italian simultaneously. I have rendered the above from the Italian version.

[21] When Savonarola entered upon the political arena, his spiritual sight was often terribly dimmed. The cause of Pisa against Florence was every bit as righteous as that of the Florentines themselves against the Medici.

[22] This Luca Landucci, whose diary we shall have occasion to quote more than once, kept an apothecary's shop near the Strozzi Palace at the Canto de' Tornaquinci. He was an ardent Piagnone, though he wavered at times. He died in 1516, and was buried in Santa Maria Novella.

[23] "He who usurpeth upon earth my place, my place, my place, which in the presence of the Son of God is vacant,

"hath made my burial-ground a conduit for that blood and filth, whereby the apostate one who fell from here above, is soothed down there below."–*Paradiso* xxvii. –Wicksteed's Translation.

Sermon on May 29th, 1496. In Villari and Casanova, *Scelte di prediche e scritti di Fra Girolamo Savonarola*.

Professor Villari justly remarks that "Savonarola's attacks were never directed in the slightest degree against the dogmas of the Roman Church, but solely against those who corrupted them." The *Triumph of the Cross* was intended to do for the Renaissance what St Thomas Aquinas had accomplished for the Middle Ages in his *Summa contra Gentiles*. As this book is the fullest expression of Savonarola's creed, it is much to be regretted that more than one of its English translators have omitted some of its most characteristic and important passages bearing upon Catholic practice and doctrine, without the slightest indication that any such process of "expurgation" has been carried out.

[26] See the Genealogical Table of the Medici.

Mr Armstrong in his *Lorenzo de' Medici*.

[28] Botticelli's brother and an ardent Piagnone, whose chronicle has been recently discovered and published by Villari and Casanova. The Franciscans were possibly sincere in the business, and mere tools in the hands of the Compagnacci; they are not likely to have been privy to the plot.

[29] The following notes make no pretence at furnishing a catalogue, but are simply intended to indicate the more important Italian pictures, especially the principal masterpieces of, or connected with the Florentine school.

See the Genealogical Table in Appendix. The elder Pier Francesco was dead many years before this picture was painted. It was for his other son, Lorenzo, that Sandro Botticelli drew his illustrations of the *Divina Commedia*.

Modern Painters, vol. ii.

[32] The eight Arti Minori not represented are the vintners (St. Martin), the inn-keepers (St. Julian), the cheesemongers (St. Bartholomew), the leather-dressers (St. Augustine), the saddlemakers (the Blessed Trinity), the joiners (the Annunciation), tin and coppersmiths (St. Zenobius), and the bakers (St. Lawrence).

There are three extant documents concerning pictures of the Madonna for the Captains of Saint Michael; two refer to a painting ordered from Bernardo Daddi, in 1346 and 1347; the third to one by Orcagna, 1352. *See* Signor P. Franceschini's monograph on Or San Michele, to which I am much indebted in this chapter.

[34] These were the burghers and lawyers of the black faction, the Podestà's allies and friends. This was in the spring of 1303.

[35] Such, at least, seems the more obvious interpretation; but there is a certain sensuality and cruelty about the victor's expression, which, together with the fact that the vanquished undoubtedly has something of Michelangelo's own features, lead us to suspect that the master's sympathies were with the lost cause.

Quoted in Mr Armstrong's *Lorenzo de' Medici*.

See Guido Carocci, *Firenze Scomparsa*, here and generally.

[38] The earliest of these mosaics are those in the tribune, executed originally by a certain Fra Jacopo in the

year 1225; those in the dome are in part ascribed to Dante's contemporary, Andrea Tafi.

Should it e'er come to pass that the sacred poem to which both heaven and earth so have set hand, that it hath made me lean through many a year, should overcome the cruelty which doth bar me forth from the fair sheepfold wherein I used to sleep, a lamb, foe to the wolves which war upon it; with changed voice now, and with changed fleece shall I return, a poet, and at the font of my baptism shall I assume the chaplet; because into the Faith which maketh souls known of God, 'twas there I entered. –Par. xxv. 1-11, *Wicksteed's translation.*

[40] By these "second gates" are of course meant Ghiberti's second gates: in reality the "third gates" of the Baptistery.

"There is only one point from which the size of the Cathedral of Florence is felt; and that is from the corner of the Via de' Balestrieri, opposite the south-east angle, where it happens that the dome is seen rising instantly above the apse and transepts" (*Seven Lamps*).

Modern Painters, vol. ii. "Of Imagination Penetrative."

[43] The Duomo has fairer memories of the Pazzi, than this deed of blood and treachery. Their ancestor at the Crusades had carried the sacred fire from Jerusalem to Florence, and still, on Easter Eve, an artificial dove sent from

the high altar lights the car of fireworks in the Piazza—the Carro dei Pazzi—in front of the church, in honour of their name.

It should be observed that Lorenzo was not specially called the "Magnificent" by his contemporaries. All the more prominent members of the Medicean family were styled *Magnifico* in the same way.

[45] "Grateful to me is sleep, and more the being stone; while ruin and shame last, not to see, not to feel, is great good fortune to me. Therefore wake me not; ah, speak low!"

Given in Addington Symonds' *Life of Michelangelo*.

"Before thee, goddess, flee the winds, the clouds of heaven; before thee and thy advent; for thee earth manifold in works puts forth sweet-smelling flowers; for thee the levels of the sea do laugh and heaven propitiated shines with outspread light" (Munro's *Lucretius*).

See *Andrea del Sarto*, by H. Guinness in the *Great Masters* series, and *G. F. Rustici* in Vasari.

Opposite the bridge, at the beginning of the Via dei Benci, is the palace of the old Alberti family; the remains of their loggia stand further up the street, at the corner of the Borgo Santa Croce. In all these streets, between the Lungarno della Borsa and the Borgo dei Greci, there are many old houses and palaces; in the Piazza dei Peruzzi the houses, formerly of that family and partly built in the fourteenth century, follow the lines of the Roman amphitheatre—the *Parlascio* of the early Middle Ages. The Palazzo dei Giudici–in the piazza of that name–was originally built in the thirteenth century, though reconstructed at a later epoch.

See Addington Symonds' *Michelangelo*. The horse in question was the equestrian monument of Francesco Sforza.

"The one was all seraphic in his ardour, the other by his wisdom was on earth a splendour of cherubic light. "Of one will I discourse, because of both the two he speaketh who doth either praise, which so he will; for to one end their works." –Wicksteed's translation, *Paradiso* xi.

[52] "I desired, and understanding was given me. I prayed, and the spirit of Wisdom came upon me; and I preferred her before kingdoms and thrones."

[53] The identification of each science and its representative is rather doubtful, especially in the celestial series. From altar to centre, Grammar, Rhetoric, and Logic are represented by Aelius Donatus, Cicero and Aristotle (or Zeno); Music, Astronomy, Geometry, Arithmetic by Tubal Cain, Zoroaster (or Ptolemy), Euclid and Pythagoras. From window to centre, Civil Law is represented by Justinian, Canon Law by Innocent III., Philosophy apparently by Boethius; the next four seem to be Contemplative, Moral, Mystical and Dogmatic Theology, and their representatives Jerome, John of Damascus, Basil and Augustine–but, with the exception of St. Augustine, the identification is quite

arbitrary. Possibly if the Logician is Zeno, the Philosopher is not Boethius but Aristotle; the figure above, representing Philosophy, holds a mirror which seems to symbolise the divine creation of the cosmic Universe.

In Richter's *Literary Works of Leonardo da Vinci*. Leonardo rather too sweepingly ignores the fact that there were a few excellent masters between the two.

The ledger and the stave (*il quaderno e la doga*): "In 1299 Messer Niccola Acciaiuoli and Messer Baldo d' Aguglione abstracted from the public records a leaf containing the evidence of a disreputable transaction, in which they, together with the Podestà, had been engaged. At about the same time Messer Durante de' Chiaramontesi, being officer of the customs for salt, took away a stave (*doga*) from the standard measure, thus making it smaller."–*A. J. Butler.*

[56] "Perfected life and high desert enheaveneth a lady more aloft," she said, "by whose rule down in your world there are who clothe and veil themselves,

That they, even till death, may wake and sleep with that Spouse who accepteth every vow that love hath made conform with his good pleasure.

From the world, to follow her, I fled while yet a girl, and in her habit I enclosed myself, and promised the way of her company.

Thereafter men more used to ill than good to reme away from the sweet cloister; and God doth know what my life then became."
—*Paradiso* iii. Wicksteed's translation.

The lover of Florentine history cannot readily tear himself away from the Casentino. The Albergo Amorosi at Bibbiena, almost at the foot of La Verna, makes delightful headquarters. There is an excellent *Guida illustrata del Casentino* by C. Beni. For the Conti Guidi, Witte's essay should be consulted; it is translated in *Witte's Essays on Dante* by C. M. Lawrence and P. H. Wicksteed. La Verna will be fully dealt with in the Assisi volume of this series, so I do not describe it here.

[58] The parentage of Ippolito and Alessandro is somewhat uncertain. The former was probably Giuliano's son by a lady of Pesaro, the latter probably the son of Lorenzo by a mulatto woman.

www.ingramcontent.com/pod-product-compliance
Lightning Source LLC
Chambersburg PA
CBHW032008220426
43664CB00006B/174